D1446781

Japanese Language and Culture
for Business and Travel

Japanese Language and Culture
for Business and Travel

KYOKO HIJIRIDA
AND
MUNEO YOSHIKAWA

 University of Hawaii Press • HONOLULU

© University of Hawaii Press 1987
All Rights Reserved
Manufactured in the United States of America

93 92 91 90 89 88   6 5 4 3 2

Library of Congress Cataloging-in-Publication Data

Hijirida, Kyoko, 1937–
  Japanese language and culture for business
and travel.

  Includes bibliographies.
  1. Japanese language—Conversation and
phrase books—English.   2. Japan—Social life
and customs—1945–   . I. Yoshikawa, Muneo,
1938–   . II. Title.
PL539.H5   1987   495.6'83421   86–30723
ISBN 0–8248–1017–1

CONTENTS

FOREWORD

The dynamics of contemporary life suggest that educators provide not only strong foundations in traditional subjects which reflect and perpetuate our basic values and beliefs, but also capitalize on new societal trends with an eye toward their integration into curricular developments and opportunities. This in turn implies that a variety of approaches and methods must be explored and an appropriate selection made in order to make specific educational experiences as profitable and purposeful as possible. Thus, in language study, considerations of these kinds have induced us to move into the area of "language for special purposes." This concept embraces the time-honored belief that communication between the peoples of nations is critical and, at the same time, provides latitude for resolving this complex issue in a variety of ways that reflect changing needs and demands.

In relatively recent times, the importance of Asia and the Pacific has received increasingly greater attention, demanding that others come to understand and be able to interact with the peoples in that broad geographical area. Japan has emerged as one of the giants. The number of students worldwide who have undertaken the study of the Japanese language has increased with the concomitant need for diversity of content and approach in the materials used.

Thus, four years ago, with these thoughts well in mind, the School of Travel Industry Management of the University of Hawaii in very close cooperation with the Faculty of Languages, Linguistics and Literature, sought to expand its curriculum in order to be able to provide its students with the opportunity to study Japanese and certain other foreign languages. It is against this background that the present textbook evolved and has now come to fruition. I personally am extremely gratified that many years of extensive research and experimentation with the Japanese language component of the curriculum in the School of Travel Industry Management (TIM) have culminated in the publication of *Japanese Language and Culture for Business and Travel.*

Professors Kyoko Hijirida and Muneo Yoshikawa have both had many years of teaching experience at the University of Hawaii. More specifically, Professor Hijirida has been active in the field of language for special purposes as well as curriculum development. Moreover, while teaching students in the TIM program, she carefully studied the TIM curriculum itself and conducted a survey of the needs of TIM students as part of extensive research in conjunction with curriculum development. Professor Yoshikawa has contributed to the expansion of the dimensions of language teaching by virtue of his research in comparative cultures, cross-cultural communication, and education. He is also actively engaged in international business communication training seminars, including the training of managers in the field of the travel industry.

The particular expertise of each author has been successfully combined in the production of this textbook. It is a valuable contribution to materials available for studying Japanese, especially because of its rather unique focus and the integration of language, culture, and communication skills. The book is the ideal vehicle for beginning students who are interested in learning Japanese language and culture as well as for individuals in the travel industry. It is my firm belief that this book will come to serve as a model for similar texts in other languages in the future.

Richard K. Seymour, Dean
Faculty of Languages, Linguistics and Literature
University of Hawaii

PREFACE

The world we live in is experiencing rapid changes in almost all aspects of its social and economic order. This emerging global transformation includes a revolution in its transportation and electronic communication systems which significantly reduces both national and cultural barriers. Whereas high mountains and vast oceans presented serious barriers to interaction between nations and their people, these obstacles to cross-cultural exchange have now been almost entirely eliminated. At this point in time, enormous numbers of people have begun to travel, both within their own societies and internationally.

Here in Hawaii, the Visitor's Bureau recently reported that approximately four million tourists come each year to the Aloha State, fully 600,000 of whom are Japanese in origin.

The increase in Japanese visitors to the Hawaiian Islands is also reflected on a larger scale by the phenomenal rate of increase in Japanese tourists world-wide. From 1960 to 1982, the number of Japanese nationals choosing to travel abroad escalated from a miniscule 75,000 to 4,086,138. This unusual growth is attributed to three major factors, cultural, political, and economic in nature.

In considering the economic reasons for this growth, we observe that between 1960 and 1974, when the oil shortage occurred, the world experienced a period of high economic growth. During this time, Japan ranked third in the world in terms of gross national product, preceded only by the United States and the Soviet Union. Japan was simultaneously becoming a world power and an increasingly affluent society.

This increasing level of both national and personal income was accompanied by a transformation in the people's lifestyle priorities. Since 1960, the goals and personal objectives of most Japanese have moved from the "Three C's" (Car, Color TV, and air Conditioner) to the "Three R's" (Residence, Range, and Recreation), and then to the "Three V's" (Villa, Visiting nationally, and obtaining Visas to visit other countries).

Borrowing from the American Greyhound Bus slogan "Discover America," the Japanese Tourist Bureau has encouraged its people to "Discover Japan." From touring their own country, the Japanese rapidly branched out and came up with a third slogan: "Discover the World." The Japanese have quickly become one of the world's great globe-trotting nationalities, to the extent that, within Japan, the common belief is that a plane crash anywhere in the world will inevitably yield one or more Japanese casualties.

The phenomenal increase in the numbers of Japanese tourists internationally has led correspondingly to a dramatic increase in the numbers of cross-cultural problems and misunderstandings. In many cases, countries frequented by large numbers of Japanese were prepared only to accommodate English-speaking visitors. This created real difficulties, not only for the host country, but for the Japanese themselves. Complaints and dissatisfactions were commonplace, at least initially. The essential problems were basically ones of communication, or miscommunication, at all levels of the cross-cultural interaction. Oftentimes, this communication breakdown was something more than a language problem. It resulted from a cultural problem—both the host country and the Japanese tourists lacked cultural understanding and sensitivity.

This situation has necessitated a training program in cross-cultural communication for managers, business people, and employees in the tourist industry–related professions. In 1982, the TIM program at the University of Hawaii had added an experimental foreign-language curriculum (Japanese, Chinese, French, and Spanish) to its program of study. After one year's experimentation, the School decided to adopt the foreign-language requirement. This decision came from the realization that TIM majors in this global and pluralistic world need to have not only knowledge and skills in their technical fields, but also language and culture skills. In response to the need for a cross-cultural communication program for those involved in tourist-related businesses and within the context of the goal of the University of Hawaii to internationalize aspects of its curriculum, a cooperative effort by the Dean and faculty of the School of Travel Industry Management, together with the Dean and faculty of the division of Languages, Linguistics and Literature, College of Arts and Sciences, made it possible to implement special foreign language curricula for Travel Industry Management majors. This textbook represents the culmination of these efforts.

We wish to express our sincere gratitude to Richard Seymour, Dean of the Faculty of Languages, Linguistics and Literature, College of Arts and Sciences; Ho-min Sohn, then Acting Chairman of the Department of East Asian Languages; Chuck Gee, Dean of the School of Travel Industry Management; and Susan Iwamura, Student Services Coordinator in the School of Travel Industry Management, for their leadership in directing the language curriculum development and for their support of this textbook project.

The authors are indebted to the following individuals for their assistance in the preparation of this textbook: Maya Tagore Erwin, Sheril Fujimoto, Diane Duffett Gruenstein, Becke S. Ishii, Joy Sekiya, and Anna Tsuchiyama.

We also wish to thank David Ashworth for reviewing the manuscript and providing valuable suggestions. Hyun Sook Chung also provided useful feedback from her experience in using the manuscript in her classes at Cannon's Business College.

Our special appreciation goes to Fred Braun and Robert Cheng, who provided encouragement and guidance during the field-testing of the original curriculum for travel industry–oriented students.

Support from the following grants made possible the preparation of this book: Center for Asian and Pacific Studies Faculty Research Fellowship; University of Hawaii President's Educational Improvement Funds; National Resource Center for East Asian Studies, Federal Support Fund; U.S. Department of Education's "Business and International Education" grant to the University of Hawaii's Center for Asian and Pacific Studies; and U.S. Department of Education grant for a "Program to Strengthen International Studies in Selected Professional Schools."

Finally we wish to acknowledge the contribution of the Travel Industry Management students who used the mimeographed version of the text and who provided invaluable suggestions and comments.

INTRODUCTION

This text was written in response to the needs and demands brought on by an emerging global transformation. It is designed to develop not only competence in language but in communication and culture skills as well. Although the target audience is those employed or planning to work in some aspect of the tourist industry, this text is for anyone interested in Japanese language and culture, whether for business or for recreational travel in Japan.

LANGUAGE SKILLS

Unlike the traditional language textbook, *Japanese Language and Culture for Business and Travel* is focused on the specific needs of travel industry–related businesses. For this reason, topics, vocabulary, and dialogue have been selected to match work situations encountered in the travel industry. At the same time, however, the basic vocabulary and approach employed in this text are applicable in any situation. The approach is the "practical and functional approach," with a focus on listening and speaking skills.

COMMUNICATION SKILLS

Effective communication, no matter what the situation, goes beyond mere language learning. It is important to know the patterns of modes of communication as well. A mode of communication may be either direct or indirect, and having an awareness of that difference has a tremendous impact upon the quality of communication. In a traditional language text, this aspect of communicative competence is generally missing.

1

CULTURE SKILLS

This aspect of language learning has a strong bearing upon the development of (1) essential cultural sensitivity and appropriate perspectives; (2) cultural understanding which includes the Japanese worldview, or Japanese cultural values and assumptions; and (3) cultural meanings of language experiences. Mere accumulation of information on Japanese culture and people is not enough for an understanding of the Japanese mind and behavior. One must understand the Japanese cultural values and the assumptions of the worldview which shapes the Japanese mind and behavior.

The culture study in this textbook therefore focuses not upon the mere accumulation of information, but rather on the understanding of the basic cultural assumptions which are manifested in the fundamental Japanese, as well as American, way of thinking, perceiving, communicating, problem-solving, learning, managing, and behaving. Furthermore, the focus is not on the accumulation of isolated pieces of information, but on the understanding of relationships among pieces of information which, when integrated, become knowledge. Also considered significant are the relationships among areas of knowledge which, when integrated, become metaknowledge (or wisdom). One of the major objectives of this text, therefore, is to help individuals develop the skills to perceive those patterns of relationships among things, rather than unrelated bits of information about things.

It must be noted here that the Japanese culture which we deal with in the textbook is not merely traditional Japanese culture, but also what is generally referred to as popular Japanese culture.

Two approaches, a comparative approach to Japanese and American cultures, and an interdisciplinary approach, are utilized in the development of culture skills. In situations where this textbook is used outside Japanese or American cultures, the Japanese and American contrasts pointed out in the text can be effectively utilized as a point of reference for further cultural comparison. Culture study becomes more valuable and meaningful when one point or issue—for example, tipping in restaurants—is observed from several different cultural perspectives.

The interdisciplinary approach may include the study of history, art, anthropology, linguistics, philosophy, religion, psychology, and sociology—all of which are meaningfully integrated.

OTHER CONSIDERATIONS

When the text is used outside Hawaii, we suggest that the Hawaii-related vocabulary items in the text be replaced by vocabulary items that are more appropriate to the local culture.

This textbook may be of interest to some native Japanese speakers as a means of enhancing their self-awareness. In this respect, they may find the culture sections of the text educational and helpful.

Kana and kan'ji transcription of the expressions and dialogue in each lesson are included in Appendix 1 for those who wish to start Japanese language study with kana and kan'ji reading and writing. We suggest that those kana and kan'ji materials be rearranged and be used according to the needs of individual institutions. Some of the kan'ji are also introduced through common Japanese signs that are considered important in the travel industry. These are included in Appendix 2. Appendix 3 is a compilation of the vocabulary for each lesson.

The level of instruction is geared toward those individuals who have no previous background in Japanese language or culture. It is also expected that each of the lessons will require four to six hours of classroom instruction.

LESSON ARRANGEMENT

The following format is used for each lesson:

1. **Useful Expressions**
   These are expressions which are frequently encountered in the particular domain which is the topic of each unit.

2. **Conversation**
   These are true-to-life conversations between Japanese tourists and travel industry personnel in their service community. English equivalents of each dialogue are given in this section.

3. **Vocabulary**
   Frequently used terms and vocabulary utilized in the domain covered are listed with their English equivalents in this section.

4. **Explanation**
   Illustrations of structural points and brief explanations are presented.

5. **Drills**
   Various types of drills are included. These are designed to increase students' fluency and understanding of sentence structures.

6. **Exercises**
   This section is designed for students to demonstrate their knowledge of the grammar and vocabulary covered in each lesson.

7. **Simulation and Skits**
   At this skill-using stage, students are expected to perform a skit by using Japanese in a given work-related situation.

8. **Culture Orientation**
   In order to help students develop the appropriate perspectives and cultural

sensitivities to Japanese culture and its people, culture information—along with behavioral characteristics of Japanese tourists—is provided in this section. In addition, when appropriate, some suggestions are presented for dealing with problems that may arise as a result of the cultural differences between Japanese and American behavior in travel industry–related situations.

9. **The Mode of Japanese Communication**
   A mode of communication may be either direct or indirect. An awareness of that difference has a tremendous impact upon the quality of communication. In this section, a mode of Japanese communication related to the lesson topics is discussed.

10. **Language and Culture**
    Language is a social mirror, reflecting the culture of the society of which it is a part. Relationships of linguistic expressions and culture are explained in this section.

11. **Culture Questions**
    Students are expected to discuss and explore culture topics of each lesson through further readings, film viewings, firsthand experiences, etc. This section is also designed for students to demonstrate their culture knowledge and skills.

12. **Suggested Resource Materials**
    Useful and pertinent resource materials which are listed in this section include films, videotapes, articles, books, and other media. These materials are expected to provide greater understanding of related topics discussed in each lesson.

13. **References**
    All books and materials used as references for each lesson are listed in this section.

Four review lessons are included to help students review major sentence patterns and vocabularies covered in previous lessons.

INTRODUCTION TO JAPANESE PRONUNCIATION

An important key to the mastery of Japanese pronunciation is an understanding of the syllabic nature of the language. Japanese view their words as being made up of distinct syllables which have the same duration. Syllables are composed of the following: a short vowel, a long vowel, combinations of a consonant and a vowel, combinations of a consonant and *y* and a vowel, a single consonant, a double consonant, and a syllabic *n*.

4

Short Vowels

There are five short vowels in Japanese. They are *a, i, u, e,* and *o.* Each short vowel can be a syllable by itself. These five vowels are pronounced respectively as follows:

a—like "a" in "ah"
i—like "i" in "image"
u—like "u" in "June"
e—like "e" in "pet"
o—like "o" in "colt"

The pronunciation of each vowel is short, clear, and even in length.

Long Vowels

A short vowel can be followed by another identical vowel, like *aa, ii, uu, ee,* and *oo.* These are called long vowels. These long vowels constitute two syllables. When they are pronounced, therefore, they must be sustained twice as long as a short vowel. They are pronounced without a pause, like "ah!" in *aa* and "eek!" in *ii.* When long vowels are made up of identical vowels, such as *aa,* they should not be pronounced separately, like *a-a.*

A short vowel can be followed by another different vowel, as in *ai, au, ie, ue, ou,* and so on. When long vowels are a composite of different vowels in sequence, as in the above examples, each vowel is pronounced separately, but with equal length, like *a-i. A-i,* however, should not be pronounced with an off-glide, as in the case of the English word "I." Remember that the pronunciation of each vowel in sequence is short, clear, and even in length.

It must be noted here that the distinction between long and short vowels is important in Japanese because the length of the vowel changes the meaning of the word.

Examples:

Short vowels	Long vowels
obasan aunt	obaasan grandmother
ojisan uncle	ojiisan grandfather
shujin husband	shuujin prisoner
e picture	ee yes
mo also	moo already

Consonant Plus Vowel

The following chart shows the consonants that may precede and form syllabic combinations with the above five vowels.

	k	g	s	z	t	d	n	h	b	p	m	y	r	w	n
a	ka	ga	sa	za	ta	da	na	ha	ba	pa	ma	ya	ra	wa	n
i	ki	gi	si	zi	ti	di	ni	hi	bi	pi	mi		ri		
			(shi)	(ji)	(chi)	(ji)									
u	ku	gu	su	zu	tu	du	nu	hu	bu	pu	mu	yu	ru		
					(tsu)	(zu)		(fu)							
e	ke	ge	se	ze	te	de	ne	he	be	pe	me		re		
o	ko	go	so	zo	to	do	no	ho	bo	po	mo	yo	ro		

Note: Syllables in parentheses indicate the spellings used in this text.

The consonant *n* can be a syllable by itself. It is called a syllabic *n*. This syllabic *n* only appears either before another consonant or at the end of a word. When it occurs in the middle of a word followed by another consonant, the syllabic *n* is followed by the apostrophe (as in kon'nichiwa) in this textbook. It is pronounced like "ng" in the English word *sing*.

Combination Sounds: Consonant Plus Consonant *Y* Plus Vowel

The combinations constitute the following syllables:

kya	gya	sya	zya	tya	nya	hya	bya	pya	mya	rya
		(sha)	(ja)	(cha)						
kyu	gyu	syu	zyu	tyu	nyu	hyu	byu	pyu	myu	ryu
		(shu)	(ju)	(chu)						
kyo	gyo	syo	zyo	tyo	nyo	hyo	byo	pyo	myo	ryo
		(sho)	(jo)	(cho)						

Note: Syllables in parentheses indicate the spellings used in this text.

Double Consonants

When a given consonant occurs in sequence, a double consonant results. The double consonants are *kk*, *ss*, *pp*, *tt*, *ssh*, and *tch*. The distinction between single and double consonant is important in Japanese because it correlates with changes in meaning.

Examples:

Single consonant	**Double consonant**
isho will (in writing)	issho together
saka slope	sakka writer
ika squid	ikka one lesson
ite kudasai please stay	itte kudasai please leave

In pronouncing the double consonant in hakkiri, to take one example, as soon as you articulate ha, you shut the glottis and hold your breath for the length of a full syllable before pronouncing the kiri.

Pronunciation of Consonants

The Japanese consonants are generally similar in pronunciation to their corresponding English consonants, with the exceptions of *r, f,* and *ts.*

One of the hardest pronunciations for speakers of English is perhaps the Japanese *r,* which is like neither the *r* nor *l* in English. It resembles a combination of the English *r* and *l.* In other words, the position of the tongue is somewhere between *r* and *l.* The tongue-tip is slightly flapped against the upper gum, as in the pronunciation of *d* in *ladder.* It is similar to the Spanish *r* in *pero;* however one should be careful not to roll one's tongue.

The *f* is pronounced by breathy air passing through the two lips slightly closed, as if you are smiling slightly. Since the upper teeth are not used at all, the pronunciation is different from the English *f.*

The sound of *ts* is like the *ts* in English *cats.* However, its pronunciation *ts* is difficult for English speakers, especially when a word starts with *ts,* because *ts* does not occur in the word-initial position in English.

Syllable Length

In order to be able to pronounce Japanese, you must learn to pronounce each syllable clearly, with even stress. And each syllable must be given the same length.

Examples:
Okinawa — o-ki-na-wa (4 syllables)
ohayoo gozaimasu — o-ha-yo-o-go-za-i-ma-su (9 syllables)
kon'ban'wa — ko-n'-ba-n'-wa (5 syllables)
sakka — sa-k-ka (3 syllables)

Remember that each syllable gets one beat; a long vowel gets counted as two syllables; the syllabic *n* gets counted as one syllable; and the first consonant of the double consonant gets counted as one syllable. It must be noted here that while syllables are pronounced with more or less equal length and stress in Japanese, the stressed syllable in English is much more clearly pronounced than other parts of the word. It is also longer in duration.

Example:
Japanese
A-me-ri-ka-n

English
A-mé-ri-can

— — — — —

Romanization

The romanization system in this text is basically the Hepburn system with a few modifications. The modifications are:

1. Long vowels are written as *aa, ii, uu, ee,* and *oo* in this text.

Hepburn	**This text**
obāsan	obaasan
ojīsan	ojiisan
shūjin	shuujin
ōkī	ookii

2. The nonfinal syllabic *n* will be written as *n'* within a word, thus en'pitsu, kon'nichiwa, shin'bun.

3. Other modifications in romanized spelling used in this text have already been spelled out in the introduction to pronunciation.

CLASSROOM INSTRUCTIONS

Yoku kiite kudasai.	Please listen carefully.
Moo ichido itte kudasai.	Please say it once more.
Yukkuri itte kudasai.	Please say it slowly.
Min'na de itte kudasai.	Please say it in chorus.
Yon'de kudasai.	Please read it.
Kaite kudasai.	Please write it.
Hanashite kudasai.	Please speak. (Please talk.)
Kotaete kudasai.	Please answer.
Yoku dekimashita.	Very good. You did a good job. You did well.
Wakarimasu ka?	Do you understand? Is that clear?
(Hai,) Wakarimasu.	(Yes,) I understand.
(Iie,) Wakarimasen.	(No,) I do not understand.
Hon o tojite kudasai.	Please close your book.
San-peeji o akete kudasai.	Please open your book to page three.
Nihon'go de hanashite kudasai.	Please speak in Japanese.

LESSON 1

GREETINGS

1.1 USEFUL EXPRESSIONS

Ohayoo gozaimasu.	Good morning.
Kon'nichiwa.	Good afternoon. Hello (when used as a greeting in the afternoon).
Kon'ban'wa.	Good evening.
Sayoonara.	Good-bye.
Oyasuminasai.	Good night. Have a good rest.
Jaa mata.	See you (again, later).
Ogen'ki desu ka?	Are you well? (How are you?)
Ikaga desu ka?	How are you?
Okagesama de.	Fine, thank you.
Maa maa desu.	OK (So so).
Odekake desu ka?	Are you going out? Are you going somewhere?
Chotto soko made.	Just down the street.
Shibaraku desu nee.	I haven't seen you in a while.

1.2 CONVERSATION

1.2.1 Meeting Someone on the Street

Suzuki: Kon'nichiwa, Yamada-san.
Yamada: Aa, Suzuki-san, kon'nichiwa.
Suzuki: Shibaraku desu nee. Ogen'ki desu ka?
Yamada: Ee, okagesama de. Suzuki-san wa?
Suzuki: Okagesama de (gen'ki desu).

Suzuki: Good afternoon, Mr. Yamada.
Yamada: Hello, Mr. Suzuki.
Suzuki: I haven't seen you in a while. How are you?
Yamada: Fine, thank you. And you?
Suzuki: I'm fine, thank you.

9

1.2.2   Meeting Your Section Chief on the Street

Uchida: Kon'ban'wa, Kachoo.
Kachoo: Kon'ban'wa, Uchida-kun.
Uchida: Odekake desu ka?
Kachoo: Ee, chotto soko made.

Uchida:	Good evening.
Section Chief:	Good evening, Mr. Uchida.
Uchida:	Are you going somewhere?
Section Chief:	Yes, just down the street.

1.3   VOCABULARY

Nouns

buchoo	department chief
fuku-shihainin	assistant manager
kachoo	section chief
sen'sei	teacher
shachoo	company president
shihainin, maneejaa	manager
Yamada-san	Mr. (Miss, Mrs., Ms.) Yamada

Others

hai	Yes (ee is less formal)
-kun	informal suffix, a form of address, used among men, equals, or towards those of lower status
-san	suffix attached to a person's name, similar to Mr., Miss, or Mrs.

1.4   EXPLANATION

1.4.1   Yamada-*san*

-san is a suffix attached to a person's name (either last or first name), which corresponds to the English titles Mr., Mrs., Ms., or Miss. It is important to note that -san must never be used with the speaker's own name.

1.4.2   Yamada-*kun*

-kun is another term of address which is used among male students and among close friends. In companies, a supervisor is entitled to use -kun to his male subordinates.

10

1.4.3 Tanaka-*kachoo*

Kachoo means *section chief.* This title alone is used as a term of address by his subordinates to the chief. Similarly, sen'sei is used for a teacher.

1.4.4 Ogen'ki desu *ka?* (Question marker)

In the above sentence, ka is a sentence particle which is placed at the end of a sentence, indicating that it is a question.

1.5 DRILLS

1.5.1 Greetings

In the following situations, provide the appropriate greeting.

Example:
> When greeting Mr. Yamada in the morning
> Yamada-san, ohayoo gozaimasu.

1. When greeting your friend Tom in the afternoon
   Tomu-kun, kon'nichiwa.

2. When greeting your manager in the evening
   Maneejaa, kon'ban'wa.

3. When saying good-bye to the company president
   Shachoo, sayoonara.

4. When saying good night to Mr. Tanaka
   Tanaka-san, oyasuminasai.

5. When greeting your teacher in the morning
   Sen'sei, ohayoo gozaimasu.

1.5.2 Greeting Someone on the Street

In the following situations, A and B will greet each other, and A will inquire if B is going somewhere.

Example: In the afternoon
> A: Kon'nichiwa.
> B: Kon'nichiwa.
> A: Odekake desu ka?
> B: Ee, chotto soko made.

1. In the morning
   A: Ohayoo gozaimasu.
   B: Ohayoo gozaimasu.
   A: Odekake desu ka?
   B: Ee, chotto soko made.

2. In the evening
   A: Kon'ban'wa.
   B: Kon'ban'wa.
   A: Odekake desu ka?
   B: Ee, chotto soko made.

1.6 EXERCISE

What do you say in Japanese when:

1. you meet someone in the morning?
2. you meet someone in the evening?
3. you meet someone in the afternoon?
4. you want to say *Hello* in the afternoon?
5. you want to say *How are you?*
6. you want to say *Thank you, I'm fine.*
7. you want to say *Goodbye.*
8. you want to say *Good night.*
9. you want to say *Are you going somewhere?*
10. you want to say *Just down the street.*

1.7 SIMULATION AND SKITS

1. You meet your business associate, Mrs. Yamamoto, on a Sunday afternoon. Greet her and exchange a few words.
2. You meet your manager, Mr. Watanabe, in the morning. After greeting him, express your concern for him because he took sick leave a couple of days ago.
3. You meet Professor Watanabe after not having seen him for a long time. Address several remarks to him.
4. You meet your close friend, Mr. Minoru Yokoda, in the late evening. Address several remarks to him.

1.8 CULTURE ORIENTATION

Japanese Culture as a "Culture of Form"

Japanese culture is known as a culture of form. It seems as though there is a proper form for everything the Japanese do. Greeting is a ritual, and ritual is very important for the Japanese. It must be executed properly, because one's greeting determines the quality of the ensuing conversation. A person is judged by how he greets another person. No matter how good the content of the conversation may be, if the ritual at the beginning is not properly observed, it is not considered adequate. One's manner of greeting is a reflection of one's family and educational background. Therefore, one is accorded trust and respect only if the ritual is properly observed.

Poor manners are perceived not only as a reflection of the individual and

12

one's family background, but also as a reflection of the organization to which one belongs. For this reason, the cultivation of employees' manners is a crucial part of the training and educational program of a company. For example, in an airline-stewardess training program, trainees must take lessons in tea ceremony and flower arrangement as a part of their flight training. The major purpose of these lessons is to help them develop correct posture, graceful bowing gestures, hand gestures, and proper social manners.

Japanese people are careful to create proper openings, and thus proper beginnings. Aisatsu means *greeting* in Japanese and is made up of two kan'ji characters. The first means *to open* and the other means *to approach*. In other words, aisatsu means *to approach the other with an open heart* (Suzuki 1981:24).

The aisatsu also confirms and signifies the two people's allegiance to a common culture and serves as a means to verify that the relationship is congenial (Tada 1980:322). Surely, two enemies would not exchange greetings. We will explore the cultural significance that takes place in the exchange of greetings between two people abiding in a common culture. The aisatsu or greeting signifies the beginning of a human relationship. It begins with the opening of one's heart. How one opens one's heart becomes crucial in the greeting.

1.9 THE MODE OF JAPANESE COMMUNICATION

Ritualistic Communication

In the Japanese culture, the significance of proper beginnings would be lost without proper endings. All that begins well must therefore end well. While the special value attached to a fresh beginning originates in the Shinto belief, the significance of the ending is influenced by Buddhist beliefs. According to Buddhist thought, death is not the end of everything. It is only part of an endless cycle of self-perpetuating reincarnation. The quality of one's life is affected by the way one brings one's life to a close. Likewise, the ending of a greeting is considered to be just as important as the beginning of it. A greeting begins and ends with verbal expression and suitable bowing.

Likewise, for American businessmen in the American context, first impressions are considered to be important. They are taught that a firm handshake creates a favorable first impression, signifying one's confidence and interest in the ensuing relationship. Needless to say, a proper greeting is important. However, what is emphasized is not so much the formality or ritualized part of the personal encounter, but rather the information actually communicated between the two parties.

Greetings for Americans are generally informal. One's manners are not generally considered to be a reflection of the organization to which one belongs, but rather a reflection of one's own personality.

From the foregoing discussion, it should be apparent that there is an extreme difference between the American concept of "greeting" and the Japanese concept of "greeting." If the Americans can show more respect for and appreciation of initial formality and apparently "empty form," the Japanese will be more comfortable. On the other hand, if the Japanese can discuss pertinent aspects of the business venture earlier in the transaction than in a comparable Japanese setting, the Americans will be more comfortable. In any case, it is important for both parties to keep their basic cultural differences in mind during international encounters, thus facilitating better communication.

1.10 LANGUAGE AND CULTURE

Language may be viewed as a mirror of culture. Let us look at the cultural assumptions and characteristics reflected in some Japanese greetings.

A. Ohayoo gozaimasu

This expression literally means *It is early.* In agrarian, premodern Japan, getting up early was a virtue. Early risers not only caught the proverbial worm, but they also won people's respect. The long, hard day started with the exchange of this expression: *It is early, isn't it! Let's work long and hard together again today.* By the exchange of this expression, the Japanese kindled their motivation.

Today, at factories and offices, this expression is exchanged unsparingly. The lively exchange of Ohayoo gozaimasu creates a spirited working atmosphere. It sets the tone for the day. Synchronization of sound and movement through greeting with a bow is believed to create the desired biorhythm. Throughout the day, other rituals are observed. These include group participation in the singing of the company song, reciting of the company motto, and exercising to music. Ohayoo gozaimasu is more than a greeting. It serves as a harmony-generating force when it is used in working situations.

As a polite expression, Ohayoo gozaimasu is generally not used with one's family members, close friends, or those who are considered members of one's ingroup. For them, the abbreviated form Ohayoo is appropriate. Osu or Ossu, which combines the first and last syllables of Ohayoo gozaimasu is a slang form used mostly by men.

B. Kon'nichiwa, Kon'ban'wa, Sayoonara, Jaa mata

These expressions literally mean: *As for this day . . . , As for this evening . . . , If so, . . . ,* and *Well, then, again,* respectively. From the standpoint of English syntax, these expressions are incomplete sentences. But in Japanese, unlike English, much is left to the imagination of the listener. Therefore, these phrases express a suitable vagueness and are viewed as complete in themselves.

14

Ohayoo gozaimasu can be used to greet anyone. However, Kon'nichiwa and Kon'ban'wa are used only with those who do not belong to one's own family or ingroup. These greetings are not exchanged among family members and among those who work at the same office because they belong to the same group. In addition, Kon'nichiwa and Kon'ban'wa are not used to greet one's superiors in business organizations (Mizutani and Mizutani 1977:17). These expressions, however, can be used among company associates, subordinates, or superiors outside the company.

C. Ogen'ki desu ka?

It means *How are you?* or *Are you in good health?* This expression is used when one has not seen the other party for a while or when one wants to inquire about someone's health. Ikaga desu ka? is equivalent to Ogen'ki desu ka? but it is less specific. It means *How are you?* or *How are things?* depending on the context. It can also serve as an invitation for refreshments. For example, Koohii, ikaga desu ka? means *How about coffee?* or *Would you care for a cup of coffee?*

D. Okagesama de

When asked Ogen'ki desu ka? a Japanese person will typically respond Okagesama de. This literally means *I am able to live with your help beneath your shadow.* It can also be interpreted as *I am able to live by your wisdom and benevolence.* At the root of this expression lies the Buddhist teaching of peaceful community living as the result of wisdom and benevolence of heart. Also, the Shinto belief of gratitude towards nature's blessings of a fruitful year and good harvest underlies the expression (Suzuki 1981:22–23). One's well-being doesn't just depend upon one's own strength and efforts; one is indebted to others around one and to nature itself. The Japanese person begins by paying his respects and expressing his indebtedness to the other individual, to the sun, water, rain, ancestors, father, mother, teacher, guest, and to all things. The expression Okagesama de includes the feeling of gratitude towards all things (Suzuki 1981:22). This signifies an extremely holistic attitude and way of thinking. Therefore, when asked Ogen'ki desu ka? the reply of Okagesama de includes a feeling of gratitude towards the other for one's very existence. Okagesama de is not merely used as a response to Ogen'ki desu ka? but it is also used in response to a friend's congratulatory remark on one's success or achievement or on the occasion of one's marriage. The underlying cultural assumption is that one's success and achievement are not solely the product of one's own ability and effort, but the result of contributions and favors on the part of many people. In the United States, where individualism is emphasized, the response would contain appreciation but not the degree of humility found in the Japanese equivalent. Okagesama de is a relational term which keeps people indebted to each other. This expression reflects the collective consciousness of the Japanese people.

E. Odekake desu ka?

This expression simply means *Are you going out?* How does one respond to this question? How much information is one expected to give? Well, first of all, this is not a question in that sense. Actually, it is a greeting, and one is not expected to say more than something like **Ee, chotto sono hen made** (*Yes, just a little ways down the street*) or **Ee, chotto dekakete kimasu** (*Yes, I'll be out briefly*). Americans often mistake this greeting for inquisitiveness. The following anecdote related by Jack Seward in *Japanese in Action* illustrates how perplexed he was by his landlady because he did not understand that **Odekake desu ka?** is simply a greeting.

Landlady: **Odekake desu ka?** *(Are you going out?)*
Seward: **Chigaimasu.** *(No, I am not.)*
Landlady: **Aa soo desu ka? Dewa, itte irassha.** (*Oh, is that so? Well, have a nice day.* [Lit. *Please go and come back.*])

Mr. Seward recalls his experience as follows:

> I tried a few times more after that, but my heart was not in it. Perhaps she did not really listen to what I said—perhaps she was making allowances, as may have been often necessary—for the caprices of a barbaric American (Seward 1969:46).

Obviously, Mr. Seward treated **Odekake desu ka?** as a personal question. He was puzzled at the landlady's response to his reply. The landlady might have been perplexed too, but she responded in accordance with appropriate form. Greeting is a ritual and a cultural form. She was not able to deviate from that form.

F. -san

Japanese people are always surprised by the way children in America address their elders by their first names. Even at a setting as formal as the university, students often address their professors by their first names. In Japan, it is impossible even to imagine workers at a company addressing their superiors by their first names. We will briefly look at the cultural significance that lies behind how people address each other in Japanese society.

It is generally said that Japan is a hierarchical/vertical society. People are sensitive to their respective ranks and constantly strive to maintain the distance between them. The use of language reflects one area through which the distances are maintained. How one addresses another becomes part of such a use of language. In Japan, the use of address terms differs according to one's position and rank. By comparison, Americans are not as sensitive to position and rank, given their rather horizontally structured society. In such a society, the value lies in the encouragement of friendliness and familiarity in order to decrease distance between positions. One often hears expressions such as "Just call me John," (rather than "Professor," or "Dr."), so that friendliness is encouraged. Even when a person of a subordinate position speaks with a person of a superior position, a degree of equality is encouraged.

In Japan, when one addresses an older person, the term san is added to the latter's last name. But when it is understood that the older person is a teacher or a doctor, the term sen'sei is added to their last name instead. (An example would be Tanaka-sen'sei.) Unlike English, where the title precedes the last name (as in "Prof. Tanaka," "Dr. Tanaka,"), the term sen'sei is always added after the last name. Sometimes the name can be altogether omitted and the term sen'sei alone used.

Within the company, the term -san is not generally used to address the section chief, department head, or president. Instead, such superiors are addressed by their position and title following their last name (thus, Tanaka-kachoo or just kachoo). Sometimes the title and the term -san are combined, as in kachoo-san, but this is mostly used as a term of address by women employees, or as a term of reference by a third person.

The term -sama is used instead of -san when the occasion is more formal. The term -chan is used for informal occasions. Generally, -chan is used to address children, added after their first names. It can also be used as a term of endearment towards older people.

For the Japanese people, who are sensitive to the hierarchical ranking system in their vertical society, terms used in addressing one another become a touchy issue. If the correct terms are not used for the correct occasions, negative feelings and impressions can result, affecting negatively the development of the relationship.

1.11 CULTURE QUESTIONS

1. Greetings are important aspects of any culture, but the reasons behind their importance vary from culture to culture. Read the culture orientation, then discuss the differences and similarities of the cultural role and meaning of greetings in Japan and in your country.

2. Discuss how you would train your employees to impart favorable impressions while dealing directly with Japanese tourists. To what sorts of things would you have to pay special attention?

3. The following morning greetings are exchanged by Miss Suzuki, a new employee to the company, and Mr. Kato, the section chief:

Miss Suzuki: Kachoo, ohayoo.
Mr. Kato: Aa, ohayoo.

In this exchange Miss Suzuki immediately gave Mr. Kato a negative impression. Discuss why.

4. The following greetings are exchanged by Mr. Yamamoto, a student, and Mr. Yoshida, a professor.

Mr. Yamamoto: Yoshida-san, kon'ban'wa.
Mr. Yoshida:　　Aa, kon'ban'wa.

Professor Yoshida was immediately offended in this exchange. Discuss why. Would Professor Yoshida's reaction be different if Mr. Yamamoto were a beginning student of Japanese?

5. A Japanese tourist commented: "The store I went to today was awful. I felt I wasn't welcome. I'll never go back to that store again." Based on what you have read in the culture orientation, discuss various possibilities for what could have occurred in the store.

6. What are some of the steps and precautions that one must take in order to impart a favorable and trustworthy impression of one's store, restaurant, or company while dealing with Japanese people?

1.12　SUGGESTED RESOURCE MATERIALS

1.12.1　Books and Magazines

A Hundred Things Japanese (Tokyo: Japan Culture Institute, 1975), pp. 125–217.
In Search of What's Japanese about Japan, John Condon and Keisuke Kurata (Tokyo: Shufunotomo Co., 1974), pp. 80–81.
Japanese Etiquette: An Introduction, The World Fellowship Committee of the Tokyo Y.W.C.A. (Tokyo: Charles E. Tuttle, 1970), pp. 3–8.
Japanese in Action: An Unorthodox Approach to the Spoken Language and the People Who Speak It, Jack Seward (New York: Walker/Weatherhill, 1969), pp. 45–50.
Kodansha Encyclopedia of Japan, vol. 2 (Tokyo: Kodansha, 1983), pp. 232–234.
Nihongo Notes 1: Speaking and Living in Japan, Osamu Mizutani and Nobuko Mizutani (Tokyo: The Japan Times, 1977), p. 17.

1.12.2　Films (16 mm) and Video Cassettes (Beta/VHS)

"Ritual: The Collective Psyche of Japan." 30 mins. Color. Psychomedic, 1977.
"Shinto: Nature, Gods, and Man in Japan." 47 mins. Color. Japan Society, 1977.

1.13　REFERENCES

Mizutani, Osamu, and Nobuko Mizutani. *Nihongo Notes 1: Speaking and Living in Japan.* Tokyo: The Japan Times, 1977.
Seward, Jack. *Japanese in Action: An Unorthodox Approach to the Spoken Language and the People Who Speak It.* New York: Walker/Weatherhill, 1969.
Suzuki, Kenji. "Kurashi no Naka ni Gosenzo kara Uketsuida Yasashisa to Chie o." *Yakushin* 1, no. 1 (December, 1981).
Tada, Michitaro. "Reigi Sahō." In *Nihonjin no Ningen Kankei Jiten,* ed. by Hiroshi Minami. Tokyo: Kodansha, 1980.

LESSON 2

INTRODUCTIONS

2.1 USEFUL EXPRESSIONS

Hajimemashite.	How do you do? (Lit. This is the first time.)
Doozo yoroshiku.	Pleased to meet you. (Lit. Please extend kindness to me. This can be used together with Hajimemashite: Hajimemashite, doozo yoroshiku. Doozo yoroshiku onegai shimasu can be used for formal introductions.)
Kochira koso.	The pleasure is mine.
(Go)shookai shimasu.	May I introduce to you . . .
Doomo.	Thanks.
Arigatoo.	Thank you.
Doomo arigatoo.	Thanks a lot.
Doomo arigatoo gozaimasu.	Thank you very much.
Doo itashimashite.	You are welcome.
(Aa,) soo desu ka?	Is that so? (Oh,) I see.
Yoroshiku onegai shimasu.	Pleased to meet you. (Lit. Please consider my request favorably.)

2.2 CONVERSATION

Introducing One Friend to Another

Watanabe: Kon'nichiwa.

Tanaka: Kon'nichiwa. Sen'jitsu wa doomo.

Watanabe: Iie, doo itashimashite. Tanaka-san, goshookai shimasu. Kochira wa Kinoshita-san desu. Kinoshita-san wa watakushi no Nihon no tomodachi desu. Kochira wa Tanaka-san desu. Tanaka-san wa Aroha Hoteru no maneejaa desu.

Tanaka: Aroha Hoteru no Tanaka desu. Doozo yoroshiku.

19

| Kinoshita: | Hajimemashite. Watakushi wa Tookyoo Tsuaa no gaido desu. (She hands her business card to Tanaka.) Yoroshiku onegai shimasu. |
| Tanaka: | Aa, doomo. Kochira koso. (He hands his card to Kinoshita.) Yoroshiku onegai shimasu. |

Watanabe:	Good afternoon.
Tanaka:	Hello. Thanks a lot for the other day (for yesterday).
Watanabe:	You're welcome. Mr. Tanaka, let me introduce you to someone. This is Miss Kinoshita. Miss Kinoshita is a friend of mine from Japan. This is Mr. Tanaka. Mr. Tanaka is the manager of Aloha Hotel.
Tanaka:	I'm (Mr.) Tanaka of Aloha Hotel. Pleased to meet you.
Kinoshita:	How do you do? I'm a guide for Tokyo Tours. *(She hands her business card to Tanaka.)* Pleased to meet you.
Tanaka:	The pleasure is mine. *(He hands his card to Kinoshita.)*

2.3 VOCABULARY

Nouns

anata	you
biichi	beach
gakusei	student
gaido	guide
hon	book
hoteru	hotel
meishi	business card
Nihon, Nippon	Japan
nihon'go	Japanese language
sen'jitsu	the previous day
shin'bun	newspaper
tomodachi	friend
watakushi	I
zasshi	magazine

Others

are	that, those (distant)
kore	this, these
sore	that, those (nearby)
kochira	this side (this person), this way, here
sochira	that side (that person), that way, there
nani (nan)	what
soo	so
iie	no

20

2.4 EXPLANATION

2.4.1 | N1 **wa** N2 **desu.** | (Identification)

Kochira *wa* Tanaka-san *desu.*   This is Mr. Tanaka.
 N1   N2

This sentence pattern can be called an identification pattern. N1, which is the subject or the topic, is identified or explained by N2. In this identification pattern, the particle wa functions as a subject- or topic-marker.

Examples:

Watakushi wa Yamada desu.	I am (Mr.) Yamada.
Are wa Waikiki Biichi desu.	That is Waikiki Beach
Yamamoto-san wa gaido desu.	(Mrs.) Yamamoto is a guide.
Are wa nan desu ka?	What is that over there?

The desu in pattern sentence 2.4.1 is the formal present (or imperfect tense) form of the copula *(to be)*. It is used in this case to equate the two nouns, that is, N1 *is* N2. The copula (desu) is conjugated as follows:

	Present	Past
affirmative	N desu.	N deshita.
negative	N $\begin{Bmatrix} \text{dewa} \\ \text{(ja)} \end{Bmatrix}$ arimasen.	N $\begin{Bmatrix} \text{dewa} \\ \text{(ja)} \end{Bmatrix}$ arimasen deshita.

Takeda-san wa shachoo desu.	Mr. Takeda is a company president.
Watakushi wa maneejaa dewa arimasen.	I am not a manager.
Yamada-san wa kachoo desu.	Mr. Yamada is a section chief.
Yoshida-san wa buchoo ja arimasen deshita.	Mr. Yoshida was not a department chief.

2.4.2 | N1 **no** N2 | (Noun modification: noun)

Yamada-san *no* zasshi   Mr. Yamada's magazines
 N1   N2

In Japanese, the particle no is used when Noun 1 modifies Noun 2 as in
Yamada-san *no* zasshi
 N1   N2

The Japanese noun modification pattern is a pre-positional modification pattern in which any noun modifier N1 *always* precedes N2 which is to be modified.

Examples:

N1		N2	
Tanaka-san	no	kuruma	Mr. Tanaka's car
Watakushi	no	tomodachi	my friend
Honoruru	no	chizu	map of Honolulu
Waikiki	no	biichi	beaches in Waikiki

Note that the English noun modification pattern can be either the pre-positional or the post-positional noun modification pattern as seen in the above examples. While N1 modifiers such as *Mr. Tanaka* and *my* precede N2 *car* and *friend*, N1 *Honolulu* and *Waikiki* occur post-positionally after N2 *map* and *beaches*.

When two or more N no nominative modifiers occur, the first nominative modifier may modify the following nominative.

Examples:

Watakushi no Nihon no tomodachi.	My friend from, or in, Japan.
Watakushi no nihon'go no sen'sei.	My Japanese language teacher.
Kochira wa watakushi no nihon'go no sen'sei desu.	This is my Japanese language teacher.

2.4.3 Anata

Anata (you) is rather limited in usage. It should not be used to address people like customers, teachers, or superiors. Instead, okyaku-sama for customers and sen'sei for teachers should be used.

2.5 DRILLS

2.5.1 Introductions

In this drill, each student will introduce himself using the following pattern:

1. _____ desu. Doozo yoroshiku.
       (name)

2. _____ no _____ desu.
       (organization)   (name)
   Doozo yoroshiku onegai shimasu.

22

2.5.2 Introducing One Friend to Another

A: Goshookai shimasu. _____, kochira wa _____ desu.
                             (name)   (name)
_____, kochira wa _____ desu.
   (name)   (name)

B: Hajimemashite. Doozo yoroshiku.

C: Kochira koso, doozo yoroshiku.

Practice the above using your business cards.

2.5.3 Response Drill

1. Are wa hoteru desu ka?
   Hai, . . .   Hai, soo desu. (Hai, hoteru desu.)
   Iie, . . .   Iie, soo ja arimasen. (Iie, hoteru ja arimasen.)
2. Kore wa nihon'go no hon desu ka?
   Hai, . . .   Hai, soo desu.
   Iie, . . .   Iie, soo ja arimasen.
3. Yamada-san wa Hiruton Hoteru no maneejaa deshita ka?
   Hai, . . .   Hai, soo deshita.
   Iie, . . .   Iie, soo ja arimasen deshita.

2.6 EXERCISES

2.6.1 Translation

What do you say in Japanese when:

1. you are introduced to someone?
2. you want to introduce Mr. Yamada, your friend, to Mrs. Smith, who is your section chief in your company?
3. you want to say *I should say so.*
4. you want to express your thanks to Mr. Uchida for the help he provided the other day?
5. you want to say *Don't mention it.*
6. you want to say *I'm Mr. Yoshida of the Hilton Hotel.*

2.6.2 Matching

Connect each item of the A group to one of the B group so that they form a set of greetings.

A
1. Ogen'ki desu ka?
2. Hajimemashite.
3. Sen'jitsu wa doomo.
4. Doozo yoroshiku.
5. Odekake desu ka?
6. Sayoonara.
7. Shibaraku desu nee.

B
a. Jaa mata.
b. Ee, okagesama de.
c. Doozo yoroshiku.
d. Iie, doo itashimashite.
e. Kochira koso yoroshiku.
f. Ee, chotto soko made.
g. Soo desu nee.

2.6.3 Scrambled Sentences

Rearrange each of the following groups of words into a Japanese sentence.

1. kore, zasshi, wa, desu
2. gakusei, ja arimasen, watakushi, wa
3. deshita, Yamada-san, sen'sei, wa
4. kore, nan, wa, desu, ka
5. Tanaka-san, desu, wa, hoteru, maneejaa, no
6. nihon'go, sore, hon, wa, desu, no

2.7 SIMULATION AND SKITS

1. As a new member of a company, introduce yourself to your associates.

2. Introduce your friend to your manager.

3. Introduce yourself by identifying the institution where you work.

4. You meet a businessman for the first time and exchange business cards.

5. You meet your former Japanese language teacher on the street while walking with a friend. Greet him and strike up a short conversation including the introduction of your friend to your teacher.

6. Introduce one friend to another, both in Japanese and American ways. Special attention should be paid to body movement, including eye contact, and to small talk.

7. Show some items such as Japanese books, magazines, etc., to your friend and ask:

Kore wa nan desu ka?
Kore wa nihon'go no hon desu ka?

24

2.8 CULTURE ORIENTATION

2.8.1 Human Relationships in Japan: **Uchi — Soto** Perspective

Japanese culture has been described as "a culture of relationship." Japanese perceive organization as an intricate network of human relationships. The success of the organization, therefore, depends on the success of human relationships. As in the old Japanese saying: **Jigyoo wa hito nari** (lit. *Business is people*), Japanese businessmen attach great significance to human relationships in business.

In Japan, human relationships are often seen to function in terms of uchi *(ingroup* or *inside)* and soto *(outgroup* or *outside)*. Japanese basically perceive the world as being either inside or outside. For example, if Japanese perceive their nation as uchi, the rest of the world is viewed as soto (to them).

The principle and structure of Japanese human relationships can be best explained from this general outlook of uchi and soto. The basic relationship of self with others is classified according to the degree of familiarity, as diagrammed below. Rules, expectations, and proper manners in dealing with others are highly structured within the framework of each domain, 1 through 3.

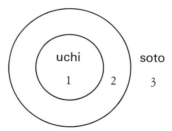

The individual enmeshed in such a human network as this is likely to react to his world and people in a compartmentalized way.

In Japan, people may find it comfortable to deal with those who come under domains 1 and 2, for they know exactly how to behave verbally as well as nonverbally within each framework of human relationships. Domain 1 is the intimate domain involving relationships among very close friends and family members, the so-called uchi members. It is the domain in which behavior is casual and even emotional, where spontaneous and honest feelings (hon'ne) are displayed. It is characterized by "social nudity" in which the natural self is disclosed, stripped of all "face" or social masks.

Anthropologist Takie Lebra refers to domain 2 as the "ritual domain," which is rather formal and normative, eliciting ritual behavior which ranges widely, from the extremely structured situation, such as a ceremony, to the accidental situation such as an unexpected encounter with an acquaintance on the street. Foreigners usually associate Japanese with the behavior of this domain: bowing, polite manners, honorific speech, humility, and reserve. The "self" is wearing a social mask and maintaining "face" in this domain. Domain 2 is not quite uchi and not quite soto, but has a form (rules and expectations) with which one must be familiar.

Domain 3 is characterized by actions toward those who are defined as soto (outsiders). The outsiders are seen by the self as strangers to whom there is no responsibility or social commitment. Lebra refers to this domain as the "anomic domain" in which there are no definite norms to control behavior. In this domain, one is not bound by "face," thus being able to afford shamelessness. Lebra elaborates further:

> If the situation happens to be totally new to Ego (self), anomic behavior is likely to emerge. Such a novel situation may be encountered by the person who has lived in a small, isolated village all his life and suddenly goes to a city; who has come into contact with a foreigner for the first time; who is travelling abroad for the first time, and so forth. In these situations, his interactions cannot be guided and controlled by a set of norms. The likely outcome would range from total inaction—a refusal to interact —to uninhibited action in a "shameless" and "heartless" manner. Japanese visiting abroad tend to suffer from the uncertainty of this anomic state but also enjoy the sense of freedom it allows, at least until they develop a new set of social relationships abroad (Lebra 1976:131).

Japanese behavior is distinguished according to domain. When one person encounters another, he quickly searches through the three domains to establish a suitable relationship, finally settling on one domain. At times, the individual may exhibit the behavior of two domains towards one person in a single meeting. For example, a stranger, who is an outsider, may suddenly become an acquaintance through introduction by a mutual friend; then the interaction changes from the anomic (3) to the ritual (2).

In American culture, there are also three such domains. However, the lines which distinguish each domain are not as clear-cut as those in Japanese culture. The use of language does not differ from one domain to the other; the behavior does not change, depending on each domain. It is much easier for strangers to meet and to get to know each other in American culture.

2.8.2 Bowing

As stated in the first chapter, Japanese culture can be said to be a culture of synchronizing movement. This can be observed in the exchange of greetings between two Japanese people. While they greet each other, they bow their heads up and down repeatedly. The synchronization of this movement provides a psychological stroking to each participant.

As stated in Lesson 1, the bow is a ritual that accompanies greeting. The greeting begins and ends with this bow, which determines whether a good impression is made, or not. Therefore, competence in this ritual becomes an indispensable skill in establishing successful human relations. Needless to say, it also plays an important role in achieving good human relations which lead to

26

success in the world of Japanese business. Let us further explore the meaning of the bow.

The bow is an act in which the Japanese people attempt to convey the resonance of their sincerity by bending their body forward. A proper and beautiful bow is said to ideally convey the resonance of a sincere heart. At the root of proper movement lies proper posture. At any given moment, if the proper posture is absent, sincerity of heart cannot be conveyed. Proper posture lies in movement and body, but even more important is the posture or attitude of the heart. In other words, if the genuine feeling of greeting is not included in the ritual of bowing, it loses its essential message. Even though greetings, such as "thank you" or "goodbye" are not verbalized, the formal ritual of bowing with a sincere heart conveys such feelings. It is said that while bowing, the timing of raising one's head at the same time as one's partner is so crucial that it can determine the course of the developing relationship (Ogasawara 1971:438).

The Japanese people believe that the beauty of a bow is similar to the beauty of a ripened stalk of rice swaying in the wind. They are taught the importance of showing respect and peace of mind by bowing more deeply and slowly than the other person (Suzuki 1981:23).

"The mature rice plant bends its head low."

As the ripened stalks of rice hang their heads, so must human beings become more humble and lower their heads further with age and material advancement. In this way, the ritual of bowing reflects the posture and attitude of one's heart. It is believed that an improper bow reflects one's poor training and education, as well as one's immaturity. Therefore, special attention must be paid to the bow upon the first and last encounter when important meetings between people take place. It is said that a proper final bow leaves behind reverberations much like the temple bell. These reverberations remain as good impressions on the hearts of the recipients.

It is difficult to expect people from other cultures, where bowing is not a part of their culture, to understand the beauty of a proper bow. Moreover, the Japanese people don't expect to see foreigners bow like the Japanese. But it can be extremely beneficial for one to be aware of the importance of the bow and to attempt to use it. In fact, one of our acquaintances couldn't speak any Japanese at all. But she was able to make many friends in Japan because she was known as "the one who has the beautiful bow." Even though her name may have been forgotten, her beautiful bow would always remain in the minds of those who had witnessed it. This is an excellent example of how the bow serves as an effective means of nonverbal communication.

2.8.3 The Japanese and the Handshake

When two people are introduced, it is customary, in America, to shake each other's right hand. During this firm and brief handshake, it is important that direct eye contact is maintained (Levine and Adelman 1982:4).

For the Japanese, who are unaccustomed to shaking hands, it is difficult to maintain direct eye contact, and the handshake becomes weak. One reason for such behavior may come from the fact that the Japanese people generally do not like to maintain direct eye contact, especially with those they have just met, fearing that it will make the other person uncomfortable. Women especially are discouraged from making direct eye contact with male strangers because it may be misinterpreted as signifying ulterior motives. For this reason, elevator girls working at department stores are trained not to maintain direct eye contact, especially with male customers.

Sometimes, one encounters a situation where the foreigner bows and the Japanese reaches his hand out for a handshake. At first glance, this looks like cross-cultural miscommunication. But when one thinks about it, both are only trying to be considerate of the other—in effect creating a situation of cross-cultural consideration! Sometimes one even encounters a Japanese who bows as he shakes hands. This may seem comical, but it represents the ingenuity of the Japanese combining both cultural elements.

Japanese businessmen often comment on the extremely firm, and even painful, handshake of the American businessmen. For the American businessmen, a firm handshake and direct eye contact are a sign of confidence and trust. But this message doesn't necessarily come across in other cultures. The Japanese people may interpret a firm handshake negatively as a sign of both aggressive behavior and aggressive character.

Generally speaking, the American handshake is not only firm, but brief. The briefness of the handshake can sometimes be interpreted by non-Americans in an unfavorable light:

> One foreign student remarked, "I'm beginning to think that there's something wrong with me. I have the impression that people in the United States don't like me. When I shake hands with them, they always pull their hands away quickly!" Is this person's impression correct or is he misinterpreting a cultural ritual? American visitors sometimes pull their hands away too quickly in countries where prolonged handshaking is common (Levine and Adelman 1982:4).

(Women in America are not expected to shake hands as firmly as men. A limp handshake from a man, especially a businessman, often signifies a weak character in the American mind.)

2.8.4   Distance as Communication

Through the act of shaking hands, a dynamic relationship may begin between strangers. At times, an introduction may even demand embracing the other person. Nevertheless, a handy rule of thumb for introductions involving strangers in Japan is that physical contact of any sort is seldom involved. Even while being introduced, the Japanese maintain a much greater distance from each other than do Americans. If this distance is decreased, the people concerned feel that their privacy has been invaded. Discomfort naturally results.

28

The distance maintained between people upon first encounter differs from culture to culture. Even within the same culture, the distance maintained differs depending upon the familiarity of the participants. It is importance to remember distance as part of communication in order to avoid uncomfortable situations.

2.8.5   Self-Introduction (Jiko Shookai)

Japanese usually meet through the introduction of a third party or a middleman. It is seen as unnatural to introduce oneself, and the Japanese try to avoid this approach as much as possible. A direct introduction such as "My name is Paul. What is yours?"—which is quite acceptable in American English—would be seen as too aggressive by Japanese, who use a more indirect method of introduction to which we shall now turn.

2.9   THE MODE OF JAPANESE COMMUNICATION

Intermediated Communication

The basic mode of meeting people in American culture is direct, whereas in Japan it is indirect. For example, in order to meet Mr. A, it is inappropriate for a businessman to go directly to him and introduce himself. He must find a "go-between" who can introduce Mr. A to him.

Japanese culture is a culture of "go-between." In order to establish a new relationship with a person or an organization, one must have a third party, an individual who knows that person or that organization. The third party, the one who pulls two different individuals together, is referred to as shookaisha *introducer.* In a formal introduction, the introducing party must generally assume responsibility for the newly established relationship. In the event that something goes wrong with that relationship, the introducing party must generally be consulted. If one has obtained a job with the assistance of an intermediary and later considers leaving the position, one must first go to the intermediary to seek his view and advice. Otherwise, that introducing party loses face and is subject to criticism.

In American culture, the introducing party generally does not assume this kind of responsibility. Strangers may meet by chance without much formality, or if an introducing party for them happens to be there, he does not play a featured role in the resulting relationship. Meeting people in American culture is generally by chance and oftentimes informal and direct.

How, then, can two businessmen meet and get acquainted without a third party who can bring them together? One needs a proper letter of introduction from a third party who knows the persons to be introduced. The letter of introduction, therefore, functions as a sort of mediator in this case. Likewise, the calling card called meishi often serves the role of a middleman. In addition to a person's name, the meishi also provides other important information. For example, it indicates his place of occupation and the position he holds. If one person is of higher social status, or holds a more respected position, the other is forewarned to use the appropriate language and manners. Without this kind of background information about the other person, Japanese businessmen find the first meeting stressful and uncomfortable. Therefore, without meishi to present, they feel unequipped to meet new people. The function of the Japanese meishi is much more broadly defined than the American's name card which is strictly used for further business reference.

It has often been noted that the Japanese culture is a culture of modesty. Perhaps that is best reflected in the manner of self-introduction. The emphasis upon personal modesty is such an important part of the Japanese society that those who are in the habit of speaking in terms of "I . . . I" are often thought to be engaging in unbecoming behavior which is both immature and childish (*The East* 1971:46).

Consequently, a variety of social techniques have evolved that permit the promotion and development of new relationships within an atmosphere that encourages both a humility of spirit and a certain modesty in mannerisms. It is merely a different form of self-assertion that Westerners are frequently prone to misinterpret as dishonest and self-effacing. For the Japanese, who place great stress on one's ability to live and work within the group, it is a social custom that serves a variety of purposes.

This custom is often best exemplified in the manner of exchanging meishi by those doing business in Japan. With a minimum of conversation, two parties meeting for the first time will, with quiet ceremony, respectfully present their cards for evaluation, allowing sufficient time for each party to come to an understanding as to the exact position and status each individual holds within his company. The meishi in almost all cases serves to establish levels of dominance and subordination within the developing relationship. Furthermore, it serves to outline areas of commonality that can be used to strengthen the new relationship. The custom of keeping conversation to a minimum during this ceremony prevents social embarrassment that may result from either boasting or acting unduly servile (Yutenji 1971:47).

The meishi also provides the opportunity of clearly defining an individual's role and status within the society. In the event that a Tokyo businessman finds himself in the embarrassing position of "running short" while entertaining clients, the presentation of his card to the club or restaurant manager serves the purpose of establishing the individual's identity as an employee of a well-known company that will subsequently "make good" on the debt that has been incurred. The proprietor is often honored to serve the representative of such a well-known firm, and frequently correctly anticipates that extending the credit of the establishment to the individual means continuing patronage by the businessman and his associates in the future (*The East* 1971:45–47).

30

2.10 LANGUAGE AND CULTURE

A. Doomo

After the movie *Shogun* was televised in the U.S., doomo became popular overnight. It was Anjin-san's pet expression. It is easy to remember and also easy to pronounce, but its usage is not as simple. Doomo changes in meaning depending not only on the situation, but also upon the tone of voice in which it is pronounced. For example, doomo means both *Thank you* and *Sorry* depending upon the situation. It also may mean *Hello, Good-bye,* and *I don't understand,* to mention just a few meanings. In some cases, Doomo kono tabi wa . . . which literally means *Indeed, at this time . . .* may serve even as an expression of condolence. Doomo is very much akin to the Hawaiian expression *aloha* whose meaning varies depending on the situation and on the tone of voice in which it is expressed. In a television program called "Studio No. 1" a whole skit, showing a man and a woman meeting in town, was carried on by merely using the word doomo. It included the greetings and even business talk, showing how versatile the word doomo is (Kindaichi 1977:40–41).

When this expression is quickly repeated (doomo, doomo), it takes on a casual note and should be used only among people with whom one is familiar. If one would like to sound more polite and sincere, it has to be repeated slowly. If one answers by saying doomo hesitantly, it is most likely that one does not know the answer or does not want to answer directly because the answer is negative. Likewise, if one wants to convey the message that one's business is not doing well, one uses doomo, expressing it rather slowly and slightly tilting the head sideways. If business is doing well, doomo is also used. Japanese love this expression, for it is ambiguous, indirect and incomplete enough to be used safely in various situations.

B. Arigatoo

Arigatoo literally means *(It) rarely exists or occurs.* According to Kunio Yanagida, a famous scholar in Japanese folklore, arigatoo was originally used to praise the deities for their wondrous acts which were indeed rare. During the Edo period (17th through 19th centuries) however, Japanese started to use arigatoo to express their gratitude and appreciation to their fellow human beings as well as to the deities (Okuyama 1972:178).

Another theory of the origin of the word arigatoo is that it came from the Portuguese word *obrigado* which means *obliged, bound, engaged,* or *grateful,* but there is not enough evidence to verify this. It might be that the Portuguese people learned the word arigatoo through the similarity in sound and meaning with their own word *obrigado* resulting in the theory that the words are somehow related.

Arigatoo gozaimasu is a polite equivalent of arigatoo. Therefore, if one is

31

talking to customers or clients, one must say arigatoo gozaimasu. This expression is considered to be one of the most beautiful expressions in the Japanese language. Company or store employees who serve clients and customers are given special training in effective pronunciation of doomo arigatoo gozaimasu.

C. Hajimemashite

For the most part, the expression hajimemashite will suffice while being introduced. It simply means *It's the first time.* Often the expression hajimete omeni kakarimasu is used in the same way. If literally translated, it becomes a silly expression meaning *For the first time I hang upon your honorable eyes.* The expressions hajimemashite or hajimete omeni kakarimasu are often followed by the expression doozo yoroshiku which literally means something like *Please be good to me,* and not much more. In Japanese, there aren't too many expressions where one's emotions can be expressed as in the English *I am happy to meet you,* or *I am pleased to meet you.* In some texts on the Japanese language, one can find the expression ochikazuki ni narete ureshii desu, literally meaning *I'm pleased to be close to you.* But such expressions are rarely used because of their unnaturalness. The Japanese people rarely express their emotions upon the first encounter. Even the words for *happy,* shiawase or koofuku are generally not used while directly speaking to another person about oneself. Usage of such expressions as *Are you happy?* (shiawase desu ka? or koofuku desu ka?) is limited to songs or questionnaires.

D. Sen'jitsu wa doomo

This expression is often used as part of a greeting or as a greeting itself, as in: Aa, Yamada-san, kon'ban'wa. Sen'jitsu wa doomo, or Aa, Yamada-san, sen'jitsu wa doomo. The meaning of this expression lies primarily in the expression doomo, in which only the two speakers will understand whether it signifies gratitude or apology. The expression sen'jitsu wa doomo reconfirms the experience of the two people at their previous meeting. It could be meant as *Thank you for the other day's treat,* in which case the expression would be used by the one who was treated. It could also be meant as *Please forgive my rudeness in taking up your precious time the last time we met,* in which case the expression would be used by the one apologizing. In other words, when two individuals meet, the one who is indebted to the other brings up the previous experience in order to show appreciation and establish continuity in the relationship. Recall that a good beginning is essential to a Japanese. So, if an expression referring to the previous meeting were not used, for example, in the case where someone had served you a meal, that person would be offended by your lack of appreciation and acknowledgement though the occasion to which it refers may have happened weeks ago. A good relationship cannot be maintained with negative feelings. Such an outcome must be avoided by an aware-

32

ness of form and politeness. One must always give verbal appreciation upon meeting a person to whom one is indebted. Such an expression should be used either as part of a greeting or as a greeting itself, even if the previous encounter took place a day, a week, or even months ago. The expression sen'jitsu wa doomo can help in establishing a good relationship while conducting business with the Japanese.

2.11 CULTURE QUESTIONS

1. During the Second World War and the Sino-Japanese War, the impression that the Japanese gave the rest of the world was very negative. The Japanese soldiers' treatment of the Chinese was brutal. They were also cruel to prisoners of war. But later, the Japanese came to be known as generous and well-mannered people. Yet, some foreigners are aghast at the Japanese lack of public manners in places such as trains. Ruth Benedict discusses this peaceful and violent nature of the Japanese people in her book, *The Chrysanthemum and the Sword.* Read Section 2.8.1 in the Culture Orientation and discuss the possible explanations for such Japanese behavior.

2. It is said that no matter how long one lives in Japan, the Japanese people will never accept a foreigner as one of themselves. Discuss possible explanations for the Japanese mentality and the resulting treatment of outsiders.

3. Having been introduced to a Japanese businessman, you are given his meishi. Unfortunately you don't have yours with you. What must you be aware of and how can you make communication smoother in such a situation?

4. It is said that American businessmen consider the first two or three minutes crucial in creating a positive impression of confidence, reliability, and trust. Attention is paid to the conversation at this time, as well as the initial handshake. Discuss how the Japanese businessman tries to create an impression of confidence, reliability, and trust. If you are from another culture, discuss how this is done in yours.

5. Discuss your observation of greetings exchanged between two Japanese people. What different types of bows are there? Is there a difference in bows between men and women? Is there a difference in bows depending upon age or social rank?

6. Bowing is not unique to Japan. It can be seen in many other cultures. Discuss when Americans bow, in what manner, and whether there is a difference from how the Japanese bow. Discuss Europeans in this context. How and under what circumstances do they bow?

7. There are different varieties of handshakes. Discuss the rules of proper handshakes: between the sexes, between young people, for women, etc. Discuss the use of embracing.

8. An American student returning to the U.S. from an exchange program stay in Japan shared with us this experience:

One day, my friend and I were walking down the street, when we happened to meet a friend of his. They struck up a conversation, but my friend didn't bother to introduce me to his friend. His friend also continued to converse with my friend without acknowledging my presence. As I waited to be introduced, the conversation abruptly ended with a "dewa." My friend turned to me, saying "Gomen nasai" ("I'm sorry.") and returned to our conversation which had been interrupted by meeting his friend. It was almost as if the conversation between my friend and his friend hadn't even taken place!

Having thus been seemingly ignored, this American student was offended by the situation. Was he really ignored? Discuss the possible explanations for what might have happened from the Japanese cultural standpoint.

2.12 SUGGESTED RESOURCE MATERIALS

2.12.1 Books and Magazines

A Hundred Things Japanese (Tokyo: Japan Culture Institute, 1975), pp. 110–111.

In Search of What's Japanese about Japan, John Condon and Keisuke Kurata (Tokyo: Shufunotomo Co., 1974), pp. 19–21.

"It's All in Your Cards—Meishi," Saburo Yutenji, *The East* 7, no. 8 (September, 1971): 45–47.

Japanese Etiquette: An Introduction, The World Fellowship Committee of the Y.W.C.A. (Tokyo: Charles E. Tuttle, 1970), pp. 3–26.

Japanese in Action: An Unorthodox Approach to the Spoken Language and the People Who Speak It, Jack Seward (New York: Walker/Weatherhill, 1969), pp. 72–77.

Japanese Patterns of Behavior, Takie S. Lebra (Honolulu: University of Hawaii Press, 1976), pp. 110–136.

Japanese: The Spoken Language in Japanese Life, Osamu Mizutani, trans. by Janet Ashby (Tokyo: The Japan Times, 1981), pp. 127–139.

The Making of James Clavell's Shōgun (New York: Dell Publishing Co., 1980).

Nihongo Notes 1: Speaking and Living in Japan, Osamu Mizutani and Nobuko Mizutani (Tokyo: The Japan Times, 1977), pp. 22–23, 46–47.

2.12.2 Films (16 mm) and Video Cassettes (Beta/VHS)

"BAFA BAFA Cross-Cultural Simulation Game." This is not a film or a video cassette. It is an effective tool to be used for enhancement of cross-cultural awareness. The kit is available at SIMILE II, 218 Twelfth Street, P.O. Box 910, Del Mar, CA 92014.

"Human Relations in Japan." 28 mins. Color. Gakken Eiga, 1978.

2.13 REFERENCES

Higuchi, Kiyoyuki. *Monoshiri Jiten: Nihonjin no Shikitari.* Tokyo: Hamato, 1981.
Kindaichi, Haruhiko. *Nihonjin no Gengo Hyōgen.* Tokyo: Kodansha, 1977.

Lebra, Takie S. *Japanese Patterns of Behavior.* Honolulu: University of Hawaii Press, 1976.

Levine, Deena R., and Mara B. Adelman. *Beyond Language: Intercultural Communication for English as a Second Language.* Englewood Cliffs, New Jersey: Prentice-Hall, 1982.

Ogasawara, Kiyonobu. "Koosai to Reigi." In *Nihon o Shiru Jiten,* ed. by Tatehiko Oshima et al. Tokyo: Shakai Shisosha, 1971.

Okuyama, Masuro. *Nihonjin to Keigo.* Tokyo: Tokyo Do, 1972.

Suzuki, Kenji. "Kurashi no Naka ni Gosenzo Kara Uketsuida Yasashisa to Chie o." *Yakushin* 1, no. 1 (December, 1981).

Yutenji, Saburo. "It's All in Your Cards—Meishi." *The East* 7, no. 8 (September, 1971).

LESSON 3

SOUVENIR SHOPPING

3.1 USEFUL EXPRESSIONS

Irasshaimase.	Welcome. Come in please.
Doozo.	Please. Please help yourself. Here you are.
Nani o sashiagemashoo ka?	What can I help you with?
Ikura desu ka?	How much does it cost?
Kore wa ikaga desu ka?	How about this?
Onegai shimasu.	Please. (Expression used when asking a favor or requesting something.)
Hoka ni nani ka?	Anything else?
Sore dake desu.	That's all.
Maido arigatoo gozaimasu.	Thank you for your continued patronage. (Used for customers who come frequently.)

3.2 CONVERSATION

3.2.1 Buying Chocolates

Situation: A customer who looks to be a tourist enters a candy shop.

Ten'in: Irasshaimase.
Kyaku: Sono chokoreeto o kudasai.
Ten'in: Hai. Doozo. Omiyage desu ka?
Kyaku: Ee, soo desu.
Ten'in: Hoka ni nani ka?
Kyaku: Sore dake desu. Ikura desu ka?
Ten'in: Roku-doru nijuuyon-sen'to desu.

. . . . . .
　　　Doomo arigatoo gozaimashita.

Clerk:	Welcome.
Customer:	(I'll) have those chocolates.
Clerk:	Will this be a gift?
Customer:	Yes.

36

Clerk: Will there be anything else?
Customer: Just that. How much is it?
Clerk: $6.24.

           . . . . . .
           Thank you very much.

3.2.2   Back at the Hotel

Situation: A tour guide meets his group members at their hotel entrance.

Gaido: Okaerinasai. Doko e ikimashita ka?
Yamada: Omiyage-ten e ikimashita.
Gaido: Nani o kaimashita ka?
Yamada: Chokoreeto o kaimashita.
Gaido: Soo desu ka? Jaa mata atode.

Guide: Welcome back. Where did (you) go?
Yamada: We went to the gift shop.
Guide: What did (you) buy?
Yamada: Chocolates.
Guide: Oh. Well, see (you) later.

3.3   VOCABULARY

Nouns

aroha shatsu	aloha shirt
chokoreeto	chocolates
depaato	department store
eigo	English language
ima	now
jimusho	office
kaisha	company
kyaku, okyaku-san	customer, guest
makademia nattsu	macadamia nuts
mise	store, shop
muumuu	muumuu
nihon'go	Japanese language
omiyage	souvenir
omiyage-ten	gift shop
shigotoba	place of work
tabako	cigarettes, tobacco
tegami	letter
ten'in	salesclerk
uchi	house, home

Verbs

dekakemasu	to go out
hanashimasu	to speak
ikimasu	to go
kaerimasu	to return
kaimasu	to buy
kakimasu	to write
kimasu	to come
shimasu	to do

Others

ano (+ noun)	that, those (distant)
kono (+ noun)	this, these
sono (+ noun)	that, those (nearby)
dono (+ noun)	which
doko	where

3.4 EXPLANATION

3.4.1 | N o kudasai. | (Request)

Chokoreeto o kudasai.   Please give me (some) chocolates.

The sentence pattern using N o kudasai is the simplest way to ask for something in Japanese. The o in chokoreeto o kudasai is a particle which indicates the direct object of the sentence.

Examples:

Tabako o kudasai.   Please give me (some) cigarettes.
Kono zasshi o kudasai.   Please give me this magazine.

3.4.2 | N_{place} (e) V_{motion} ni | (Directional particles)

Depaato e ikimasu.   (I) am going to the department store.

The e is a particle that denotes direction. It follows place nouns or other nouns that may indicate places. The particles ni and e are used interchangeably with locomotive verbs that indicate movement from one place to another, such as ikimasu *go*, kimasu *come*, or kaerimasu *go back, come back*.

The -masu ending seen in verbs such as ikimasu occurs in formal style statements. The form -masu is the affirmative present (or imperfect) tense form ending of a formal verbal predicate. The conjugation of V-masu is as follows:

	present	past
affirmative	V-masu	V-mashita
negative	V-masen	V-masen deshita

Kaisha e ikimasu.	(I) go (will go) to the company.
Hoteru e ikimashita.	(He) went to the hotel.
Jimusho e kaerimasen.	(She) won't return to the office.
Waikiki e ikimasen deshita.	(They) didn't go to Waikiki.

The subjects in parentheses indicate that they are omitted in the Japanese rendition of the sentences. Subjects as well as objects are frequently omitted in Japanese sentences. Please note that after this lesson subjects and objects which appear in English sentences but which are omitted in Japanese sentences will not appear within parentheses.

3.4.3 $\boxed{\text{N}_{\text{place}} \textbf{ de N o V-masu}}$ (Do such and such in or at a particular place.)

Depaato de muumuu o kaimasu.	(I) will buy a muumuu at the department store.

A place nominative followed by the particle de indicates the place where an action takes place. This particle precedes an action verb or a verb of happening. The o in muumuu o kaimasu is the object marker, which precedes an action verb.

Examples:

Nani o kaimashita ka?	What did (you) buy?
Aroha shatsu o kaimashita.	(I) bought an aloha shirt.
Doko de kaimashita ka?	Where did (you) buy (it)?
Waikiki no mise de kaimashita.	(I) bought (it) at a store in Waikiki.
Omiyage-ten de chokoreeto o kaimasu.	(I) will buy (some) chocolates at the souvenir shop.
Hoteru de tegami o kakimasu.	(I) will write a letter at the hotel.

3.4.4 Koko/Soko/Asoko

Places near or around the speaker, near the listener, and away from both are, respectively, referred to with koko, soko, and asoko. Following is a chart summarizing the ko-, so-, a-, do- words. Kono, sono, ano, and dono must always take a noun, as in: kono hon, sono hon, ano hon, dono hon.

Near the Speaker	Near the Listener	Away from Both	Question Words
kore - this (one)	sore - that (one)	are - that (one)	dore - which (one)?
kono N - this N	sono N - that N	ano N - that N	dono N - which N?
koko - this place, here	soko - that place, there	asoko - that place, over there	doko - which place? where?
kochira - this way, this person	sochira - that way, that person	achira - that way	dochira - which way?

Examples:

Kore wa hon desu.   This is a book.
Anata no pen wa dore desu ka?   Which is your pen?
Sono hon o kudasai.   Please give me that book.
Dono zasshi desu ka?   Which magazine is it?
Doko de sore o kaimashita ka?   Where did (you) buy that?
Kochira wa Yamada-san desu.   This (person) is Mr. Yamada.
Achira e ikimasu.   (I'll) go that way.

3.4.5 Numbers and Counting

Counting Numbers	Dollars (doru)	Cents (sen'to)
1 ichi	ichi-doru	issen'to
2 ni	ni-doru	ni-sen'to
3 san	san-doru	san-sen'to
4 shi, yon	yon-doru	yon-sen'to
5 go	go-doru	go-sen'to
6 roku	roku-doru	roku-sen'to
7 shichi, nana	nana-doru	nana-sen'to
8 hachi	hachi-doru	hassen'to
9 ku, kyuu	kyuu-doru	kyuu-sen'to
10 juu	juu-doru	jussen'to jissen'to

As you note in the above chart, there are some numbers (4, 7, and 9) which can be read in two different ways. Study further the list below:

11 juu-ichi	21 ni-juu-ichi	31 san-juu-ichi
12 juu-ni	22 ni-juu-ni	32 san-juu-ni
13 juu-san	23 ni-juu-san	33 san-juu-san
14 juu-shi	24 ni-juu-shi	34 san-juu-shi
15 juu-go	25 ni-juu-go	35 san-juu-go
16 juu-roku	26 ni-juu-roku	36 san-juu-roku
17 juu-shichi	27 ni-juu-shichi	37 san-juu-shichi
18 juu-hachi	28 ni-juu-hachi	38 san-juu-hachi
19 juu-ku	29 ni-juu-ku	39 san-juu-ku
20 ni-juu	30 san-juu	40 yon-juu
41 yon-juu-ichi	51 go-juu-ichi	61 roku-juu-ichi
42 yon-juu-ni	52 go-juu-ni	62 roku-juu-ni
43 yon-juu-san	53 go-juu-san	63 roku-juu-san
44 yon-juu-shi	54 go-juu-shi	64 roku-juu-shi
45 yon-juu-go	55 go-juu-go	65 roku-juu-go
46 yon-juu-roku	56 go-juu-roku	66 roku-juu-roku
47 yon-juu-shichi	57 go-juu-shichi	67 roku-juu-shichi
48 yon-juu-hachi	58 go-juu-hachi	68 roku-juu-hachi
49 yon-juu-ku	59 go-juu-ku	69 roku-juu-ku
50 go-juu	60 roku-juu	70 nana-juu
71 nana-juu-ichi	81 hachi-juu-ichi	91 kyuu-juu-ichi
72 nana-juu-ni	82 hachi-juu-ni	92 kyuu-juu-ni
73 nana-juu-san	83 hachi-juu-san	93 kyuu-juu-san
74 nana-juu-shi	84 hachi-juu-shi	94 kyuu-juu-shi
75 nana-juu-go	85 hachi-juu-go	95 kyuu-juu-go
76 nana-juu-roku	86 hachi-juu-roku	96 kyuu-juu-roku
77 nana-juu-shichi	87 hachi-juu-shichi	97 kyuu-juu-shichi
78 nana-juu-hachi	88 hachi-juu-hachi	98 kyuu-juu-hachi
79 nana-juu-ku	89 hachi-juu-ku	99 kyuu-juu-ku
80 hachi-juu	90 kyuu-juu	100 hyaku
200 ni-hyaku	2,000 ni-sen	20,000 ni-man
300 san-byaku	3,000 san-zen	30,000 san-man
400 yon-hyaku	4,000 yon-sen	40,000 yon-man
500 go-hyaku	5,000 go-sen	50,000 go-man
600 roppyaku	6,000 roku-sen	60,000 roku-man
700 nana-hyaku	7,000 nana-sen	70,000 nana-man
800 happyaku	8,000 hassen	80,000 hachi-man
900 kyuu-hyaku	9,000 kyuu-sen	90,000 kyuu-man
1,000 sen or issen	10,000 ichi-man	100,000 juu-man

1,000,000	hyaku-man
10,000,000	sen-man
100,000,000	ichi-oku

3.5 DRILLS

3.5.1 Question–Answer Drill

Example:
    Doko e ikimasu ka?
    Cue: Department store   Depaato e ikimasu.

1. Ima doko e ikimasu ka?
   Cue: Souvenir shop   Omiyage-ten e ikimasu.

2. Ima doko e ikimasu ka?
   Cue: Just down the street   Chotto soko made.

3. Ima doko e ikimasu ka?
   Cue: Home   Uchi e kaerimasu.

4. Ima doko e ikimasu ka?
   Cue: Company   Kaisha e ikimasu.

5. Doko e ikimashita ka?
   Cue: Workplace   Shigotoba e ikimashita.

6. Higa-san wa doko e ikimashita ka?
   Cue: Department store in Ala   Ara Moana no depaato e iki-
        Moana   mashita.

7. Yamamoto-san wa doko e ikimashita ka?
   Cue: A friend's house   Tomodachi no uchi e ikimashita.

8. Anata wa doko e ikimashita ka?
   Cue: Store   Mise e ikimashita.

9. Doko e ikimashita ka?
   Cue: Just down the street   Chotto soko made.

3.5.2 Question–Answer Drill

Example:
    Nani o sashiagemashoo ka?
    Cue: Cigarette   Tabako o kudasai.
                      (Tabako o onegai shimasu)

1. Nani o sashiagemashoo ka?
   Cue: Muumuu   Muumuu o kudasai.
                      (Muumuu o onegai shimasu)

2. Nani o sashiagemashoo ka?
   Cue: This chocolate   Kono chokoreeto o kudasai.

3. Nani o sashiagemashoo ka?
   Cue: Macadamia nut chocolate Makademia nattsu chokoreeto o
                            kudasai.

42

4. Nani o sashiagemashoo ka?
   Cue: That muumuu over there

   Ano muumuu o kudasai.

5. Nani o sashiagemashoo ka?
   Cue: That one

   Sore o kudasai.

6. Nani o sashiagemashoo ka?
   Cue: This one

   Kore o kudasai.

7. Nani o sashiagemashoo ka?
   Cue: This cigarette

   Kono tabako o kudasai.

3.5.3 Question–Answer Drill

Example:
   Doko de kaimasu ka?
   Cue: Department store

   Depaato de kaimasu.

1. Doko de tegami o kakimasu ka?
   Cue: Company

   Kaisha de kakimasu.

2. Doko de eigo o hanashimasu ka?
   Cue: Work place

   Shigotoba de hanashimasu.

3. Doko de omiyage o kaimasu ka?
   Cue: Souvenir shop

   Omiyage-ten de kaimasu.

4. Doko de nihon'go o hanashimasu
   ka?
   Cue: Company

   Kaisha de hanashimasu.

5. Doko de shimasu ka?
   Cue: Home

   Uchi de shimasu.

3.5.4 Question–Answer Drill

Example:
   Ima muumuu o kaimasu ka?

   Ee, kaimasu.
   Iie, kaimasen.

1. Kaisha e kimasu ka?

   Ee, kimasu.
   Iie, kimasen.

2. Omiyage o kaimasu ka?

   Ee, kaimasu.
   Iie, kaimasen.

3. Nihon'go o hanashimasu ka?

   Ee, hanashimasu.
   Iie, hanashimasen.

4. Kaisha de nihon'go o
   hanashimashita ka?

   Ee, hanashimashita.
   Iie, hanashimasen deshita.

5. Uchi e kaerimasu ka?

   Ee, kaerimasu.
   Iie, kaerimasen.

6. Waikiki e ikimashita ka?   Ee, ikimashita.
                               Iie, ikimasen deshita.

3.5.5 Question–Answer Drill

Answer the question Ikura desu ka? with the following prices.

1.	$1.00	Ichi-doru desu.
2.	$2.00	Ni-doru desu.
3.	$3.00	San-doru desu.
4.	$4.00	Yon-doru desu.
5.	$5.50	Go-doru gojissen'to desu.
6.	$7.28	Nana-doru nijuuhassen'to desu.
7.	$8.40	Hachi-doru yon'jissen'to desu.
8.	$9.65	Kyuu-doru rokujuugo-sen'to desu.
9.	$10.01	Juu-doru issen'to desu.
10.	$17.89	Juunana-doru hachijuukyuu-sen'to desu.
11.	$19.99	Juukyuu-doru kyuujuukyuu-sen'to desu.
12.	$47.10	Yon'juunana-doru jissen'to desu.
13.	$100.00	Hyaku-doru desu.
14.	$233.40	Ni-hyaku san'juusan-doru yon'jussen'to desu.
15.	$1,350.97	Sen san-byaku gojuu-doru kyuujuunana-sen'to desu.

3.6 EXERCISES

3.6.1 Situational Practice

Say it in Japanese.

1. Where did you buy this souvenir?
2. Is this your book?
3. I am going to the beach.
4. Do you speak Japanese?
5. This pack of cigarettes is $1.50.
6. How much was it? It was $6.00
7. What did you do at the office?
8. I went to the department store in Waikiki.

3.6.2 Situational Practice

What would you say in Japanese when:

1. you welcome (greet) your customer as he/she enters?
2. you want to ask a price?
3. you thank your customer?
4. you want to make a suggestion: *How about this?*
5. you want to ask a favor?

44

3.6.3 Completion

Fill in the blanks with the appropriate particle from the following list: wa, de, o, e, no.

1. Jimusho _____ tegami _____ kakimashita.

2. Shigotoba _____ hon _____ yomimashita.

3. Ara Moana _____ depaato _____ ikimashita.

4. Ima kore _____ shimasu ka?

5. Ima jimusho _____ ikimasu.

6. Kore _____ Yamada-san _____ zasshi desu.

3.6.4 Questions and Answers

Answer the following questions in Japanese.

1. Nani o shimashita ka?
2. Ima doko e ikimasu ka?
3. Doko de kono zasshi o yomimashita ka?
4. Depaato de nani o kaimashita ka?
5. Doko de tegami o kakimasu ka?
6. Kore wa ikura desu ka? ($776.89)

3.7 SIMULATION AND SKITS

1. Make up a list of Hawaiian souvenirs and prices to go with them. With one student playing the role of customer and another the role of salesclerk, simulate sales transactions in a souvenir shop.

2. One student holds up a certain item. Another student will ask where he/she bought the item and how much it cost.

3. Using the price list from a newspaper advertisement, have one student ask the salesclerk for the price of the product and for an explanation about the item.

4. Using the price list from a newspaper advertisement, have one student ask the salesclerk to explain about the product and tell where certain products come from.

5. A customer has entered the store in hopes of buying some souvenirs. However, she doesn't know what to buy. Have the salesclerk help her by introducing various products of Hawaii to her.

6. Two students meet early one afternoon after class on their way to their jobs in Waikiki. They stop to talk briefly about where they are going and what they

will do when they arrive at their workplace. Both students are curious about the language spoken in their respective workplaces. Create a conversation between the students where these major points are discussed.

3.8 CULTURE ORIENTATION

3.8.1 Omiyage

In the past, the Japanese have rather unkindly been labeled as "economic animals." Still, in many parts of the world, they are referred to as "shopping animals" or "gift-buying animals." One example of this perception is that of honeymoon couples spending at least two days of their busy four-day stay doing nothing but shopping! It has been estimated that Japanese visitors in Hawaii spend, on the average, almost nine times as much money on gifts and souvenirs as visitors from the U.S. mainland. This Japanese mania for souvenir buying may give people the impression that all Japanese tourists have a lot of money to throw away, or to spend on themselves. But in actuality, gifts are often bought as a form of reciprocation for gifts of money received from friends and relatives prior to leaving Japan. These monetary gifts are known as sen'betsu. The sen'-betsu places an obligation on the recipient to return the favor with appropriate souvenirs, known as omiyage. In the case of honeymoon couples, they buy souvenirs not only for their families, but also for their go-between, to whom they are indebted. Businessmen or company employees never forget to buy appropriate souvenirs for their colleagues or superiors. Thus, omiyage shopping is a very important concern for the Japanese tourists.

Historically, under the Tokugawa feudal system, it is recorded that travel was only permitted for those with an official pass. People could not travel freely or to an area of their own choosing. Travel was strictly prohibited for peasants. Merchants had to carry an official pass at all times. Even samurai, who were the highest in social rank, were required to carry an official pass while traveling from one area to another.

The feudal system strictly limited the travel of the general populace who were neither samurai nor merchants. But, an official pass could be issued to the general populace under one condition, which was to pay homage to the Ise Shrine. Under such a guise, one could travel with an official pass.

Those who paid homage to the Ise Shrine would come back with the Shrine's sacred amulets, special almanacs, or local products (such as facial powder, combs, or ornamental hairpins), and give them as omiyage. The sacred amulets from Ise served as important evidence that the person had gone there (Higuchi 1980:93–95).

Traveling was an expensive affair in those days. Not everyone who wished to travel could do so. But, by obtaining a sacred amulet from Ise, anyone could benefit: peasants in villages, merchants in towns, all could pray for a good rice harvest and prosperity in business. In order to pay homage to the Shrine and

46

obtain the sacred amulet, the peasants in the villages and employers and employees among the merchants in towns collected money to send a few people from among themselves. This collection of money was called osen'betsu. Although the custom of giving osen'betsu has become less common, it is still practiced today. A person fulfills various obligations by bringing back omiyage from the places to which he has traveled.

The people receiving the osen'betsu to travel to the Ise Shrine carried a miyake (container) filled with local products as offerings to the deities. On the way back, they carried the sacred amulets, sacred arrows, and other local products from Ise Shrine as omiyage. The omiyage consisted not only of material goods, but also of tales to be told, tales which originated in different provinces, and interesting anecdotes of experiences along the way. These tales were called miyage-banashi. A modern form of miyage-banashi is the numerous photographs Japanese people take.

Periodically, there were explosive occurrences of collective groups paying homage to Ise Shrine. These occurred when the people attributed their rich harvest or business prosperity to a sacred amulet or arrow brought by one of their travelers from the Ise Shrine. In 1771, an estimated two million people visited the Shrine, and in 1830, the number had risen to five million! In 1867, rumor began in Edo, spreading across the nation, that sacred amulets and arrows had fallen from the heavens at the Ise Shrine. Hearing this, there was a nationwide rush to pay homage at Ise Shrine with people arriving in great processions. Such mass demonstrations of homage to the Shrine were called okage mairi (Higuchi 1980:95). It is these periodic displays from which the modern expression okagesama (covered in Lesson 1) is believed to be derived. Okage-sama literally means *because of the deities' favor.*

As travel became more accessible to the general populace, the meanings associated with the word miyage (including the miyake *container,* the miyaka *storage house,* and omiage *to look carefully and to choose a gift for others*), blended together and, even to this day, are hard to separate.

Also, during this period, an important factor that changed the omiyage from mere gift giving of local products, to the status of souvenir, was the san'kin kootai system. This system required that the local lords (daimyoo) of various provinces attend the Shogun's court at Edo, with the purpose of paying homage and rendering service to him.

Depending upon the different daimyoo, the homage to Edo was paid either once every two years, or once or twice a year. When traveling to Edo, the daimyoo went in a procession consisting of about 1500 people. During the course of a year, daimyoo from 245 provinces all over Japan came to Edo. This caused a temporary mass exodus from the countryside. During the 17th century and continuing to the end of the 19th century, Edo steadily became the largest city in the world. It was estimated that every year approximately 250,000 samurai visited Edo, purchasing omiyage as gifts for family and friends prior to their return to their respective provinces (Nawabuchi 1980:76).

During the Meiji period, as Japan westernized, the main purpose of travel was to go to the West in order to return to Japan and assist in the modernization process. **Omiyage**, in this case, was not something concrete, but rather knowledge and technology learned and brought back to Japan from the West. But when Japan achieved a high level of economic development in the 1960s, the purpose of travel (especially abroad), shifted anew to pleasure and entertainment. At this point, there was rapid development in the tourism industry.

During the **okage mairi** in the feudal period, the Japanese people released their repressed energy by means of travel. After the Second World War the Japanese people's energy was directed to reconstructing their country. In the 1960s, their energy was released in various other ways. Businessmen worked hard to achieve economic growth. Student energy was directed toward protests and rallies. In 1962, the Japanese masses participated in the Tokyo Olympics. And in 1970, many people traveled to the World Exposition, as if it was another **okage mairi**. The growth in the rate of Japanese tourists abroad was no exception. Traveling abroad for the Japanese people was not only a way to obtain new knowledge, but it was a way of obtaining pleasure, and it served as an outlet for their restrained energies.

Looking at Japanese gift-giving behavior from a cultural perspective, we find that **giri** and **on** or *social obligations and a sense of debt and gratitude* also play an important role in the gift-buying custom. For the traveler, bringing gifts from the places he visited is a good way to repay his social obligations or debts, and to show gratitude to his relatives, friends, colleagues, or superiors.

Giri can be incurred in any number of ways, and the Japanese are very punctilious about returning such favors—often to the extent that they would rather not establish new social relationships because they may incur so many debts that they would be a burden.

In any case, gift giving is one relatively simple and socially approved way of reciprocating favors, whether they are tangible or intangible. It would be in poor taste not to reciprocate a gift received from someone else. Reciprocity is one of the crucial patterns of Japanese social interaction.

In Japan, gift exchange has become a highly conventionalized custom and has become an integral part of Japanese life. Gifts are generally exchanged three times a year: at the beginning of the year (**onen'shi**), mid-year (**ochuugen**), and year-end (**oseibo**). Generally, mid-year and year-end gifts are exchanged more commonly, probably due to the big bonuses given at these times. Gifts are exchanged, back and forth, much like the Japanese bowing movement. This basic synchronizing movement, which was described before as the basic Japanese rhythm, must be maintained in order to insure the continuation of the friendship and a good working relationship with others. The gift-exchange practice serves as an important social lubricant for the Japanese people today, even though many find the practice a burden.

Despite the complaints and criticisms against the highly ritualized and conventionalized gift-exchange practice described above, there are no signs of its disappearance. The exchange of gifts is considered as one of the concrete and simple ways in which one can pay back debts and express gratitude.

The conventional system of giving gifts two or three times a year still serves as an important social lubricant. But a less formal gift-giving custom in Japan comprises an important part of social etiquette. When one visits a home, it is customary that one brings a **temiyage** (hand-carried **omiyage**) for his host or hostess. Most commonly, this consists of sweets that can accompany tea or coffee which will probably be served. This **temiyage** expresses the guest's thoughtfulness towards his host/hostess. It would create an embarrassing situation, for both the guest and the host, if there were nothing appropriate to accompany the tea or coffee.

To prevent such a situation from occurring, the **temiyage** (bringing sweets or fruit) custom is both pragmatic and thoughtful. This creates a harmonious context for social interaction. Gift giving can be seen as a form of nonverbal communication in which the gifts serve as intermediaries to express the joys of reunion and the sharing of friendship.

We will look at the Japanese **omiyage** custom from a different perspective now. The customs of **omiyage** reflect the collective consciousness of the Japanese culture. When one steps outside the community (such as family, neighborhood, or company) to which one belongs, one attempts to share one's new experiences with those left behind. One way to share these experiences is with **omiyage** *local products* or **miyage-banashi**. In doing this, the collective consciousness or group spirit can be maintained.

If the new experiences undergone by a member who left the community are not shared, a distance is created between him and the other members of the community. The balance that was maintained within the community before he left is thereby disrupted. To avoid such disturbances, the custom of **omiyage** was created. Therefore, the **omiyage** can be said to reflect a spirit of equality and familiarity within a community. Because of this spirit of equality, a Japanese boss tends to buy the same **omiyage** in quantity, and to distribute them to his subordinates equally upon his return. No one is discriminated against. Thus group harmony is maintained. The Japanese culture maintains its unique spirit of equality in an industrialized nation.

Since the spirit and essential purpose of the **omiyage** lies in the act of sharing new experiences with the community, the content of the **omiyage** becomes a secondary issue. It can be said, therefore, that the **omiyage** has a symbolic meaning.

As mentioned before, one of the possible origins of the word **omiyage** is that it came from the expression **omiage**, meaning *to look carefully and choose an article to present to a person*. But this does not necessarily mean choosing a gift to suit the likes and dislikes of an individual. Rather, effort is made to choose a gift that best represents the experience encountered, such as a famous product of the locality which was visited. Thus, **omiyage** reflect the cultural elements of the whole society.

3.8.2 Businessmen and Gift Giving

Every year, on the fifth day of the New Year, businessmen, many of whom are top executives of large corporations, pay annual courtesy visits to their customer corporations, banks, and governmental officials to exchange ritual celebrations for the New Year and good wishes for continued patronage and good fortune for the coming year. During their visit, they leave their seasonal gift with their proper identification on it. This type of behavior by businessmen, wishing to receive the favor of continued patronage in the coming year, is viewed as bribery in the United States. For example, government officials receiving such conventional gifts from businessmen would be subject to prosecution in the United States. However, in Japan, such an act is generally accepted in the business community as a social custom. In fact, to ignore such customs would not only be rude, but could even result in the opinion that such a person is behaving in a socially unacceptable manner.

There are situations when the distinction between gifts given with good intentions (supported by the socially acceptable custom), and those given for personal reasons, or as bribes, can be very ambiguous. But in Japan, this very ambiguity becomes a virtue which serves as the basis for the continued business relationship. Such acts are often identified by Americans, accustomed to clearly delineating right from wrong, as bribes and, therefore, in violation of business ethics. If a favor is asked immediately after a gift is received, it becomes apparent that the gift was given as a bribe. But if a history of gift exchange has been established, in spite of the danger of being bribed, the Japanese will consider it a sincere token of a good and ongoing business relationship. Over the years, the custom of gift exchanging has served as a lubricant in order to create the foundation for a good business relationship. When such a foundation has been established, the Japanese feel that in times of emergency, difficult favors can be requested. Therefore, in the back of the Japanese mind, there is an assumption that establishing a good business relationship is both a time-consuming and money-consuming process (Takeuchi 1981:39).

3.9 THE MODE OF JAPANESE COMMUNICATION

Symbolic Communication

It was mentioned in Lesson 2 that meishi serve as a go-between for individuals. A gift functions in a similar manner. In other words, the Japanese will choose to express his own feelings and thoughts through a material object such as a gift, rather than through face to face verbal communication. The gift serves as a cue to the receiver to understand the thoughts of the one who gave the gift. Therefore, one tries to choose a gift that best expresses his feelings. In America, this type of gift-giving communication exists between lovers and people very fond of each other. This type of communication pattern can be characterized as an

50

intermediated communication pattern. It is a symbolic way of expressing one's feelings or ideas through the intermediation of a nonlinguistic object.

(The seasonal gift giving is more conventionalized and its significance lies more in what is appropriate to be given in that particular season, rather than to express personal feelings. When choosing a seasonal gift, one generally does not pay attention to the receiver's individual tastes.)

3.10 LANGUAGE AND CULTURE

A. Irasshaimase

Irasshaimase is a greeting word, equivalent to English *hello* or *hi,* used when a customer enters a store. Unlike English, where the *Hello* is followed by *May I help you?* irasshaimase doesn't need to be followed by anything else. In fact, by saying *May I help you?* or *Can I get you this (or that)?* customers may shy away because they feel the shopkeeper is pushy rather than helpful. There is no appropriate expression that the customer can use such as *No, thanks, I'm just looking.* This leaves the customer feeling uneasy. Japanese people become extremely self-conscious when they feel someone is watching them. Also they are often sensitive not to trouble the employees of the store! As a rule, it is best to leave the customers alone after pleasantly welcoming them. It is important to be constantly sensitive and aware of the customers' needs without making it obvious that you are watching them. This certainly requires skill!

(What has been covered above applies primarily to stores catering to the middle and upper classes. For general stores, even the greeting changes from irasshaimase to a less formal irasshai. The irasshai is repeated two or three times in a rapid and lively tone, especially for stores dealing with fresh produce such as fish, vegetables, and fruit. The lively tone of voice almost seems to exemplify the freshness of the produce.)

B. Shimasu

In the Japanese language, a single word, whether a verb or noun or adjective, can be a complete statement in an ordinary conversation. For example, shimasu, which simply means *to do,* cannot without the subject, be regarded as a complete sentence or statement in English. On the other hand, shimasu in Japanese is considered a complete sentence or statement. Without the actual context, we may of course not know the subject and the object of the verb shimasu. If, however, those who are engaged in the conversation understand the subject and the object being referred to, it is more natural for the interlocutors to omit the subject and the object.

Even in writing, subjects like *I, you, he, she, they* and objects like *it, this, that, they* are often omitted if they are understood in context. Inclusion of these subjects and objects renders the statements and sentences unnatural. The omission of subjects and objects, in conversation and in reading, perplexes the beginning students of Japanese, particularly native speakers of English, whose syntax requires, in its construction, distinct and full indication of the subject-object relation.

Why are subjects and objects often omitted in the Japanese language? One consideration may be related to the mode of thinking of the Japanese people. Japanese may generally be considered as visual and concrete thinkers, who are interested in the domain of the immediate and concrete experience (Kishimoto 1967:246). They are not inclined to analyze the immediate and concrete situation into a subject-object predicate relation. Rather than enhancing the distinction between subject and object, Japanese tend to perceive the subject as inextricably bound up with the surrounding and to perceive or experience a situation holistically. The language enables them to express their immediate experience in concrete terms without making a dichotomy between subject and object. This mode of Japanese thinking is well reflected in the Japanese poem, or haiku, in which subject-object distinction rarely occurs. Given this holistic cultural orientation of the Japanese people, it is understandable why they can often communicate meaningfully without the use of subjects and objects in their language.

3.11 CULTURE QUESTIONS

1. In the Culture Orientation, the influence of omiyage on Japanese culture was discussed. Discuss American gift-exchange practice or the gift-exchange practice in your own country, and describe how it reflects cultural values. Compare it with the case of Japan.

2. According to the 1980 Visitor Expenditure Survey by the Hawaii Visitors Bureau, all visitors other than the Japanese spend 9 percent of their money buying gifts and souvenirs daily while Japanese spend 36 percent. Explain why the Japanese spend such a large amount.

3. Assuming that you are working in a store, what kinds of products would you stock to appeal to the Japanese people? Which make the best omiyage? Is there a difference in taste depending upon age, sex, or occupation?

4. There are plans for a joint venture with a Japanese company and the one at which you work. Although the Japanese company is interested in the joint venture, there are several issues and problems that need to be discussed and resolved beforehand between your company and theirs. For this purpose, two representatives from their company fly to your country. They bring valuable Mikimoto pearls to your company president's wife (a common Japanese practice) and gifts to the businessmen with whom they will be directly negotiating. Since problems still remain to be discussed, your company has yet to approve the joint venture. How would you, being a culturally sensitive manager, deal with the valuable gifts brought over by the Japanese businessmen?

5. After reading the Culture Orientation, the Mode of Japanese Communication, and Language and Culture sections in this lesson, what kind of recommendations and advice can you give to omiyage shop owners and managers, in order to deal effectively with Japanese visitors?

3.12 SUGGESTED RESOURCE MATERIALS

3.12.1 Books and Magazines

"Gifts and Bribes in Japanese Environment," Sumio Takeuchi, *The Japan Economic Journal* (June 9, 1981), pp. 39–40.

"Gift-Giving in a Modernizing Japan," Harumi Befu, *Monumenta Nipponica* 23 (1968): 445–456.

A Hundred More Things Japanese, ed. by Hoyoe Murakami and Donald Richie (Tokyo: Japan Culture Institute, 1980), pp. 106–107, 134–135.

A Hundred Things Japanese (Tokyo: Japan Culture Institute, 1975), pp. 92–93.

In Search of What's Japanese about Japan, Jack Condon and Keisuke Kurata (Tokyo: Shufunotomo Co., 1974), pp. 14–18.

Kodansha Encyclopedia of Japan, vol. 3 (Tokyo: Kondansha, 1983), pp. 30–31.

Mock Joya's Things Japanese, Mock Joya (Tokyo: Tokyo News Service, 1968), pp. 695–696, 721.

3.12.2 Films (16 mm) and Video Cassettes (Beta / VHS)

"We Sell Everything—The Japanese Department Store." 90 mins. Color. TBS, 1980.

3.13 REFERENCES

Higuchi, Kiyoyuki. "Tabi." *Tabi to Nihonjin.* Tokyo: Kodansha, 1980.

Inagaki, Shisei. "Tabi to Omiyage Kō." *Nihon Hyakkei to Omiyagehin.* Tokyo: Heibonsha, 1980.

Kishimoto, Hideo. "Some Japanese Cultural Traits and Religions." In *The Japanese Mind,* ed. by Charles A. Moore. Honolulu: East-West Center Press, 1967.

Nawabuchi, Kenjo. "Miyage no Rekishi Jōron." *Nihon Hyakkei to Omiyagehin.* Tokyo: Heibonsha, 1980.

Takeuchi, Sumio. "Gifts and Bribes in Japanese Environment." *The Japan Economic Journal* (June 9, 1981).

LESSON 4

SOUVENIRS

4.1 USEFUL EXPRESSIONS

Shooshoo omachi kudasai.	Wait just a moment please.
Omatase itashimashita.	Sorry to have kept you waiting.
Omachidoo-sama deshita.	Thank you for waiting.
Soo desu nee.	Let me see.
Chotto chiisai desu.	It's a little small.
Saizu wa choodo ii desu.	The size is just right.
Sore o misete kudasai.	Please show me that.
Yon-paasen'to (4%) no zeikin ga tsukimasu.	Four percent tax will be added.
Kashikomarimashita.	Certainly.

4.2 CONVERSATION

4.2.1 Shopping for an Aloha Shirt

Situation: The salesclerk assists the customer in finding the proper size shirt.

Ten'in: Irasshaimase.
Kyaku: Aroha shatsu o misete kudasai.
Ten'in: Doozo kochira e. Saizu wa chuu desu ka?
Kyaku: Hai, soo desu.
Ten'in: Kore wa ikaga desu ka?
Kyaku: Soo desu nee. Sore wa ikura desu ka?
Ten'in: San'juu-doru desu.
Kyaku: Jaa, sore o ichi-mai kudasai.
Ten'in: Hai, kashikomarimashita.

Clerk: Welcome.
Customer: Please show me some aloha shirts.
Clerk: Please come this way. Is medium your size?
Customer: Yes, it is.
Clerk: How about this one?
Customer: Hmmm . . . How much is it?
Clerk: Thirty dollars.
Customer: Okay, I'd like one of those, please.
Clerk: Yes, certainly.

4.2.2   Shopping for Perfume

Kyaku: Koosui ga arimasu ka?
Ten'in: Hai, arimasu. Kochira wa Furan'su no koosui desu. Sochira wa Hawai no koosui desu.
Kyaku: Kono Shaneru Faibu (5) wa ikura desu ka?
Ten'in: San'juugo-doru desu. Sore ni yon-paasen'to no zeikin ga tsuki-masu.
Kyaku: Sore o ikko kudasai.
Ten'in: San'juuroku-doru nijissen'to desu. Tsutsumimashoo ka?
Kyaku: Hai, onegai shimasu.
Ten'in: San-doru hachijissen'to no otsuri desu. Doomo arigatoo gozaima-shita.

Customer: Do you carry perfume?
Clerk: Yes, we do. Here you are. These are French perfumes. Those are Hawaiian perfumes.
Customer: How much is this Chanel No. 5?
Clerk: It's thirty-five dollars. And four percent tax will be added.
Customer: Please give me one of those.
Clerk: It'll be thirty-six dollars and twenty cents. Shall I wrap it?
Customer: Yes, please.
Clerk: Here's your change, three dollars and eighty cents. Thank you very much.

4.3   VOCABULARY

Nouns

Amerika	America
ashita	tomorrow
baggu	bag
chuu	medium
dai	large
daigaku	university

Furan'su	France
Hawai	Hawaii
Itarii	Italy
kaimono	shopping
kinoo	yesterday
koosui	perfume
kyoo	today
otsuri	change
saizu	size
san'go	coral
seeru	sale
shoo	small
toshokan	library
uisukii	whiskey
zeikin	tax

Verbs

arimasu	to exist (inanimate), to have
ben'kyoo shimasu	to study
imasu	to exist (animate)
kaimono shimasu	to go shopping
tsutsumimasu	to wrap
yomimasu	to read

Adjectives

chiisai	small
ii (yoi)	good
muzukashii	difficult
omoshiroi	interesting
ookii	large, big
takai	expensive, high
tsumaranai	uninteresting
warui	bad
yasashii	easy, gentle
yasui	inexpensive, cheap

Adverbs

chotto	a little bit
totemo	very, quite

Counters

-ko	counter used for number of pieces
-mai	counter used for flat pieces

56

4.4 EXPLANATION

4.4.1 | N ga V (arimasu/imasu) | (Existence of something or someone)

This pattern | N ga arimasu/imasu | expresses the following ideas:

Existence: *There is a hotel* or *There is Mr. Tanaka.*
Location: *The hotel is at (someplace)* or *Mr. Tanaka is at (someplace).*
Possession: *We have a hotel* or *We have Mr. Tanaka.*

This pattern, therefore, expresses the existence, possession, or location of something or someone. If the N is inanimate (like a hotel), the verb is arimasu, and if the N is animate (like Mr. Tanaka), the verb is imasu.

Examples:
Uisukii ga arimasu.
inanimate ——↑

There is (some) whiskey.
We have (some) whiskey.

Okyaku-san ga imasu.
animate ———————↑

There are (some) customers.
We have (some) customers.

4.4.2 | N_place ni N ga arimasu/imasu | (Existence of something or someone in or at a particular location)

| N_place ni | indicates the particular location of something or someone, as in
Koko ni uisukii ga arimasu. *In here* (or *at this place*), *there is (some) whiskey* or
Here (or *at this place*), *we have (some) whiskey.*

Examples:
Koko ni hon ga arimasu.

There are (some) books here.
We have (some) books here.
Books are here.

Mise ni okyaku-san ga imasu.

There are (some) customers in (at) the
store.
We have (some) customers in the
store.
(Some) customers are in the store.

So when we hear Tookyoo ni, we expect the speaker is trying to say that *in this particular place*, *Tokyo*, he has something or someone.

Examples:
Tookyoo ni watakushi no uchi ga arimasu.
In Tokyo, there is my house.

Tookyoo ni, tomodachi ga imasu.
In Tokyo, I have a friend.

4.4.3 | N wa N_{place} ni arimasu/imasu |

This pattern is an alternate pattern of | N_{place} ni N ga arimasu/imasu | . In

this pattern, | N ga | became topicalized and changed to | N wa | . So, if
you want to talk about N as a topic of the sentence, you start with the topical-

ized N as in | N wa N_{place} ni arimasu/imasu | .

Examples:

Asoko ni Tanaka-san ga imasu.	There is Mr. Tanaka over there.
Tanaka-san wa asoko ni imasu.	As for Mr. Tanaka, he is over there.

4.4.4 | V-mashoo | (Let's do such and such.)

Furan'su e ikimashoo.	Let's go to France.
Nihon'go o hanashimashoo.	Let's speak Japanese.

The V-mashoo in ikimashoo is the OO form or the "tentative form" of ikimasu. In this lesson, this form means *Let's do* . . . The V-mashoo form, followed by the sentence particle ka, corresponds to the English *Shall I/we
(do) . . . ?*

Examples:

Tsutsumimashoo ka?	Shall I wrap it up?
Ikimashoo ka?	Shall we go?
Uchi e kaerimashoo ka?	Shall we go home?
Soo shimashoo.	Let's do so.
Ee, kaimashoo.	Yes, let's buy it.

4.4.5 Adjectives

Japanese adjectives have one of these endings: -ai, -ii, -ui, and -oi. These adjective endings express the present tense form of the adjective.

Examples:

takai	is expensive	samui	is cold
ookii	is big	chiisai	is small
yasui	is inexpensive	ii (yoi)*	is good
omoshiroi	is interesting	warui	is bad

*Ii is the colloquial usage for yoi meaning *good.*

The copula **desu** occurring after the adjective makes the sentence formal or more polite. In this sense, **desu** following an adjective can be viewed as the "formality marker" of the adjective.

Examples:

Informal	Formal or polite	
Takai.	Takai desu.	It's expensive.
Yasui.	Yasui desu.	It's inexpensive.

Unlike English adjectives, Japanese adjectives take new forms to indicate past and negative. The past and negative endings, namely -katta and -ku arimasen respectively, are added to the adjective stem (the part which precedes the final -i of adjectives). To make a negative past, **deshita** is added to the negative ending, -ku arimasen.

The following chart indicates the conjugation of adjectives (formal or polite forms):

	Present	Past
Affirmative	**A - (ai, ii, ui, oi) desu.** Takai desu. It is expensive.	**A - katta desu.** Takakatta desu. It was expensive.
Negative	**A - ku arimasen.** Takaku arimasen. It is not expensive.	**A - ku arimasen deshita.** Takaku arimasen deshita. It was not expensive.

4.5 DRILLS

4.5.1 Substitution Drill

Example:

koosui	Soko ni koosui ga arimasu.

1.	tabako	Soko ni tabako ga arimasu.
2.	otsuri	Soko ni otsuri ga arimasu.
3.	gakusei	Soko ni gakusei ga imasu.
4.	tegami	Soko ni tegami ga arimasu.
5.	sen'sei	Soko ni sen'sei ga imasu.
6.	shin'bun	Soko ni shin'bun ga arimasu.
7.	maneejaa	Soko ni maneejaa ga imasu.
8.	zasshi	Soko ni zasshi ga arimasu.
9.	omiyage	Soko ni omiyage ga arimasu.

10. shachoo	Soko ni shachoo ga imasu.
11. san'go	Soko ni san'go ga arimasu.
12. uisukii	Soko ni uisukii ga arimasu.
13. toshokan	Soko ni toshokan ga arimasu.

4.5.2 Question–Answer Drill

Example:
  Doko e ikimashoo ka?
  biichi   Biichi e ikimashoo.

1. Nani o kaimashoo ka?
   san'go   San'go o kaimashoo.

2. Nani o shimashoo ka?
   kaimono   Kaimono o shimashoo.

3. Nani o tsutsumimashoo ka?
   sono koosui   Sono koosui o tsutsumimashoo.

4. Doko de hanashimashoo ka?
   jimusho   Jimusho de hanashimashoo.

5. Doko de kakimashoo ka?
   toshokan   Toshokan de kakimashoo.

6. Kyoo doko e ikimashoo ka?
   Waikiki no biichi   Waikiki no biichi e ikimashoo.

4.5.3 Question–Answer Drill

Example:
  Kono saizu wa ookii desu ka?   Hai, ookii desu.
                                         Iie, ookiku arimasen.

1. Kono hon wa omoshiroi desu ka?   Hai, omoshiroi desu.
                                         Iie, omoshiroku arimasen.

2. Sono san'go wa yasukatta desu ka?   Hai, yasukatta desu.
                                         Iie, yasuku arimasen
                                             deshita.

3. Nihon'go wa muzukashii desu ka?   Hai, muzukashii desu.
                                         Iie, muzukashiku arimasen.

4. Kono koosui wa ii desu ka?   Hai, ii desu.
                                         Iie, yoku arimasen.

5. Sore wa Furan'su no koosui desu ka?   Hai, soo desu.
                                         Iie, soo dewa arimasen.

60

6. Are wa Hawai daigaku desu ka?   Hai, soo desu.
                                                 Iie, soo dewa arimasen.
7. Kono muumuu no saizu wa chuu desu ka?   Hai, chuu desu.
                                                 Iie, chuu dewa arimasen.

4.5.4   Response Drill

Example:
    Tabako ga arimasu ka?
    Cue: Ee   Ee, arimasu.

1. Kyoo uchi ni imasu ka?
   Ee
                                                 Ee, imasu.
2. Ashita omiyage o kaimashoo ka?
   Ee
                                                 Ee, kaimashoo.
3. Nihon'go no shin'bun ga arimasu ka?
   Iie
                                                 Iie, arimasen.
4. Kore wa takakatta desu ka?
   Iie
                                                 Iie, takaku arimasen deshita.
5. Kinoo biichi e ikimashita ka?
   Iie
                                                 Iie, ikimasen deshita.
6. Are wa Hawai no koosui desu ka?
   Hai
                                                 Hai, soo desu.
7. Sono mise wa yasui desu ka?
   Iie
                                                 Iie, yasuku arimasen.
8. Are wa toshokan desu ka?
   Iie
                                                 Iie, toshokan dewa (ja) arima-
                                                 sen.

4.6   EXERCISES

4.6.1   Matching

Using lines, connect the antonymous expressions.

1. takai   muzukashii
2. ookii   ii
3. warui   yasui
4. yasashii   chiisai
5. tsumaranai   omoshiroi

4.6.2 Scrambled Sentences

Compose short sentences in Japanese using the words given below.

chotto   choodo   totemo   zeikin   tsumaranai   ichi-mai   ni-ko

4.6.3 Transformation

Transform the following into their negative equivalents.

1. Omoshiroi desu.
2. Terebi o mimashita.
3. Totemo gen'ki desu.
4. Tanaka-san wa hoteru no maneejaa deshita.
5. Sono hon wa yokatta desu.
6. Sono omiyage o tsutsumimashita.
7. Nihon'go o hanashimashita.

4.6.4 Situational Practice

Say it in Japanese.

1. Let's go to Italy.
2. Shall we watch TV at Taro's house tomorrow?
3. Did you speak Japanese at the office?
4. This perfume is made in France.
5. Is this coral expensive?
6. This aloha shirt was very cheap.
7. Are there souvenir stores in the hotel?
8. Mr. Yamada was over there.
9. The size of this muumuu is just right.
10. Four percent tax will be added.

4.7   SIMULATION AND SKITS

1. Using the words you have already learned, ask your classmate what he/she did yesterday or plans to do today or tomorrow. Students who are asked these questions must respond.

2. Choose a place from the following list and ask your classmate what you do there: department store, supermarket, office, home, souvenir shop, hotel, library.

3. A customer is looking for a specific souvenir but does not see it anywhere in the store. Have her ask the salesclerk if they sell it or not. This customer

knows exactly what she is looking for. Therefore, have her describe it to the salesclerk.

4. A customer has chosen many souvenirs that he wishes to buy. He would like to know the cost of each item and the total cost that he is to pay. The salesclerk will respond and give him the total cost, which includes the sales tax.

5. During a transaction between a customer and a salesclerk, integrate the use of counters: -mai, -ko, -doru, -sen'to, etc.

4.8   CULTURE ORIENTATION

Japanese Culture as a "Wrapping Culture"

In Lesson 1, Japanese culture was referred to as a "culture of form." By explaining the term "culture of form," we were able to see how Japanese perceive, understand, and interact with their surroundings. In this lesson, we will explore the Japanese culture as a "wrapping culture," which looks at "culture of form" from another perspective.

Both the beginning and the ending of a process signify importance for a culture that emphasizes form. For example, the content of a speech may be well organized and well presented, yet if either the beginning or the ending is not satisfactory, the entire speech will be perceived as having been unsatisfactory. Similarly, in a "wrapping culture," if the outside wrapping of a gift is not done properly, regardless of its content, the value of the gift depreciates. Therefore, in Japan, as much importance is placed on external aspects as on internal aspects. To illustrate this importance, it is said that no matter how great a sword, if it does not possess a sheath, it is no sword at all. Miyamoto Musashi, a famous swordsman, was said to have no opponent to match him in strength. But he was once also said to resemble a "sharp sword without a sheath." In other words, a good swordsman required not only strength, but also something else in which to wrap that strength. Musashi was able to discover his real strength through studying Zen. It was mental growth and maturity that was able to "wrap" him.

In the "wrapping culture" of Japan, it is said that the more important an entity is, the less visible it is to the naked eye. Historically, the Japanese Emperor and the Shogun were invisible to the common person. In 1853 Commodore Perry, having studied this Japanese propensity for secrecy, negotiated with Japanese officials at Edo Bay as an invisible entity by using his men as go-betweens. As a result, Perry's existence was made more dynamic to the Japanese officials.

Just as objects are judged both externally and internally, so are people. If one asks a Japanese what the three basic human needs are, he will probably answer: clothing (i), food (shoku), and shelter (juu). He will most likely mention clothing first. Japanese will spend money on clothing even if it means cutting down expenses on food or shelter. In this culture, everyone "wraps" himself according to his role and needs. Women dress in a feminine fashion, men dress in a masculine fashion, teachers dress as teachers should, students dress as students should, children dress as children, and businessmen dress as businessmen. This phenomenon can explain why the Japanese culture is often thought of as a "culture of roles," consisting of a certain form that must be met.

The importance attached to wrapping extends, literally, to wrapping merchandise. Japanese department stores pay much attention to their wrapping paper. Each department store has its own wrapping paper through which it portrays its identity. It must design a wrapping paper which is in good taste and which can be appreciated by everyone. Yet, having a favorable wrapping paper alone is still inadequate if the gifts themselves are wrapped unsatisfactorily. Every department store employee receives training in how to wrap gifts. The ability to wrap gifts quickly and beautifully is indispensable for store employees. Japanese children are indirectly trained to master such dexterity through learning how to fold origami.

Stores that cater to the upper middle class and above wrap gifts in paper imprinted with their trade marks and place them in a special paper handbag of their own design. (Most of the time such services are free of charge.) Japanese tourists who are accustomed to such treatment at home are sometimes surprised and complain of inadequate service in foreign countries which do not have these customs.

In an American department store, gifts are generally wrapped at a special gift-wrapping counter, and often a minimal fee is charged. Otherwise, the customer may wrap it himself at home. In the Japanese "wrapping culture," such a situation generally does not occur.

Some critical attitudes towards this "wrapping culture" have recently been observed in Japan. Critics say that there is no need to wrap each gift meticulously and that it is a waste of paper, time, and energy. They suggest that by cutting costs from such external matters, the product itself can be made cheaper. Others say, in rebuttal to this, that if the wrapping process is put to an end, the Japanese sense of beauty, dexterity, and consideration for customers would slowly disappear. This would be considered a great loss to Japanese culture.

It seems that the wrapping process constitutes one of the core Japanese values which has been assimilated into all aspects of life, and such a value cannot easily be abandoned.

On formal gift-giving occasions, such as special seasons and weddings, Japanese generally wrap gifts properly and then wrap them once again with special rice paper, a very beautiful and strong paper made entirely by hand. There are about eight different types of rice paper. Depending upon the occasion, different types are used, along with a particular wrapping style. For example, according to the book *Japanese Etiquette,* wrapping paper is usually folded so that the last fold comes on top of the package at the right hand edge of the package. However, the last fold comes on top of the package at the left hand side for unhappy occasions. This custom regarding folding also applies to the direction in which a kimono is folded. If an improper wrapping style is used on certain occasions, it can be a cause for embarrassment. Japanese people are sensitive to such detail.

The carefully wrapped gift is next tied with a special cord called **mizuhiki.** These cords come in different colors, and each one is used for a different occasion. For example, red and white or gold and red cords are used for festive occasions. Gold and silver cords are used for funeral ceremonies.

Once the **mizuhiki** is properly tied, a special folded paper called **noshi** is attached to the upper right corner of the gift. (Originally, **noshi** was made of ear-shell, a kind of abalone stretched and dried. This symbolized a festive occasion in that the receiver of the gift need not abstain from consumption of meat as he would on occasions of death or other misfortunes in accordance with the Shinto custom.)

The elaborately wrapped gift is finally wrapped in a **furoshiki** (silken cloth wrapper). At the appropriate time, the gift is taken out of the **furoshiki** and is presented with a statement appropriate for the occasion. This description shows how complex and elaborate the Japanese gift-exchange custom is. It is almost an institution in itself with complex rules defining who should give to whom, what occasions require gifts, what sort of gift is appropriate on a given occasion, and how the gift should be wrapped and presented.

4.9   THE MODE OF JAPANESE COMMUNICATION

Circling-Around-the-Point Communication

As mentioned, in Japan, objects of importance are often wrapped. How is this custom of wrapping related to the Japanese mode of communication? If the American mode of communication can be described as *coming-to-the-point,* the Japanese mode of communication can be said to be *going-around-the-point.* Graphically, it can be thus shown:

(American mode of communication)   (Japanese mode of communication)

65

In other words, in the American mode of communication a point is made as simply and directly as possible. But in Japan, the actual point to be expressed is treated very much like a gift. In order for a point to be presented, it must be "wrapped." In America, a person who can express his thoughts clearly, directly, and quickly is considered to be articulate in a positive light. But in Japan, such an articulate person is perceived as being immature. The Japanese feel that a child can express his feelings and thoughts directly, but a mature adult should be sensitive to the listener's feelings and be able to detect his needs. Indirectness becomes inevitable in such a mode of communication.

This basic difference of communication between the Japanese and American can be seen in the following illustration.

A visitor from America to Japan decided to climb up a mountain after having heard that there was a famous shrine at its peak. Having reached the top after spending hours of climbing, he was disappointed at seeing an old and barren shrine. The actual walk up the mountain was only of secondary importance, merely a means to an end. The shorter the means, the better it would have been for him.

On the other hand, there was a Japanese person who felt that the winding road and the process of getting to the shrine was most important. On the way to the shrine, he was able to enjoy the beautiful scenery around him. He ended up spending more time getting to the shrine than he expected. He almost didn't make it to the shrine because he was satisfied with the experiences along the way. He enjoyed the process so much that the joy of discovering the simple and unostentatious shrine at the top of the mountain came, so to speak, as a by-product. He rested his tired body by the corner of the shrine and was thankful for its existence.

For the Japanese, *HOW* one gets to the top of the mountain becomes most important. The quality of the means determines the quality of the end. Even if one reaches the top, if the experience of getting there was not satisfactory, it often loses its meaning.

Similarly, in the Japanese mode of communication, attention is focused on the process of how the point is made rather than what the point being articulated is. In this respect, the Japanese mode of communication can be said to be process oriented, whereas in America, the primary focus seems to be placed on *WHAT* is being presented rather than on how it is presented. It can thus be said that Americans are more oriented toward a purpose or task. The Japanese often enjoy the process of getting to the point so much that they sometimes even lose their original point! After being exposed to such a situation, the task-oriented American becomes thoroughly frustrated because he is unable to accomplish anything visible. When a coming-to-the-point person attempts to communicate with a circling-around-the-point person, he ends up commenting "What is your point?" "What are you trying to say?" or "I lost you. I don't know where you are." Not being able to catch the main point creates a sense of frustration. On the other hand, for the circling-around-the-point person, frustration is created by the constant interruption in the flow of the process of getting to the point. What is most frustrating to the task-oriented American is, after waiting patiently for the process-oriented Japanese to get to the point, the conversation ends with the point never being verbalized. To the Japanese, the essential point is understood intuitively or psychically. What is essential is often inaudible. The technical term for this mode of communication is haragei; it requires considerable skill to use haragei effectively.

There is a generation gap in this indirect Japanese process-oriented, or circling-around-the-point, mode of communication. Although not as extreme as the Americans, Japanese youths are identifying more with a direct task-oriented and coming-to-the-point mode of communication. There is also a certain amount of regional difference in how people communicate. Generally speaking, people in Tokyo are more direct and to the point compared to people in Kyoto. In order to smoothly communicate with a Japanese person, it is essential to be aware of the indirect Japanese mode of communication.

4.10 LANGUAGE AND CULTURE

A. Depaato

In this section we will see what the Japanese depaato is and what caused it to catch the attention of foreigners, not only in Japan, but around the world.

When one enters a depaato, one is politely greeted with irasshaimase *(welcome)* by elevator girls dressed in uniform and white gloves. If one enters the depaato at opening time (usually 10:00 a.m.), not only elevator girls, but all the employees at their separate corners bow and greet the entering customers in unison. One can't help but feel like a king or a queen at this red carpet treatment! The first floor is usually filled with displays of deluxe and luxury items, such as perfumes, cosmetics, neckties, and pianos. There may even be some light classical music playing. The depaato invites people to an altogether different world.

The Japanese depaato has been described as a place to relax. Some people go there to see what the newest products are; in fact, many, instead of shopping at the depaato, shop at smaller stores where products are much cheaper. There are numerous coffee shops and tea houses in the depaato and these serve as places for people to meet. Sometimes, business even takes place in such locations. Every depaato has a floor of restaurants where customers can choose from a variety of different foods, such as Japanese, Western, and Chinese. The depaato also provides various types of entertainment. At times, they hold art exhibits and archeological exhibits. Also, when space is available, they offer it to small colleges which utilize it to teach courses. The depaato serves to provide cultural and educational programs for their customers' benefit. The roofs of the depaato provide a children's amusement center with rides, games, and sometimes even a miniature zoo. There are special cases where one may find a depaato with free nursery service. In a way, the depaato can be said to be a community in itself.

The concept of the department store originally came from abroad, and the Japanese people adopted it to suit their own culture and turned it into something distinctly Japanese.

B. Shooshoo omachi kudasai

This expression, which means generally *Please wait for a moment,* can be used as a means of avoiding a situation requiring a direct refusal.

In America, when a customer at a store requests something, and the employee knows that it has been sold out, he will be told, "I'm sorry, it has been sold out." The customer will understand and leave saying, "Oh, well. That's too bad." However, a Japanese customer may feel somewhat insulted by such a direct reply. He would feel as though his request was directly refused. For this reason, employees are specially trained not to directly reply "No," or "It's sold out," though such may indeed be the case. Instead, they are taught to reply, "I think that it's sold out, but I shall check once again for you." After such a reply, the customer has a while to prepare himself for a negative reply. The initial "No," to the request is made less direct in this manner. This can be described as providing a "cushion" for the customer. Rather than the final result, the process of getting there becomes important. In America, customers would readily accept the fact that a product was sold out, and being told so from the beginning would save time for both parties, making the process more efficient. But for the Japanese, the time he has available is better spent on emotional satisfaction than for material satisfaction. The employee also considers the extra time spent in looking for something he knows isn't there, not as a waste of time, but as an important service for the customer. Once the employee double-checks the storage for the requested item and is absolutely sure that it is not in stock, he may refer the customer to another branch of the same store. By doing this, the employee believes that rather than losing a customer, he will retain a customer by leaving a favorable impression of the store and their services. With such considerations, the phrase shooshoo omachi kudasai is used in Japanese stores.

C. Soo desu nee

This expression is one of the Japanese people's favorite expressions. It provides a pause in a conversation which allows the speakers to think aloud. Rather than directly confronting the listener with the speaker's opinion, this pause provides a cushion to the listener allowing him to prepare for the speaker's response.

68

Along with **soo desu nee** . . . , the expression **chotto** . . . is also used for refusal. When translated into English as *A little bit* . . . it forms an incomplete sentence. But in Japanese, this grammatically incomplete expression completes the intended message, and it is entirely up to the sensitivity of the listener to be able to catch it. Both the expressions **soo desu nee** and **chotto** are relational terms subject to interpretation according to the context where it is used. The Japanese language encourages the use of indirect means of expression as being more polite. Ambiguity is exalted as a virtue.

D. Otsuri

How one hands over change to a customer is different in Japan and America. American cashiers are instructed to state the amount of the purchase and then to count the change into the customer's palm, announcing each subsequent addition until the original amount handed over by the customer has been reached. For example, if a customer gives the cashier a ten-dollar bill for a $6.39 total purchase, he will first give the customer the proper change saying, six dollars and thirty-nine cents and 61 cents makes seven dollars." Then counting three one-dollar bills into his hand, he will add, "8, 9, and 10 dollars." However, the Japanese cashier, while handing over the change, will say something like, "You gave me ten dollars. The purchase price was six dollars and thirty-nine cents, so your change is three dollars and sixty-one cents." The change is often placed in a small tray rather than directly handed over by hand. With such differences, the Japanese person may find the American system rather confusing. Some Japanese people believe that the cashier is insulting their intelligence in basic arithmetic.

E. Saizu

The word **saizu** is a loanword which came from the English word *size*. The Japanese borrowed the word but not its measuring system. Being a clerk, you must be aware that the system of marking sizes is different, for example, in America a pair of women's shoes sized $7\frac{1}{2}$ would be a size 25 in Japan. So, Japanese tourists may need special help in finding the correct size, especially when it comes to shoes, dresses, shirts, trousers, and the like. A store that has available a chart converting the Japanese system to American will provide a helpful service for its customers. For your reference, the following chart lists size conversions.

A Comparison of Japanese and American Sizes

WOMEN						

| Blouse, Sweater | J | M | ML | L | LL | |
| | A | 34 | 36 | 38 | 40 | |

| Dress | J | 7 | 9 | 11 | 13 | 15 |
| | A | 8 | 10 | 12 | 14 | 16 |

| Hosiery | J | $20^{1}/_{4}$ | $21^{1}/_{2}$ | $22^{3}/_{4}$ | 24 | $25^{1}/_{4}$ | $26^{1}/_{2}$ |
| | A | 8 | $8^{1}/_{2}$ | 9 | $9^{1}/_{2}$ | 10 | $10^{1}/_{2}$ |

| Shoes | J | 22 | 23 | 24 | 25 | 26 |
| | A | $4^{1}/_{2}$ | $5^{1}/_{2}$ | $6^{1}/_{2}$ | $7^{1}/_{2}$ | $8^{1}/_{2}$ |

| Ring | J | 6 | 7 | 8 | 9 | 10 | 11 | 12 | 13 | 14 |
| | A | $3^{1}/_{2}$ | 4 | $4^{1}/_{2}$ | 5 | $5^{1}/_{2}$ | — | 6 | $6^{1}/_{2}$ | 7 |

MEN						

| Sport Shirts | J | S | M | L | LL | LLL |
| | A | XS | S | M | L | XL |

| Dress Shirts | J | 36 | 37 | 38 | 39 | 40 | 41 | 42 |
| | A | 14 | $14^{1}/_{2}$ | 15 | $15^{1}/_{2}$ | 16 | $16^{1}/_{2}$ | 17 |

| Socks | J | 23 | $24^{1}/_{2}$ | $25^{1}/_{2}$ | $26^{3}/_{4}$ | 28 | $29^{1}/_{4}$ |
| | A | 9 | $9^{1}/_{2}$ | 10 | $10^{1}/_{2}$ | 11 | $11^{1}/_{2}$ |

| Shoes | J | 24 | $24^{1}/_{2}$ | 25 | $25^{1}/_{2}$ | 26 | 27 |
| | A | 6 | $6^{1}/_{2}$ | $7-7^{1}/_{2}$ 8 | | $8^{1}/_{2}$ | $9-9^{1}/_{2}$ |

4.11 CULTURE QUESTIONS

1. The Culture Orientation described the circling-around-the-point mode of Japanese communication. Discuss whether the same can be said of business communication with the Japanese people.

2. What kinds of advantages would a manager have, who is aware of the different modes of communication in Japan?

3. Most travelers who have gone to Japan appreciate the Japanese department stores. Based on your readings in the Culture Orientation and your own experience (if any), compare your country's department stores with those in Japan and discuss why foreigners are attracted to them. In addition, discuss what could be learned from the Japanese department stores.

4. The Japanese people, who prefer to use an indirect mode of communication, are careful about the manner in which they make refusals. One may lose a customer merely by the manner of his refusal. Every culture has its way of refusing. Discuss how your culture facilitates communication between customers and store employees, especially in the area of refusals.

5. Discuss how store managers or giftshop employees can best provide and improve services for tourists. During the discussion, please bear in mind that the Japanese culture is a wrapping culture. Also consider the services offered by the department stores in Japan as discussed in our reading.

4.12 SUGGESTED RESOURCE MATERIALS

Books and Magazines

A Hundred More Things Japanese, ed. by Hoyoe Murakami and Donald Richie (Tokyo: Japan Culture Institute, 1980), pp. 74–75, 134–135.

Japanese Etiquette: An Introduction, The World Fellowship Committee of the Tokyo Y.W.C.A. (Tokyo: Charles E. Tuttle, 1970), pp. 42–47.

Kodansha Encyclopedia of Japan, vol. 2 (Tokyo: Kodansha, 1983), p. 87.

Nihongo Notes 1: Speaking and Living in Japan, Osamu Mizutani and Nobuko Mizutani (Tokyo: The Japan Times, 1977), pp. 144–145.

4.13 REFERENCES

Hayashiya, Tatsusaburo, Tadao Umesao, Michitaro Tada, and Hidetoshi Kato. "Depaato." *Nihonjin no Chie.* Tokyo: Chuokoronsha, 1974.

Japanese Etiquette: An Introduction. The World Fellowship Committee of the Tokyo Y.W.C.A. Tokyo: Charles E. Tuttle Co., 1970.

Kaplan, Robert B. "Cultural Thought Patterns in Intercultural Education." In *Readings on English as a Second Language,* ed. by Kenneth Craft. Cambridge, Mass.: Winthrop Publishing, 1972.

Murakami, Hoyoe, and Donald Richie, eds. *A Hundred More Things Japanese.* Tokyo: Japan Culture Institute, 1980.

LESSON 5

BRAND-NAME PRODUCTS

5.1 USEFUL EXPRESSIONS

Kochira wa ima *seeru (baagen seeru)* desu.

We have a *sale* going on here now.

Ni-waribiki de sashiagemasu.

A 20 percent discount will be given to you.

Don'na mono ga yoroshii deshoo ka?

What type of items do you have in mind?

Don'na *iro* ga yoroshii deshoo ka?

What kind of *color* would you prefer?

Kon'na mono wa ikaga deshoo ka?

How would you like something like this?

Shichaku shitsu (kitsuke shitsu) wa sochira desu.

The dressing room is that way.

Totemo oniai desu yo.

That really looks good on you.

Ryokoo kogitte (Toraberaa chekku) de (mo) ii desu ka?

Do you accept *traveler's checks?*

Ee, kekkoo desu.

Yes, that's fine.

Sore wa ima gozaimasen ga . . . sumimasen.

I'm sorry we don't have it . . . please excuse the inconvenience.

Chotto sumimasen . . .

Excuse me.

Nanika omise shimashoo ka?

Can I show you something? (May I help you?)

72

5.2   CONVERSATION

Shopping for Brand-name Products

Ten'in: Irasshaimase.
Kyaku: Fen'dii no han'dobaggu ga hoshii n'desu ga . . .
Ten'in: Okyaku-sama no desu ne?
Kyaku: Ee, watakushi no desu. Sore o misete kudasai.
Ten'in: Doozo. Kochira wa zen'bu Fen'dii desu. Achira wa Jiban'shii to
           Kurisuchan Deooru desu.
Kyaku: Kirei na baggu desu nee. Kono baggu wa ikura desu ka?
Ten'in: Fen'dii desu ne. 160-doru de gozaimasu ga, ichi-waribiki de sashi-
           agemasu. Desukara 144-doru desu.
Kyaku: Tabako mo arimasu ka?
Ten'in: Hai, gozaimasu. Dan'hiru mo Raaku mo gozaimasu ga . . .
Kyaku: Dewa, Dan'hiru o kudasai. Kono baggu mo issho ni onegai
           shimasu.
Ten'in: Doomo arigatoo gozaimasu. Dan'hiru wa 15-doru desu. Zen'bu de
           $165.36 desu.
Kyaku: Ryokoo kogitte de mo ii desu ka?
Ten'in: Ee, kekkoo desu yo. Pasupooto o onegai shimasu.
Kyaku: Doozo . . .
Ten'in: Doomo arigatoo gozaimashita.

Clerk: Welcome.
Customer: I would like a Fendi handbag.
Clerk: Is it for you?
Customer: Yes, it's for me. May I see that one please?
Clerk: Please do. These here are all Fendi handbags. Those over there are
              Givenchy and Christian Dior.
Customer: It's a beautiful bag, isn't it? How much is this bag?
Clerk: Do you mean the Fendi? Let me see now . . . that would be $160
              but I'll give you a 10 percent discount on it. So it'll be $144.
Customer: Do you also have some cigarettes?
Clerk: Yes, we do. We have Dunhill and Lark.
Customer: OK, please let me have a Dunhill. And also this bag as well.
Clerk: Thank you very much. The Dunhill is $15 a carton, that makes it
              $165.36 all together.
Customer: May I pay with traveler's checks?
Clerk: Yes, that'll be fine. May I see your passport please?
Customer: Here you are.
Clerk: Thank you very much.

73

5.3 VOCABULARY

Nouns

baagen seru	bargain sale
buran'do seihin	brand-name products
buran'do hin	brand made
fasshon	fashion
gen'kin	cash
han'dobaggu,	
han'do bakku	handbag
hito	person
iro	color
katachi	shape
on'na mono	things for women
oouri dashi	big sale
otoko mono	things for men
ryokoo kogitte	traveler's checks
ryuukoo	fashion
sutairu	style
tabako	cigarettes, tobacco
tokoro	place
toraberaa chekku	traveler's checks
waribiki	discount
zen'bu	all

Adjective Nouns

hade	loud (color)
jimi	conservative (color)
joobu	strong
nigiyaka	lively
shin'setsu	kind, polite
shizuka	quiet

Pre-Nouns

an'na	that kind of . . . over there
don'na	what kind of
kon'na	this kind of
son'na	that kind of

Adjectives

akai	red
atarashii	new
furui	old
kuroi	black

mezurashii	unusual
shiroi	white
yasashii	gentle, kind, easy

Adverbs

issho ni	together
zuibun	very, relatively

5.4 EXPLANATION

5.4.1 | N ga hoshii desu. | I want something.

Hoshii is an adjective meaning *wanted* or *desired*. The item that is wanted is followed by the particle ga. When it is necessary to identify by whom that desire is held, wa usually follows the person or animate nominative. Thus:
Watakushi wa han'dobaggu ga hoshii desu.
I want a handbag.

Yamada-san wa nani ga hoshii n'desu ka?
What would Mr. Yamada like?

The n' sometimes occurs between an adjective and the copular desu:
Hoshii n'desu.
Omoshirokatta n'desu yo.

In this case, n' is called the precopula. The difference between desu and n'desu is that n'desu is a little more emphatic, colloquial, and elucidative.

5.4.2 | A-i + N | (Noun modification: adjective)

A nominative may be modified by an immediately preceding adjective.

Examples:	chiisai saizu	small size
	omoshiroi zasshi	interesting magazine
	ii omiyage	good souvenirs
	atarashii mise	new store
	furui shin'bun	old newspaper
	mezurashii omiyage	rare souvenir
	akai shatsu	red shirt
	kuroi iro	black color
	shiroi han'kachi	white handkerchief

5.4.3 | Kirei and joobu | (Adjective nouns)

Words like kirei *pretty* and shizuka *quiet* are adjectives in English. However, in Japanese, they are classified as a different type of adjective called adjective nouns, NA. As was covered in Lesson 4, the regular adjectives end in one of four endings, namely -ai, -ii, -ui, and -oi. Adjective nouns do not usually have such endings. (However, kirai *disliked*, which is classified as NA, is an exception.) Some other adjective nouns are hade *flashy*, shin'setsu *kind*, teinei *polite*, and nigiyaka *lively*. The difference between regular adjectives and adjective nouns shows up in the case of noun modification. The former precedes a noun immediately, without any particle as in omoshiroi hon; the latter takes na as in kirei na hon. Compare these examples with those in 5.4.2.

Examples:
hade na muumuu — a colorful (flashy) muumuu
shin'setsu na hito — a kind person
teinei na ten'in-san — a courteous salesclerk
nigiyaka na biichi — a lively beach

The difference between adjective nouns and regular nouns in the pattern of modification is as follows:

Regular nouns

N no N

nihon'go *no* hon
a Japanese book

Adjective nouns

AN na N

kirei *na* hon
a pretty book

5.4.4 Particles: mo, to, ka, ya

The particle mo means *also* or *too* in English. In a sentence mo replaces the following particles: o, ga, wa.

Examples:

Watakushi wa muumuu *o* kaimasu.

I am going to buy a muumuu.

Watakushi wa muumuu *mo* kaimasu.

I am going to buy a muumuu *also*.

Tabako *ga* arimasu ka?
Do you have some cigarettes?

Tabako *mo* arimasu ka?
Do you *also* have some cigarettes?

Watakushi *wa* biichi e ikimasu.
I am going to the beach.

Watakushi *mo* biichi e ikimasu.
I am *also* going to the beach.
I *too* am going to the beach.

However, mo cannot replace particles like e, ni, and de. Mo occurs together with these particles.

76

Examples:

Watakushi wa biichi *e* ikimasu.
I am going to the beach.

Watakushi wa biichi *e mo* ikimasu.
I am going to the beach *also.*

Koko *ni* shin'bun ga arimasu.
There is a newspaper here.

Koko ni *mo* shin'bun ga arimasu.
There is a newspaper here *also.*

Kono mise *de* kaimasu.
I'll buy it at this store.

Kono mise *de mo* kaimasu.
I'll buy it at this store *also.*

Furthermore, when A mo B mo occurs in a positive sentence, it means *both* A *and* B; in a negative sentence, it means *neither* A *nor* B.

Examples:

Muumuu *mo* aroha shatsu *mo* kaimashita.
I bought *both* a muumuu *and* an aloha shirt.

Yamada-san *mo* Tanaka-san *mo* sen'sei dewa arimasen.
Neither Mr. Yamada *nor* Ms. Tanaka are teachers.

The particle to that occurs between nouns joins these nouns and is equivalent to the English *and.*

Examples:

Depaato de muumuu *to* aroha shatsu o kaimashita.
I bought a muumuu *and* an aloha shirt at the department store.

To is never used to join sentences or predicates. Soshite is used instead.

Example:

Biichi e ikimashita. Soshite ben'kyoo shimashita.
I went to the beach. And then I studied.

The particle ka which appears between nouns is used like the particles to and ya. Ka, however, is used as an equivalent of *or.*

Kyoo *ka* ashita shimasu.
I'll do it today *or* tomorrow.

The particle ya is used in a manner similar to the particle to *and.* Both to and ya may correspond to *and* in English, but ya is used to indicate some items representative of a larger group of items, while to is used when relating the entire list of items. Compare the following:

Hon *to* zasshi o kaimashita.
I bought a book *and* a magazine.

Hon *ya* zasshi o kaimashita.
I bought a book, a magazine, *and some other things* (such as a notebook).

5.4.5 Particle **wa** and **ga**

The particle wa may be used as a subject marker, topic marker, or contrast marker. These are explained further in this section.

1. The subject marker **wa** can be used in the sentence structure N *wa* N *desu*.

Examples:

Kore *wa* hon desu.	This is a book
Watakushi *wa* gakusei desu.	I am a student.

2. Topic marker **wa** can be used in the following sentence structures:

Hon *o* kaimashita.	Hon *wa* kaimashita.
I bought a book.	As for the book, I bought it.
Nihon ni tomodachi *ga* imasu.	Tomodachi *wa* Nihon ni imasu.
I have a friend in Japan.	As for my friend, (Speaking of my friend,) he is in Japan.

Wa is also used to replace the object marker, especially in negative answers.

Examples:

Hon *o* kaimasu.	Hon *wa* kaimasen.
I'm going to buy a book.	I'm not going to buy any books.
Tomodachi *ga* imasu.	Tomodachi *wa* imasen.
I have a friend.	I don't have any friends.
Ocha *o* nomimasu ka?	Iie, ocha *wa* nomimasen.
Will you drink some tea?	No, I don't drink tea.

3. Contrast marker **wa** can be used in the following sentence structures:

Hon *o* kaimashita ga, shin'bun *wa* kaimasen deshita.
I bought a book, but I didn't buy a newspaper.

Hon *wa* kaimashita ga, shin'bun *wa* kaimasen deshita.
Although I bought a book, I didn't buy a newspaper.

Kyoo ikimashita.	I went today.
Kyoo *wa* ikimashita.	I went today (but not the other days).
Kyoo *wa* ikimashita ga kinoo *wa* ikimasen deshita.	I went today but yesterday I didn't.
Tomodachi *ga* imasu.	He has friends.
Tomodachi *wa* imasu.	He has friends (but lacks something else).
Tomodachi wa imasu ga okane *wa* arimasen.	He has friends but he has no money.

It must be noted that **wa** in **Tomodachi wa imasu** can also be a topic marker.

The particle **wa** also serves as a subject marker in simple identifications.

Examples:

Kore *wa* Nihon no kamera desu.	This is a Japanese camera.

78

This answers the question, Sore wa nan desu ka?	*What is that?*
Watakushi wa Tanaka desu.	I am Tanaka.
This answers the question, Anata wa donata desu ka?	*Who are you?*

When this subject marker wa is replaced by a particle ga, the subject is emphasized.

Examples:

Kore *ga* Nihon no kamera desu.	This one is a Japanese camera.
This answers the question, Dore *ga* Nihon no kamera desu ka?	*Which one* is a Japanese camera?

The question focuses on one particular object, in this case the camera made in Japan.

Watakushi *ga* Tanaka desu.	*I* am Tanaka.
This answers the question, Donata *ga* Tanaka-san desu ka?	*Which one* (of you) is Mr. Tanaka?

This question focuses on one particular person, in this case Mr. Tanaka, among more than two individuals.

5.4.6 Particle **ne** (Tag Question)

Ne, said with a rising intonation, is a sentence particle, and implies the strong expectation of the hearer's agreement to what the speaker has mentioned. It often corresponds to *isn't it?, aren't you?, don't you think so?,* and so forth.

Omiyage desu ne?	It's a souvenir, isn't it?
Anata wa gakusei desu ne?	You are a student, aren't you?

When the ne is said lightly, it merely functions to add softness or friendliness to speech. This is a common practice in informal speech.

5.4.7 Particle **nee** (Exclamation marker)

Nee is a sentence particle that stands at the end of a sentence and is used to express admiration, surprise, or other similar exclamations, usually expecting the hearer's concurrence. Nee follows, among others, predicates of description, consisting of objective or adjectival nominatives.

Takai desu nee!	How expensive it is!
Kirei desu nee!	How pretty it is!

5.4.8   Particle yo (Emphatic)

Yo is an emphatic sentence particle that occurs at the end of a sentence and is used to call the hearer's attention to a statement giving warning, new information, assurance, and so forth. It corresponds to English *you know, I'll tell you, say,* or *certainly.*

Soko ni Yamada-san ga imasu yo.	Mr. Yamada is over there, you know.
Ashita toshokan e ikimasu ka?	Are you going to the library tomorrow?
Ee, ikimasu yo.	Yes, I certainly am.

5.4.9   Zen'bu de (Totalizing)

Zen'bu de means *for everything* or *for all.* The function of the particle de after a quantity nominative is often to totalize.

Zen'bu de ikura desu ka?	How much for everything?
Kore wa yottsu de juu-doru desu.	It is 10 dollars for the four.

5.4.10   Particle ga *(but)*

Ga that occurs at the end of a nonfinal clause, or before a comma, is the clause particle corresponding to *but* or *although.* The particle ga is used to connect two sentences like a conjunction in English.

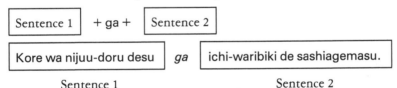

Sentence 1	+ ga +	Sentence 2

Kore wa nijuu-doru desu	*ga*	ichi-waribiki de sashiagemasu.
Sentence 1		Sentence 2

This costs 20 dollars but I'll give you a 10 percent discount on it.

Sometimes, ga appears without any clause following it. In such cases, ga is used to soften the directness of the expression, to show the speaker's hesitation, or to suggest an implication of the statement.

Uisukii ga hoshii n'desu ga . . .	I want a bottle of whiskey (but will you let me see some?).

5.4.11   Don'na

Don'na is a prenominative meaning *What sort of . . . ?* It matches kono, sono, ano, and dono. Following is another group of prenominatives:

Kon'na	This sort of
Son'na	That sort of

80

| An'na | That sort of |
| Don'na | What sort of |

| Anata no han'dobaggu wa don'na sutairu desu ka? | What sort of style bag do you have? |
| Yamada-san wa don'na kata desu ka? | What sort of person is Mr. Yamada? |

5.4.12 Okyaku-sama no desu ka?

Okyaku-sama no desu ka? means *Is it the customer's?* or *Is it (one) for you (the customer)?* A nominative han'dobaggu after no has been omitted when the han'dobaggu is understood. When the implication is clear, a nominative following no may be omitted.

Study the following:

Muumuu ga hoshii n'desu ga . . .	I'd like a muumuu.
Okyaku-sama no desu ka?	For yourself? (Your own?)
Ee, watakushi no desu.	Yes, for myself. (Yes, my own.)
Kono hon wa *dare (donata)* no desu ka?	Whose book is this?
Ni-doru no koosui ga arimasu ka?	Do you have a two-dollar perfume?
Iie, ni-doru no wa arimasen.	No, we don't have a two-dollar one.

Okyaku-sama may be said to a second person who is a customer or a guest.

5.5 DRILLS

5.5.1 English–Japanese Mixed Drill

1. Hoshii (n')desu.	Responses:
koosui	Koosui ga hoshii (n')desu.
I	Watakushi wa koosui ga hoshii (n')desu.
wanted	Watakushi wa koosui ga hoshikatta (n')desu.
2. Hoshii (n')desu.	
don't want	Hoshiku arimasen.
tabako	Tabako ga hoshiku arimasen.
Tomoko	Tomoko-san wa tabako ga hoshiku arimasen.
3. Hoshiku arimasen.	
didn't want	Hoshiku arimasen deshita.
san'go	San'go ga hoshiku arimasen deshita.
okyaku-san	Okyaku-san wa san'go ga hoshiku arimasen deshita.

5.5.2   Transformation Drill

Change the following adjectives to the past tense.

Example:
atarashii (desu)   atarashikatta (desu)

1. takai (desu)   takakatta (desu)
2. omoshiroi (desu)   omoshirokatta (desu)
3. furui (desu)   furukatta (desu)
4. ii (desu)   yokatta (desu)
5. atsui (desu)   atsukatta (desu)
6. yasui (desu)   yasukatta (desu)
7. muzukashii (desu)   muzukashikatta (desu)

5.5.3   Transformation Drill

Change the following to the past tense.

A. Example:
   Atarashii hon desu.   Atarashii hon deshita.

1. Yasui zasshi desu.   Yasui zasshi deshita.
2. Omoshiroi hito desu.   Omoshiroi hito deshita.
3. Ii hito desu.   Ii hito deshita.
4. Akai san'go desu.   Akai san'go deshita.
5. Kirei na on'na no kata desu.   Kirei na on'na no kata deshita.
6. Hade na shatsu desu.   Hade na shatsu deshita.
7. Otoko mono desu.   Otoko mono deshita.

B. Example:
   Yasashii kata ja arimasen.   Yasashii kata ja arimasen deshita.

1. Yasui tabako ja arimasen.   Yasui tabako ja arimasen deshita.
2. Hade na muumuu ja arimasen.   Hade na muumuu ja arimasen deshita.

3. Jimi na shatsu ja arimasen.   Jimi na shatsu ja arimasen deshita.
4. Teinei na hito ja arimasen.   Teinei na hito ja arimasen deshita.
5. Shizuka na hoteru ja arimasen. Shizuka na hoteru ja arimasen deshita.

6. Shin'setsu na kata ja arimasen. Shin'setsu na kata ja arimasen deshita.

7. Nigiyaka na tokoro ja arimasen. Nigiyaka na tokoro ja arimasen deshita.

5.5.4 Transformation Drill

Repeat each sentence, deleting the modified noun.

1. Okyaku-sama no baggu desu ne? Okyaku-sama no desu ne?
2. Anata no tabako desu ka? Anata no desu ka?
3. Doko no tokei desu ka? Doko no desu ka?
4. 10-doru no koosui o kudasai. 10-doru no o kudasai.
5. On'na mono no seetaa o misete On'na mono no o misete kudasai.
   kudasai.
6. Eigo no shin'bun o yomimasu. Eigo no o yomimasu.
7. Ikura no uisukii ga hoshii desu Ikura no ga hoshii desu ka?
   ka?

5.5.5 English–Japanese Drill

1. Kore wa dare no zasshi desu ka?
   Mine. Watakushi no desu.

2. Kore wa tsutsumimashoo ka?
   Please do so. Soo shite kudasai.

3. Kore wa otoko mono desu ka?
   No, for women. Iie, on'na mono desu.

4. Nani o sashiagemashoo ka?
   Please give me two of these kinds Kon'na shatsu o ni-mai kudasai.
   of shirts.

5. Don'na hoteru desu ka?
   A pretty hotel. Kirei na hoteru desu.

6. Don'na biichi desu ka?
   A quiet beach. Shizuka na biichi desu.

7. Don'na kata desu ka?
   A kind person. Shin'setsu na kata desu.

8. Don'na hon o yomimashita ka?
   A Japanese book. Nihon'go no hon o yomimashita.

9. Don'na tokoro ga ii deshoo ka?
   A lively place. Nigiyaka na tokoro ga ii desu.

10. Nani o kaimashita ka?
    An expensive (piece of) coral. Takai san'go o kaimashita.

5.6 EXERCISES

5.6.1 Questions and Answers

Answer the following questions in Japanese.

1. Kore wa ikura desu ka?
   670 yen
2. Ikura no seetaa ga hoshii (n')desu ka?
   for $15.00
3. Zen'bu de ikura desu ka?
   $240.51
4. Soko ni okane ga ikura arimasu ka?
   590 yen
5. Saizu wa nan deshoo ka?
   medium
6. Dore ga baagen seeru desu ka?
   This one is 20 percent off.
7. Ryokoo kogitte de mo ii desu ka?
   Yes, it is alright.
8. Don'na iro ga yoroshii desu ka?
   White or black

5.6.2 Translation

Express the following in Japanese.

1. This (item) is on sale now with a 20 percent discount.
2. This person wants an unusual item.
3. What color do you like?
4. You speak both Japanese and Hawaiian, don't you?
5. Mr. Tanaka and Mr. Yamada bought some Dunhill tobacco.
6. Let's go today or tomorrow.
7. Who bought a muumuu and an aloha shirt?
8. Four percent tax will be included. That makes $89.24 altogether.
9. Is this (person) Mr. Tanaka?

5.7 SIMULATION AND SKITS

1. Create a dialogue in which you and your friend talk about favorite brand-name items in terms of styles, colors, prices, and so forth.

84

2. Create a dialogue between a salesclerk and a Japanese customer who is looking for some buran'do-hin for omiyage to give his/her special friend in Japan.

3. Create a conversation between two people incorporating the topic of "color." Be creative, for example, talk about the rainbow, the flags of different nations, and so forth.

4. List a few products (European or brand-name) which are popular among females, and among males.

5. Identify the following brands in terms of products they sell. Come up with characteristics unique to each brand.

Kariche	Dan'hiru	Fira
Fen'dii	Omega	Deooru
Gucchi		

6. Have a conversation take place between a salesclerk and a Japanese customer. Let the salesclerk inquire as to why Japanese tourists prefer to buy brand-name products for omiyage, or have two people discuss their ideas about why Japanese tourists prefer to buy brand-name products.

5.8 CULTURE ORIENTATION

Brand-name Products

The Japanese people have a tendency to emphasize specific brand-name products. If it's perfume, it must be Chanel or Guerlain. If it's handbags, it must be Gucci. And if it's alcoholic beverages, it must be Napoleon! It is said that the best customers at the duty free stores all around the world are the Japanese. What makes the Japanese people so brand conscious? This lesson looks at such Japanese psychology and their mode of behavior.

It can be said that most people have some degree of curiosity toward things that are new to them. But the Japanese people's curiosity seems to exceed the ordinary degree. We will look into some possible reasons why this may be true. First, the Japanese characteristic of being curious can be traced back to the ancient Japanese myths. Second, Japan's geographical situation as an island has affected the Japanese personality. Third, the formation of the Japanese personality was highly influenced by the dual elements of nomadic and agrarian social structure. Finally, the Japanese tendency to constantly open and close their nation to outside influence had an effect on the formation of its people's national character.

According to the Japanese *Kojiki,* Amaterasu Omikami (the Sun Goddess), for some reason, had enclosed herself in a cave in heaven. As a result, the world became wrapped in darkness. The startled gods of heaven got together to think of a way to bring her out. Finally, they decided to cause a merry riot outside of the cave. One god began to dance and the other gods and goddesses seeing this began to roar with laughter and shout with merriment. The Sun Goddess became extremely curious about the noise and carefully peeked out to see. Just then two giants hiding on both sides of the cave's opening pushed open the huge rock closing the cave, grabbed the Sun Goddess by the arm and pulled her out. As a result, light shone once again in the world. In this way, the goddess Amaterasu Omikami brought light and happiness into the world (Toya 1982:136–140). According to one theory, the curiosity that began with the Sun Goddess was the prototype of the extreme curiosity of the Japanese personality. Many such instances of peeking out to the outside out of curiosity can be found in Japanese stories throughout history.

Japan is an island nation. Generally speaking, it is said that islanders idealize the flourishing continent across the sea. In the case of Japan, the continental civilizations of China and India were idealized. But by saying that the islanders of Japan have an extreme curiosity, it cannot be concluded that other islanders are equally curious. There must be something essentially Japanese that creates the Japanese personality.

According to cultural anthropologist, Eiichiro Ishida, the elements of curiosity can be traced to the character of the ancient Japanese people (Tsurumi 1972:28–29). It then can be characterized as being either nomadic or agrarian. It is said that the nomadic people were equestrian people from Northeast Asia who entered northern Kyushu in the beginning of the 4th century A.D. According to this theory, these nomadic people conquered the indigenous agrarian people of Japan and established the Japanese nation. The nomadic people can be characterized as being extremely curious and easily adapting to the culture of other people. On the other hand, the agrarian people can be characterized as being conservative, self-sufficient, and preoccupied with the preservation of tradition. Ishida explains that the Japanese personality is made up of both of these characteristics. When Japan opened her doors to the rest of the world, it may be attributed to the nomadic characteristic of curiosity and energy that led them to expand outward. When she closed her doors, on the other hand, it may be attributed to the agrarian characteristic of protectionism.

Both the element of seclusion and the tendency to open its doors to foreign influence coexist in the Japanese society influencing the development of the national character. There are strict barriers between ingroup and outgroup in human relations, but the Japanese put no limits on borrowing elements of the three basic human needs (clothing, food, and shelter) or ideology from abroad.

We will next briefly look at the evolution of the element of seclusion and the tendency to open its doors to foreign influence in Japanese society from a historical perspective and see how it relates to the national characteristic of being curious.

The glorious culture of China shone like a bright star in the eyes of the Japanese people during the Nara period in the 7th century. Japan opened her doors and hungrily borrowed from and immersed herself into the Chinese culture. It was during this time that the city of Kyoto was built, modeled after the Chinese city. But towards the end of the 8th century, the Japanese people began to realize that their own culture was being overwhelmed by the Chinese culture. During the Heian period, Japan closed her doors from outside influence and began to "Japanize" the elements of Chinese culture that had been brought in. "Japanization" is a process through which all the heterogeneous elements are adjusted to Japanese values and needs. As a result of the Japanization of these cultural elements, the Heian period produced many things that became distinctly Japanese. For example, Murasaki Shikibu's famous *Tale of Genji* was a product of this period. New writing systems called hiragana and katakana were also developed from the Chinese kan'ji script.

By the 12th century, during the Kamakura period, even Buddhism, which had entered Japan in the 5th and 6th century through Asashio Peninsula, had developed into a Japanese Buddhism with various sects. (There were two Mongol invasions during the Kamakura period [1192–1333] and the winds that helped to defeat them on both occasions were called kamikaze *divine wind*).

In the 14th century, during the Muromachi period, Japan opened her doors once again to acquire elements of Western culture, namely from the Dutch and the Portuguese. Contact was made with the Dutch and Portuguese with the primary interest of commerce and trade. Goods brought by ship into Japan were highly valued. With the arrival of the Dutch and Portuguese, the advent of Christianity became inevitable. There were some people among the Japanese that became firm believers of the Christian faith.

The 16th century, during the Muromachi and Momoyama period, was called Sengoku Jidai (warring period) when all parts of the country were at war with each other. Western influence in weapons could be seen at the time; guns and cannons were used on the battle ground. It was during this period of wars that the spiritual culture of the Japanese arts developed. The physically exhausted samurai and warriors sought spiritual comfort and peace. It was through elements such as tea, flowers, drama, and gardening that such spiritual comfort could be found. What had previously come in from China became transformed into Japanese forms, including tea ceremony (chadoo), flower arrangement (kadoo), and gardening, including bon'sai.

In the 17th century, Japan closed her doors again, fearing the number of those that believed in Christ's superiority over the Shogun and the Emperor would increase. This was the famous strict seclusion policy during the Edo period which lasted for about two and a half centuries. During this period all the cultural elements taken from outside were completely "Japanized" creating such distinctly Japanese things as kabuki and bun'raku.

However, Japan was not completely closed off to other countries during this time. It was through the port of Dejima in Nagasaki, on the island of Kyushu, that the Japanese maintained some contact with the Dutch and Portuguese. In other words, Dejima served as the single window through which the Japanese could observe the rest of the world. Finally, the seclusion, which had lasted for almost two and a half centuries, came to an end when Commodore Perry, aboard his "black ship," forced the country open. Having observed the "black ship," the Japanese were amazed at the West's technological superiority. They decided, at this point, that it was imperative for the Japanese to industrialize and become a stronger nation.

Edo period came to an end towards the end of the 19th century. With the start of the Meiji period, Japan adopted the model of **wakon-yoosai** *(Japanese spirit and Western technology)* to develop and strengthen the nation. **Wakon-yoosai** was a model in which the Western knowledge and technology would be combined with the Japanese spirit in order to strengthen the country. As a result, Japan's doors were flung open, especially to the cultures of England, France, Germany, and the United States. Japan absorbed many things from these cultures following the motto, *Catch up, catch up with the West!*

By the end of the Meiji period and Taisho period, Japan had reached considerable levels of industrialization. But in 1941, with its entry into World War II, it closed its doors to the West again. The Second World War came to an end in 1945. With Japan's defeat, it was not Commodore Perry aboard his "black ship," but General MacArthur aboard his warship that entered Tokyo (formerly Edo) Bay. It had been approximately 100 years since Commodore Perry had last entered the same bay. After the war, Japan once again opened up her doors to Western culture, especially the culture of the United States. It adopted the model of **wakon-yoosai**, showing remarkable growth in its economic development to the degree where Japan became one of the world's economic giants. In this way, Japan caught up with Western cultures and in some areas even overtook them. Japan's westernization began to exceed the degree to which it could be controlled. But it had become nearly impossible to close its doors once again to "Japanize" the foreign cultural elements.

Thus, Japan's contacts with the outside world have alternated in a pattern of numerous seclusion policies and open-door policies.

The Japanese people's sense of curiosity was exemplified further by this repetitive policy of being shown and then not being shown the outside world. Historically speaking, the Japanese people have always valued things coming from outside, referring to them as **hakurai-hin** (meaning *things brought by ship*). Strictly speaking, **hakurai-hin** nowadays refers to products of Western civilization, and the demand for these products seems to signify a certain amount of an inferiority complex the Japanese harbor toward the West. Placed in a hierarchical social structure, the Japanese people have a tendency to see the world with a vertical view with the Western civilization above its own.

The use of the policy of "quality control (QC)," as part of the model of **wakon-yoosai**, enabled the quality of Japan's products to reach international

88

standards. However, in spite of this fact, the Japanese people still have a weakness for products with famous foreign labels, calling them "brand products."

By merely possessing a brand-name product, some Japanese people feel a sense of uplifting of status, as though, for a moment, they had joined the upper rungs of society. Some describe this as the vanity of the Japanese people. Others describe it as a middle-class mentality. The cultural influence of form, name, and external appearances can also be observed. By molding oneself into the "form" of a brand-name product, the person can be seen as *appearing to* possess the quality of the particular product. For many people, the label of Johnny Walker Black is more important than its content. Essentially they are "drinking" the label! Some bars in Japan go to the extent of using empty Napoleon brandy bottles and filling them up with Japanese whiskey. The bottle is then placed on a shelf, not to be consumed, but to be seen. However, it is also important to realize that not everybody purchases brand-name products out of vanity; some people sincerely appreciate the quality of the product. They say that brand-name products last longer than others and that it is worth paying the high prices in the long run.

There is one more reason why the Japanese people are so attracted to brand-name products when they go abroad. Although the same brand-name products are sold in Japan, the Japanese people prefer to purchase them abroad where the prices are almost half or even one-third the price of those sold in Japan. A brand-name product bought in Japan becomes a luxury item difficult for most people to afford, whereas the same product becomes accessible to more people when purchased abroad. If one pursues this reason in depth, one may come to the conclusion that the Japanese people are attracted to these expensive brand-name products not from being wealthy enough to possess them, but rather often from their frugal characteristics. Some people say that Japan is, after all, still fundamentally a poor nation. Psychologists have said that such expensive brand-name products fulfill the Japanese people's psychological need that the possession of one's own house used to fulfill, prior to the tremendous increase in land and housing prices.

5.9   THE MODE OF JAPANESE COMMUNICATION

Semblance-type Communication

The Japanese people put much emphasis on form and outward appearance. A child should be childlike, a woman womanly, a boy boyish, an adult adultlike, a student studentlike, a mother motherly, a father fatherly, and a businessman businessmanlike. Each of these forms has its appropriate dress, language, gesture, and manner of speech which must be maintained. Therefore, it becomes necessary to stay within the given form in order to communicate. It is important that respect for one another's form is shown. Stores carry an image of their own.

This image of the store is yet another reason why employees must behave and communicate with the customer in an appropriate manner. However, even before the manner of speech or language is observed, the appearance of the person is noticed. How one dresses becomes extremely important in order to portray one's attitude. There is a saying in Japanese that *One is evaluated even before opening one's mouth.* A person's attitude can be detected by merely observing his/her personal appearance. One of the reasons why the Japanese people so often use uniforms is because a given form can be easily determined. This attention to form dictates that a language of respect (honorific style of speech) must be employed toward the customers. An employee must address the customers as an employee should. Otherwise, he may lose his precious customers. This maintenance of form is often difficult for an individualistic American to understand.

5.10 LANGUAGE AND CULTURE

A. Seeru and Baagen Seeru

The words seeru *(sale)* and baagen seeru *(bargain sale)* are words of foreign origin used in place of the Japanese words yasuuri *(sale)* and ooyasuuri *(grand bargain sale)*. Why do the Japanese choose to use such foreign words when they have their own? One important reason is to appeal to the public by using foreign words making the products seem more classy or fashionable. Using the Japanese word yasuuri or ooyasuuri seems to make the products cheaper in quality, much like the American psychology of saying *lingerie* instead of *underwear!* In order to create a better image, such foreign words are used. Department stores and stores generally dealing with products catering to the middle and upper class tend to do this more often.

However, in the city of Osaka where people tend to be more down-to-earth, the Japanese words yasuuri and ooyasuuri are used in order to appeal directly to the human desires, even at department stores.

B. Kon'na mono wa ikaga deshoo ka?

The Japanese people prefer to use the expression kon'na mono wa ikaga deshoo ka? rather than kore wa ikaga desu ka? while offering or suggesting items to customers. The expression kore wa specifies a specific object while kon'na mono wa is a less direct expression referring to *something like this,* thus giving the customer more to choose from. Also deshoo ka at the end of the expression is more indirect compared to desu ka, making the expression less harsh. The less direct an expression, the less harsh and more polite it becomes for the Japanese people.

90

C. Shichaku Shitsu

One must be very careful when buying clothing in a foreign country, since many countries have their own scale of sizes. Oftentimes, rather than relying on the size, one has to actually try it on. Unfortunately some people don't realize that many stores have shichaku shitsu *dressing rooms.* In Japan most wives, knowing their husband's taste, do all the husband's shopping for clothing. Often older people and people coming from rural areas in Japan have never used a shichaku shitsu. Such people have difficult times while in a foreign country trying to buy clothes for themselves. Sometimes one can observe such tourists trying on clothes right in the middle of the store to see if they fit! This can create an embarrassing situation for both the customer and the employee. It would be a good idea to mention in the beginning the existence of a shichaku shitsu by saying, shichaku shitsu wa sochira desu, to the customers in order to avoid such embarrassing situations. One can't assume all customers are aware of such things as the shichaku shitsu.

D. Ryokoo Kogitte or Toraberaa Chekku

The Japanese are known to carry cash. In fact, they are known to carry large sums of cash. Although the use of charge cards is increasing, Japan still remains largely a cash-oriented society. Since purchases are made in cash, most companies pay their employees' salaries or bonuses in cash. Japanese people often carry cash even while going abroad. Travel agencies dealing with Japanese tourists have had to forewarn them to try not to carry cash, after several Japanese tourists were robbed of all their money in foreign countries. Travel books also often advise Japanese tourists not to carry cash. As a result, an increasing number of Japanese tourists have begun to carry ryokoo kogitte (*traveler's checks,* often also known as toraberaa chekku). Not being used to using checks some people often forget to sign their names! In addition, the older people, not being accustomed to signing their names in English, have an even more difficult time while using traveler's checks. Sometimes, seeing the Japanese tourist not being able to properly sign even his own name on his check, the employee at the store will ask, "Do you have an I.D.?" in English. Not knowing that I.D. stands for identification, even a Japanese person who has studied English for several years will look puzzled. Most likely, even if the word *identification* or mibunshoomeisho (translated into Japanese) were used, many Japanese tourists would probably not understand what was being asked of them. This reaction is rooted in the lack of necessity for the average citizen to use any form of I.D. while purchasing goods in Japan. The Japanese people are just not used to producing an identification while simply shopping. Many of them don't carry their passports everywhere, and, therefore, may not be able to produce identification when requested. While dealing with Japanese tourists fumbling over their traveler's checks, an employee who understands and acknowledges what they are normally accustomed to can help create positive feelings.

E. Kekkoo desu

The use of the expression **kekkoo desu** can be difficult. In this lesson we will deal with the use of this expression as an answer to requests or offers. If a request is made, the answer **kekkoo desu** means, *Yes, that's fine*, granting permission. However, if an offer is made such as, "Would you like some coffee?" and the answer is in the affirmative, it should take the form **kekkoo desu nee**, with the **nee** added to the end. If the answer is in the negative, it should take the form, **Iie, kekkoo desu**, *No thank you*. The rules governing usage of this expression become increasingly complex when **hai**, **ee**, or **iie** are omitted. Its usage varies according to the situation. Although the expression is somewhat complicated, it is a useful one to learn since it is so often used. Here are some tips in learning the expression:

1. When the expression **kekkoo desu** follows a request, it is safe to assume that permission was granted, regardless of the absence of **hai**, or **ee** at the beginning of the expression.

2. When the expression **kekkoo desu** follows an offer, it is safe to assume that the answer was a *No thank you* even if the expression did not follow **iie**. If the answer was an affirmative one, it will usually be expressed as **kekkoo desu nee** with the **nee** following.

5.11 CULTURE QUESTIONS

1. Japanese culture was described as a culture of form in Lesson 1, a wrapping culture in Lesson 4, and a culture of appearance in this lesson. Describe how these three analyses of Japanese culture relate to one another.

2. It has been discussed in this lesson how the Japanese people are very conscious of brand-name products. Discuss how the Japanese people compare with people from other countries in this respect.

3. With the emergence of brand-name product look-alikes, the Japanese people have begun to be more cautious of what they buy. Discuss from where and from whom the Japanese people purchase brand-name products.

4. Discuss how one would design a store and display items that would appeal to Japanese people, taking cultural considerations into account.

5. Purchasing clothes in a foreign country can sometimes be difficult. If you were a culturally sensitive store employee, how would you help a Japanese customer do his/her shopping?

6. Visit some of the stores which sell brand-name products. Find out which products are particularly popular, and identify them with their nationalities, for example, French-made perfumes sell well, while leather products made in Italy are popular.

5.12 SUGGESTED RESOURCE MATERIALS

Books and Magazines

A Hundred Things Japanese (Tokyo: Japan Culture Institute, 1975), pp. 94–95.
Japan: Past and Present, Edwin O. Reischauer (New York: Alfred A. Knopf, 1962).
Kodansha Encyclopedia of Japan, vol. 8 (Tokyo: Kodansha, 1983), pp. 24–29.
Nihongo Notes 1: Speaking and Living in Japan, Osamu Mizutani and Nobuko Mizu-
    tani (Tokyo: The Japan Times, 1977), pp. 138–139.

5.13 REFERENCES

A Hundred Things Japanese. Tokyo: Japan Culture Institute, 1975.
Toya, Manabu. *The Shinto.* Tokyo: AA Shuppan Co., 1982.
Tsurumi, Kazuko. *Kōkishin to Nihonjin.* Tokyo: Kodansha Gendai Shinsho, 1972.

LESSON 6

REVIEW

6.1

N1 wa N2	desu / dewa (ja) arimasen.
N wa N1 no N2	deshita / dewa (ja) arimasen deshita.

kochira		Tanaka-san			desu.
sochira		shachoo			dewa ⎱ arimasen
achira		tomodachi			ja ⎰
- - - - - -	wa	kachoo	- - - - - - - - -		deshita.
kore		mise		toraberaa chekku	dewa ⎱ arimasen.
sore		hoteru		zasshi	ja ⎰ deshita.
are		buchoo	no	meishi	
		maneejaa		baggu	
				mono	

6.2

Place de N o V	masu / masen.
	mashita / masen deshita.

biichi		omiyage			
hoteru		tabako			
mise		baggu			masu.
furon'to		shin'bun			mashita.
depaato	de	kore	o	kai	masen.
Amerika		uisukii			masen deshita.
Hawai		biiru			
Nihon		sore			
Furan'su		are			
Itarii					

94

6.3 | N1 o kudasai. | N1 ga hoshii (n')desu.

	otoko mono	
	gen'kin	
	shin'bun	
	toraberaa chekku	
	chokoreeto	
	makademia nattsu	o kudasai.
yasui	tabako	ga hoshii desu.
takai	uisukii	
	koosui	
akai	aroha shatsu	
shiroi	muumuu	
ookii	baggu	
chiisai	san'go	

6.4 | Place ni N1 ga imasu/arimasu.

biichi		kachoo		
hoteru		tomodachi		
depaato	ni	Yamada-san		imasu.
jimusho		maneejaa		
mise		okyaku-san	ga	
furon'to		shin'bun		
		tabako		arimasu.
		makademia nattsu		

95

LESSON 7

DINING AT A RESTAURANT

7.1 USEFUL EXPRESSIONS

Itadakimasu.	(Said before eating or drinking.)
Gochisoo-sama (deshita).	It was delicious, thank you.
Yoyaku onegai shimasu.	I'd like to make a reservation please.
Yoyaku nasaimashita ka?	Do you have reservations?
Nan-ji ni irasshaimasu ka?	What time do you expect to come?
Nan-nin-sama desu ka?	How many people is this for?
Omachi shite imasu.	I will be waiting for you.
Nan ni nasaimasu ka?	What may I get for you?
Shokken o omochi desu ka?	Do you have a meal card?
Byuffe (baikin'gu) wa serufu saabisu desu.	The buffet is self-service.
Okan'joo (chekku) wa issho desu ka, betsubetsu desu ka?	Will the check be together or separate?
Sugu motte mairimasu.	I'll bring it right away.
Moshi moshi, Kotobuki Resutoran desu ga . . .	Hello, this is Kotobuki Restaurant. (What can I do for you?)
Suteeki no yakiguai wa?	How do you want your steak cooked?

7.2 CONVERSATION

7.2.1 At the Breakfast Table

Hosutesu: Irasshaimase. Ofutari-sama desu ne. Doozo kochira e.
Morita: Doomo.
Hosutesu: Menyuu o doozo.

      . . . . . .

Ueitoresu: Irasshaimase. Shokken o omochi desu ka?
Morita: Hai.

96

Ueitoresu:	Dewa sono shokken o kudasai.
	Chuushoku wa byuffe desu. Menyuu kara mo chuumon
	dekimasu.
Morita:	Watakushi wa byuffe.
Uchida:	Watakushi wa menyuu kara chuumon shimasu.
Ueitoresu:	Nan ni nasaimasu ka?
Uchida:	Soo desu nee. Papaiya ga suki desu kara,
	papaiya to toosuto to koohii o onegai shimasu.
Ueitoresu:	Hai, sugu motte mairimasu. (to Mrs. Morita) Byuffe wa serufu
	saabisu desu kara, doozo.
Morita:	Hai. Doomo.

Hostess:	Welcome. Table for two? Come this way please.
Mrs. Morita:	Thank you.
Hostess:	Here's your menu.
	. . . . . .
Waitress:	Welcome. Do you have any meal tickets (coupons)?
Mrs. Morita:	Yes. I do.
Waitress:	You can hand those tickets to me.
	Lunch is buffet (style). You can also order from our menu.
Mrs. Morita:	I'll go with the buffet.
Mrs. Uchida:	I'll order from the menu.
Waitress:	And what'll you have?
Mrs. Uchida:	Well, let me see . . . I like papayas
	so I'll order a papaya, toast, and coffee.
Waitress:	Okay, I'll bring them over right away. *(to Mrs. Morita)* The buffet
	is self-service. You may go ahead and serve yourself.
Mrs. Morita:	Thank you.

7.2.2 Taking a Dinner Reservation

Hosutesu:	Moshi moshi, Kotobuki Resutoran desu ga . . .
Nakada:	Yoyaku onegai shitai n'desu ga.
Hosutesu:	Hai. Nan-ji ni irasshaimasu ka?
Nakada:	Roku-ji han ni ikitai n'desu.
Hosutesu:	Nan-nin-sama desu ka?
Nakada:	San-nin desu.
Hosutesu:	Onamae o onegai shimasu.
Nakada:	Nakada Harue desu.
Hosutesu:	Arigatoo gozaimasu. Omachi shite imasu.

Hostess:	Hello. Kotobuki Restaurant.
Mrs. Nakada:	I'd like to make reservations please.
Hostess:	What time will you be coming in?
Mrs. Nakada:	I'd like to be there at 6:30.

Hostess:	How many people in your party?
Mrs. Nakada:	Three.
Hostess:	May I have your name please.
Mrs. Nakada:	Harue Nakada.
Hostess:	Thank you very much. We'll be looking forward to seeing you.

7.2.3   At the Dinner Table

Hosutesu:	Irasshaimase. Yoyaku nasaimashita ka?
Nakada:	Hai. Nakada desu.
Hosutesu:	San-nin-sama desu ne. Kochira e doozo.
	(After the customers are seated, the cocktail waitress comes to take their order.)
Kakuteru Ueitoresu:	Kakuteru wa ikaga desu ka?
Nakada:	Biiru, Miraa o ni-hon kudasai.
Kakuteru Ueitoresu:	Hai, sugu motte mairimasu.
	(The waitress returns with the drinks.)
Ueitoresu:	Omatase shimashita.
Nakada:	Kono saaroin suteeki o san-nin'mae kudasai.
Ueitoresu:	Yakiguai wa?
Nakada:	Midiamu desu.
Ueitoresu:	Sarada no doresshin'gu wa nan ni nasaimasu ka?
Nakada:	Furen'chi desu.
Ueitoresu:	Raisu to poteto, dochira ni nasaimasu ka?
Nakada:	Raisu o onegai shimasu.
Ueitoresu:	Hai, wakarimashita. Shooshoo omachi kudasai ne.
	(After the guests have eaten . . .)
Nakada:	Okan'joo onegai shimasu.
Ueitoresu:	Hai. Achira no reji de onegai shimasu. Arigatoo gozaimashita.

Hostess:	Welcome. Do you have reservations?
Mrs. Nakada:	Yes. I'm Mrs. Nakada.
Hostess:	For three? Please come this way.
	(After the customers are seated, the cocktail waitress comes over to take their order.)
Cocktail Waitress:	Would you care for some cocktails?
Mrs. Nakada:	Two bottles of Miller please.
Cocktail Waitress:	OK, I'll bring them over right away.
	(The waitress returns with the drinks.)

98

Waitress:	Sorry to have kept you waiting.
Mrs. Nakada:	We'll have three of these sirloin steaks.
Waitress:	How would you like them done?
Mrs. Nakada:	Medium.
Waitress:	What kind of dressing would you like on your salad?
Mrs. Nakada:	French.
Waitress:	Would you like rice or potatoes?
Mrs. Nakada:	Rice, please.
Waitress:	Please wait a moment.
	(After the guests have eaten . . .)
Mrs. Nakada:	Our bill please.
Waitress:	Please pay at the register. Thank you very much.

7.3 VOCABULARY

Nouns

asa	morning
asagohan, chooshoku	breakfast
ban'gohan, yuushoku	supper, dinner
biiru	beer
byuffe, baikin'gu	buffet
chippu	tip
dezaato	dessert
dochira	which one, which side
doresshin'gu	dressing
gogo	p.m., afternoon
gozen	a.m., morning
han'baagaa	hamburger
hima	free time
hiru	afternoon
hirugohan, chuushoku	lunch
ima	now
juusu	juice
kakuteru	cocktails
kan'joo	account, bill
koocha	black tea
koohii	coffee
kudamono	fruit
mae	front, before
menyuu	menu
nomimono	drinks
ocha	green tea
papaiya	papaya

99

reji	register
resutoran, shokudoo	restaurant
sarada	salad
serufu saabisu	self-service
sugi	past (in telling time)
suteeki, bifuteki	beef steak

Verbs

chuumon shimasu	to order
nomimasu	to drink
tabemasu	to eat

Adjectives

mazui	not delicious
oishii	delicious, tasty

Adjective Nouns

suki	like

Adverbs

betsubetsu ni	separately
issho ni	together
sugu	right away

Counters

-fun	counter for minutes
-hai	counter for glasses of drinks
-hon	counter for slender objects
-ji	counter for time
-jikan	counter for hours
-nin	counter for people
-nin'mae	counter for portions of food

7.4 EXPLANATION

7.4.1

Cause	*Effect*
Subordinate clause + **kara,**	main clause

(Cause or reason)

Kara, which occurs after a subordinate clause, is a clause particle meaning *cause* or *reason* and is equivalent to the conjunctions *because* or *since* in English.

Examples:
1. Nihon'go ga suki desu kara, ben'kyoo shimasu.
     (Noun clause)
   Because I like the Japanese language, I'll study it.

2. Nihon'go wa omoshiroi desu kara, ben'kyoo shimasu.
   (Adjectival clause)
   Since Japanese is interesting, I'll study it.

3. Ben'kyoo shimashita kara, yoku wakarimasu.
   (Verb clause)
   Because I studied, I understood well.
                    or
   I understood well *because* I studied.

As you notice from the above examples, the subordinate clause with kara at the end *always* precedes the main clause stating the effect. However, in English, the clause indicating cause may occur either before or after the clause stating effect, as shown in example 3. All three examples above show how the formal patterns of N, A, and V (N + desu + kara, and V + masu + kara) are used. The informal patterns of N, A, and V + kara will be explained in the next lesson.

7.4.2 | **V (pre-masu form) + tai** | (Someone wants to do such and such)

Yoyaku shitai means *want to make reservation,* and is the combination form (or pre-masu form) of the verb **yoyaku shimasu** and the -tai *want to,* or *would like to.* Like adjectives, -tai is followed by the copula **desu** or **n'desu** in normal style, and conjugates in the following manner:

(tabe)tai (n')desu.	want to (eat)
(tabe)taku arimasen.	do not want to (eat)
(tabe)takatta (n')desu.	wanted to (eat)
(tabe)taku arimasen deshita.	did not want to (eat)

The -tai desu phrase usually represents the speaker's desire to do something. There is some limitation in use when referring to a second or third person's desire. When the verb before -tai requires a direct object, the particle o following the direct object may be replaced by the particle ga. However both o and ga may be used interchangeably.

Hawai no kudamono ga (o) tabetai desu.
Kaisha e ikitaku arimasen.

7.4.3 Polite Forms

The form mairimasu is a humble equivalent of kimasu and ikimasu.

The honorific or "elevating" form is irasshaimasu. To be polite, the two forms, elevating and humble, should be used appropriately. Study the following chart and examples.

101

Plain formal form	Polite Humble form	Polite Honorific, elevating form
kimasu *come*	mairimasu	irasshaimasu
ikimasu *go*	mairimasu	irasshaimasu
imasu *be*	orimasu	irasshaimasu
shimasu *do*	itashimasu	nasaimasu
tabemasu *eat*	itadakimasu	meshiagarimasu

Example:

Q: Doko e irasshaimashita ka?

A: Hanauma Bei e mairimashita (ikimashita).

Q: Kono han'baagaa o meshiagarimasen ka?

A: Ee, itadakimasu yo. Arigatoo.

7.4.4 Numbers and Counters

	Native Numbers	Counting People (-nin)	Glassfuls or Cupfuls (-hai)	Slender Objects (-hon)	Servings (-nin'mae)
1	hitotsu	hitori	ippai	ippon	ichi-nin'mae
2	futatsu	futari	ni-hai	ni-hon	ni-nin'mae
3	mittsu	san-nin	san-bai	san-bon	san-nin'mae
4	yottsu	yo-nin	yon-hai	yon-hon	yo-nin'mae
5	itsutsu	go-nin	go-hai	go-hon	go-nin'mae
6	muttsu	roku-nin	{ roku-hai { roppai	roppon	roku-nin'mae
7	nanatsu	nana-nin	nana-hai	nana-hon	nana-nin'mae
8	yattsu	hachi-nin	{ hachi-hai { happai	happon	hachi-nin'mae
9	kokonotsu	{ ku-nin { kyuu-nin	kyuu-hai	kyuu-hon	{ ku-nin'mae { kyuu-nin'mae
10	too	juu-nin	{ jippai { juppai	{ jippon { juppon	juu-nin'mae
How many?	ikutsu	nan-nin	nan-bai	nan-bon	nan-nin'mae

102

7.4.5 Ni (Specific time indicator)

The particle ni as in roku-ji ni or nan-ji ni is used to indicate a specific point in time.

Nan-ji ni hoteru e ikimashoo ka?   What time shall we go to the hotel?
Hachi-ji han ni ikimashoo.   Let's go at 8:30.

7.4.6 Jikan (Counter for amount of time)

Jikan is used for counting time spans, such as ni-jikan *two hours*. Ni is not to be used to indicate spans of time.

Span of time:
Ichi-jikan machimashita.
I waited for one hour.

Point in time:
Ichi-ji ni machimashita.
I waited at one o'clock.

7.4.7 -fun (Counter for minutes)

-fun is used for counting minutes.

Study the following pronunciation list. Watch the phonetic change which occurs in 1, 3, 4, 6, 8, and 10.

ip-pun	one minute
ni-fun	two minutes
san-pun	three minutes
yon-pun	four minutes
go-fun	five minutes
rop-pun	six minutes
nana-fun	seven minutes
hap-pun	eight minutes
(hachi-fun)	
kyuu-fun	nine minutes
jip-pun	ten minutes
(jup-pun)	

san-ji go-fun (sugi)	3:05
ku-ji yon'juugo-fun	9:45
(or juu-ji juugo-fun mae)	

To indicate a time span measured in minutes, -fun or -fun'kan may be used.

Go-fun matte kudasai.   Please wait for five minutes.
    or
Go-fun'kan matte kudasai.

7.5 DRILLS

7.5.1 Question–Answer Drill

Answer each of the following questions, first in the affirmative, then in the negative.

Example: Kono koohii wa oishii desu ka?
       Hai, oishii desu.
       Iie, oishiku arimasen.

1. Kono biiru wa yasui desu ka?
  Hai, yasui desu.
  Iie, yasuku arimasen.

2. Kono mise no koohii wa mazui desu ka?
  Hai, mazui desu.
  Iie, mazuku arimasen.

3. Papaiya wa suki desu ka?
  Hai, suki desu.
  Iie, suki ja arimasen.

4. Kono zasshi wa omoshiroi desu ka?
  Hai, omoshiroi desu.
  Iie, omoshiroku arimasen.

5. Kyoo wa hima desu ka?
  Hai, hima desu.
  Iie, hima ja arimasen.

6. Biichi e ikitai desu ka?
  Hai, ikitai desu.
  Iie, ikitaku arimasen.

7. Waikiki biichi wa kirei desu ka?
  Hai, kirei desu.
  Iie, kirei ja arimasen.

8. Hoteru wa shizuka deshita ka?
  Hai, shizuka deshita.
  Iie, shizuka ja arimasen deshita.

9. Baikin'gu wa oishikatta desu ka?
  Hai, oishikatta desu.
  Iie, oishiku arimasen deshita.

10. Kinoo no shin'bun o yomimashita ka?
  Hai, yomimashita.
  Iie, yomimasen deshita.

11. Bifuteki o chuumon shitai n'desu ka?
  Hai, chuumon shitai n'desu.
  Iie, chuumon shitaku arimasen.

7.5.2 Substitution Drill

Example: Yasui shatsu o *(one)* kaimashita.
         Yasui shatsu o *ichi-mai* kaimashita.

1. Oishii koohii o *(two)* nomimashita.
   Oishii koohii o *ni-hai* nomimashita.

2. Ii okyaku-san ga *(three)* kimashita.
   Ii okyaku-san ga *san-nin* kimashita.

3. Omoshiroi hito ga *(four)* imasu.
   Omoshiroi hito ga *yo-nin* imasu.

4. Ookii han'baagaa o *(two)* tabemashita.
   Ookii han'baagaa o *futatsu* tabemashita.

5. Tabako o *(one)* kudasai.
   Tabako o *ippon* kudasai.

6. Suteeki o *(two)* chuumon shimashita.
   Suteeki o *ni-nin'mae* chuumon shimashita.

7.5.3 English–Japanese Mixed Drill

Example: Ano gakusei wa don'na
         hito desu ka?   Cue: an interesting man
         Omoshiroi hito desu.

1. Don'na hoteru ga ii desu ka?   Cue: a quiet hotel
   Shizuka na hoteru ga ii desu.

2. Omiyage wa nani ga ii desu ka?   Cue: pretty muumuu
   Kirei na muumuu ga ii desu.

3. Asagohan wa nan ni nasaimasu ka?   Cue: toast and coffee
   Toosuto to koohii ni shimasu.

4. Nani o tabemashita ka?   Cue: a delicious salad
   Oishii sarada o tabemashita.

5. Don'na tokoro deshita ka?   Cue: a quiet place
   Shizuka na tokoro deshita.

7.5.4 English–Japanese Mixed Drill

Example: Dooshite kaimasen deshita ka? Cue: It was expensive.
         Takakatta (desu) kara kaimasen deshita.

1. Dooshite kyoo Ara Moana e
    ikimasu ka?   Cue: I'll buy drinks.
   Nomimono o kaimasu kara ikimasu.

2. Dooshite kore o kaimashita ka?   Cue: It was pretty.
   Kirei deshita kara kaimashita.

3. Dooshite nihon'go o ben'kyoo
      shimasu ka?   Cue: I like Japanese.
   Nihon'go ga suki desu kara ben'kyoo shimasu.

4. Dooshite Nihon e ikitai n'desu ka?   Cue: I want to study Japanese.
   Nihon'go o ben'kyoo shitai (desu) kara ikitai n'desu.

5. Dooshite sono biichi e ikitai
      desu ka?   Cue: It's a quiet beach.
   Shizuka na biichi desu kara ikitai desu.

6. Dooshite sugu toshokan e ikitai   Cue: There's a book which
      n'desu ka?   I want to read.
   Yomitai hon ga arimasu kara ikitai desu.

7. Dooshite kaitaku arimasen ka?   Cue: It's an expensive book.
   Takai hon desu kara kaitaku arimasen.

7.5.5 Substitution Drill

Ima nan-ji desu ka?

It's   one o'clock.   Ichi-ji desu.
       two   Ni-ji desu.
       four-thirty   Yo-ji han desu.
       (and so forth)

7.6 EXERCISES

7.6.1 Question–Answer

Ima nan-ji desu ka?

 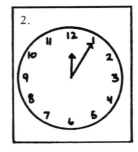 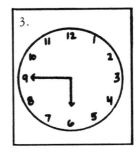

7.6.2 Completion and Translation

Insert a particle in each blank. Then give an English equivalent for each sentence.

1. Go-ji _____ kaisha e ikimasu.

2. Dare _____ shimasu ka? Yamada-san _____ shimasu.

3. Hoteru _____ resutoran _____ hirugohan _____ tabemashita.

4. Paatii _____ shichi-ji han _____ irasshaimasu ka?

5. Kyoo _____ ashita shimasu.

6. Yamada-san _____ tenisu _____ suki desu.

7. Suki _____ nomimono _____ biiru desu.

8. Watakushi _____ dezaato _____ tabetai n'desu.

9. Nani _____ chuumon nasaimashita ka?

7.6.3 Transformation

Transform the following into the negative past tense form.

1. Omoshiroi desu.
2. Terebi ga mitai desu.
3. Koocha ga suki desu.
4. Nihon'go no sen'sei deshita.
5. Takusan tabetakatta desu.
6. Kinoo wa hima deshita.
7. Kore wa suki na nomimono desu.

7.6.4 Translation

Carry on the following dialogue in Japanese.

A: Did you have breakfast?
B: Yes, I did.
A: Where did you have it?
B: I had it at the East-West Center cafeteria.
A: What did you have?
B: I had a piece of toast and a cup of coffee. Oh, I ate papaya too.
A: Was it good (delicious)?
B: Yes, it was.
A: What time do you go to school?
B: I am going now.
A: Let's go together.

7.7   SIMULATION AND SKITS

1. The scene is a restaurant in Waikiki. Two students playing the role of customers enter the restaurant. They explain that they have a reservation and are seated by the hostess, played by a third student. Student #4, the waitress (or waiter), comes to take the order. These customers are very hard to please! The waitress makes many suggestions to them (. . . wa ikaga desu ka?), but they still have difficulty making up their minds. Try to be as imaginative as possible and make use of food names and adjectives in your conversation. When the customers finally come to a decision, have the waitress bring their order and assist them further, if necessary.

2. Later on, in the kitchen of the same Waikiki restaurant, two employees do an inventory of the food supplies remaining in the pantry.

   Below is a possible conversational exchange. Translate, or make up your own dialogue.
   A: Are there any hot dogs?
   B: Yes, there are lots of hot dogs.
   A: How many are there?
   B: There are six large hot dogs and fifteen small ones.
   A: Tomorrow we'll buy some more. What time are you coming tomorrow?
   B: I'll come at 9 o'clock.
   A: Since I'm going shopping at the supermarket, I'll come at 10:30.
   B: I understand. Thank you.

3. Two students, one from Japan and one from the U.S., talk together about the different foods that they eat. Some possible questions are:
   1. Where do you eat breakfast?
   2. What do you have for breakfast?
   3. Do you drink black tea in the morning?
   4. How many hot dogs do you eat for lunch?
   5. Where do you eat dinner?

   Think in terms of **what** you eat, **how much** you have, **what kind** you have, **where** you eat, **when** you eat, and **why** you eat the food you do. You may want to visit a Japanese food store or the Oriental food section in a supermarket to become more acquainted with varieties of Japanese food, if you're not already.

4. Discuss with your partner your schedule for one day, explaining what you do at a certain time and for how long.

108

7.8 CULTURE ORIENTATION

7.8.1 Japanese Eating Habits

Japan has a unique geographical setting; it is an island and has a land mass, 84 percent of which is mountainous. As a result, the ocean and the mountains have greatly influenced the Japanese people's eating habits. Traditionally, Japan was an agricultural society, and the Japanese people's staple food has always been rice. They have various ways of referring to rice because it is such a valuable commodity in their society. For example, ine refers to the unharvested rice plant. Kome refers to uncooked rice. Gohan refers to cooked rice, and okoge to partially scorched boiled rice. In addition, there are various types of rice such as hakumai *(white rice)*, gen'mai *(brown rice)*, mochi gome *(sticky cake rice)*.

Japanese rice is different from the dry long-grain variety often found elsewhere. It has a sticky consistency and is oval in shape. Many Japanese people feel Japanese rice is the only real rice! As a result, some Japanese tourists, especially older people, will carry Japanese rice with them even when they go abroad. Even within Japan, there are different types of rice grown in different areas, such as sasanishiki and koshihikari (from the Sendai and Niigata areas). The Japanese are rather selective when it comes to choosing rice.

In Japan, rice is considered a sacred commodity according to Shinto belief. The word musubi referring to *rice balls* has its origin in the name of the god next in rank to Amaterasu Omikami called Musubi. According to myth, Musubi was a god of production. It is written in the *Kojiki,* an ancient chronicle, that Musubi created the Japanese Islands (Toya 1982:120–121). Musubi, the god of production, was devoutly worshipped in Japan. It can be said that the value of production is ingrained in the Japanese national character as if it were their second nature. Perhaps it can be said further that the present Japanese worship of their GNP is a reflection of this second nature! In olden times the rank of the samurai was determined by how much rice he produced in his region. The Japanese people believed that every grain of rice contained an element of the god Musubi. As a result, they believed that eating rice produced life energy. Thus, the rice ball came to be known as musubi, a source of life energy.

Although rice became central to Japanese life, not everybody was able to eat it. Farmers producing rice had to give most of it away as payment to their local lords. A poor peasant, for example, had to resort to eating barley mixed with radish gruel. It has only been in the past forty years, following World War II, that rice has become accessible to everybody in Japan (*Nihon o Shiru Jiten* 1972:333).

The Japanese people ate rice and barley produced in the fields as staple food. Fish, shellfish, mushrooms, and zen'mai *(young fern)* gathered from the ocean and mountains were secondary foods. Meat was available in the mountains; however, due to the influence of Buddhist teachings that perceived four-legged animals as impure, eating meat was strictly forbidden. Meat from birds was limited to wild birds found in the mountains. Chickens were not raised for consumption because they were considered to be the sacred conveyers of time. It can be said that the Japanese people were historically not meat-eaters.

Although Kobe beef has become famous all over the world, it was not until the Meiji period began (in 1868) that meat was available to the common people (*Nihon o Shiru Jiten* 1972:330). Foods, such as sukiyaki, which are now eaten with high quality beef, used to be eaten with fish. Although meat-eaters have increased in the past 100 years or so, there are still some people who feel nauseated at the sight of rare beef served at buffets and dinners.

Due to the Western influence, breakfast with coffee and ham and eggs has become increasingly popular among the younger generation in Japan. But among the older generation, Japanese foods, such as rice, miso soup, fish, tsu-kemono *(pickles)*, and tea, are still preferred.

Japanese eating habits became progressively Westernized as Japan's level of modernization increased under the model of wakon-yoosai *(Japanese spirit/ Western knowledge or technology)*. For example, ten'pura, a dish known to be traditionally Japanese, is believed to be of foreign origin. There are many theories about the derivation of the word tempura. It is generally thought to be the derivation of either the Portuguese word *tempero* for *cooking* or the Spanish word *templo* for *temple* (Kodansha Encyclopedia of Japan, 1983:3). It is a case of a Western dish that has been adapted to Japanese taste.

Even sushi, generally believed to be a pure Japanese food, originated in China. The Chinese placed rice and fish in a bamboo barrel or tub, pressing it down with a heavy weight, preserving it for a long time. This was eaten as it fermented. It is said that this was the prototype of sushi. Although this fermented fish probably came from China, it can also be found in various parts of Southeast Asia (*Nihon o Shiru Jiten* 1972:348). The Japanese adapted this recipe to their own taste, creating sushi, known today as the most representative of Japanese foods.

Japan is now expanding raamen *(noodle dish)* restaurant chains abroad. But the noodles used in raamen also originated in China. Although raamen sounds somewhat Chinese, it is a word coined by the Japanese to sound Chinese. In actuality, there is no such thing as raamen among Chinese dishes. Generally speaking, Chinese dishes brought into Japan were altered to suit Japanese tastes.

In 1958, instant raamen was invented by Hyakufuku Ando. It was advertised in a commercial which said, in part: "three minutes after pouring hot water . . . ," and it was an instant success (Kato 1978:265). Later, the Japanese began to export instant raamen in much the same way Sony exported transistor radios: both products were compact and portable. Now, this technology of making instant products has been adopted by the Chinese and people of Hong Kong, and they have come out with their own instant noodles.

Karee raisu or raisu karee *(curry rice)*, originally Indian, has been adopted by the Japanese, who have turned it into something uniquely Japanese. Many Japanese love curry rice and assume that it originated in Japan! Today both karee raisu and raamen are favorite lunch dishes of office employees. The French *croquette* became the Japanese korokke, and many people believe it to be a Japanese original (*Nihon o Shiru Jiten* 1972:333).

Even the eating of steak, a rather recent phenomenon, is undergoing Japanization. Teppan-yaki steak is an example. It is eaten using chopsticks, and is served from a special pan and with a special sauce. With the slogan, *Bring the kitchen to you,* the meat is cooked before the customers, who are thrilled with the performance of the "samurai cook" with his knife. Cooking becomes not just a means of food preparation but also a show itself. In this manner, the senses are stimulated through the eyes, nose, ears, and mouth, allowing the customers to enjoy and feel satisfied with their meal. The teppan-yaki steak, known as the "Japanese steak," has become increasingly popular among Americans.

The Japanese were able to transform the taste and appearance of foods to their liking through the utilization of the model of wakon-yoosai. But due to the influences of the "instant-speed-age," Japanese tastes are also changing. American fast food chains, such as McDonalds and Kentucky Fried Chicken, are mushrooming all over the world and have quickly invaded the Japanese market as well. Yet, it is said that even these fast food chains have slowly begun to go through the Japanization process.

It was stated earlier in the text that the basic needs of the Japanese people were clothing, food, and housing, in that order. Next to clothing, the second priority for the Japanese people is food. There are many Japanese people who feel it is worth sacrificing comfort to be able to eat good food. Most Japanese tourists feel that since they have come all the way to a foreign country, away from their home community, they should make the trip worthwhile by eating good food as opposed to merely satisfying their hunger by keeping their stomachs filled with something. The impression most Japanese tourists have of American food is that it is generous in its quantity but, generally speaking, bland in quality.

According to a survey of 100 Japanese tourists (both male and female, between the ages of 20 and 30), their decision to return to Hawaii was strongly influenced by factors such as variety, price, and the quality of food service. For example, 57 percent of the people answered "yes" to the question: "Did the quality of service provided by restaurants in Hawaii influence your decision to come back to Hawaii?" The percentage of people that cared more about the taste of the food increased with the age of the person being surveyed (Liao 1983).

7.8.2 The Japanese and Their Sense of Taste

Generally speaking, the Japanese people are very particular about the taste of their food. They have a particular taste that suits them. The one thing that a Japanese person absolutely requires while eating is shooyu *(soy sauce)*. This is similar to the way in which many Americans find it necessary to use tomato ketchup on their food. For example, a Japanese person will not be satisfied without shooyu while eating broiled fish. Sashimi can't be eaten without shooyu. They even use shooyu on their steak, which has developed into what is called teriyaki steak, and is becoming a popular item on some American menus. They even developed teri-burgers, which are hamburgers seasoned with shooyu, in areas with a concentration of Japanese-Americans, as in Hawaii and California.

With the development of the Kikkoman Shoyu Company, shooyu has become more widely used under the name soy sauce in America. Interestingly, the term *soy sauce* resulted when a Dutch person romanized shooyu as *shzoya* in Japan. This *shzoya* was taken into Europe and was gradually changed to *shoya* and *soya*. In Britain, it is still referred to as *soya*. In America, *soya* became *soy* with the word *sauce* added to it. The beans that produce soy sauce came to be called *soy bean* (Kato 1978:103). The word shoyu didn't come from the word *soy* but rather, it was *soy* that came from shoyu.

Sukiyaki, ten'pura, and sashimi, well-known representative Japanese foods, cannot be eaten without shooyu. It wouldn't be an exaggeration to say that the Japanese taste is essentially based on the taste of shooyu. After the war, when white rice became accessible, there were many people who ate it with shooyu alone, not being able to afford anything else. There was a time when a whole meal consisted of rice, seaweed, and shooyu. The fundamental Japanese taste can be represented by the preparation of mochi *(rice cake)* wrapped with seaweed and eaten with a dip in shooyu. Although the number of Japanese tourists who carry rice, seaweed, and shooyu while traveling has declined in recent years, there are still people who take osen'bei (rice crackers with shooyu flavoring, often wrapped in seaweed) instead. It seems the Japanese people just can't go without this Japanese taste! It would be a good idea to keep a bottle of shooyu at restaurants where Japanese tourists visit.

Generally speaking, Japanese people say that American food has a flat taste. Unlike Americans, who prefer to eat fish or vegetables grown to maturity, Japanese prefer to eat fish or vegetables when they are still younger and smaller in size. They say that the more mature or large the fish or vegetable is, the less tasty it is. Fish eaten in America are usually those that are fully grown. Vegetables, such as eggplants or cucumbers are huge compared to those found in Japan. Of course, this does not necessarily indicate that all fully grown foods are less tasty.

American people often do not use much seasoning in their cooking. For example, they say that a high-quality steak should be just as good when eaten without sauce or seasoning. It is the choice of the individual consuming the food whether to season it or not. As a result, there are a variety of sauces available to choose from. Japanese people, not used to the concept of seasoning their own food when served, often don't season it at all. It is no wonder that they conclude that American food tastes flat!

There are others in Japan who say that American foods are too oily and rich. Some people find it hard to swallow rich foods after having indulged two or three times. Not being able to eat the rich American food after their arrival and suffering from jet lag and indigestion from the long flight, Japanese tourists often end up eating lighter Japanese foods. In addition, there are many that choose to go to Japanese restaurants simply because they can't understand English menus.

Japanese people often find American sweets and desserts too sweet for their taste. The sugar content of cakes bought in Japan is considerably lower than in America. Eating sweets after a meal was not a Japanese custom; there are still people, especially in the older generation, who can't eat sweets after a meal. They say that the good taste of a meal becomes lost if one takes sweets, such as cake or ice cream, after it. Many Japanese people prefer to finish their meal with a cup of green tea enjoying the good taste of the meal still lingering in their mouths. Japanese green tea is especially suitable for bringing out the taste of food. Japan, originally a culture of tea, has, in recent years, also become a culture of coffee. Perhaps we are in an age with no time to fuss over the lingering aftertaste of our meals.

7.8.3 Tea and Coffee

In Japan, tea ocha refers specifically to green tea. If one wants black tea, one must ask for koocha. In a Western restaurant, if one asks for "tea," he will get black tea.

Japan is definitely a culture of tea. The Japanese like tea so much that they continue to drink tea day and night. A meal is never complete without tea. It is even said that, for the Japanese, life without tea would be unthinkable.

However, as mentioned before, the Japanese have also begun to enjoy coffee in recent years. According to a survey on personal possessions conducted by the Scientific Institute for Commercial Products of the C.D.I. Company in 1976, 90 percent of people in urban and surrounding areas had instant coffee in their possession. Of these, 80 percent said that they often used it (Kato 1976:256). The number of coffee users may still be on the rise.

Interestingly, instant coffee was the invention of a Japanese! In 1899, Satori Kato successfully experimented and invented instant coffee. But due to the lack of a market in Japan, he had to sail to the United States. Satori Kato did not obtain a patent at the time and never received official recognition for his invention (it was not until 1906 that G. Washington, an American, obtained an official patent for instant coffee) (Kato 1976:258).

As the cases of Sony's transistor radio, instant raamen, or instant coffee show, the Japanese are not only good at adapting foreign-made products and making them into something unique in themselves, but are also ingenious at making something large and complex into something more compact and handy. One can say the Japanese people like simple and handy things. Japan remains a culture of tea, as well as a culture of coffee.

7.8.4 Typical Japanese Dishes

Sukiyaki –	Thin slices of beef and various vegetables, bean curd, and vermicelli usually fried on the table in front of the customer or guest.
Ten'pura –	Prawns, fish in season, vegetables, and dried seaweed coated with a mixture of egg, water, and wheat flour then deep-fried in vegetable oil.
Sushi –	There are three main types: makizushi, nigirizushi, and inarizushi. Makizushi is rolled vinegared rice, usually filled with cucumber, fresh water eel (unagi), sweet omelet, dried gourd slices (kan'pyoo), and colored dried shrimp shavings, then wrapped in dried seaweed. Nigirizushi is a ball of vinegared rice topped with a little horseradish and a slice of raw fish. Tuna, cuttlefish, and prawn are most commonly used. Inarizushi is fried beancurd (aburage) shaped like a cone and filled with vinegared rice. Often the rice is mixed with minced boiled vegetables such as carrots and string beans.
Sashimi –	Raw fish eaten with soy sauce and horseradish.
Yakitori –	Small pieces of deboned chicken, liver, and vegetables skewered on a bamboo stick and grilled on an open fire.
Ton'katsu –	Pork rolled in bread crumbs and deep fried. It is similar to the American pork cutlet.
Shabu-shabu –	Tender, thin slices of the choicest beef held with chopsticks and boiled in water at the diners' table.
Soba and udon –	Two kinds of Japanese noodle. Soba is thin noodles made from buckwheat flour. Udon is thick noodles made from wheat flour. They are served either in a broth or dipped in a sauce.

7.8.5 Food Models

In most Japanese restaurants, plastic models of the dishes are usually beautifully displayed in show windows outside the entrance. They look quite real. They are made so skillfully that each dish could almost be called a work of art. Generally, it can be said of the Japanese that they distrust abstractions. Customers are not satisfied merely with an abstract name of a dish on a menu.

114

Rather than not being satisfied, it would be more accurate to say that if they cannot see the dish before them, they feel uneasy about ordering it.

According to the observation of one businessman, there is a noticeable increase in the number of customers in restaurants which provide the show window food displays. It is for this reason that there are many specialists whose business it is to make these show window displays as attractive as possible. Because the number of customers increases with the quality of the display, as well as the existence of the display, there is a direct relationship between the show window food display and the profits of the restaurant. In department store cafeterias for the general public, there is a number for each dish in the window, so that one need only say the number when placing one's order. Thus, one can easily appreciate the indispensability of the show window food displays to the restaurant business.

7.9 THE JAPANESE MODE OF COMMUNICATION

Feeling-oriented Communication

Japanese people often look for a kissa-ten *coffee shop* when they travel outside of their country. But they are all disappointed when they can't find any like those in Japan. What difference could there be between the Japanese kissa-ten and the Western or American coffee house? We will examine the Japanese mode of communication by studying the Japanese kissa-ten.

The coffee served at a kissa-ten is much tastier than instant coffee. However, the Japanese people do not visit kissa-ten for the purpose of good coffee alone. Why is it that Japanese people miss this kissa-ten away from home? The answer is that they miss a certain atmosphere it provides. Every kissa-ten carries an atmosphere of its own. In a "classic" kissa-ten one can listen to classical Western music. Even the atmosphere of the shop itself—the furniture and decor—is fashioned to create the atmosphere of a "classic" kissa-ten. Similarly, there are "rock-kissa" (short for Rock-n-Roll kissa-ten), "jazz-kissa" and other music-related kissas.

The name kissa-ten can be traced to 1925 in the Showa period. At that time kissa came to be used instead of "milk hall" which had been used in the Taisho period (1910–1920s). The essential atmosphere of the "milk hall" also changed. The "milk hall" was a place where one could get healthy, delicious food and drink. But the kissa-ten created an atmosphere of Western civilization, serving as a window to the West. Classical Western music was played—like Beethoven and Mozart—and famous Western paintings decorated the walls (Tada 1981:211). The kissa-ten provided a Western atmosphere. Coffee, which symbolized Western culture, was served there, and cakes were served with black tea. (Even now, green tea is not served at kissa-ten).

Today kissa-ten provide many different types of atmosphere. For example, there are traditional Japanese style kissa-ten called wafuu-kissa, where the waitresses greet customers wearing their kimonos, and the decor and music both contribute to the Japanese atmosphere. Each kissa-ten has an atmosphere of its own, and a person can choose whichever one he likes depending upon his mood at the time.

The kissa-ten serves many purposes. It serves as a meeting place for friends, providing a relaxed atmosphere suited for their moods. The kissa-ten serves as a meeting place and a "hang out" for young people. It also serves as a location for lovers to meet. Due to the lack of space for privacy in the big cities, there are special kissa-ten called doohan-kissa for couples which offer "the ground for testing the new way of romantic love" (A Hundred Things Japanese 1975:86). Kissa-ten also serve as places to conduct business, an indispensable role in the urban life of Japan. There is even a kissa-ten which provides music through individual earphones to allow the customer the music of his choice. There are some people who listen to their music and write poetry while immersed in their "solitude." Kissa-ten called waapuro kissa (word processor kissa-ten) and eikaiwa kissa (English conversation coffee shop) are some of the popular new-comers to Japan. Young people go to a waapuro kissa to use a word processor to write something like their personal letters, essays, even poems, over coffee. They go to eikaiwa kissa to meet foreigners and to practice English with them over coffee. This type of kissa-ten is good, not only for eager students of English, but also for foreigners who want to meet young Japanese people. The great variety of coffee shops (kissa-ten) in Japanese society is a good reflection of the modern current of Japanese social life.

Generally speaking, one can say that the Japanese are sentimental, easily controlled by feelings and emotions. It is not much of an exaggeration to say that Japanese people can't communicate without the appropriate atmosphere. Atmosphere constitutes an important aspect of the Japanese mode of communication. The Japanese people have a feeling-oriented mode of communication. It is said in Japan that man is essentially an animal of emotion where emotion constitutes 80 percent of him and rationality the other 20 percent. With such a view of man, it is no wonder that feelings and emotions control the Japanese mode of communication. The kissa-ten provides an atmosphere conducive to communication, whether between business associates or between friends. The kissa-ten is indispensable in order for the Japanese people to communicate successfully.

7.10 LANGUAGE AND CULTURE

A. Itadakimasu and gochisoo-sama deshita

The expression itadaki refers to the motion of bowing one's head and raising gifts received from the dieties. Therefore, the essential meaning of the expression itadakimasu, said before eating a meal, is to express gratitude upon receiving something. This expression is used before a meal, serving much the same purpose as saying grace, expressing gratitude for the meal. However, compared to grace, which is an expression directly thanking God, the expression itadakimasu has become more of a custom where the gratitude is not really expressed to God but to the person who prepared the meal, or to the person who is paying for the meal. For this reason, it would not be at all strange if a Japanese Christian said itadakimasu after saying his grace.

Nowadays itadakimasu is generally said before a meal even if there isn't anybody to express gratitude to. This expression also serves, in a sense, to mentally demarcate the beginning of the act of eating. Similarly, in order to mentally demarcate the end of the meal, the expression gochisoo-sama deshita is used. This expression also originally had a deep cultural meaning. Gochisoo-sama originates from the word chisoo, meaning *running together*. The honorific prefix go- was added to the beginning, forming the expression gochisoo-sama to express gratitude for "making so many people run around to prepare this meal" (Suzuki 1982:23). In time, this expression also became part of the custom used after meals. But it is important to know the original meaning and purpose of the expression and, at times, to see it in that light.

B. Shokken

The Japanese people are accustomed to using shokken *food tickets*. Shokken are often included in group tour tickets along with the airfare and hotel expenses. This is a way in which the tour agency can arrange discount food prices from restaurants by securing customers.

Shokken are used for other purposes as well. For example, at large restaurants in department stores, the customers decide what they want to eat by looking at the food models displayed in a showcase. Each item is designated by a number; so, before entering the restaurant, the customer buys a shokken with the number of the item he wants. Having bought the shokken, he will sit at an open table where the waitress comes and picks up half of the shokken. Time is saved ordering because the waitress knows immediately what the customer wants by looking at the number on the shokken. Shokken are often used in Japan in order to simplify certain procedures.

C. Byuffe and Baikin'gu

Recently the word byuffe has been added to the Japanese vocabulary, borrowed from the English word *buffet*. In addition to byuffe, the word baikin'gu is also often used to refer to a "smorgasbord," a word too long and unfitting to Japanese. Why, then, was the word baikin'gu used rather than *smorgasbord*? A manager from Hotel Viking, located in Oslo, came to Japan to teach at a Japanese culinary school. One of the things he prepared was a smorgasbord, and the Japanese, rather than calling it that, named it baikin'gu *(Viking)*, after the name of the hotel where the manager worked. When one thinks of *Viking*, one is reminded of a scene from a movie where tough-looking Viking men pile their plates full of food. The word baikin'gu probably came from the very fitting image of Vikings and smorgasbords. However, baikin'gu is still a rather new word in Japan and its self-service method is not as popular in Japan as it might be in the United States. Many older people don't know what baikin'gu style refers to.

D. Suki

The expression suki, when used in connection with an object, corresponds to the English expression *to like*. However, when suki is used as an expression of love, it connotes a meaning culturally different from the English word *like*. In English, the expressions *I like you* and *I love you* have a definite difference in sense and meaning. The Japanese often use the word suki in order to express love even though there is another word to specifically express love (aishimasu). Therefore, when the expression Anata ga suki desu is used, it can be taken as meaning *I like you* or *I love you*. The ambiguity of the word suki seems to be the reason why it is used to express feelings both of fondness and of love.

Often confrontations with very personal expressions create embarrassing situations in the Japanese cultural framework. The use of ambiguous terms such as suki is preferred over explicit expressions of feeling such as aishimasu in order to avoid such embarrassing situations. Moreover, the Japanese people perceive love as something, not to be expressed in words, but to be felt between each other. Therefore, the use of the word suki between lovers would be easily understood to express love. For these reasons, the meaning of the word suki, used in connection with an object, would be clear, but one has to be careful when using it with people.

E. . . . wa ikaga desu ka? and . . . tabetai desu ka?

In order to express the question, *Would you like to eat?*, the form tabetai desu ka is suitable only when used between good friends. The tai form is used to express desire. If the expression tabetai desu ka? were directed toward customers, with the intent of asking *Do you have a desire to eat?*, the connotation would be too direct, even rude. The indirect expression of X wa ikaga desu ka? *(How about x?)* would be more polite. (The less explicit an expression, the more polite it becomes in Japan.) Unless one is with close friends, the use of expressions such as tabetai desu ka? or nomitai desu ka? should be avoided. Although the message would be communicated, it would not be in proper cultural form.

F. Yakiguai (well done? medium? or rare?)

The Japanese people generally eat only certain types of fish as sashimi, such as tuna, yellow fin, and salmon. However, they are not so accustomed to red

118

meat, as we mentioned in the culture orientation. The Japanese familiarity with meat is historically still rather brief. There are still many people who cannot eat a piece of rare steak without feeling sick, although the number of people able to eat rare steak has been increasing. For the Japanese, yakiguai becomes very important while ordering steak. Most people order it cooked medium, but the older generation makes it a point to order it cooked well done by asking yoku yaite kudasai.

G. Raisu

As mentioned in the culture orientation, the Japanese have numerous ways of referring to rice. Usually cooked rice is called gohan. However, cooked rice served with a Western-style dish is often called raisu rather than gohan, which conjures up the image of rice in a Japanese rice bowl. When the Japanese use the word raisu, it may sound like *lice*. This is because the *r* and *l* sounds are not distinguished in the Japanese language. Therefore, raisu may be pronounced with an *r* or an *l* without much distinction placed upon it. It is a useful aspect of Japanese language to be aware of if you are ever confronted with an order of "fried lice, preez!"

H. Teishoku

The Japanese people generally do not like to spend time ordering items from each category of food, such as meat or fish, starches, and vegetables while at a restaurant. They prefer to just order teishoku, which is an already planned meal. (The reasons for this will be discussed in the next lesson.) However, teishoku also come with different combinations which gives the customer some choice in the combination of foods.

I. Chippu

The American tipping system seems to cause some difficulty for the Japanese. This is largely because there is no tipping system in Japan as it exists in the United States. One Japanese tourist explained: "I had once offered a tip to a stewardess working very hard in a Western airplane. I had thought it was a customary practice, but she refused to accept it. However, having disembarked from the airplane, I was required to tip four to five times before I was able to sit and relax in my hotel room. I tipped the porter, taxi driver, hotel doorboy and the bell-boy." He said that it completely wore him out to have to calculate in his head the proper amount to tip and then convert it into dollars.

Another example of confusion with respect to American tipping customs is this quote from a waitress at a restaurant: "There are those Japanese tourists who leave a generous tip on the table and those that are so stingy that they leave nothing at all!" This situation requires some explanation. More often than not, the tips that Japanese tourists leave have no connection to their generosity or stinginess. Rather, it is a direct reflection of their lack of understanding of the system of tipping. There are some people who completely forget to tip and some who pay too much without having any intension of being overly generous.

In Japan, rather than paying separately for services, in the form of tips, a service charge is already included in the total price. In a sense, the payment for service is made compulsory in Japan. But Japanese people prefer not to trouble themselves with the evaluation of services every time they enter a restaurant. A compulsory price is clearer and more efficient. The Japanese people do not seem to be too adept at evaluating services; it is not encouraged because it might be viewed as creating disharmony. (Similarly, for the purpose of maintaining harmony between people, companies in Japan do not base their salary scale on personal merits or distinctions.) A pervasive tipping system will probably never take root in Japanese society as long as emphasis is placed on social harmony.

This is not to say that there is no tipping system in Japan. The custom continues in Japanese ryokan *(inns)* where money is wrapped in paper and given to those who will be taking care of you. Unlike the American tip, this money is given in advance, to insure good service. Sometimes this is done by giving a small gift rather than money. Tipping in the United States is done after the service has been rendered serving as an evaluation. But giving money ahead of time is a way of expressing one's gratitude before the service begins. Perhaps the tipping system as developed in the United States is a natural consequence of a culture built on the principle of checks and balances.

7.11 CULTURE QUESTIONS

1. Discuss what types and qualities of restaurants a Japanese tourist would feel comfortable in.

2. Compare rice as eaten in Japan with how it is eaten in your country. How is it cooked? How much is eaten?

3. The Japanese taste for food revolves around shooyu. What ingredient does your country's taste for food revolve around? How do you think a Japanese person would react to it?

4. Compare and contrast your country's taste and perception of food to that of the Japanese, as was discussed in the Culture Orientation. Discuss how the knowledge of Japanese taste and perception of food may help in your work situation.

5. Discuss how a waitress may effectively deal with the situation in a restaurant when a Japanese fails to include the tip, or, on the other hand, when a Japanese customer tries to tip in a fast food restaurant where a tip is not expected.

6. Go to a Japanese restaurant, order from the menu, and return to class to discuss your experiences with the other members of the class.

120

7.12 SUGGESTED RESOURCE MATERIALS

7.12.1 Books and Magazines

A Hundred Things Japanese (Tokyo: Japan Culture Institute, 1975), pp. 32–33, 58–59, 60–63, 82–83, 86–87, 90–91, 94–95.

Kodansha Encyclopedia of Japan, vol. 2 (Tokyo: Kodansha, 1983), pp. 304–307.

Kodansha Encyclopedia of Japan, vol. 6 (Tokyo: Kodansha, 1983), pp. 308–310.

Mock Joya's Things Japanese, Mock Joya (Tokyo: Tokyo News Service, 1968), pp. 275–330.

"A Taste of Japan: Sukiyaki," Donald Richie, *Winds* 3, no. 11 (April, 1982): 14–19.

7.12.2 Films (16 mm) and Video Cassettes (Beta / VHS)

"Japan's Food from Land and Sea." 12 mins. Color. Itraw, 1962.

7.13 REFERENCES

A Hundred Things Japanese. Tokyo: Japan Culture Institute, 1975.

Kato, Hidetoshi. *Shoku no Shakai Gaku.* Tokyo: Bungei Shunju, 1978.

Kodansha Encyclopedia of Japan, vol. 8. Tokyo: Kodansha, 1983.

Liao, Linda. "Survey on Food-service and Tourism in Hawaii." Paper prepared for Japanese 197, University of Hawaii, 1983.

Oshima, Tatehiko, et al., eds. *Nihon o Shiru Jiten.* Tokyo: Shakai Shiso sha, 1971.

Seward, Jack. *Japanese in Action: An Unorthodox Approach to the Spoken Language and the People Who Speak It.* New York: Walker / Weatherhill, 1969.

Suzuki, Kenji. *Yakushin.* Tokyo: Koosei Shuppan sha, 1982.

Tada, Michitaro. *Shinpen no Nihon Bunka.* Tokyo: Kodansha, 1981.

Toya, Manabu. *The Shinto.* Tokyo: Shuppan, 1982.

LESSON 8

DINING AT A JAPANESE RESTAURANT

8.1 USEFUL EXPRESSIONS

Gohan ga tabetai naa!	I really want to eat rice!
Onaka ga suite imasu.	I'm hungry
Onaka ga ippai desu.	I'm full.
Nodo ga kawaite imasu.	I'm thirsty.
Ocha o moo ippai ikaga desu ka?	Would you like another cup of tea?
Iie, moo kekkoo desu.	No, thank you. (I've had enough.)
Osumi desu ka?	Are you through?
Kashikomarimashita.	Yes, I understand.
Watakushi ga ogorimasu.	I'll treat (you).
Gochisoo ni narimasu.	Thank you for your treat. (This expression is used before you start the meal or after you have accepted someone's invitation or treat. And after the meal, the expression Gochisoo-sama (deshita) is used for thanking the host for the treat.)

8.2 CONVERSATION

8.2.1 At a Japanese Restaurant

Situation: A young couple enter a restaurant.

Ueitoresu: Irasshaimase.
Yoshio: Aa, gohan ga tabetai naa.
Jun'ko: Atashi mo.
Ueitoresu: Kyoo wa kan'koo deshita ka?
Jun'ko: Soo desu. Hanauma Bei e ikimashita.
              Sumimasen, ohiya o kudasai.
Ueitoresu: Doozo.
              . . . . . .
Ueitoresu: Nan ni nasaimasu ka?
Yoshio: Boku wa teishoku B.
Jun'ko: Atashi wa osushi, nigiri no Take o onegai shimasu.
Ueitoresu: Hai. Onomimono wa?
Jun'ko: Kirin ippon to guaba juusu o ippai onegai shimasu.
Ueitoresu: Hai, kashikomarimashita.
              (After they have eaten)
Jun'ko: Nee, chippu wa ikura gurai oku no?
Yoshio: 10% kara 15% kurai da yo.
              . . . . . .
Jun'ko: Dewa ikimashoo. (to waitress) Gochisoo-sama deshita.
Ueitoresu: Doomo arigatoo gozaimashita.

Waitress: Welcome.
Yoshio: Boy, would I like to eat some rice.
Junko: Me too.
Waitress: Have you been sight-seeing today?
Junko: Yes, we went to Hanauma Bay.
              Excuse me. Could I have some cold water please?
Waitress: Certainly. Here you are.
              . . . . . .
Waitress: What would you like to order?
Yoshio: I'll have the set menu B please.
Junko: I'll have the sushi and nigiri no Take please.
Waitress: All right. Can I get you anything to drink?
Junko: Yes. One bottle of Kirin beer and a glass of guava juice please.
Waitress: Thank you.
              (After they have eaten)
Junko: Well, I wonder how large a tip we should leave?
Yoshio: Isn't it between 10 and 15 percent?
              . . . . . .

123

Junko: Well, let's leave. *(to waitress)* Thank you.
Waitress: Thank you very much.

8.2.2   Meeting a Friend at a Restaurant

Situation: A young man sees his friend (senior) as he enters a restaurant.

Yamada: Sen'pai, nani o tabete imasu ka?
Sato: Ten'don da. Boku ga ogoru yo, Yamada-kun. Issho ni doo?
Yamada: Doomo arigatoo gozaimasu. Dewa sen'pai, gochisoo ni nari-
            masu.
Sato: *(to waitress)* Chotto sumimasen. Ten'don o moo hitotsu motte
            kite kudasai.
Ueitoresu: Kashikomarimashita.

Yamada: Mr. Sato (senior person), what are you eating?
Sato: Oh, a bowl of rice and fish. Let me treat you, Yamada. How about
          joining me?
Yamada: Gee, thanks. I'll accept that offer!
Sato: *(to waitress)* Excuse me. Please bring another bowl of **ten'don.**
Waitress: Certainly.

8.3   VOCABULARY

Nouns

arubaito	part-time job
gochisoo	feast
inarizushi	fried bean curd stuffed with sushi rice
ippin ryoori	ala carte
kan'koo	tour
makizushi	rolled sushi
nigirizushi	hand-rolled sushi with raw fish
(o)hashi	chopsticks
ohiya	cold water
omiotsuke, misoshiru	miso soup
onaji	same
raamen	Chinese-style noodles
sake	Japanese rice wine
sashimi	sliced raw fish
seki	seat
sen'pai	senior person
soba	buckwheat flour noodles
sushi	rice with vinegar

124

tabemono	food
teishoku	a meal of set items
ten'don	a bowl of rice with fried shrimp or fish on top
ten'pura	tempura, deep fried Japanese foods
ton'katsu	pork cutlet
tsukemono	pickled vegetables
udon	thick wheat flour noodles

Verbs

agemasu	to give
kekkon shimasu	to marry
ogorimasu	to treat
okimasu	to place
shirimasu	to know
sumimasu	to finish
tsukimasu	to include, to attach

Others

goro	approximate (point of time)
gurai	approximate (amount, quantity)
moo hitotsu	one more

8.4 EXPLANATION

8.4.1 Formal and Informal Forms of Nouns, Adjectives, and Verbs

Nouns and Adjective Nouns

The form of the copula determines whether the sentence ending with a noun or adjective noun is formal or informal. The formal form of the copula is desu and its informal form is da.

Examples:

	Formal	**Informal**
Noun:	Yamada-san wa sen'pai *desu.* Mr. Yamada is my senior.	Yamada-san wa sen'pai *da.*
Adjective Noun:	Koko wa shizuka *desu.* This place is quiet.	Koko wa shizuka *da.*

Adjectives

	Formal	**Informal**
	Kore wa oishii *desu.* This is delicious.	Kore wa oishii.

Note that the formal form of the copula desu is simply omitted in the informal form of the sentence ending with an adjective. Therefore, any sentence completed by adjective endings such as -oi, -ai, -ui, and -ii is considered to be in informal form.

Verbs

Any sentence ending with the -masu form of the verb is considered to be in formal form. For example, Sumisu-san wa Tookyoo e iki*masu*, *Mr. Smith will go to Tokyo*. In order to make the sentence ending with V-masu informal, V-masu form must change to V-u form, for example, ikimasu becomes iku, tabemasu becomes taberu.

Formal	Informal
Sumisu-san wa Tookyoo e *ikimasu*.	Sumisu-san wa Tookyoo e *iku*.
Mr. Smith is going to Tokyo.	
Watakushi wa kore o *tabemasu*.	Watakushi wa kore o *taberu*.
I'll eat this.	
Tanaka-san wa koohii o *nomimasu*.	Tanaka-san wa koohii o *nomu*.
Mr. Tanaka will drink coffee.	

The verb form V-u in iku, taberu, and nomu can be called the dictionary form, because this is the form which you find in a dictionary. This form is also called a citation form or a plain form. This informal form of verbs is important, because it not only signifies an informal speech form but is also a basis upon which various sentence patterns can be constructed. The other usage for the informal form of verbs will be covered in later lessons.

The formal speech forms should be used:

1. When you are in the "ritual domain" as explained in Lesson 2. In other words, desu form and masu form are generally used when you talk to someone whom you know, but you do not feel close enough to be informal.

2. When you talk to a superior, such as your immediate boss at work.

As a matter of fact, the desu form and masu form can be called "safe" forms, because they are safe to use in ordinary social situations.

Informal speech form should be used:

1. When you are in the intimate domain discussed in Lesson 2, in which you feel intimate enough to be informal, as with very close friends and family members.

2. When you talk to your subordinates at work.

In the dialogue of this lesson, Mr. Sato, who is a sen'pai *senior* talking to Mr. Yamada, a koohai *junior,* used informal forms such as ten'don da and boku ga ogoru yo. The use of informal form by Mr. Sato indicates the closeness of the relationship between the two men.

8.4.2 Verb Classification

All verbs are basically classified into three categories, namely, vowel verbs, consonant verbs, and irregular verbs. To simplify the verb classification, the following practical hints are suggested:

1. *Vowel Verbs:* Most verbs, whose dictionary form (the form that appears in dictionaries) ends in -eru or -iru, can be said to belong to this set. There are, however, several exceptions. They are kaeru *to return,* hairu *to enter,* hashiru *to run,* kiru *to cut,* and chiru *to fall.* These verbs end with -eru and -iru, but do not belong to the vowel verb class. Instead, they belong to the consonant verb class.

2. *Consonant Verbs:* All the other verbs, whose dictionary form does not end in -eru or -iru, belong to the consonant verb set.

3. *Irregular Verbs:* There are only two irregular verbs, namely, kuru *to come* and suru *to do.* Because of irregularities in their conjugation, these two verbs should be handled separately. This verb classification becomes important for forming various grammatical forms such as the te (gerund) form, informal past tense, and negative forms, all of which will be presented later.

Each verb, whether vowel verb or consonant verb, has its base form and stem form. The base form represents the part that stays constant, after deleting the inflected part. For example, tabe of taberu and mi of miru, are the base forms of two vowel verbs. Similarly, nom of nomu and hanas of hanasu are the base forms of two consonant verbs. Note here that, since the final segment of the vowel verb is a vowel, either *e* or *i,* it is called a vowel verb, and since the final segment of the consonant verb is a consonant, like *m* or *s,* it is called a consonant verb. Also, each verb has its stem form, to which the formal ending masu is attached, as in tabe-masu and nomi-masu. Note that the stem form and the base form of the vowel verbs are identical. For the consonant verbs, *i* is added to the base form, which becomes the stem, as in nomi-(masu) and hanashi-(masu).

The following table is a partial listing of some forms of vowel verbs and consonant verbs.

Classification	Dictionary form		Base form	Stem form	Pre-Nai[1] form
Vowel Verbs	taberu	*eat*	tabe	tabe-(masu)	tabe-(nai)
	miru	*see*	mi	mi-(masu)	mi-(nai)
	iru	*be*	i	i-(masu)	i-(nai)
Consonant Verbs	nomu	*drink*	nom	nomi-(masu)	noma-(nai)
	hanasu	*speak*	hanas	hanashi-(masu)	hanasa-(nai)
	asobu	*play*	asob	asobi-(masu)	asoba-(nai)
	kaeru	*return home*	kaer	kaeri-(masu)	kaera-(nai)
	kaku	*write*	kak	kaki-(masu)	kaka-(nai)
	oyogu	*swim*	oyog	oyogi-(masu)	oyoga-(nai)
	matsu	*wait*	mat	machi-(masu)	mata-(nai)
	ka(w)u[2]	*buy*	ka(w)	ka(w)i-(masu)	kawa-(nai)
Irregular Verbs	suru	*do*		shi-(masu)	shi-(nai)
	kuru	*come*		ki-(masu)	ko-(nai)

1. The pre-nai form is the form that appears before -nai, the informal negative ending.
2. Verbs like kau, which have vowel–vowel combinations are assumed to have an intervening consonant. The consonant is silent (ka[w]u) except in the informal negative form (kawanai), which will be covered in the following lesson.

Some additional practical hints for the classification of a verb as either a consonant verb or a vowel verb are:

1. If a verb ends in -eru or -iru, you cannot be sure whether it is a consonant verb or a vowel verb until you check the te form or the plain perfect tense form (ta form) of the verb.

2. The suffixes -masu and -nai can be used as criteria for determining whether a verb is a vowel verb or a consonant verb. If the two forms before -masu and -nai are identical, it is a vowel verb. If the two forms are not identical, the verb is classified as a consonant verb.

8.4.3 The te Form (the Gerund Form)

1. The te form of each verb is formed in one of the following manners:
   (a) Vowel Verb: Stem form + te
   Examples:

i-(masu)	ite	be
mi-(masu)	mite	see
tabe-(masu)	tabete	eat

(b) Consonant Verb:

When the final syllable of the stem form is:

(1) -i-(masu), -tte replaces -i

Examples:

kai-(masu)	katte	buy
narai-(masu)	naratte	learn

(2) -ki-(masu), -ite replaces -ki

Example:

kaki-(masu)	kaite	write

Iki-(masu) is the only exception to this rule; it becomes itte.

(3) -gi-(masu), -ide replaces -gi

Examples:

oyogi-(masu)	oyoide	swim
isogi-(masu)	isoide	hurry

(4) -chi-(masu), or -ri-(masu), -tte replaces -chi or -ri

Examples:

machi-(masu)	matte	wait
kaeri-(masu)	kaette	return

(5) -shi-(masu), add -te to -shi

Example:

hanashi-(masu)	hanashite	speak

(6) -bi-(masu), -mi-(masu), or -ni(masu), -n'de replaces -bi, -mi, or -ni

Examples:

asobi-(masu)	ason'de	play
nomi-(masu)	non'de	drink
shini-(masu)	shin'de	die

(c) Irregular Verb:

(1)	shimasu	shite	do
(2)	kimasu	kite	come

2. The dictionary form of a verb is formed in one of the following ways:

(a) The dictionary form of a vowel verb is formed by attaching -ru to the stem form of the verb.

tabe-(masu)	taberu	eat
age-(masu)	ageru	give
deki-(masu)	dekiru	be able to
sashiage-(masu)	sashiageru	give
i-(masu)	iru	be
mi-(masu)	miru	see
mise-(masu)	miseru	show

(b) The dictionary form of a consonant verb is formed by attaching -u to the base form of the verb.

ik-(imasu)	iku	go
tsuk-(imasu)	tsuku	arrive
ar-(imasu)	aru	be, have
tsutsum-(imasu)	tsutsumu	wrap
nom-(imasu)	nomu	drink
hanash-(imasu)	hanasu	speak
ka-(imasu)	kau	buy
mach-(imasu)	matsu	wait
moch-(imasu)	motsu	hold

(c) Irregular Verbs

shimasu	suru	do
kimasu	kuru	come

8.4.4 Verb (-te) kudasai

The te form of a verb plus the predicate extender kudasai formulates the polite imperative, *Please do such and such.*

Sore o misete kudasai.	Please show that to me.
Kore o tsutsun'de kudasai.	Please wrap this up.
Chotto matte kudasai.	Please wait for a minute.

8.4.5 Verb (-te) imasu

Tabete imasu means *is eating* and is the combination of the te form of the verb tabemasu—taberu—and the imperfect tense form of the predicate extender imasu—iru.

(Predicate Modifier) + Verb (-te) + {
imasu
imasen
imashita
imasen deshita
imashoo
ite kudasai
}

(Verbs such as arimasu and imasu cannot be used in this combination.)

1. This form may mean an action is continuing or going on: *Someone is doing such and such.*

ben'kyoo shimasu	ben'kyoo shite imasu	is studying
hanashimasu	hanashite imasu	is talking
hatarakimasu	hataraite imasu	is working

130

kaimasu	katte imasu	is buying
kaimono shimasu	kaimono shite imasu	is shopping
kakimasu	kaite imasu	is writing
kikimasu	kiite imasu	is listening
machimasu	matte imasu	is waiting
mimasu	mite imasu	is watching
misemasu	misete imasu	is showing

2. This form may also mean that the result of an action exists or the state resulting from an action exists: *Something has been done, and the result of that action exists.* or *Something is done.* This usage is common among verbs which are not continuative.

chigaimashita	chigatte imasu	is different
kekkon shimashita	kekkon shite imasu	is married
kikimashita[a]	kiite imasu	have heard
kimashita[a]	kite imasu	wear
mochimashita	motte imasu	have
shirimashita	shitte imasu[b]	know
wakarimashita	wakatte imasu	is understood
wasuremashita	wasurete imasu	have forgotten

a. Most of the verbs listed under the first usage may also indicate the result of an action under certain limited circumstances. Verbs such as kikimasu and kimasu, however, are used in either one of the two meanings rather regularly. The context usually makes it clear which meaning is called for.

Boku wa ima arubaito o shite imasen.
I'm not working (I don't have a part-time job) now.

Sono shokudoo de matte ite kudasai.
Please be waiting at the restaurant.

Kinoo no ku-ji goro nani o shite imashita ka?
What were you doing around nine o'clock yesterday?

Terebi o mite imashita.
I was watching television.

b. Shitte imasu means *(I) know it.* The verb shirimasu is somewhat different in usage from other verbs. Shirimasu means *get to know* or *come to know.* But *someone does not know it* or *you have not come to know* is expressed by the negative present shirimasen.

Nihon'go o shitte imasu ka?	Do you know Japanese?
Hai, sukoshi shitte imasu.	Yes, I know a little.
Iie, shirimasen.	No, I don't know it.

8.4.6 Informal Speech

In informal conversation, both men and women use informal speech styles, in which sentence particles such as no, yo, wa, ka, and so forth, are added after informal verbs, adjectives, or nouns. (The dictionary form is the present tense of informal form, and only this form is presented in this lesson.)

	Formal	Informal	
		Men	**Women**
Verbs:	wakarimasu	wakaru	wakaru
		wakaru yo	wakaru wa
			yo
		wakaru -?	wakaru -?
		ka?	no?
		no?	
Adjectives:	omoshiroi desu	omoshiroi	omoshiroi
		omoshiroi yo	omoshiroi noyo
		no	wayo
		omoshiroi -?	omoshiroi -?
		ka?	no?
Nouns:	kamera desu	kamera da	kamera
		kamera dane	kamera ne
		kamera dayo	kamera dawa
			dawayo
		kamera ka?	kamera -?
			kamera na no?

The informal form can be used before -kara in a subordinate clause.

Compare:

1. *Ben'kyoo shimasu* kara wakarimasu.
   Ben'kyoo suru kara wakarimasu.
   Because I study, I understand.

2. Sugu *ikimasu* kara matte ite kudasai.
   Sugu *iku* kara matte ite kudasai.
   Since I'm coming, please be waiting.

8.5 DRILLS

8.5.1 Transformation Drill

1. Kore o misemasu.   Kore o misete kudasai.
2. Kono seetaa o urimasu.   Kono seetaa o utte kudasai.

3. Nihon'go o hanashimasu.	Nihon'go o hanashite kudasai.
4. Ashita jimusho ni imasu.	Ashita jimusho ni ite kudasai.
5. Koko e kimasu.	Koko e kite kudasai.
6. Depaato de kaimasu.	Depaato de katte kudasai.
7. Sugu ikimasu.	Sugu itte kudasai.
8. Kore o tsutsumimasu.	Kore o tsutsun'de kudasai.
9. Ohiya o nomimasu.	Ohiya o non'de kudasai.
10. Chippu o okimasu.	Chippu o oite kudasai.
11. Omiyage o agemasu.	Omiyage o agete kudasai.

8.5.2 Response Drill

1. Nani o kaimashoo ka?
   Kono hon o katte kudasai.

   Cue: this book

2. Ashita doko e ikimashoo ka?
   Biichi e itte kudasai.

   Cue: the beach

3. Nani o shimashoo ka?
   Tegami o kaite kudasai.

   Cue: write a letter

4. Nani o chuumon shimashoo ka?
   Nigirizushi o chuumon shite
      kudasai.

   Cue: nigirizushi

5. Chippu o ikura okimashoo ka?
   Ni-doru oite kudasai.

   Cue: two dollars

6. Nani o ogorimashoo ka?
   Sushi o ogotte kudasai.

   Cue: sushi

7. Doko de oyogimashoo ka?
   Hanauma Bei de oyoide kudasai.

   Cue: Hanauma Bay

8.5.3 Transformation Drill

1. Nihon'go o hanashimasu.	Nihon'go o hanashite imasu.
2. Sono mise de machimasu.	Sono mise de matte imasu.
3. Shin'bun o yomimasu.	Shin'bun o yon'de imasu.
4. Kekkon shimasu.	Kekkon shite imasu.
5. Wakarimasu.	Wakatte imasu.

8.5.4 Response Drill

1. Ima nihon'go o ben'kyoo shite imasu ka?
   Hai, ben'kyoo shite imasu.
   Iie, ben'kyoo shite imasen.

2. Okane o motte imasu ka?
   Hai, motte imasu.
   Iie, motte imasen.

3. Ten'pura o meshiagatte imasu ka?
   Hai, tabete imasu.
   Iie, tabete imasen.

4. Uchi de nihon'go o hanashite imasu ka?
   Hai, hanashite imasu.
   Iie, hanashite imasen.

5. Kinoo no asa terebi o mite imashita ka?
   Hai, mite imashita.
   Iie, mite imasen deshita.

8.5.5   Substitution Drill

Informal form practice:

Example: Ashita ikimasu kara.
           Ashita iku kara.

1. Tanaka-san ga kimasu kara.
   Tanaka-san ga kuru kara.

2. Ashita shimasu kara.
   Ashita suru kara.

3. Gakusei desu kara.
   Gakusei da kara.

4. Biichi de oyogitai desu kara.
   Biichi de oyogitai kara.

5. Asoko de matte imasu kara.
   Asoko de matte iru kara.

6. Sugu motte kimasu kara.
   Sugu motte kuru kara.

7. Watakushi ga yoyaku shimasu kara.
   Watakushi ga yoyaku suru kara.

8. Moo ippai nomitai desu kara.
   Moo ippai nomitai kara.

9. Kono hon wa omoshiroi desu kara.
   Kono hon wa omoshiroi kara.

10. Yamada-san o machimasu kara.
    Yamada-san o matsu kara.

8.6 EXERCISES

8.6.1 Completion

Complete the following, based on the English equivalent provided.

1. Hiru gohan wa nani o . . .
   What did you eat for lunch?

2. Kinoo no ku-ji goro, nani o . . .
   What were you doing at about 9 o'clock yesterday?

3. Dare o . . .
   For whom are you waiting?

4. Nani o . . .
   What are they selling?

5. Tanaka-san wa . . .
   Mrs. Tanaka is drinking black tea.

6. Nanigo o . . .
   What language do you speak?

7. Nanigo o . . .
   What language do you know? (shirimasu)

8. Shoo wa . . .
   The show was very interesting.

9. Osake ga . . .
   I wanted to drink sake.

10. Nakada-san wa kinoo . . .
    Nakada was not reading a book at the library yesterday.

8.6.2 Situational Practice

What do you say in Japanese when:

1. You are thirsty.
2. You are hungry.
3. You really want to drink beer.
4. You are full.
5. You want to tell your friend that you'll treat him or her.
6. You accept your friend's treat.
7. You want to thank your friend for the treat. (It was a feast.)
8. You want to order two portions of sushi. (Specify your favorite type of sushi.)
9. You want to know how much tip you should leave.

8.6.3 Situational Practice

As a waitress, you want to say to your Japanese customer:

1. How many people are in your party?
2. Did you make reservations?
3. What would you like to order?
4. Please wait for a moment.
5. I'll bring it right away.
6. I'm sorry to have kept you waiting.
7. Yes sir or I understand.
8. Please pay your check at the register over there.
9. Are you through?

8.7 SIMULATION AND SKITS

1. A small group of students visited a local Japanese restaurant with their teacher. They learned about the different kinds of meals served at Japanese restaurants by observing what each other ordered and by asking their teacher and waitress questions. They came back and shared with the rest of their class what they learned from the outing.

2. Two owners of Japanese restaurants visit the class. Each explains his menu to the class. The class asks the two owners questions about their menus.

3. A foreign student goes to a Japanese restaurant and orders nigirizushi and miso soup. He does not know how it should be eaten, so he asks the waitress to explain Japanese table manners to him.

4. A student studied Japanese cooking and presented a "cooking show" to the class. He chose to demonstrate preparation of one of the following meals to the class: sukiyaki, shabushabu, makizushi, or nigirizushi.

8.8 CULTURE ORIENTATION

8.8.1 The Japanese Revealed Through Their Cookery

This lesson will study Japanese values and national characteristics by looking at their attitude towards cookery. This will be done by contrasting Japanese attitudes towards cookery with American and Chinese attitudes. We will especially focus on the underlying cultural values and orientations that affect the Japanese method of food preparation.

136

Nature and art of cookery. What are some of the important variables which have affected and influenced the basic attitudes of people towards eating? Since food is a product of nature, we will begin by studying the basic attitudes towards nature that the Americans, Chinese, and Japanese have developed over time. We will do this by briefly looking at the geographical and historical conditions that affected their views of nature.

Japan. Approximately 84 percent of Japan is mountainous, providing the Japanese islanders with a rich and beautiful natural setting. As a result of its geographical location, Japan has four very distinct seasons in a year. The Japanese sense of aesthetics has revolved around nature and its four seasons. For 1200 years, aesthetics has played a major role in Japanese life, placing much emphasis on sensitivity to beauty and the development of an aesthetic sensitivity in each individual.

In Japan, with cultural value based on the aesthetic appreciation of and sensitivity to nature, art forms such as flower arrangement, flower viewing, moon viewing, autumn leaves viewing, brush painting, and tea ceremony developed. Natural beauty becomes a criterion for judging the beauty of anything. Business conduct and eating habits are also judged according to this criterion of beauty. Next we will look at Japan's neighbor, China, and Chinese attitudes towards nature.

China. There are many similarities between Japanese and Chinese attitudes towards nature. However, there is one big difference between the two. While the Japanese accept nature and attempt to become one with it, the Chinese resist and challenge it. This is probably due to the constant, gigantic floods of the Yellow River, which destroyed numerous cities and caused famines each time they occurred. Against this geographical and historical setting, the Chinese people naturally developed a degree of mistrust of nature.

Methods of flood control requiring human effort were developed. This led the people to believe in the power of human capacity rather than in a supernatural being such as an almighty god. Many sacred men were worshipped like gods for their success in controlling the floods. Mao Tse Tung can be looked upon as a man who was worshipped as being sacred in modern Chinese history. He not only "moved the mountain" and controlled the flood, but he also moved the whole nation. No wonder he was worshipped like a god! The Chinese perceived human beings as capable of doing anything if they really tried. This brought about their notion of human supremacy. As a result, the Chinese perceived nature to be an entity man could control.

At the same time, Chinese people were down-to-earth people. They developed and invented many things to enrich and enjoy their lives on earth, whether it was in the area of food, or of games, or even of sex. The Chinese attitude towards nature influenced their methods of preparing food. We shall discuss how this was done after we look at the American attitude towards nature.

137

America. For the immigrants that came to the American continent, the frontier meant physical danger, grinding toil, and hardship. But for those immigrants who left the European continent, which symbolized oppression and poverty, the frontier also symbolized opportunity, adventure, and independence. For these people, nature was, on the one hand, an enemy to contend with, but, on the other hand, an opportunity they could never have imagined. The presence of the native Indians added to the danger and hostility of the natural environment that the immigrants faced.

In order for man to survive in this hostile environment, he had to be creative, quick to take advantage of opportunities, adventurous, willing to try new things, intelligent, and able to predict and control events. In this way, the American propensity for change and progress had a natural beginning. For the American, progress did not entail changing oneself, but rather manipulating, controlling, and changing one's environment—nature itself. Under such circumstances, the abilities to control, manipulate, predict, solve problems, invent, and achieve became important values. One can say the American people highly value the scientific approach to problem solving. Against such a geographical and historical setting, work habits and personalities of individuals were affected. Such values as industry, efficiency, and speed became important. Such American values and characteristics influenced their method of preparing food and habits of eating it.

We have briefly discussed how each of the three countries perceived nature in order to understand how attitudes towards nature affect attitudes towards eating habits. Next, we will look at specific aspects of eating and food preparation in each of the three cultures and think about the cultural orientations of each.

Appearance. Japanese people place much value on the appearance of prepared food. It must be aesthetically beautiful in appearance. It is believed that the color scheme and arrangement of food is directly related to the stimulation of appetite. When a Japanese person exclaims oishii as he eats a meal, it compliments the beauty of the taste as well as the beauty of the appearance, in a literal translation of the Japanese.

On the other hand, to Chinese people, the amount and different varieties of food stimulate their appetite. Not much emphasis is placed on an aesthetically beautiful appearance.

The American people place importance on recognizing the content by the appearance of food. In other words, a reliable and dependable appearance is valued in food: meat should look like meat, fish should look like fish, and one should be able to tell what vegetable is served on a plate. In addition, a nutritious and sanitary appearance is also important.

The Japanese attempt to become one with nature to the extent of bringing nature to the dining table. For example, a river fish served on a plate will not only look like a fish on a plate but it will be cooked in such a way as to make it look like it is swimming and a rectangular chinaware plate will be used to serve the river fish to make it look like the fish is still swimming in the river. In addition, bits of condiments will be placed on the plate to make it look like moss on the riverbottom. Some people go to the extent of placing inedible pebbles to make the appearance more riverlike. In this way the Japanese people enjoy their meals by bringing nature to their tables and attempting to become one with it. The Japanese people attempt to interact with nature through their palates. This gives them a sense of harmony between nature and man (Higuchi 1975:199).

In some high-class restaurants seasonal flowers, such as plum blossoms, camellias, or a yamabuki flower *(Japanese rose)*, is placed by the dish in order to bring the feeling of the different seasons to the table. The appearance of the meal becomes more aesthetically beautiful if nature can be recreated as it naturally exists.

Chinese cooking allows one to experience the transformation of nature through one's tongue. The transformation of natural materials (mastery of nature) into food seems almost an act of the cook's skill and magical power. The Chinese are known to use everything for their cooking and the transformation of these materials into food depends upon the skill of the cook, who is even able to conceal what the original material was.

Similarly, American cooking allows one to experience the conquest of nature through one's palate. Great pains are taken to create sauces which, in fact, cover up the natural taste of the food. Even vegetables which can be eaten raw are covered with dressing to conceal the natural taste.

In contrast, the Japanese cooking emphasizes the maintenance of the natural taste and appearance of foods. Next, we look at the approach to food preparation in these three cultures.

Approach. The Japanese take extra pains to retain the original taste and appearance of natural ingredients. The cook, in a sense, attempts to attain oneness with nature. If the cook wants to have his guests experience nature through the meal, the cook himself must be one with nature. In order to achieve this, the cook must be able to capture the very essence of each of the materials he is dealing with. The Japanese expression ono ono no motte iru mochi aji o ikani ikasuka (literally, *how to draw out the essence of each taste*) sums up how the essential taste of each material must be acknowledged and drawn out. The cook cannot merely display his ability. He must be able to control his personal skills to accommodate the essential tastes of each food. If a cook can attain this ability, he can be said to be a master of the art of cooking.

In this way, one can look at flower arrangement as an art of being able to bring out or express the individual flower's essence. How does one learn the essence of each individual flower? A master in the art of flower arrangement may answer that his/her own master was the flower itself and the flower taught him/her everything about the flower. Likewise, a chinaware craftsman learns from the soil, and a good sculptor learns from trees and other natural elements.

The good cook learns from his ingredients. A cucumber has a special taste that he can only learn from the cucumber. And a fish may have a special taste only it has, which one can only learn from that particular fish. The motto of the Japanese cook is not to kill the natural taste of the food, but to draw it out. The Japanese seasonings of ajinomoto or shooyu do not have very strong tastes of their own. But they were designed to bring out the natural taste of the ingredients used. Thus, the Japanese people do not often use Western sauces, which dominate the original taste of the ingredients.

The Chinese cook likes to display his skills. The Chinese people are proud of the human power and capacity to transform natural ingredients with their craftsmanship and skill in cooking. They are proud of the fact that they can make fish taste like chicken or chicken taste like duck. Guests can fill their bellies with delicious food without really knowing what they are eating. Those who eat the food are often amazed by the cook's skill that transforms ordinary natural ingredients into delicious foods.

The American cook, like the Japanese, likes to maintain the original taste, but for different reasons. As mentioned before, the Americans like to have their foods dependable and readily identifiable. They like to maintain the original taste in order for the taste to be dependable and consistent. Chicken should taste like chicken. Even food products must be dependable and reliable. For example, people like to know exactly what is contained in the products and exactly what it does. If the manufacturer has altered or improved its content, the word *improved* is mentioned on the wrapping. Why is dependability of food so important to Americans? One of the reasons is to save time. An American housewife saves time if the products she uses are dependable, and she can plan her schedule ahead of time in order to do other things besides housework. If the product fails in its performance, she ends up wasting time to patch up the horrible mess. Therefore, it is important for food products to be dependable. The American people are also sensitive to weight and nutrition; products usually mention their caloric content, vitamin content, and other nutritional information. The American housewife likes to know she can prepare a quick and easy meal and have it nutritionally sound as well. Reliance on recipes is also important, and they include information such as preparation time, calories per serving, and cooking time.

Food preparation in different countries is very much influenced by their cultural values. We will next explore the method of preparing foods by the Japanese cook, comparing it to the Chinese and American methods.

Method. One can describe the Japanese cooking method as "watercolor painting technique." This method requires the artist not to go back and patch up his mistakes. As in watercolor painting, water is used as the base medium in Japanese cooking, and the mixing of ingredients and taste is kept to a minimum. Japanese cooking has traditionally used very little oil, and instead, has used water as its base (Umesao 1972:48). The result is a very simple, plain, and light dish. If the cook makes a mistake, he cannot easily go back and patch it up.

In contrast, it can be said that Chinese cooking uses "oil painting technique." It uses oil as its base medium, and the ingredients are mixed together to create a balanced taste. The result is a heavy and oily dish. Even if the cook makes mistakes, they can be readjusted by increasing or decreasing ingredients and spices.

The American cooking method can be described as "mosaic painting technique." This method requires a recipe with well-ordered and sequential instructions. Each ingredient is added step-by-step following these instructions. The result should be reproducible by anybody just like a scientific experiment. The taste and method is standardized. One can describe this method as being scientific with its qualities of reliability, dependability, predictability, and control.

Japanese food prepared by the watercolor technique loses its taste when mixed with a different dish. Chinese food, on the other hand, can mix well with different foods without disrupting its taste too much. For example, Chinese food can be served in a plate lunch with a variety of dishes without disrupting the taste of each dish. However, Japanese food cannot be piled together in one plate lunch as easily as Chinese food. This is one reason why partitions are made for Japanese food sets such as the teishoku and also why the Japanese serve their meals in separate containers for every dish.

As in the method of their food preparation, the Japanese people themselves do not mix very well with others. In this respect, they can be said to lack an international character. Perhaps one can say that the Chinese people, as in their food preparation, are able to mix easily with others without losing their individuality, thus being more international in character. The "paint by number" method of preparing American food seems to reflect the American nation. Here the people do not create a melting pot, but do still create one single nation. Each piece of mosaic consists of individual characteristics, but all of them together make up the whole entity called the United States of America. America has a quality of unity and diversity both at the same time.

Next we will look at the attitudes of the Japanese towards the behavior of eating. We will do this by comparing them to Chinese and American attitudes.

Eating behavior. The Japanese people are basically passive when it comes to eating. Even now, some traditional Japanese restaurants do not carry menus, and the customer leaves the ordering of food completely up to the expert cook. There are no menus even for large-scale dinners with entertainment, such as the Japanese-style dinner party, or en'kai, and kaiseki ryoori, which consists of a set menu of selected dishes served on an individual tray to each member of a party. Even the items in the teishoku, mentioned in Lesson 7, are already chosen ahead of time. Generally speaking, the Japanese people lack the initiative to say "I will eat this today," and choose exactly what they want.

Chinese and Americans, in comparison to the Japanese, are active in their eating behavior. They both choose exactly what they want and eat the exact amount that they desire.

We will look at the Japanese people's attitudes toward tableware next, and explore the position tableware plays in Japanese cooking.

Tableware. The taste of food alone does not make up the whole aesthetic experience of eating. The tableware plays an important role in completing the experience. As mentioned earlier, the Japanese value the concept of bringing nature to the dining table. The taste of the food alone does not complete the meal. It must be served in a proper dish to highlight the ingredients used. For example, fish should be served on a plate which is suggestive of the river or ocean or lake where the fish was found.

By comparison, the Chinese and Americans do not pay so much attention to tableware. The main concerns in Chinese cooking are taste and quantity. Eating is a physical experience for the Chinese, rather than an aesthetic experience as it is for the Japanese. Similarly, for the American, eating is a physical experience where the emphasis lies on the efficient use of time and the nutritional value of the meal. Very little time is spent on tableware. Thoughts of bringing inedible pebbles to the table would be out of the question! At most, they will arrange flowers at the table.

The custom of inviting guests over for dinner is seldom practiced. However, the Japanese take the utmost care and spend much time on choosing the proper tableware when such an occasion does occur.

The Chinese spend time on the dinner menu rather than on the tableware. Once the menu has been decided, they look for the proper ingredients to be used. Often a whole day is spent on cooking the dinner. One Chinese woman said that she had a repertoire of 260 dishes. She chose several dishes from the list for each dinner. She recorded which items were used for each dinner so that she wouldn't repeat the same combination again.

Americans also spend much time on dinner parties. But rather than spending the whole day cooking, time is spent on cleaning and preparing the house for a congenial atmosphere for the guests. A good host and hostess should be able to interact and socialize with their invited guests. Time is spent efficiently for eating and serving food. The dining table serves as an area for eating, and after they complete the meal, they all move to the living room for socializing. The process of eating is not where the main focus lies at the dinner party; rather, it is in the socializing.

Table manners. The Japanese people are very particular when it comes to table manners. One Chinese person commented, "Japanese food tastes good but the quantity is too little. And the table manners and the atmosphere is too

142

tense to be able to thoroughly enjoy the food." Such a complaint is understandable coming from a Chinese, for they emphasize enjoying one's meal. Food spilled on the table proves that the meal was enjoyed. It is even appreciated as a compliment to the host and hostess!

The Japanese have many rules of table manners, for example, some sauces can only be used for certain items. One can only use one's own hashi *chopsticks* for certain items and not for others. Some items must not be mixed with certain other items. The list goes on and on.

Formal dinners in America also require very specific table manners. Soup must be eaten with the spoon moving away from the body; a salad fork must be used with the salad and the longer fork with the entree. For the Chinese person, whose primary concern is to enjoy the meal, such strict table manners must certainly spoil his enjoyment.

The eating of Japanese food can be described both as an aesthetic experience and as a total physical experience, where the food is prepared to appeal to all five senses: taste, smell, appearance, touch, and even sound. Few things are held in the hand directly. Among these would be musubi and nigiri rice balls. As for sound, one cannot eat a takuan *(Japanese pickled radish)* without hearing it crunch. A bowl of soba or udon *(noodles)* cannot be eaten without the noisy slurps. Slurping noodles is considered natural and the only way to enjoy them. If one doesn't slurp one's noodles, one may be asked, "Aren't you enjoying your noodles?" Appealing to all five senses is a special characteristic of Japanese food.

However, cultural problems can arise when some of these table manners clash with others. Slurping noodles at an American home would be considered rather rude. Having to be aware of different table manners while eating can even spoil the entire meal!

8.8.2   The Accommodating Culture and the Choosing Culture

Japanese people prefer to solve their problems through accommodating and adapting themselves to the needs of others and to various situations. The Japanese have an accommodating culture. In some ways, American culture is also accommodating. The big difference in the American culture is that one doesn't accommodate oneself to the situation, but rather the situation is accommodated to oneself. This difference probably stems from what we discussed earlier: the immigrants' need to confront the wilderness in order to survive in a new environment. As a result, a self-assertive approach to problem solving evolved. The self-assertive approach symbolizes more a choosing culture than an accommodating culture.

The American choosing culture can be illustrated by how a meal might be ordered in a group of five travelers. Each person is asked individually what is desired for breakfast:

Coffee or tea?
Coffee? Regular or Sanka?
Cream and sugar in your coffee?
How about some juice?
Orange juice? Tomato juice? Grapefruit juice?
Large, medium, or small?
How many eggs would you like?
Sunny-side up or scrambled?
Bacon, ham, or sausage with your eggs?
Do you want your bacon crispy? and so forth . . .

Respecting each person's preference takes a lot of time. Imagine spending five minutes for each order. It would take 25 minutes just to order breakfast!

A Japanese group of 50 travelers, on the other hand, would take a few seconds to order their breakfast. The managing treasurer or the representative from the group would leave the ordering of breakfast up to whomever is in charge. Most of the time, the breakfasts are ordered in sets (**teishoku**) of A and B, or by some other designation. Even if a certain person might prefer something other than set A or B, he will most probably keep this to himself, valuing the efficiency and speed in serving the whole group above his own preferences. The individual will sacrifice his small desire for the benefit of the larger group. This attitude is the key to Japanese efficiency and the harmony maintained in personal relationships. If the harmony of the entire group is lost, the result is the ultimate downfall of the individual, who is only a part of the whole community.

Therefore, while dealing with a group of Japanese tourists, the best way to accomplish things is to go directly through the managing representative of the group. To make ordering of meals easier, one should either go through the managing representative or prepare a smorgasbord to enable everybody to choose what he likes (Kobayashi 1980:214–216).

8.9   THE MODE OF JAPANESE COMMUNICATION

Accommodating Communication

As mentioned earlier, the Japanese people enjoy a rich and beautiful natural environment surrounded by mountains that make up about 84 percent of the Japanese archipelago. Natural features, such as rivers and mountains, are generally not gigantic nor monumental in scale. Although natural disasters do occur, such as typhoons, storms, and earthquakes, the general natural setting is moderate and comfortable for the people. As a result, the natural environment acts, not as an enemy, but as a friend to the Japanese people. It was necessary for them to adjust to their environment in order to survive rather than to challenge it.

144

This is one of the reasons why the Japanese approach to problem solving also tries to avoid confrontation and challenge. It also avoids perceiving the problem as merely a negative thing to be fought against. The Japanese problem-solving method is to approach the problem with an accommodating attitude and a willingness to adapt to the situation. Through this approach even physical illness does not have to be perceived negatively as something to be confronted; it can be seen positively as a danger signal for the body. The word kiki *crisis* in Japanese consists of the characters meaning *danger* and *opportunity*. In other words, a crisis can be seen, not only as a dangerous situation, but as an opportunity for further growth. Physical illness or other crises become situations to be accepted rather than avoided. In accepting the situation, it is not to be confronted and challenged, but to be dealt with as a chance to improve the original situation. The main focus lies on the positive aspect of improvement, which itself can help in curing the illness or preventing a crisis.

The Japanese mode of communication can also be said to be one of accommodation and adaptation, rather than of confrontation and challenge. The Japanese mode of communication calls for one speaker to adapt to the other. For example, if two people have opposing opinions, neither will confront the other with his opinion. Some people may completely forego their own opinion to accommodate another's, while others may tactfully bring out another perspective to the issue. The main focus lies in avoiding situations of confrontation mainly from fear of disrupting the relationship. The Japanese perceive that if the relationship is gone, the problem itself will become impossible to solve.

The Japanese mode of communication can be frustrating to those who have a confrontative mode of communication. The latter may perceive the former as being boring, avoiding challenge, and having no personal opinion. On the other hand, the Japanese find confrontative people too aggressive and difficult to deal with, and they attempt to avoid these people.

The Japanese people enjoy and have a special knack for accommodation. They accommodate their clothing, food, and food preparation to the various seasons. They accommodate their language to social status, age, and sex.

8.10 LANGUAGE AND CULTURE

A. Hashi

The best way to eat and appreciate Japanese food is by using hashi *chopsticks*. Hashi enables one to eat various items of food, which are often sliced and cut into small pieces, without mixing them all together. Japanese food is often prepared in small bite-sized pieces. Even when they prepare Western food, such as steak, they slice it into small pieces, making it easier to be eaten with hashi. Soup is eaten by directly taking the bowl to one's mouth and picking out the contents using the hashi. Although chopsticks were invented in China, the Japanese changed them somewhat to suit their own needs and taste. Chinese chopsticks are usually longer and thicker, often made of ivory or plastic. The Japanese find it difficult to use Chinese chopsticks compared to their own smaller wooden ones.

The Japanese are very sensitive when it comes to the use of hashi. Each member of the family has a pair kept in an individual box. They consider hashi used by others very unsanitary and prefer to use wari-bashi *(disposable wooden chopsticks)* when they eat out. One can immediately tell if wari-bashi have been used by the simple fact that they are broken into two sticks. Wari-bashi guarantee that nobody else has used them before. They can be considered as one of the ingenious Japanese inventions, being small, light, clean, and convenient to carry anywhere.

There are numerous traditional legends pertaining to the use of hashi. For example, if hashi are used to eat one's ben'too *(packed lunch)* in the mountains, the hashi should be broken in half and thrown away. Otherwise, evil spirits will haunt one and make one sick (Higuchi 1981:53). There are also taboos concerning the use of hashi at the table. For example, food should not be passed from hashi to hashi, primarily because it reminds one of the passing of a dead person's bones into the burial jar from hashi to hashi by family members. Hashi should not be stuck vertically in a bowl of rice because that is the way food is offered to dead ancestors.

Hashi are not merely tools for eating, but an extension of the Japanese people's hands. The wooden hashi, a natural material, is an ideal medium to use between oneself and the food being eaten, for the Japanese feel that direct contact with food is unclean. The effect would not be the same if the hashi were made of metal, ivory, or plastic because they would somehow feel too cold and insensitive. The Japanese people always try to maintain a close tie with nature. Traditional houses were built of natural materials such as wood, paper, and mud, retaining the contact between man and nature. Similarly, the wooden hashi maintain man's contact with the food he eats which comes from nature. Many Japanese people say that they don't feel as though they have eaten unless they have used hashi.

B. **Oshibori**

Oshibori are small, wet towels tightly wrung out (often slightly scented), offered as a refresher to guests and customers. Most Japanese restaurants offer oshibori to enable their customers to wipe their faces and hands. Cool oshibori are extremely soothing when one is perspiring and hot in the summer. All fatigue and stress seem to melt away when using an oshibori. In the winter, they are served steaming hot. It has the same sensation as when one goes to the barber and is given a hot towel over one's face.

Oshibori wipe away more than grime. (They) warm or cool, soothe and refresh at least temporarily expunging care and stress. In its combination of practical function and

146

psychological effect, the *oshibori* can be seen, indeed, as an outgrowth of the same mentality that created such Japanese arts as the tea ceremony (Trumbull 1980:64–65).

One Japanese tourist in the United States explained her experience of being disappointed at not being offered an **oshibori** at a coffee shop. She was more tired than thirsty and had wanted a refreshing **oshibori**, but she realized America isn't Japan! The **oshibori** is really a very simple thing when one thinks about it. But it functions as an indispensable service for guests.

Recently non-Japanese airline carriers have started to offer **oshibori** to their customers. One can say that it is another ingenious invention of the Japanese people. It would be a good suggestion to restaurants abroad to experiment by offering **oshibori** to their customers.

C. Sen'pai

Generally speaking, **sen'pai** refers to the older graduates of one's school. Those who graduated after the **sen'pai** are all junior to him and are referred to as **koohai**. The **sen'pai-koohai** relationship naturally evolves in a company regardless of whether the individuals knew each other prior to being employed or not. The **sen'pai-koohai** relationship continues even outside of the company with the understanding that the **sen'pai** will take care of and look after the **koohai**. Similarly the **koohai** demonstrates his loyalty and respect for the **sen'pai**. This relationship is often referred to as the **amae** relationship of mutual dependency.

Recall the dialogue earlier in this lesson between Sato-san, the **sen'pai**, and Yamada-san who is, in turn, his **koohai**. Yamada-san is very typical of the **koohai** in a **sen'pai-koohai** relationship. The **koohai** pays proper respect to his **sen'pai**, who treats him to lunch, and accommodates the **sen'pai** by accepting the same meal.

D. Arubaito

Arubaito means *part-time work*, and is borrowed from the German word *arbeit* meaning *work*. Recently the word **arubaito** has been abbreviated to **baito** by younger people.

The Japanese have a knack for creating or "Japanizing" foreign words into their own vocabulary. There are many such foreign words that have virtually become understandable only as Japanese words.

8.11 CULTURE QUESTIONS

1. Discuss among yourselves whether or not the use of **wari-bashi** or **oshibori** are desirable in a reastaurant dealing with Japanese tourists. Give your reasons.

2. A group of 30 Japanese tourists enters a restaurant. You are the only waiter/waitress able to take orders. What is the best thing for you to do?

147

3. What should one keep in mind while communicating with a Japanese person who has an accommodating mode of communication, as we discussed earlier in the lesson?

4. It is often said that the McDonald's food chain is reflective of American culture. List as many American cultural values as you can see reflected in McDonald's.

5. Many adjustments and changes had to be made when Kentucky Fried Chicken was brought into Japan in order to appeal to the Japanese. Having watched the film "The Colonel Comes to Japan," discuss what adjustments and changes had to be made.

8.12 SUGGESTED RESOURCE MATERIALS

8.12.1 Books and Magazines

"Feasts for the Eye," Donald Richie *Winds* 5, no. 8 (January, 1984): 30–35.
A Hundred Things Japanese (Tokyo: Japan Culture Institute, 1975), pp. 48–49.
In Search of What's Japanese About Japan, John Condon and Keisuke Kurata (Tokyo: Shufunotomo Co., 1974), pp. 36–38.
The Japanese, Jack Seward (Tokyo: Simpson-Doyle & Co., 1971), pp. 12–29.
Kodansha Encyclopedia of Japan, vol. 2 (Tokyo: Kodansha, 1983), pp. 20–25.
Things Japanese in Hawaii, John DeFrancis (Honolulu: The University Press of Hawaii, 1973), pp. 161–168.

8.12.2 Films (16 mm) and Video Cassettes (Beta / VHS)

"Mangetsu Bentō." *Full-Moon Lunch: The Life of a Japanese Family: An Intimate Portrait.* Video. 57 mins. Color. John Nathan, 1975.
"The Colonel Comes to Japan." 28 mins. Color. WGBH, 1982.

8.13 REFERENCES

Higuchi, Kiyoyuki. *Monoshiri Jiten: Nihonjin no Shikitari.* Tokyo: Yamato Shuppan-sha, 1981.
Higuchi, Kiyoyuki. *Zoku Umeboshi to Nihontō.* Tokyo: Non Books, 1975.
Kobayashi, Kaoru. "Shokuba no Ningen Kankei." In *Nihonjin no Ningenkankei Jiten,* ed. by Hiroshi Minami. Tokyo: Kodansha, 1980.
Trumbull, Suzanne. "Oshibori." *A Hundred More Things Japanese.* Tokyo: Japan Culture Institute, 1980.
Umesao, Tadao et al. *Nihonjin no Kokoro.* Tokyo: Asahi Shinbun sha, 1972.

LESSON 9

SERVING DRINKS

9.1 USEFUL EXPRESSIONS

Hisashiburi ni ippai yarimashoo.
Ohiya o moo ippai itadakemasu ka?
Osake ni tsuyoi desu nee.
Soo desu ka?
Soo desu nee.

(Kore de) yoroshii desu ka?
Itsumo osewa ni natte imasu.
Kore kara mo doozo yoroshiku
 onegai shimasu.
Otagai ni gan'barimashoo.
Kore wa nan de dekite imasu ka?
Kakuteru wa sugu dekimasu.
Pan'chi wa furuutsu juusu de dekite
 imasu.
Shikata ga arimasen.
Kan'pai!

Let's go drinking for a change.
Can I get another glass of water?
You're a heavy drinker, aren't you?
Is that so?
That's right, isn't it. Let's see.
 Well . . .
Will this be all?
You have been very helpful.
I hope I can count on your continued
 support.
Let's do our best.
What is this made of?
The cocktail will be ready soon.
The punch is made with fruit juice.

It can't be helped.
Your health! Cheers! (a toast, drink to
 the health)

149

9.2 CONVERSATION

9.2.1 At Brown's Office

Situation: Brown, an American hotel manager, meets with Kobayashi, who is with a Japanese tour company.

Brown: Aa, Kobayashi-san, shibaraku deshita nee.

Kobayashi: Aa, Brown-san, hon'too ni shibaraku deshita. Itsumo osewa ni natte imasu. Brown-san, kon'ban wa ohima desu ka?

Brown: Ee.

Kobayashi: Jaa, kon'ban issho ni nomimasen ka? Kin'yoobi desu kara . . .

Brown: Ii desu nee. Hisashiburi ni ippai yarimashoo.

Kobayashi: Ii tokoro o shitte imasu ka?

Brown: Soo desu nee. Aa, Club Sunshine e ikimashoo. Karaoke mo arimasu yo.

Kobayashi: Soo desu ka? Jaa, soko ni shimashoo.

(Later, at the club)

Kobayashi: Brown-san, nan ni shimasu ka?

Brown: Soo desu nee, watakushi wa mizuwari.

Kobayashi: Jaa, watakushi mo mizuwari.

(After the drinks are served)

Brown: Jaa, mizuwari de kan'pai shimashoo.

Kobayashi and Brown: Kan'pai!

Brown: Kore kara mo doozo yoroshiku onegai shimasu.

Kobayashi: Kochira koso.

Brown: Nihon no keiki wa doo desu ka?

Kobayashi: Amari yoku nai desu ne.

Brown: Soo desu ka? Kochira mo kibishii desu yo.

Kobayashi: Saa, doozo, doozo.

Brown: Aa, doomo, doomo.

Kobayashi: Maa, otagai ni gan'barimashoo.

Kobayashi and Brown: Kan'pai!

Brown: Well, Mr. Kobayashi, I haven't seen you for ages.

Kobayashi: Why, Mr. Brown, it has been a long time, hasn't it? I'm really very much indebted to you. Are you free tonight?

Brown: Yes.

Kobayashi: Well, let's go out for a drink, then. Since it's Friday . . .

Brown: That's fine. Let's celebrate our reunion after so long!

Kobayashi: Do you know of a good place?

Brown: Hum. Let's try Club Sunshine. They have a mike with taped music we can sing along with there.

Kobayashi: Really? All right. Let's go there.

(Later, at the club)

150

Kobayashi: What will you have, Mr. Brown?
Brown: Hum. I'll have a whiskey and water.
Kobayashi: All right. I will too.
           (After the drinks are served)
Brown: Well, let's toast.
Kobayashi and Brown: Cheers!
Brown: Here's to our continued good business.
Kobayashi: I'll second that.
Brown: So, how are business conditions in Japan?
Kobayashi: Oh, not very good.
Brown: Really? It's pretty tight here too.
Kobayashi: Please, have another one.
Brown: Thank you. Thank you.
Kobayashi: Well, we'll have to do our best.
Brown and Kobayashi: Cheers!

9.2.2 Tropical Drinks

Kyaku: Mai Tai wa nan de dekite imasu ka?
Baaten'daa: Mai Tai desu ka? Ramu-shu de dekite imasu. Hawai no yuumei
             na kakuteru desu. Sukoshi tsuyoi desu yo.
Kyaku: Chi Chi wa nan de tsukurimasu ka?
Baaten'daa: Wokka, kokonatsu shiroppu, furuutsu juusu nado de tsukuri-
             masu. Oishii desu yo.
Kyaku: Mai Tai o ippai non'de mimashoo.
Baaten'daa: Hai, doozo.

Customer: What is in a Mai Tai?
Bartender: A Mai Tai? Rum. It's a famous Hawaiian cocktail.
           But it is a strong drink.
Customer: What's in a Chi Chi?
Bartender: Vodka, coconut syrup, and fruit juice. It's quite delicious.
Customer: I think I'll try the Mai Tai.
Bartender: Here you are.

Below are descriptions in Japanese and English of three popular tropical drinks.
Use this information and what you have learned from the previous dialogue to
answer questions for a Japanese customer who wants to try an exotic drink.

Chi Chi: Wokka, kokonatsu shiroppu to furuutsu juusu o buren'do shita
           Hawai no kakuteru desu.
Blue Hawaii: Hawai no sora *(sky)* no iro o doozo, ramu to buruu kurasao no
           kakuteru desu.
Mai Tai: Ramu o beesu ni shite tsukutta kakuteru de Hawai no besuto wan
           desu. Takusan nomanai de kudasai.

151

Chi Chi: A subtle blending of vodka, coconut syrup, and fruit juices.

Blue Hawaii: Blue curaçao gives it color; light rum gives it kick.

Mai Tai: Large portions of fine rums and a delicate touch of the lesser ingredients makes this the best in Hawaii. Not too many, please!

9.3   VOCABULARY

Nouns

arukooru	alcoholic beverages
dooryoo	colleagues
en'kai	dinner party
fune	boat, ship
hana	flower
hikooki	airplane
iroiro	variety
kan'pai	a toast
karaoke	taped music for singing along
keiki	business condition
kissa-ten	coffee shop
makunouchi	makunouchi dish
mizuwari	whiskey and water
nama biiru	draft beer
niku	meat
nin'ki	popularity
nomiya	drinking place
ryootei	a Japanese teahouse (with **tatami** rooms)
setsumei	explanation
shokuji	meal
sunakku	snack bar
tabemono	food
tan'joobi	birthday
tsukiai	association, company
tsumami	hors d'oeuvres
uisukii	whiskey
uta	song
wain	wine
yasai	vegetables
zen'sai, apetaizaa	appetizer

Verbs

dekimasu	can do, possible
shokuji shimasu	to dine

152

tsukurimasu	to make	
utaimasu	to sing	

Adjectives

amai	sweet, flat taste
atsui	hot (weather, heat)
karai	hot (taste)
katai	hard
kibishii	harsh, severe, strict
tanoshii	joyous
tsumetai	cold
tsuyoi	strong
yawarakai	soft, tender
yowai	weak, mild

Adjective Nouns

yuumei	famous

Adverbs

chittomo	(not) at all
amari-nai	not very

Others

-nado	et cetera, and so forth

9.4 EXPLANATION

9.4.1 Verb Conjugation

Plain Negative Form (Present Tense)

Vowel Verbs:
The stem form plus -nai

iru	inai	be
miru	minai	see
taberu	tabenai	eat

Consonant Verbs:
The base form plus -anai

iku	ikanai	go
kaeru	kaeranai	return
hanasu	hanasanai	speak
ka(w)	kawanai	buy

The verb of existence aru is irregular here, and its negative informal form is nai. Also, arimasen and dewa arimasen become -nai and dewa nai (the latter) contracted to ja nai.

Irregular Verbs:

suru	shinai	do
kuru	konai	come

Uchi e kaeranai no?	Don't you go home?
Ee, kaeranai wa.	Yes, (your guess is right,) I do not go home.
Iie, kaeru wa.	No, (your guess is not right,) I will go home.
Wakaranai kara oshiete kudasai.	Since I don't understand, please teach me.

Plain Perfect Tense

This tense is formed in the same manner for both the **te** form and **ta** form.

Vowel Verbs:

imasu	iru	ita	be
dekimasu	dekiru	dekita	be able to
mimasu	miru	mita	see

Consonant Verbs:

arimasu	aru	atta	be, have
kakimasu	kaku	kaita	write
yomimasu	yomu	yon'da	read
ikimasu	iku	itta	go
kaimasu	ka(w)u	katta	buy
oyogimasu	oyogu	oyoida	swim

Irregular Verbs:

kimasu	kuru	kita	come
shimasu	suru	shita	do

Nani o non'da no?	What did you drink?
Buruu Hawai o nomimashita.	I drank a Blue Hawaii.

Plain Negative Past Tense

This tense is formed by changing the adjective derivative -nai into -nakatta.

Vowel Verbs:

Present Tense (V-nai)	Past Tense (V-nakatta)
inai	inakatta
minai	minakatta
tabenai	tabenakatta
agenai	agenakatta

154

Consonant Verbs:

nomanai	nomanakatta
ikanai	ikanakatta
kawanai	kawanakatta
hanasanai	hanasanakatta
nai	nakatta

Irregular Verbs:

konai	konakatta
shinai	shinakatta
kan'koo shinai	kan'koo shinakatta

Kinoo paatii e ikanakatta no?	Didn't you go to the party yesterday?
Ee, ikanakatta no yo.	Yes, (you're right,) I didn't go, you know.
Iie, itta no yo.	No, (you're not right,) I went, you know.

9.4.2

$$\left. \begin{matrix} V \\ A \\ N \end{matrix} \right\} \text{informal form} \Big\} + \textbf{deshoo} \qquad \text{(probably)}$$

Karaoke mo aru deshoo means *There will be* karaoke also. Deshoo is a tentative form of the copula desu. While desu makes a statement definite, deshoo makes it suppositional or less confirmative, and it might be expressed as *I suppose, will probably be,* and so forth. Deshoo follows the informal form of the verb and adjective. The informal form of the copula desu is da. When a sentence N-da is embedded into the sentence pattern N-deshoo, da is dropped. However, the past tense datta is not dropped. Study the following example sentences.

Verbs

Shimada-san wa kuru deshoo.	Mr. Shimada will probably come.
Tanaka-san wa paatii e ikanai deshoo.	Mr. Tanaka probably will not go to the party.

Adjectives

Ano hoteru wa takai deshoo.	That hotel is probably expensive.
Kono wain wa amari amakunai deshoo.	This wine will not be very sweet.

155

Copula

Keiko-san no tan'joobi wa shi-gatsu yooka deshoo.	Keiko's birthday will probably be April 8th.
Haruo-san wa mizuwari ga suki deshoo.	Haruo probably likes whiskey with water.
Tanaka-san wa shihainin dewa nai deshoo.	Mr. Tanaka probably is not a manager.

If **deshoo** is combined with the question marker **ka**, the meaning becomes *I wonder (if)* . . .

Tanaka-san wa shihainin deshoo ka?	I wonder if Mr. Tanaka is a manager.

When **deshoo** is uttered with a rising intonation, it is a question seeking the listener's agreement like **desu ne?**, but with a little less certainty.

Tanaka-san wa shihainin deshoo?	Isn't Mr. Tanaka a manager?
Iie, fuku-shihainin desu.	No. He is an assistant manager.
Paatii e iku deshoo?	You're going to the party, aren't you?
Ee, ikimasu yo.	Yes. I will go.

9.4.3 | **N ga dekimasu.** | (Potential)

Gorofu ga dekimasu.	I can play golf.

The verb **dekimasu** means *be able to (do)*, *be possible*, *can (do)*, and so forth. The thing one can do is followed by the particle **ga**, and the one who can do it, if mentioned, is followed by the particle **wa**: (N wa) N ga dekimasu.

Tanaka-san wa tenisu ga dekimasu.	Mr. Tanaka can play tennis.
Sugu gohan ga dekimasu.	The meal (or rice) will be ready soon.

9.4.4 | **N wa N o V-(r)u koto ga dekimasu.** | (Potential)

Tanaka-san wa gorufu o suru koto ga dekimasu.	Mr. Tanaka can play golf.
Susan-san wa osake o takusan nomu koto ga dekimasu.	Susan can drink a lot of sake.
John-san wa nihon'go o hanasu koto ga dekimasu.	John can speak Japanese.

156

9.4.5 De (made of)

The particle de may be used to list ingredients.

Furuutsu pan'chi wa iroiro na kudamono to sebun appu to aisukuriimu *de*
    dekite imasu.
Fruit punch is made of various fruits, 7-Up, and ice cream.

Kore wa nan *de* dekite imasu ka?
What is this made of?

Karee raisu wa karee ya niku *de* tsukurimasu.
Curry rice is made of curry, meat, and things like that.

9.4.6 De (by means of)

The particle de may be used to indicate *by means of.*

Ohashi *de* tabemasu.	I eat with chopsticks.
Sutoroo *de* nomimashoo.	Let's drink it with a straw.
Suteeki wa naifu to fooku *de* tabemasu.	I eat steak with a knife and fork.
Takushii *de* kaerimashita.	I went home by taxi.

9.4.7 Calendar Words

Months	
ichi-gatsu	January
ni-gatsu	February
san-gatsu	March
shi-gatsu	April
go-gatsu	May
roku-gatsu	June
shichi-gatsu	July
hachi-gatsu	August
ku-gatsu	September
juu-gatsu	October
juuichi-gatsu	November
juuni-gatsu	December
nan-gatsu	which month?

Dates			
1	tsuitachi	17	juushichi-nichi
2	futsu-ka	18	juuhachi-nichi
3	mikka	19	juuku-nichi
4	yokka	20	hatsu-ka
5	itsu-ka	21	nijuuichi-nichi
6	mui-ka	22	nijuuni-nichi
7	nano-ka	23	nijuusan-nichi
8	yoo-ka	24	nijuuyokka
9	kokono-ka	25	nijuugo-nichi
10	too-ka	26	nijuuroku-nichi
11	juuichi-nichi	27	nijuushichi-nichi
12	juuni-nichi	28	nijuuhachi-nichi
13	juusan-nichi	29	nijuuku-nichi
14	juuyokka	30	san'juu-nichi
15	juugo-nichi	31	san'juuichi-nichi
16	juuroku-nichi	what date?	nan-nichi

Days of the Week	
nichi-yoobi	Sunday
getsu-yoobi	Monday
ka-yoobi	Tuesday
sui-yoobi	Wednesday
moku-yoobi	Thursday
kin-yoobi	Friday
do-yoobi	Saturday
nan-yoobi	what day of the week?

Years	
sen kyuuhyaku hachijuuyo-nen	1984
sen kyuuhyaku hachijuugo-nen	1985
nan-nen	what year?

Examples:

Kyoo wa nan-yoobi desu ka?	What day of the week is it today?
Moku-yoobi desu.	It's Thursday.
Kyoo wa nan-nichi desu ka?	What's the date today?
Shigatsu yoo-ka desu.	It's April 8th.
"Kodomo no hi" wa itsu desu ka?	When is Children's Day?
Go-gatsu itsuka desu.	It's May 5th.
Itsu Hawai e irasshaimashita ka?	When did you come to Hawaii?
Sen kyuuhyaku hachijuusan-nen juu-gatsu hatsuka ni mairi-mashita.	I came on October 20th, 1983.

9.4.8 | **amari** / **chittomo** } + Negative predicate { not very . . . / not at all . . . . }

Some adverbs, such as **amari** *(not) very*, **chittomo** *(not) at all*, are used with negative predicates. Since these adverbs are used mainly in negation, they may also carry a negative connotation when they are used alone.

Osake wa suki desu ka?	Do you like sake?
Iie, amari (suki ja arimasen).	No, I don't like it very much.
Totemo isogashii desu ka?	Are you very busy?
Chittomo (isogashiku arimasen).	I'm not busy at all.
Tooi desu ka?	Is it far away?
Iie, amari tooku arimasen yo.	No, it's not far away.

158

9.4.9 | V-te + mimasu | (Try and see)

Non'de mimashoo means *I think I'll try drinking (it)*. The V-te form plus the predicate extender mimasu *try* implies someone will give something a try. The extender mimasu conjugates like a verb.

V-te
{
mimasu
mimasen
mimashita
mimasen deshita
mimashoo
mite kudasai
}

Kore o tabete mimashoo.

Let's eat this one and find out how it is.

Asoko e itte mimasen ka?

Won't you go over there and find out?

9.5 DRILLS

9.5.1 Question–Answer Drill

Think of as many answers to the question Nani ga dekimasu ka? as you can.

Example: Nani ga dekimasu ka?
Taipu ga dekimasu.   Cue: type

1. Nani ga dekimasu ka?
Gorufu ga dekimasu.   Cue: golf

2. Nani ga dekimasu ka?
Tenisu ga dekimasu.   Cue: tennis

3. Nani ga dekimasu ka?
Suiei ga dekimasu.   Cue: swim

4. Nani ga dekimasu ka?
Saafin'gu ga dekimasu.   Cue: surf

5. Nani ga dekimasu ka?
Piano ga dekimasu.   Cue: piano

6. Nani ga dekimasu ka?
Gitaa ga dekimasu.   Cue: guitar

7. Nani ga dekimasu ka?
Ukurere ga dekimasu.   Cue: ukulele

8. Nani ga dekimasu ka?
Futto booru ga dekimasu.   Cue: football

159

9.5.2 Question-Answer Drill

Think of as many questions as possible to ask your partner about what he or she knows how to do. Then let him or her respond.

Example: A: Saafin'gu o suru koto ga dekimasu ka?
          B: Iie, dekimasen. (or Hai, dekimasu.)

1. Kuruma o un'ten suru koto ga dekimasu ka?
   Iie, dekimasen. (or Hai, dekimasu.)

2. Sono biichi de oyogu koto ga dekimasu ka?
   Iie, dekimasen. (or Hai, dekimasu.)

3. Sukeeto o suru koto ga dekimasu ka?
   Iie, dekimasen. (or Hai, dekimasu.)

4. Sushi o tsukuru koto ga dekimasu ka?
   Iie, dekimasen. (or Hai, dekimasu.)

5. Kan'ji o kaku koto ga dekimasu ka?
   Iie, dekimasen. (or Hai, dekimasu.)

6. Nihon'go o hanasu koto ga dekimasu ka?
   Iie, dekimasen. (or Hai, dekimasu.)

7. Chuugokugo o yomu koto ga dekimasu ka?
   Iie, dekimasen. (or Hai, dekimasu.)

8. Fujisan ni noboru koto ga dekimasu ka?
   Iie, dekimasen. (or Hai, dekimasu.)

9.5.3 Question-Answer Drill

Example: Kono karee raisu wa nan de dekite imasu ka?
          Cue: curry, rice, meat, and vegetables.
          Karee (to), gohan (to), niku (to), yasai de dekite imasu.

1. Chi Chi wa nan de dekite imasu ka?   Cue: vodka, coconut syrup, and fruit juices
   Wokka to kokonatsu shiroppu to furuutsu juusu de dekite imasu.

2. Buruu Hawai wa nan de dekite imasu ka?   Cue: rum and blue curaçao
   Ramu-shu to buruu kurasao de dekite imasu.

3. Osake wa nan de tsukurimasu ka?   Cue: uncooked rice
   Kome de tsukurimasu.

4. Wain wa nan de dekite imasu ka?   Cue: grapes
   Budoo de dekite imasu.

5. Biiru wa nan de dekite imasu ka?   Cue: barley
   Mugi de dekite imasu.

160

6. Mai Tai wa nan de tsukurimasu
   ka?
   Ramu-shu de tsukurimasu.

   Cue: rum

7. Makizushi wa nan de tsukurimasu ka?
   Gohan (to), nori (to), kan'pyoo nado de tsukurimasu.

   Cue: rice, nori, kan'pyoo, and so
   forth.

9.5.4 Question–Answer Drill

Example: En'pitsu de kakimasu ka?
   Cue: no, with a pen
   Iie, pen de kakimasu.

1. Takushii de kaerimasu ka?
   Iie, basu de kaerimasu.

   Cue: no, by bus

2. Ohashi de tabemasu ka?
   Iie, fooku de tabemasu.

   Cue: no, with a fork

3. Fune de ikimasu ka?
   Iie, hikooki de ikimasu.

   Cue: no, by airplane

4. Roomaji de kakimasu ka?
   Iie, kana to kan'ji de kakimasu.

   Cue: no, with kana and kan'ji

5. Nihon e wa nan de ikimasu ka?
   Hikooki de ikimasu.

   Cue: by airplane

9.5.5 Substitution Drill

A. Example: Let's try *writing* Japanese.
   Nihon'go o *kaite* mimashoo.

1. Let's try *speaking* Japanese.
   Nihon'go o *hanashite* mimashoo.

2. Let's try *reading* Japanese.
   Nihon'go o *yon'de* mimashoo.

3. Let's try *listening to* Japanese.
   Nihon'go o *kiite* mimashoo.

B. Example: Let's try *drinking* this.
   Kore o *non'de* mimashoo.

1. Let's try *eating* this.
   Kore o *tabete* mimashoo.

2. Let's try *studying* this.
   Kore o *ben'kyoo shite* mimashoo.

3. Let's try *making* this.
   Kore o *tsukutte* mimashoo.

161

9.5.6 Question-Answer Drill

Answer the following questions according to the cues provided.

1. Anata no tan'joobi wa itsu desu ka?
   Cue: May 5   Gogatsu itsuka desu.

2. Otoosan no tan'joobi wa itsu desu ka?
   Cue: December 2   Juunigatsu futsuka desu.

3. Okaasan no tan'joobi wa itsu desu ka?
   Cue: April 3   Shigatsu mikka desu.

4. Sen'sei no tan'joobi wa itsu desu ka?
   Cue: October 20   Juugatsu hatsuka desu.

5. Tomodachi no tan'joobi wa itsu desu ka?
   Cue: June 15   Rokugatsu juugonichi desu.

6. Nihon e ikitai hi wa itsu desu ka?
   Cue: January 10   Ichigatsu tooka desu.

7. Kekkon shita hi wa itsu desu ka?
   Cue: June 3   Rokugatsu mikka desu.

8. Kurisumasu wa itsu desu ka?
   Cue: December 25   Juunigatsu nijuugonichi desu.

9. Oshoogatsu *(New Year's Day)* wa itsu desu ka?
   Cue: January 1   Ichigatsu tsuitachi desu.

9.5.7 Verb Conjugation Drill

Verb	*V-dic*	*V-(a)nai*	*V-ta*	*V-(a)nakatta*
tabemasu	taberu	tabenai	tabeta	tabenakatta
nomimasu	nomu	nomanai	non'da	nomanakatta
yomimasu	yomu	yomanai	yon'da	yomanakatta
kakimasu	kaku	kakanai	kaita	kakanakatta
hanashimasu	hanasu	hanasanai	hanashita	hanasanakatta
oyogimasu	oyogu	oyoganai	oyoida	oyoganakatta
machimasu	matsu	matanai	matta	matanakatta
kaimasu	kau	kawanai	katta	kawanakatta
mochimasu	motsu	motanai	motta	motanakatta
kimasu *(come)*	kuru	konai	kita	konakatta
shimasu	suru	shinai	shita	shinakatta
tsutsumimasu	tsutsumu	tsutsumanai	tsutsun'da	tsutsumanakatta
ben'kyoo shimasu	ben'kyoo suru	ben'kyoo shinai	ben'kyoo shita	ben'kyoo shinakatta
ikimasu	iku	ikanai	itta	ikanakatta
kaerimasu	kaeru	kaeranai	kaetta	kaeranakatta
arimasu	aru	nai	atta	nakatta
utaimasu	utau	utawanai	utatta	utawanakatta

162

9.5.8 Transformation Drill

Change the following sentences into the tentative form using deshoo.

Example: Mai Tai wa tsuyoi desu.   Mai Tai wa tsuyoi deshoo.

1. Tanaka-san ga kaimasu. — Tanaka-san ga kau deshoo.
2. Kono hoteru wa yuumei desu. — Kono hoteru wa yuumei deshoo.
3. John-san wa ikimasen. — John-san wa ikanai deshoo.
4. En'kai wa omoshiroku arimasen. — En'kai wa omoshiroku nai deshoo.
5. Sato-san wa hoteru ni imasu. — Sato-san wa hoteru ni iru deshoo.
6. Yamada-san wa gitaa ga dekimasu. — Yamada-san wa gitaa ga dekiru deshoo.
7. Maneejaa ga shimasu. — Maneejaa ga suru deshoo.
8. Are wa mizuwari desu. — Are wa mizuwari deshoo.
9. Are wa Nihon no kamera desu. — Are wa Nihon no kamera deshoo.
10. Sono resutoran wa tooku arimasen. — Sono resutoran wa tooku nai deshoo.

9.5.9 Response Drill

1. Nihon'go wa muzukashii desu ka?
   chittomo   Iie, chittomo muzukashiku arimasen.

2. Ano mise wa kirei desu ka?
   amari   Iie, amari kirei ja arimasen.

3. Sono koocha wa oishii desu ka?
   chittomo   Iie, chittomo oishiku arimasen.

4. Onaka ga suite imasu ka?
   amari   Iie, amari suite imasen.

5. Nihon'go ga joozu desu nee.
   chittomo   Iie, chittomo joozu ja arimasen.

6. Yamada-san wa karaoke ga suki desu ka?
   amari   Iie, amari suki ja arimasen.

7. Nihon ryoori ga tabetakatta desu ka?
   amari   Iie, amari tabetaku arimasen deshita.

8. Ten'in wa shin'setsu deshita ka?
   amari   Iie, amari shin'setsu ja arimasen deshita.

9. Sono eiga wa omoshirokatta desu ka?
   chittomo   Iie, chittomo omoshiroku arimasen deshita.

163

9.6 EXERCISES

9.6.1 Completion

Fill in each blank with an appropriate word to match the idea expressed in English.

1. A: _____ wa doo desu ka?   How is your business?
   B: _____ yoku arimasen.   It's not very good.

2. A: Kore ga _____ Waikiki   This is the famous
   Biichi desu yo.   Waikiki Beach.
   B: _____   Is that so?

3. A: Mizuwari o _____ kudasai.   Please give me another glass of whiskey and water.
   B: _____.   Yes, I understand.

4. A: _____ suki desu ka?   Do you like singing along with taped music?
   B: Hai, _____ suki desu.   Yes, I like it very much.

5. A: Gorufu ga _____ desu ka?   Are you good at playing golf?
   B: Iie, _____   No, not at all.

6. A: Ano kata wa _____ desu ka?   Is that person your colleague?
   B: _____.   No, he isn't.

7. A: Nama biiru o _____ ?   Shall we try drinking draft beer?
   B: Ee, _____ .   Yes, let's try.

9.6.2 Multiple Choice

Choose the appropriate response for speaker B in each item.

1. A: Otagai ni gan'barimashoo ne.
   B: a. Soo desu ka?   b. Soo desu nee.

2. A: Kon'ban ippai yarimasen ka?
   B: a. Ii desu nee.   b. Soo desu ka?

3. A: Keiki wa doo?
   B: a. Amari . . .   b. Doomo.

4. A: Kyoo wa nan-nichi desu ka?
   B: a. Yooka desu.   b. Doyoobi desu.

5. A: Suiei ga dekimasu ka?
   B: a. Iie, amari dekimasen.   b. Iie, sukoshi dekimasen.

164

9.6.3 Translation

Express the following in English.

1. Kon'ban ippai yarimasen ka?
2. Mizuwari o moo ippai kudasai.
3. Shigoto wa kibishii desu ga, gan'batte kudasai.
4. Gohan wa dekite imasu ka?
5. Takada-san wa osake ni yowai kara shikata ga nai wa. Juusu o motte kite ne.
6. Min'na de biiru de kan'pai shimashoo.
7. Kyoo wa kugatsu tsuitachi, kayoobi desu ne.

9.6.4 Translation

Express the following in Japanese.

1. Do you come to school by car?
2. Can you speak Japanese?
3. There are a variety of flowers in Hawaii.
4. I was very hungry, so I wanted to go home right away.
5. I can make makizushi.
6. Can you write your name in Japanese?
7. I do not have a car, so I will go by bus.
8. My friend and I sang along with Japanese karaoke songs.
9. Mr. Yamada, my colleague, also joined us in drinking, so we had a good time.
10. I tried drinking sake, but it was not very good.
11. Today is Wednesday, July 5, 1984.
12. I ate ten minutes ago, so I am not hungry at all.
13. Since I did not eat, I am very hungry.
14. I will not go to the dinner party, so I'll stay home.
15. John will probably return on November 1.

9.7 SIMULATION AND SKITS

1. A honeymoon couple from Japan wants to order exotic Hawaiian drinks. As a waiter or waitress, explain to them what each tropical drink, such as Chi Chi, Mai Tai, and Blue Hawaii, is made of and what it's like.

2. You meet a friend you haven't seen for a while and invite him to have a few drinks with you at a karaoke bar. Ask him about his business while you are drinking.

3. A friend from Japan is not familiar with some of the holidays we celebrate in America such as Easter, Presidents' Day, and Thanksgiving Day. Tell him what dates the various holidays fall on, so he'll know what days he will not have to go to school.

4. A visitor from the mainland visits a Japanese restaurant for the first time and wants to know what the various Japanese foods are made of. As a waiter or waitress explain what makizushi, shabushabu, ten'pura, and so forth, is made of.

5. You are with a close friend drinking at a bar. Use informal speech in your conversation with him.

9.8 CULTURE ORIENTATION

9.8.1 Hare and Ke Consciousness

Since ancient times the Japanese have lived with the dual consciousness of hare and ke. The hare consciousness is felt during holidays and special occasions, whereas ke refers to the consciousness felt in the everyday routine of life. Originally, the days of hare were set aside for religious purposes. On such days, the people were released from the tensions of daily life, and they would thoroughly enjoy themselves by eating the foods and drinking the drinks of hare and wearing hare-gi (hare *clothes*). When the days of hare were over, the people would return to their ke food and drink and wear their ke clothes and go back to the tension and hardships of their daily work. There were distinct differences in the food, drink, and clothes of hare days and ke days.

However, in this day and age, it cannot be denied that the distinctions between hare and ke are no longer as clear as they used to be. Other than on special holidays, including New Year's Day, where special food and drink is consumed and special clothes are worn, the distinctions between hare and ke have become less precise. With increased material wealth, the Japanese now enjoy a hare life every day: sake can be bought in vending machines; good food can be eaten at restaurants; and good clothes can be purchased in abundance. Nevertheless, the desire of the workers to escape their daily routine full of tension remains unchanged. In order to accommodate such needs, the company, for example, which comprises a small community of its own, will hold hare activities such as en'kai *parties,* boonen'kai *year-end parties,* kan'soogeikai *welcome or farewell parties,* and hanami *flower-viewing parties.* Such parties constitute a type of hare ritual within the community.

The company resembles a traditional village community. As in village hare activities, the company party has seat assignments arranged hierarchically for its members. The person with highest status sits at the head of the table and is assigned the task of opening the party with a greeting. He is the one who will

166

introduce a newcomer in the community and pass the sake. There is drink and song, and gaiety fills the air.

The purpose of en'kai is to maintain group harmony. These occasions are designed to heighten the sense of community and encourage the emotional unity of the community. Just as there are certain people in the villages assigned to organize and plan hare activities, the companies also assign this role to some of its members. Those assigned to plan and organize special activities are also in charge of making them successful and enjoyable; their achievements are judged by others in the company. In other words, the role of the organizer is a serious task and is considered part of their professional ability.

Such formal, often public, special activities can become tense and not fulfill the purpose of allowing members to release their work tension. In such cases, a nijikai *second party* is held. Normally good friends get together at these nijikai, which are more private than public. It is often said that even sake tastes bad at the formal en'kai, so a nijikai has to be held between good friends where the sake would taste better. These nijikai serve to release work tension; workers can speak ill of their boss and criticize fellow workers. Often, company superiors join these nijikai, so a further san'jikai *third party* is held exclusively for close friends. By the time san'jikai comes along, the level of alcoholic consumption escalates considerably.

Often, superiors or senior workers take some of their workers on a nijikai for the purpose of creating a closer relationship. A special bond is created where the drinking takes place in a certain location, designating a certain territorial boundary, and often takes place at a specific bar. Although, from the outside, these nijikai look private in nature they are often an extension of the organizational setup and serve to enhance human relations within the work place. The Japanese people place much emphasis on the emotional ties between workers as well as the occupational ties. Japanese workers often prefer a sympathetic and understanding kachoo rather than a merely occupationally capable kachoo.

Even at nijikai, where the purpose is to release one's tension, self-control is absolutely necessary in order not to jeopardize human relationships. There are limits within which sake can be an excuse for certain types of behavior, but beyond these limits, there are no excuses (Sakada 1980:285–287).

9.8.2 The Makunouchi Ben'too and the Japanese People

The expressions isshooken'mei and gan'batte kudasai are extremely important if one intends to communicate with Japanese people. Literally translated, the first expression means *to place one's entire life into one purpose, object, or place*. The second expession can be translated as *please do one's best*. Both of these expressions represent the diligent character of the Japanese people. The first expression, to place one's entire life into one purpose, expresses the characteristic of the rural Japanese people. In other words, their goal was to maximize the fruits of their limited land resource. This type of reasoning can be found in the idea of the Japanese makunouchi ben'too. A ben'too is divided into four squares. The goal of the chef is to maximize the effect of the food—its beauty and quality—in the limited available space.

Another characteristic of the makunouchi ben'too is to accommodate as many items as possible in this limited space. In some ways, the island of Japan can be seen as a makunouchi ben'too where the Japanese people adapt and import foreign goods and culture and skillfully arrange them according to their needs. In the process of adapting these foreign elements, they have had to miniaturize them to fit the available space. Miniaturization also reminds one of the makunouchi ben'too, where each part is compactly and efficiently placed. The Japanese are able to fit their desires and needs into a small framework, as can be seen in everything from makunouchi ben'too to automobiles, and are able to put the various different elements into a whole (Ekuan 1981:100).

Makunouchi ben'too represents more Japanese cultural elements if one takes a further look. For example, when one orders a makunouchi ben'too, one has the reassuring feeling that at least one of the many items included will be to his/her liking. For this reason, makunouchi ben'too are often appreciated on group excursions. Since Japanese society is not a dichotomy of "winners" and "losers," the system accommodates everybody. The way in which Japanese people hope to retain everything is akin to the Buddhist thought of saving everybody, including the villain. The makunouchi ben'too can be seen as the embodiment of such Japanese thought and their unique skill in its achievement.

9.8.3 Japanese and Dinner Entertainment

In America, parties are often held at private homes. American homes are often architecturally planned for entertaining. Generally speaking, they are arranged in a comfortable manner for anyone to be able to relax and feel at home. In contrast to the American situation, parties are seldom held at private homes in Japan. In most urban homes, there isn't enough space to hold large parties. But most importantly, a home, for the Japanese people, is a very private place, open only to relatives, long-time friends, children's friends, and sometimes to the husband's subordinates. For this reason, most entertaining done between business associates takes place at restaurants.

When formal entertainment for company occasions takes place, the Japanese prefer to entertain at Japanese-style restaurants (called ryooriya or ryootei) rather than at Western-style restaurants. There are several reasons for this preference. First, Japanese people don't find sitting at the table on chairs, as one does at a Western restaurant, very comfortable. The most relaxing for the Japanese is to sit Japanese-style on the floor. Second, every party is designated a separate room at a Japanese ryootei. To each of these rooms separate waitresses are

168

assigned, and they become an integral part of the dinner entertainment itself. The task of these waitresses is not merely to transport food but to assist in creating a congenial atmosphere. Furthermore, an advantage to choosing a Japanese ryootei is that a sense of group cohesion can be established. This is possible because, unlike Western-style restaurants, everybody eats the same food. Rather than preserving individualism through ordering food independently, the Japanese all share the same food regardless of the rank or position of the individuals. An order is usually made over the phone prior to the dinner engagement. A sense of cohesion is established through sharing the experience of eating the same food. Likewise, when the company takes their employees on social trips, every person wears the same yukata (kimono) which is provided by the Japanese inn and eats the same food, precisely for the purpose of establishing group cohesion.

Generally speaking, sake and beer are served at en'kai rather than whiskey or other cocktail drinks. This is largely because an individual's taste for a certain variety of whiskey would disrupt the cohesiveness. Most people begin with beer and switch to sake later on.

Sake serves as the most effective catalyst to establish group cohesion. Sake was once a drink consumed for religious rituals and ceremonial occasions. For example, it was believed that shamans could become mediators between heaven and earth, between God and man, if they consumed sake. They would enter a trancelike consciousness and would be able to convey God's wishes (Mochizuki 1976:20). Later on, sake was consumed in the village at special occasions in order to reaffirm communal mutuality. A similar form of this utilization of sake can be observed in the company, which is a modern embodiment of a community, in order to strengthen group cohesion.

The value of sake as a unifying force remains unchanged in Japanese culture. For example, even now a bride and groom share a cup of sake as part of the marriage ceremony to symbolize the union of their lives, as well as the union of heaven and earth.

Drinking sake requires adherence to certain rules of etiquette. The first rule requires that the drinker must not pour sake for himself. This means that drinking sake requires a partner to keep pouring for the drinker. This symbolically indicates that each is at the other's service (Befu 1974:200). Pouring one's own sake only destroys the sense of togetherness. Since sake cups (ochoko) are small and therefore easy to empty, one must constantly watch to see if the other's cup needs refilling. This brings out the drinker's care for and attentiveness to the other's needs. The person having the sake poured for him must hold his cup up as the sake is carefully poured in midair. Immediately after his cup is filled, he takes the tokkuri *sake container* and, in turn, pours for his partner. This rhythmical motion of filling and refilling each other's cup contributes to group cohesion. In addition, the person who pours the sake says saa saa, doozo doozo while the other expresses his gratitude by saying doomo doomo

169

doomo and otto to to while they both carefully balance this act in midair. These verbal expressions also contribute toward establishment of a cooperative atmosphere.

In order to avoid isolated groups in an en'kai some people will carry a tokkuri and walk around offering sake. As a general rule, a person holding a lower position pours sake for his superiors. In doing so, he asks his superior's permission for the privilege of pouring sake for him. A customary action at an en'kai is for the person holding a superior position to offer the person holding a lower position the privilege of drinking out of the superior's sake cup. It must be kept in mind that one must not wipe the other's cup before drinking. Once one has emptied the cup, he must immediately return the cup and pour the sake. "Each such exchange is a symbolic handshake or embrace and a reaffirmation of the social pact uniting those exchanging the cup" (Befu 1974:201).

Through such repeated exchanges, the en'kai has a tremendous impact on the group. The exchanges between the higher and lower rank as well as among equals have a psychological and physical effect that strengthens group cohesion and consciousness.

As the party continues, the people become lively and extremely loud with dancing and singing and clapping. Many people become drunk. As mentioned earlier, the Japanese believe their shamans are able to communicate with the gods through drinking sake. This brought about a certain permissiveness in Japanese society toward the behavior of drunkenness. In a sense, the Japanese people have traditionally allowed misbehavior under the influence of alcohol. Because of this attitude an en'kai with drunken people can become very loud. Complaints against such behavior are commonplace when tourists unluckily run into an en'kai at Japanese restaurants.

9.8.4 Hastiness: A Japanese National Characteristic

The Japanese people are generally known for their perseverance. On the other hand, they sometimes act hastily. Compared to other nationalities, the Japanese have no patience while shopping or waiting to be served at a restaurant. It's true that nobody likes to wait, but the Japanese people quickly show signs of irritation when they have to wait. Some begin to complain and even get angry. Fast service, therefore, is looked upon as good service. If the quality of the food is good at a restaurant, but the service is slow, the restaurant may be rated low. As a result, restaurants with tasty food, as well as fast service, become most popular in Japan. Teishoku and other combination sets are popular partly because of this emphasis on speed. Perhaps one of the reason why items like raamen and curry rice are so popular is because of the emphasis on immediate service.

The characteristic of hastiness can be observed, not only while the Japanese people wait, but also while they eat. They often gobble up their food in a matter of minutes! According to one source, this characteristic originated in the times when the samurai code of ethics and rules required them not to waste time eating their food, for it would keep them off guard from their enemies. It was considered a manly virtue to be on guard at every minute; therefore, a minimum amount of time was allotted to eating (Kato 1980:93–94). In addition, the value of eating hastily originates in the Japanese agricultural society where food was quickly consumed in order to get back to work in the fields. To this day, this hasty eating behavior of the Japanese people can be observed everywhere except at special occasions when the act of eating becomes the medium of communication.

If Japanese tourists are made to wait at a restaurant, it may be a good idea to suggest they have a drink or two at the bar. In addition, a few words of apology for making them wait would be appreciated. Since waiting is a painful experience for the hasty Japanese people, a thoughtful and polite apology would aid in easing their irritation or even anger.

The national characteristic of hastiness may be a contributing force in their creation of the compact, simple, instant, portable, and convenient products that they are famous for. Perhaps even the accuracy and punctuality of their transportation schedule may be a reflection of the hasty character of the Japanese people.

9.9 THE MODE OF JAPANESE COMMUNICATION

"Nominication"

Nominication is a special loanword which has been coined by Japanese. It is made up of two words—nomi meaning *drinking* and *-nication* the last part of *communication*. Nomination therefore refers to *communication through drinking*. It is meant to be humorous.

Nomination is usually performed through otsukiai which refers to occasions when a superior or senior worker takes his workers out to drink after the day's work is over. Even those who don't drink or can't drink must accompany their superiors because the purpose of these outings is not merely to drink and eat but to enhance group consciousness and emotional unity. The members of the group must often sacrifice their own desires to the building of group cohesiveness.

The word tsukiai connotes *sacrificing one's own will for something.* These occasions, much like the nijikai, allow casualness and openness to discuss anything, including work. Things that couldn't be said at work can be said here with the help of sake. It becomes important for senior workers to conduct these otsukiai to understand the thoughts and feelings of their workers which aren't ordinarily expressed at work. These otsukiai are equally important for the junior workers to understand what their authorities are thinking and to be able to convey their true feelings in a casual manner to their authorities. It can be said that these otsukiai are an important part of organizational life and not merely conducted for the fun of drinking and eating.

Otsukiai, which is conducted on a rather regular basis, is a good example of how a hare occasion became more of a ke occasion in recent times. Most of the time, the superiors or senior workers take on the responsibility of paying for these otsukiai. However, they would all be "in the red" if the money came out of their own pockets all the time! To prevent this, the company has a monthly expense account where a certain amount is set aside for the purpose of otsukiai, communication, and entertaining company clients. The expense account facilitates a smooth interaction between the workers and serves to promote the company. In spite of this expense account, the senior workers often have to pay out of their own pockets. The junior workers realize this, and a sense of dependency and followership is created which extends itself even into the work situation (Sakada 1980:287).

9.10   LANGUAGE AND CULTURE

A.   Ippai yarimashoo

The gesture of holding a sake cup (ochoko) often accompanies the phrase Ippai yarimashoo, exchanged between men. Often this gesture alone can indicate that the speaker means to say Kon'ban doo desu ka? *How about drinking tonight?* In response to this gesture, one may say kyoowa . . . *today* and display the gesture of the American OK sign with a turn of the head from left to right. In Japan, the American OK sign is the sign for money. In other words, turning one's head and displaying this sign means *I don't have money today, so I can't go drinking.*

B.   Osake ni tsuyoi desu nee

This phrase, which means *You are a heavy drinker, aren't you?*, can often be interpreted negatively in the American cultural context. However, if it is rephrased into *You can hold liquor quite well, can't you?*, it can be interpreted positively. Likewise, in the Japanese cultural context, the phrase Osake ni tsuyoi desu nee has a positive connotation. As mentioned in the culture orientation earlier, sake plays various roles in Japan. It is generally advantageous for a man to be able to drink because this indicates that he can socialize well. The phrase not only has a positive connotation but includes even a touch of admiration!

C.   Soo desu nee

This phrase is a favorite among Japanese people because it is such a convenient phrase. If an immediate answer can't be given to a question or request, one can

172

answer **soo desu nee** and either watch for reactions from the speaker so that one can answer according to their reaction, or take time to think of an appropriate answer. Through the use of this phrase one can answer "yes" or "no" in an indirect manner. And one can be extremely vague by not giving an exact answer. When the Japanese people use this phrase, it usually indicates their intentional avoidance of having to give an immediate answer, or that they may be having difficulty giving an answer.

D. Itsumo osewa ni natte imasu

This phrase is difficult to translate into English. **Osewa ni natte imasu**, translated literally, means *to be taken care of.* This might carry a negative connotation for Americans, who value independence. However, for the Japanese people, whose culture is based on mutual dependency, to take care of one another is an important value. Gratitude must be expressed in some way to those that have taken care of one or one's family members. For example, the wife of an employee may use this phrase to his boss, and the boss may reciprocate the gratitude with praise for the wife's husband. In this way, smooth human relations can be conducted. Expressions as **itsumo osewa ni natte imasu** serve as important social lubricants.

E. Korekara mo doozo yoroshiku onegai shimasu

Translated literally **korekara mo** means *from now onward* and **doozo yoroshiku** is a phrase used to introduce oneself at a first meeting. **Doozo yoroshiku onegai shimasu** is not the same as the English phrases *I am happy to see you* or *I am pleased to meet you,* but indicates a request for continued friendship in the future. This establishes a relationship between the two parties. In response to this phrase, one may answer **kochira koso**, thereby reciprocating the request. This phrase also serves as a social lubricant allowing a smooth establishment of human relationships.

F. Otagai ni gan'barimashoo

This phrase indicates the industrious nature of the Japanese people. **Otagai ni** means *each other, you and I,* expressing a sense of togetherness. This indicates the Japanese collective consciousness, where nobody stands completely alone.

The expression **gan'barimashoo** means *do one's best.* However, examining the etymology of the word **gan'baru** reveals that it came from the phrase **ga o haru** which refers to a person who will not agree with others and insists on his own views.

One wonders how such a word came to be valued when the insistence on one's personal view was not a highly valued quality in the village social structure. The change in its value probably came about when the ability to exert one's maximum capacity of energy gradually came to be highly valued. To **gan'baru** meant that each person would perform to maximum capacity in their

173

respective fields. This indicated that each person would excel in his or her field, whether it was in academia, warfare, or sports. When the field of warfare or sports began to involve the whole nation as its audience, the value of gan'baru became a national value (Tada 1981:55). When the expression otagai ni was added to gan'barimashoo, the value of collective consciousness was incorporated, serving as a propelling force for the Japanese people. In Japan, the value of the process leading to a goal is often valued over the goal itself. Japanese perceive one's exertion of maximum capacity as being a valuable trait. To recall a point made earlier: the Japanese people can be said to be a process-oriented people rather than a goal-oriented people.

The expression gan'barimashoo is often stated as gan'batte kudasai in the form of a request to people who are about to compete in some event or who are about to begin something new. For example, it is used for a student who is about to take an exam, or to a newlywed couple just beginning their new lives.

The Japanese were able to overcome the struggling postwar period and the period of economic growth of the 1960s with this gan'barimashoo spirit. No doubt this spirit served as a major force in the shaping of Japan as it is now. However, the Japanese people, driven by this gan'barimashoo spirit, have often been criticized from outside for being workaholics and accused of waging an economic war. A Southeast Asian person once asked a Japanese, "When do you ever have time to worship if you work all the time?" Working hard was an important part of the American puritan work ethic. But as America became a postindustrial nation, this quality of working overly hard began to take on a negative connotation, and people even began to perceive this quality in others as a possible threat to their own well-being. Many Japanese people feel that the accusation that they are waging an economic war is unfair, especially after all the hard work they have put in. However, they have also recently begun to ask themselves what they are living for and what they are working for.

G. Shikata ga arimasen

This expression embodies a sense of resignation that accepts that things will only be as they will be. It is often perceived as a fatalistic attitude by Western people, who believe strongly that life is what the individual makes it. There is a fundamental difference in approach to problem solving between the Western view of life and the Japanese view of life. Japanese people believe that there is a framework of life given to every individual and the task of the individual is to "live it up" with dedication. The Japanese people have traditionally solved their difficulties by accepting them as they are and adjusting themselves to harmonize with them. Things will be as they will; this is shikata ga arimasen.

On the other hand, Americans have favored a confrontative approach to problem solving. Rather than acccept the situation by saying, *It can't be helped,* they search for ways to solve a problem by saying, *If there is a will, there is a way.* The expression shikata ga arimasen is typically Japanese if one looks at the people's view of life.

174

H. Kan'pai

Kan'pai literally means *to dry one's cup*. It is similar to the English expression *Bottoms up*. However, unlike drinking out of a large mug or glass, it was easier for the Japanese to "dry out" the small sake cup that they drank out of originally. Now the literal meaning of *drying out one's cup* is not emphasized so much, and the expression kan'pai is used in the same way the Americans may use the expression *Cheers!*

9.11 CULTURE QUESTIONS

1. Compare and contrast the occasions for having dinner entertainment in an American company and a Japanese company. Use the information from the section on en'kai. If you are not American, discuss how your culture organizes such activities as en'kai.

2. Discuss what American cultural values are reflected in an American cocktail party. In what ways are cocktail parties related to business? Discuss what observations a Japanese person may make at an American cocktail party.

3. Family members are not included in recreational trips organized by the company. For example, the husband will leave his wife and children at home while he joins the company trips. Discuss why this is done.

4. Americans are well known for their various clubs. The Rotary Club, the Lion's Club, and so forth, were all established by Americans. Why are such clubs so important for Americans? Discuss the relationship between these clubs and business.

5. Many Japanese businessmen relax and overcome stress by drinking sake. What do American businessmen and businessmen of other countries do in order to relax and overcome stress and tension?

9.12 SUGGESTED RESOURCE MATERIALS

9.12.1 Books and Magazines

From Bonsai to Levi's, George Fields (New York: Macmillan Co., 1983), pp. 122–131.
Getting Your Yen's Worth: How to Negotiate with Japanese, Inc., Robert T. Moran (Houston: Gulf Publishing Co., 1985).
Japanese Tourists Abroad, Kazuo Nishiyama (Honolulu: International Management Consultant, 1973), pp. 29–31.
Kodansha Encyclopedia of Japan, vol. 2 (Tokyo: Kodansha, 1983), p. 218.
Managing Cultural Differences, Philip R. Harris and Robert T. Moran (Houston: Gulf Publishing Co., 1979), p. 297.
Nihongo Notes 3: Understanding Japanese Usage, Osamu Mizutani and Nobuko Mizutani (Tokyo: The Japan Times, 1980), p. 131.

9.12.2 Films (16 mm) and Video Cassettes (Beta / VHS)

"The Colonel Comes to Japan." 28 mins. Color. WGBH, 1982.
"Kachō-san: The Section Chief and His Day." 30 mins. Color. Yomiuri Eigasha.

9.13 REFERENCES

Befu, Harumi. "An Ethnography of Dinner Entertainment in Japan." *Arctic Anthropology* 11, supplement (1974).

Ekuan, Kenji. "Makunouchi Bentōteki Hassō to Seikatsu Bunka." *Nihon to Chie to Dentoo.* Tokyo: Kodansha, 1981.

Kato, Hidetoshi et al. "Shoku no Shakaigaku." *Shoku no Bunka.* Tokyo: Kodansha, 1980.

Mochizuki, Mamoru. *Kojin Kūkan no Naka de.* Tokyo: Buren Shuppan, 1976.

Sakada, Minoru. "Asobi no Ningen Kankei." In *Nihon no Ningen Kankei Jiten,* ed. by Hiroshi Minami. Tokyo: Kodansha, 1980.

Tada, Michitaro. *Shinpen no Nihon Bunka.* Tokyo: Kodansha, 1981.

LESSON 10

REVIEW

10.1 $N \left\{ \begin{array}{l} \text{o} \\ \text{ga} \\ \text{wa} \end{array} \right\}$ **V-tai desu.**

| resutoran hoteru kissa-ten ryootei | de | raamen chuushoku chooshoku yuushoku sushi apetaizaa tsumami suteeki | o | tabe | -tai desu. -taku arimasen. -takatta desu. -taku arimasen deshita. |
| | | ocha koocha nama biiru sake wain Buruu Hawai | ga wa | nomi | |

10.2 | **V-te + mimashoo.**

kudamono sushi teishoku papaiya ten'pura	o	chuumon shite	mimashoo.
wain sake mizuwari		non'de	
shokudoo ryootei kissa-ten	e	itte	

LESSON 11

CHECKING IN AT THE HOTEL

11.1 USEFUL EXPRESSIONS

Yoyaku ga gozaimasu ka?	Do you have a reservation?
Hai, yoyaku shite arimasu.	Yes, I have made a reservation.
Itsu made gotaizai desu ka?	How long will you be staying?
Umi(te)gawa ga ii desu ka,	Would you prefer (a room) on
yama(te)gawa ga ii desu ka?	the ocean side or mountain side?
Goan'nai shimasu.	I'll show you.
Hawai wa hajimete desu ka?	Is this your first visit to Hawaii?
Umi ga yoku miemasu.	I can see the ocean clearly.
Kono kagi o doozo.	Here, this is your key.
Doozo goyukkuri.	Please relax.
Okokorozuke (o) doomo arigatoo.	Thank you for the tip.
Oyasuminasai.	Good night.

11.2 CONVERSATION

11.2.1   Check-in at the Hotel

Furon'to: Irasshaimase.

Kyaku: Heya o onegai shimasu. Satoo Haruo desu. Yoyaku shite
          arimasu.

Furon'to: Shooshoo omachi kudasai. Satoo Haruo-san desu ne.
          Itsu made gotaizai desu ka?

Kyaku: Kyoo kara gogatsu kokonoka made desu.

Furon'to: San-paku desu ne. Oheya wa 531-goo desu. Go-kai no umi(te)-
          gawa desu. Kono kagi o doozo. Beruman ga goan'nai shimasu
          kara, shooshoo omachi kudasai.

Kyaku: Doomo.

Front Desk

Clerk: Welcome.

Guest: May I have a room, please? My name is Haruo Sato, and I should
        have a room reservation.

Clerk: Just a minute please. Your name is Mr. Haruo Sato, right? How long will you be staying?

Guest: From today until the ninth of May.

Clerk: That's three nights, isn't it? Your room will be 531. That's the fifth floor facing the ocean. Here's your key. Just wait a moment, and the bellman will show you to your room.

Guest: Thank you.

11.2.2 Conversation with the Bellman

Beruman: Kono onimotsu desu ne. Doozo. Erebeetaa wa migi no hoo desu.

Kyaku: Shokudoo wa nan-gai ni arimasu ka?

Beruman: Ikkai desu. Yonaka no ni-ji made aite imasu.

Kyaku: Puuru wa dochira desu ka?

Beruman: Hoteru no yoko no hoo desu. Hawai wa hajimete desu ka?

Kyaku: Iie, mae ni ichido kita koto ga arimasu.

Beruman: Soo desu ka? Saa, kochira desu. Ea kon no aru oheya desu yo. Doozo goyukkuri.

Kyaku: Doomo arigatoo. Kore wa sukoshi desu ga doozo.
(The guest hands the bellman a tip.)

Beruman: Okokorozuke arigatoo gozaimasu.

Bellman: Is this your baggage? Please come with me. The elevator is to our right.

Guest: On what floor is the dining room?

Bellman: The first. It is open until 2 a.m.

Guest: Where is the pool?

Bellman: On the side of the hotel. Is this your first trip to Hawaii?

Guest: No, I came here once before.

Bellman: Is that right? This way please. Your room has air conditioning. Please enjoy your stay.

Guest: Thank you so much. Here's a small tip for you.
(The guest hands the bellman a tip.)

Bellman: Thanks for your thoughtfulness.

11.3 VOCABULARY

Nouns

ban'goo	number
ea kon	air conditioner
eiga	movie
furon'to	front desk

180

gogo	afternoon (p.m.)
gorufu	golf
gozen	morning (a.m.)
heya	room
hidari	left
kagi	key
kokorozuke, chippu	tip
mae	front, before
migi	right
nimotsu	baggage
ryokan	Japanese-style inn
ryokoo	trip
suiei	swimming
tsuin	twin, double occupancy
uketsuke	receptionist
umi	ocean, sea
umi(te)gawa	ocean side (view)
yama(te)gawa	mountain side (view)
yoko	side
yonaka	midnight
yoru	night

Verbs

akimasu	to open
an'nai shimasu	to guide, to show the way
miemasu	is visible, can see
oyogimasu	to swim
ryokoo shimasu	to travel
taizai shimasu	to stay over
tomarimasu	to sleep over

Adjectives

chikai	near
hayai	early, fast
osoi	late, slow
tooi	far

Adverbs

choodo	just right, just about
itsu	when
sukoshi	a little, a few
takusan	a lot, many, much
yoku	well, frequently
(yoi-yoku)	
yukkuri	slowly, leisurely

181

Counters

-ban	counter for night
-do	counter for repetitions
	(ichido = once)
-goo (shitsu)	room number
-haku	counter for night's lodging
-kai	counter for floors

Others

hoo	side, direction
-kara	from
-made	until

11.4 EXPLANATION

11.4.1 Noun modification: verb

We have so far learned the following basic noun modification patterns:

1. 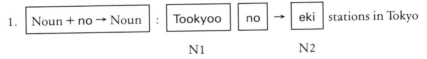 stations in Tokyo

The noun Tookyoo takes the particle no and modifies the other noun, eki. Tookyoo no eki must be differentiated from Tookyoo Eki, which means *Tokyo Station*. NN combinations without the particle no, like Tokyo Eki, are generally proper nouns.

2.  an interesting book

Adjectives modify nouns directly without any particles

3.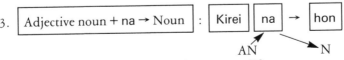

Adjective nouns take the particle na to modify a noun.

Notice that the above modifiers precede the noun. One ground rule for noun modifiers in Japanese is that the modifier *always* precedes the noun directly whereas noun modifiers in English may precede or follow the noun.

182

Examples:

Japanese
Tanaka-san no uchi.

English
Mr. Tanaka's house.

or

The house which Mr. Tanaka owns.

Yasui kamera.

A cheap camera.

or

The camera which is cheap.

This ground rule also holds true when a noun is modified by a verb-final sentence modifier.

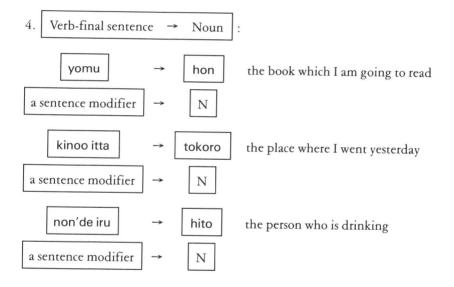

4. | Verb-final sentence → Noun | :

yomu → hon   the book which I am going to read

a sentence modifier → N

kinoo itta → tokoro   the place where I went yesterday

a sentence modifier → N

non'de iru → hito   the person who is drinking

a sentence modifier → N

Another ground rule for the noun modifier in Japanese is that the form of verb in the sentence must be the plain, or informal form, V (-u, -nai, -ta, and -nakatta) + Noun.

Examples:

taberu hito
the person who is going to eat

koohii o *nomanai* hito
the person who doesn't drink coffee

mita eiga
the movie that I saw

gakkoo e *konakatta* gakusei
the student who didn't come to school

When a sentence that modifies a noun includes the subject, the subject is followed either by the subject particle **ga** or by **no**.

183

The time when Mr. Yamada checks in is three o'clock.

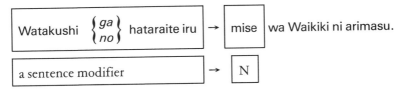

The store where I am working at is located in Waikiki.

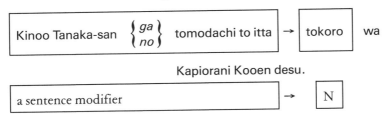

The place where Mr. Tanaka went with his friend yesterday is Kapiolani Park.

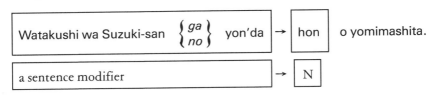

I read the book which Mr. Suzuki read.

Again, the above examples show that any type of modifier *always* precedes the noun.

Study the following:

1. Watakushi ga yon'de iru shin'bun wa *Asahi Shin'bun* desu.
   The newspaper to which I subscribe is the *Asahi Shinbun*.
2. Yamada-san ga kinoo oyoida biichi wa Hawai no yuumei na biichi desu.
   The beach where Mr. Yamada swam yesterday is a famous Hawaiian beach.
3. Sono yama(te)gawa no heya kara mieru chiisai ryokan wa watakushi ga ni-nen mae ni hitoban tomatta tokoro desu.
   The small inn you can see from that room facing the mountain is the place where I spent one night two years ago.

11.4.2 | (Person **wa**) + (Predicate modifier) + V-ta koto $\begin{Bmatrix} ga \\ wa \end{Bmatrix}$ $\begin{Bmatrix} arimasu. \\ arimasen. \end{Bmatrix}$

(Past experience)

Mae ni Hawai e kita koto ga arimasu means *I have come to Hawaii before* or *I've had the experience of coming to Hawaii before*. This pattern conveys the experience of having done something, whereas mere occurrence in the past is expressed by the past tense form -mashita. The predicate modifiers such as ichido *once*, nido *twice*, mae or mae ni *before* may be used in this pattern.

Nomoto: Nakada-san wa Oosutoraria e ryokoo shita koto ga arimasu ka?
Nakada: Iie, arimasen. Nomoto-san wa?
Nomoto: Itta koto ga arimasu.

Mr. Nomoto: Mrs. Nakada, have you ever traveled to Australia?
Mrs. Nakada: No, I haven't. How about you?
Mr. Nomoto: I have been there.

11.4.3 Counters

Counting numbers are followed by different counters, depending on the items being counted.

-goo (shitsu) used for counting room numbers
-kai used for counting floors or stories of a building
-ban used for counting nights with hito-, futa-, mi-, which are derived from
    the native number system (hitotsu, futatsu, mitsu, . . .)
-haku used for counting night's lodging

Study the following:

	-goo(shitsu)	-kai	-haku	-ban
1	ichi-goo	ikkai	ippaku	hito-ban
2	ni-goo	ni-kai	ni-haku	futa-ban
3	san-goo	san-gai	san-paku	mi-ban*
4	yon-goo	yon-kai	yon-haku	
5	go-goo	go-kai	go-haku	
6	roku-goo	rokkai	roppaku	
7	nana-goo	nana-kai	nana-haku	
8	hachi-goo	hakkai	happaku	
9	kyuu-goo	kyuu-kai	kyuu-haku	
10	juu-goo	jikkai	juppaku	
How		jukkai		
many?	nan-goo	nan-gai	nan-paku	iku-ban

*The counter -ban is not commonly used for counting higher than mi-ban. Instead, the counter -haku is used.

185

Examples:

1. Oheya no ban'goo wa nan-ban desu ka?

   What is your room number?

   Ni-ni-ichi-yon desu (or Nisen nihyaku juuyon-goo desu.)

   It is room 2214.

2. Hoteru ni nan-paku nasaimasu ka?

   How many nights are you staying (lodging) at the hotel?

   Gohaku desu.

   Five nights.

3. Sono hoteru wa hitoban ikura desu ka?

   How much is it for one night at that hotel?

   Kyuujuu-doru desu.

   It is 90 dollars.

4. Shokudoo wa nan-gai desu ka?

   What floor is the restaurant on?

   Nanakai desu.

   On the 7th floor.

11.5   DRILLS

11.5.1   Transformation Drill

Give the plain (informal) equivalent.

1. ikimasu — iku
2. kimasu — kuru
3. ryokoo shimasu — ryokoo suru
4. an'nai shimasu — an'nai suru
5. kaimasu — kau
6. mochimasu — motsu
7. tomarimasu — tomaru
8. imasu — iru
9. hatarakimasu — hataraku
10. oyogimasu — oyogu

11.5.2   Transformation Drill

Give the plain (informal) equivalent.

1. wakarimasen — wakaranai
2. machimasen — matanai
3. shimasen — shinai
4. kaimasen — kawanai
5. arimasen — nai
6. hanashimasen — hanasanai
7. kimasen — konai

186

8. tomarimasen	————	tomaranai
9. nomimasen	————	nomanai
10. mimasen	————	minai

11.5.3 Transformation Drill

Give the plain (informal) equivalent.

1. ikimashita	————	itta
2. yomimashita	————	yon'da
3. kikimashita	————	kiita
4. kakimashita	————	kaita
5. mochimashita	————	motta
6. ryokoo shimashita	————	ryokoo shita
7. kaimashita	————	katta
8. tabemashita	————	tabeta
9. arimashita	————	atta
10. kaerimashita	————	kaetta

11.5.4 Transformation Drill

Give the plain (informal) equivalent.

1. oyogimasen deshita	————	oyoganakatta
2. hanashimasen deshita	————	hanasanakatta
3. kimasen deshita	————	konakatta
4. ikimasen deshita	————	ikanakatta
5. kaimasen deshita	————	kawanakatta
6. ryokoo shimasen deshita	————	ryokoo shinakatta
7. nomimasen deshita	————	nomanakatta
8. tomarimasen deshita	————	tomaranakatta
9. tabemasen deshita	————	tabenakatta
10. wakarimasen deshita	————	wakaranakatta

11.5.5 Substitution Drill

Replace the sentence modifiers in the following pattern sentences.

A. *Ashita kan'koo suru* tokoro wa doko desu ka?

1. Tomodachi ga taizai shimasu   *Tomodachi ga taizai suru* tokoro wa doko desu ka?

2. Masao-san ga ikimasu   *Masao-san ga iku* tokoro wa doko desu ka?

3. Kyoo tomarimasu   *Kyoo tomaru* tokoro wa doko desu ka?

4. Tanaka-san ga matte imasu   *Tanaka-san ga matte iru* tokoro wa doko desu ka?

B. Kore wa *ea kon ga (no) nai* heya desu.

1. den'wa ga arimasen   Kore wa *den'wa ga (no) nai* heya desu.
2. amari ikimasen   Kore wa *amari ikanai* heya desu.
3. umi ga miemasen   Kore wa *umi ga (no) mienai* heya desu.
4. watashi wa tomatta   Kore wa *watashi ga (no) tomatta koto*
   koto ga arimasen   *ga nai* heya desu.

C. *Ryokoo shita* hito wa Yamada-san desu.

1. Omiyage o kaimashita   *Omiyage o katta* hito wa Yamada-
   san desu.
2. Tegami o kakimashita   *Tegami o kaita* hito wa Yamada-san
   desu.
3. Paatii e ikimashita   *Paatii e itta* hito wa Yamada-san
   desu.
4. Uta o utaimashita   *Uta o utatta* hito wa Yamada-san
   desu.

D. *Watakushi ga kan'koo shinakatta* tokoro wa Furan'su *(France)* desu.

1. Watakushi wa tomarimasen   *Watakushi ga tomaranakatta* tokoro
   deshita   wa Furan'su desu.
2. Watakushi wa mimasen deshita   *Watakushi ga minakatta* tokoro wa
   Furan'su desu.
3. Watakushi wa ikimasen deshita   *Watakushi ga ikanakatta* tokoro wa
   Furan'su desu.
4. Watakushi wa an'nai shimasen   *Watakushi ga an'nai shinakatta*
   deshita   tokoro wa Furan'su desu.

11.5.6   Response Drill

Answer the following questions using the English cues as your guide.

1. Dono gakusei ga John-san   Cue: the student who is over there
   desu ka?
   Asoko ni iru gakusei ga John-san desu.
2. Don'na heya ni tomaritai   Cue: a room with TV and air
   desu ka?   conditioner
   Terebi to ea kon no aru heya ni tomaritai desu.
3. Doko e ikitai desu ka?   Cue: the place where there is a pretty
   beach
   Kirei na biichi no aru tokoro e ikitai desu.
4. Nani o kikimashita ka?   Cue: the time when Mr. Yamada
   leaves
   Yamada-san ga dekakeru jikan o kikimashita.

188

5. Nani ga yomitai desu ka?   Cue: the book you have
   Anata ga motte iru hon ga yomitai desu.

6. Don'na kata ga ii desu ka?   Cue: the person who speaks Japanese
   Nihon'go o hanasu kata ga ii desu.

7. Nani o ben'kyoo shite imasu ka?   Cue: the lesson which I did not
                                             understand
   Wakaranakatta ressun o ben'kyoo shite imasu.

11.5.7   Response Drill

Answer each of the following questions, first in the affirmative, then in the negative.

1. Nihon e itta koto ga arimasu ka?
   Hai, itta koto ga arimasu.
   Iie, itta koto wa (or ga) arimasen.

2. Hon'kon *(Hong Kong)* e itta koto ga arimasu ka?
   Hai, itta koto ga arimasu.
   Iie, itta koto wa arimasen.

3. Arubaito o shita koto ga arimasu ka?
   Hai, shita koto ga arimasu.
   Iie, shita koto wa arimasen.

4. Makizushi o tsukutta koto ga arimasu ka?
   Hai, tsukutta koto ga arimasu.
   Iie, tsukutta koto wa arimasen.

5. Sheraton Hoteru ni tomatta koto ga arimasu ka?
   Hai, tomatta koto ga arimasu.
   Iie, tomatta koto wa arimasen.

11.6   EXERCISES

11.6.1   Translation

Say the following in Japanese.

1. The Japanese restaurant is on the second floor in this hotel.
2. The movie that I saw yesterday was interesting.
3. I want to stay here until May ninth.
4. The bellman will show you to your room.
5. The check-in time is three o'clock in the afternoon.
6. The beer which John is drinking now is not very popular.
7. I have never been to Kyoto.
8. I have worked at McDonald's before.
9. The hotel which Mr. Yasuda wants to stay in is very old.

11.6.2 Matching

Connect related words with a line.

1. migi	a. maneejaa
2. suiei	b. chippu
3. taizai suru	c. umitegawa
4. ryokan	d. imasu
5. shihainin	e. hidari
6. utau	f. oyogu
7. koohai	g. furon'to
8. uketsuke	h. karaoke
9. kokorozuke	i. sen'pai
10. yamategawa	j. hoteru

11.6.3 Multiple Choice

Find the appropriate counter for each sentence, making a phonetic change if necessary.

-goo shitsu	-kai	-nin'mae	-ji
-mai	-ban	-haku	-hai	-hon

1. Kawai Saafu Hoteru (*Kauai Surf Hotel*) ni hito-_____ tomatta koto ga aru.
2. Sono heya wa 22-_____ ni arimasu.
3. Sumida-san no oheya wa 235-_____ desu.
4. Shin'kon ryokoo wa Rosu (*Los Angeles*) ni 3-_____ shimashita.
5. Sashimi o 4-_____ onegai shimasu.
6. Omizu o moo 1-_____ itadakemasu ka?
7. Kon'na en'pitsu o 3-_____ kudasai.
8. Kissa-ten wa nan-_____ ni arimasu ka?
9. Nan-nichi Hawai ni taizai nasaimashita ka?
   Mikka futa-_____ taizai shimashita.

11.6.4 Completion

Insert an appropriate particle into each of the following blanks.

1. Kinoo Yamada-san _____ yon'da hon _____ doo deshita ka?
2. Asoko _____ aru chiisai kamera _____ misete kudasai.
3. Kono nomimono _____ nan _____ dekite imasu ka?
4. Kabuki _____ mita koto _____ arimasu ka?
5. Kono sutoroo (*straw*) _____ non'de kudasai.
6. Anata _____ motte iru zasshi _____ yomitai desu.
7. Kono kan'ji _____ setsumei suru koto _____ dekimasu ka?

11.7 SIMULATION AND SKITS

1. As a hotel front desk clerk, help a guest who has just arrived and wants to register. The guest has made a reservation.

2. As a front desk clerk, help a couple who has not made a reservation. Ask their preference about type of room, location of room, cost of room, and so forth.

3. As a bellboy, help carry a guest's luggage to his room.

4. You've just met a tourist from Japan and you ask him if this is his first visit to Hawaii. You also want to know if he's had the experience of traveling to other places.

5. You and your friend are talking about your interesting past experiences. In the conversation, use the different noun modification patterns where applicable.

11.8 CULTURE ORIENTATION

11.8.1 The Japanese and Travel

Japanese culture is a culture of **michi** or **doo** *the way or path*. The Japanese people once perceived travel as a painstaking and laborious struggle. The origin of the words for travel and trouble was the same. Traveling was a task, and the traveler was a hard worker. Until recently, travel and death were considered two sides of the same coin in Japan. In villages, the departure of a person going on a trip would be celebrated by the whole village. In some areas of Japan, these parties were called **tachibi**, which referred to the farewell party for the dead. Travel was a serious endeavor, involving the possibility of death (Kato 1982: 14–15).

Travel is symbolic of life for the Japanese people. Human life is a temporary phenomenon in the eternal spectrum of time, and the Japanese look upon life as a journey. The journey begins with birth and ends with death. With the introduction of the concept of reincarnation, death came to be perceived as another journey. The 16th-century Romantic poet Matsuo Basho epitomized this concept of life as a journey. Basho traveled all over Japan and wrote numerous haiku. To learn something from daily experiences was what made up a journey. Basho experienced joy in the peace of mind that travel provided.

Basho left many masterful haiku and ended his life in journey. However, he continues to live in the hearts of the Japanese people who still read and love his poetry.

> Old pond
>> Frog jumped in
>>> The sound of water

191

This is a very famous haiku which almost every Japanese person knows by heart. There are people in Japan who travel where Basho once did. The spirit of the traveler that Basho left behind still lingers on in the hearts of the Japanese. The haiku Basho wrote on his travels have been collected in a book titled *Oku No Hosomichi (The Deep Narrow Path)*. As the title suggests, Basho's life was a journey in itself. Basho was able to express himself through the concrete artistic medium of haiku and was able to grow and mature through it. He lived "the path of haiku."

This *path* (michi) in Chinese is the *Tao* in *Taoism*. This expresses the spiritual "way" of life. In Japanese this *Tao* is referred to as doo, found in the words juudoo, ken'doo *the way of the sword*, chadoo *the way of tea—tea ceremony*, kadoo *the way of flower—flower arrangement*, shodoo *the way of writing—calligraphy*, and haidoo *the way of haiku*. Doo also refers to the *way of life*.

Just as every person has a different journey, every person also has a different path of life. In the case of Basho, haidoo, *the way of haiku*, was his path. However, there are many other paths like kadoo, chadoo, shodoo, and juudoo. Although these all seem like hobbies, one may pursue them throughout one's entire life. The Japanese do not perceive these as merely acquiring certain skills. All of these paths serve as concrete mediums of expressing one's way of life. One must be able to go beyond the level of mastering the skill to express the spiritual attitude toward one's own life.

The Japanese perceive a journey as representative of life itself; it also represents the path of life which one must take step-by-step. The journey serves as a teacher which assists man to mature. This concept is well expressed in the old Japanese saying *let the precious child travel*.

11.8.2   The Concept of **Doo (Michi)** and the Japanese Mode of Learning

When a Japanese learns something, the form is given to him by his master or teacher. Having repeatedly practiced this form, he is to strive toward mastery. There are two ways to translate the English word *form* into Japanese. One way is kata, and the other is katachi. According to one theory, the difference between katachi and kata is that the chi can be written by using several different kan'ji. For example, the characters for *blood, milk, earth, soul,* and *wind* can all be used. However, all of these connote a certain element of energy or life-force. Katachi, as opposed to kata, is a more holistic form incorporating a certain element of life-energy. Kata, on the other hand, is merely the form itself. There is an expression in Japan which states *Enter through the form* (kata) *and transcend it (into* katachi). In other words, learning is a process through which one begins with a given form and, by repeatedly practicing this form, sometimes for years, one can reach the holistic stage of achieving katachi. This process of entering through the kata and transcending into the katachi represents the doo, or the *way*.

192

When one begins to learn juudoo, one begins with the kata which his master demonstrates. This is then practiced over and over until the physical form and the spiritual form can harmonize into a holistic katachi where the life-energy can flow through.

The Japanese people have created many forms of art through this mode of learning. For example, by utilizing the modernization model of wakon-yoosai, the Japanese obtained the form (kata) of the watch from Switzerland. By utilizing their mode of learning, the Japanese studied the Swiss watch for nearly twenty years until they were able to produce a comparable watch of their own called Seiko. It is said that the present Swiss watch is a result of 200 years of work and study. Some other examples of the utilization of the Japanese mode of learning can be observed in the production of transistor radios, cameras, and automobiles.

Man's life, beginning with birth, and his growth represent one path. Man's journey through life is another path. But every path begins with a form (kata), and one must transcend this form into a holistic and balanced form (katachi) full of life-energy.

11.8.3   The Japanese and the "This-worldly" Way of Thinking

The Japanese people tend to be more concerned with worldly matters than with abstract concepts. This characteristic can be traced to the Japanese environment. Recall that 84 percent of Japan's land mass consists of mountains. Although not rich in natural resources, natural beauty abounded in Japan, and although cultivatable land was scarce, the land itself was fertile. Japan always had an abundance of seafood from its surrounding ocean, and water was always plentiful. Japan's geographic isolation as an island provided protection and security from outside forces. The Japanese people, under these conditions, perceived nature as a benevolent force and strove to harmonize with it. Nature was perceived, not as a negative force to contend with, but as an instructor of how to live and survive. The Japanese perceived the relationship between man and nature as one of trust and security. Thus, the Japanese began to believe in a phenomenological world that was here and now.

It is said, in the Shinto religion, that God exists in 8 million forms. In other words, God exists in everything in this world. Rather than portraying the gods as overseeing man from above, the ancient Japanese texts, the *Kojiki* and *Nihon Shoki,* portrayed them as existing along with man. For example, Ama-terasu Omikami, the main goddess in the Shinto pantheon of gods, expresses herself in the concrete form of the sun. The sun shines upon all mankind, and this force of Amaterasu Omikami is a very real experience for the Japanese people. Even with the introduction of Buddhism and its concept of the divided world of paradise and hell, the highly speculative element of Buddhism from India did not pervade the Japanese culture. Instead, the more down-to-earth interpretation of Buddhism coming from China took root in Japan. Zen, with its element of immediacy and concreteness, flourished in Japan. The present Shingon Buddhism in Japan also seems less abstract and speculative and more concrete, concerned with daily aspects of life. Japanese religion's emphasis on the practical aspects of life probably can be traced back to the Japanese "this-worldly" way of thinking and emphasis on immediacy and concreteness.

Just as the Japanese values and way of thinking are affected by an emphasis on immediacy and concreteness, their mode of communication is equally affected. This emphasis on immediacy places importance on the appreciation of every moment which, having passed, can never be recaptured. This concept is closely related to the discussion, in this lesson, of the importance placed on every process that is involved in following the path (michi). In the realm of human relations, every meeting becomes precious and important. The expression ichigo ichie *one lifetime (in) one meeting* embodies this concept.

Japanese stay away from purely theoretical discussions for the sake of argument. Unless there is some concreteness involved in the discussion, they will not respond. In some respects, Japanese are not too keen on abstract thinking and are therefore not too adept at it. They generally avoid asking "why." In some ways, one can venture to say that the Japanese people are not too philosophical. Their preference for haiku, a poetical style with immediacy and concreteness, over Western poetry is related to the fact that the Japanese people would prefer not to overly philosophize and make abstractions. Use of concrete examples in speech and manners would be highly conducive to successful communication with a Japanese person.

11.8.4   The Japanese and the Quality Control Circle

The Japanese are known as innovators, rather than as inventors. This is related to the Japanese mode of learning discussed earlier, where one enters through a given form and transcends it (from the kata to the katachi). However, the earlier kata and the transcended katachi form are similar in outer appearance, with no major discoveries taking place.

Lately, however, there have been several inventions the Japanese people have come up with. Several explanations can be made for this phenomenon; the most important being the use of the quality control technique. In origin, the quality control concept and technique is American. After World War II, the American quality control expert William Deming came to teach the Japanese about quality control in conjunction with their economic revival programs. The Japanese adopted the quality control concept by applying their own modernization model of wakon-yoosai, which was discussed in Lesson 5. They learned the concept of quality control, given the form (kata) from the United States; after 30 years of experimentation and research, they developed the form (katachi) of quality control for which they became famous. In 1974, quality control was exported back to the United States and was experimented with by Lockheed Corporation and Honeywell. Positive results from these experiments led other American corporations and organizations to adopt quality control circles. Now, both small and large businesses are enthusiastically utilizing the quality control approach to solve productivity problems. The concept of quality control is rapidly spreading to other nations of the world.

Brainstorming is one of the quality control techniques. This technique involves pooling together innovative ideas from all individuals, regardless of their status, specialty, or degree of involvement in the project. Generally speaking, Japanese culture discouraged any action or thought that exceeded the limits of a given kata. Japanese society has always had a clear-cut social hierarchy and, because of this, creativity and innovation coming from the lower ranks was discouraged, lest it cause embarrassment to a person of higher status. As the old Japanese saying goes, *The nail that protrudes must be hammered down.* From such a cultural background, one would not imagine that a technique like brainstorming would have grown. However, once it was introduced as part of the program for quality control, it was easily accepted by the Japanese companies.

One of the reasons for the success of brainstorming lay in the strengthening of group spirit. In Japanese society, where the seniority system is so strong, brainstorming evolved from an individual merit system into a group project. The various ideas pooled together were looked upon as a group accomplishment rather than an individual accomplishment. And these groups were recognized for their ideas and rewarded accordingly. This system strengthened the group spirit within the company. In this manner, the seemingly inappropriate mechanism of brainstorming was assimilated and developed in the Japanese corporate system.

There are other reasons for the success of brainstorming; one lies in the fact that it came from outside. It was immediately pigeonholed as being a foreign system which had no pressing urgency to be accepted into the existing system. Brainstorming also helped encourage creativity from employees whose creativity was suppressed under the seniority system. Because of the seniority system in Japan, regardless of whether an employee gave an outstanding performance or not, promotion was gradual and definite. Under this system, it did not matter if individuals contributed new and creative ideas to a project. Since the American system is an individual merit system, brainstorming would successfully encourage individuals to be creative and compete with one another for credit. However, since individual creativity did not lead to promotion or individual recognition in the Japanese system, there was a tendency for individuals not to go out of their way to be creative. With the introduction of brainstorming, this tendency was reversed and many new ideas were pooled together. As a result, these ideas led to many new inventions and innovations.

Many times, in order to create new things, old frameworks must be destroyed and new ones created. In other words, creativity often involves the ability to destroy. The Japanese people have an ability to adopt and improve things, but on a cultural level they lack an ability to destroy because of their heavy emphasis on the maintenance of kata (form or framework). The Japanese mode of learning also often involves remaining within a given framework. Unless the Japanese can adopt a style of learning and thinking that extends beyond a given framework, utilized in the field of education as well as standardized for society, they will always be looked upon as innovators and not inventors.

11.9   THE JAPANESE MODE OF COMMUNICATION

The Process-oriented Mode of Communication

The Japanese emphasize the importance of the process of reaching a goal. As mentioned earlier, Japanese culture is a culture of michi *way.* Every person's life is a michi which becomes mature as one walks straight along it. There is no end to this michi and the importance lies in valuing every step of the way. The Japanese people can be said to emphasize and value the small steps taken on the way rather than the goal itself. They believe that the goal will naturally be good if every step to get there is good. Because of this cultural orientation, *how* one conveys rather than *what* one conveys is emphasized. This mode of communication can be called the process-oriented mode of communication, and it explains the Japanese emphasis on form and ritual as a natural form of expression.

11.10   LANGUAGE AND CULTURE

A.   **Umi(te)gawa**

The Japanese often confuse the phrases *ocean view* and *ocean front.* One tourist from Japan said, "I had reserved an umitegawa (or umigawa) *(ocean-view)* room in Hawaii from Japan, but when we got there only a glimpse of the ocean could be seen from our room!" This tourist had gone to argue with the manager of the hotel, saying the hotel had made a mistake. However, the manager replied that the reservation was made for the "ocean view" and not the "ocean front." *Ocean view,* to the manager, meant that the ocean is merely visible from the room, while *ocean front* calls for a room fronting the ocean, with a panoramic view of it. Since the Japanese do not make this distinction in their language, it is important that the distinction be made very clear when hotel reservations are made for a Japanese tourist.

196

B. Doozo goyukkuri

This expression is often literally translated as *please take your time*. However, when the expression is used at a private home or by a representative at a company compound, it reflects hospitality toward the guest or visitor. The expression connotes *please relax* or *please make yourself at home*.

C. Ea kon

The Japanese people are experts at transforming foreign words into their own vocabulary. For example, English *air conditioner* was abbreviated as ea kon and is commonly used as part of current Japanese vocabulary. The name *Los Angeles* is abbreviated in Japan as Rosu ("Los") rather than "L.A." Problems arise when the Japanese try to communicate with Americans using the word rosu and find they can't be understood! Ea kon also can't be understood by English speakers. Another example is the abbreviated word for *word processor.* The Japanese way is to say waa puro! An older example, which is no longer used by the younger generation, is moga for *modern girl* and mobo for *modern boy*.

11.11 CULTURE QUESTIONS

1. The Japanese concept of travel and journey was discussed in the culture orientation. Compare and contrast the concept of travel in Japan with the concept of travel in your country.

2. How does the Japanese mode of learning—entering from the kata (form) and transcending it into the katachi—compare with the American mode of learning? Some of you may have seen the movie "Karate Kid." The way the hero, the Karate Kid, was trained under his master reflects this particular Japanese mode of learning. Use this movie as a point of reference for discussion.

3. Twenty years ago, products "Made in Japan" were known for their poor quality. Now products "Made in Japan" are known for their high quality. What are some of the causes for this transformation?

4. What qualities can be developed in order to have a hotel front desk manager who can be appreciated by non-English-speaking Japanese tourists? Utilize brainstorming to come up with some good ideas.

11.12 SUGGESTED RESOURCE MATERIALS

11.12.1 Books and Magazines

"The Acceptance of Phenomenalism," *Ways of Thinking of Eastern Peoples: India, China, Tibet, Japan,* Hajime Nakamura (Honolulu: The University Press of Hawaii, 1981), pp. 350–406.

A Hundred Things Japanese (Tokyo: Japan Culture Institute, 1975), pp. 196–197.
In Search of What's Japanese about Japan, John Condon and Keisuke Kurata (Tokyo: Shufunotomo, 1974), pp. 109–115.
Kodansha Encyclopedia of Japan, vol. 6 (Tokyo: Kodansha, 1983), pp. 272–274.
Kodansha Encyclopedia of Japan, vol. 8 (Tokyo: Kodansha, 1983), p. 24.
"Some Japanese Cultural Traits and Religions," Hideo Kishimoto, *Philosophy and Cultures: East and West.* Ed. by Charles A. Moore (Honolulu: East-West Center Press, 1962), pp. 245–254.

11.12.2   Films (16 mm) and Video Cassettes (Beta/VHS)

"Judo." 27 mins. The Ministry of Foreign Affairs, 1970.
"Kyūdō: Japanese Ceremonial Archery." 10 mins. Color. ACI, 1969.

11.13   REFERENCE

Kato, Hidetoshi. *Shin Ryokō Yōjinshū.* Tokyo: Chuko Shinsho, 1982.

LESSON 12

ASKING FOR FRONT DESK SERVICES

12.1 USEFUL EXPRESSIONS

Hai, nan deshoo ka? Nani ka goyoo desu ka?	Yes, what can I help you with?
Kichoohin o azuketai n'desu ga . . .	I would like to leave my valuables (with you) . . . but (what should I do?)
Watakushi ni nani ka den'gon ga arimasu ka?	Do I have any messages?
Oheya no ban'goo wa?	What is your room number?
Oisogi desu ka?	Are you in a hurry?
Kagi o nakusanaide kudasai.	Please do not lose the key.
Dame desu.	It's not good (or OK).

12.2 CONVERSATION

12.2.1 Checking for Mail

Furon'to: Hai, nan deshoo ka?
Kyaku: Tegami ga kite imasu ka? 342-goo shitsu no Suzuki desu ga . . .
Furon'to: Otegami wa kite imasen ga, den'gon ga gozaimasu.
Kyaku: Doomo.

Front Desk
Clerk: Can I help you?
Guest: I wonder if I have any mail? My name is Suzuki, Room 342 . . .
Clerk: You don't have any mail, but you do have a message.
Guest: Thank you.

199

12.2.2 Pharmacy Information at the Front Desk

Kyaku: Atama ga itai n'desu ga, kono hen ni kusuriya ga arimasu ka?
Furon'to: Ano robii no iriguchi no hoo ni arimasu yo.
Kyaku: Doomo.

Guest: I have a headache. Is there a pharmacy around here?
Clerk: Yes, there's one at the entrance to the lobby.
Guest: Thank you.

12.2.3 Currency Exchange at the Front Desk

Kyaku: Ryoogae dekimasu ka?
Furon'to: Hai, dekimasu yo.
Kyaku: Reeto wa ikura desu ka?
Furon'to: Ichi-doru wa 160-en desu.
Kyaku: Ichiman-en onegai shimasu.
Furon'to: Hai, 62-doru 50-sen'to desu. Doozo.
Kyaku: Doomo.

Guest: Can you exchange money?
Clerk: Yes, we can.
Guest: What is the rate today?
Clerk: One dollar is 160 yen.
Guest: Please change 10,000 yen.
Clerk: That will be 62 dollars and 50 cents.
Guest: Thank you.

12.2.4 Taxi Information at the Front Desk

Kyaku: Anoo, Ara Moana Sen'taa e ikitai n'desu ga, takushii wa doko
          de norimasu ka?
Furon'to: Takushii o yobimasu kara, hoteru no iriguchi no mae de
          omachi kudasai.
Kyaku: Doomo arigatoo.

Guest: I would like to go to Ala Moana Center. Where can I catch a taxi?
Clerk: I'll call the taxi. Please wait at the hotel entrance.
Guest: Thank you.

12.2.5 Renting a Safety Deposit Box

Kyaku: Kashikin'ko o karitai n'desu ga . . .
Furon'to: Tonari no kaun'taa e doozo.
Kyaku: A, soo desu ka?
Kyaku: Anoo, kashikin'ko o karitai n'desu kedo . . .
Kaikei: Hai. Kore o yon'de kara, shita ni sain shite kudasai.
Kyaku: Kan'ji de kaitemo ii desu ka?

Kaikei:	Iie, roomaji de kaite kudasai. Sorekara, kono kagi o nakusanai de kudasai. Soshite, kin'ko o aketai toki ni wa kagi o watashite, ona-mae o itte kudasai ne.
Kyaku:	Wakarimashita. Doomo arigatoo.

Guest: I would like to leave some things in a safety deposit box please.
Front Desk
Clerk: Please go to the next counter.
Guest: I see.
Guest: I would like to leave some things in a safety deposit box, please.
Cashier: I see. After reading this, please sign here.
Guest: May I write in kan'ji?
Cashier: No, please write in Roman letters. Please be careful not to lose this key. And when you want to open the box, just give us the key and tell us your name.
Guest: All right. Thank you.

12.3 VOCABULARY

Nouns

asatte	day after tomorrow
atama	head
deguchi	exit
den'gon, messeeji	message
den'poo	telegram
iriguchi	entrance
kan'ji	Chinese character
kashikin'ko	deposit box (for valuables)
kichoohin	valuables
kusuri	medicine
kusuriya	drug store
mado	window
onaka	stomach
ototoi	day before yesterday
reeto	rate
robii	lobby
roomaji	Roman letters (romanization)
ryoogae	currency exchange
shita	beneath, under
shomei, sain	signature
toki	time, when
tonari	next door
ue	above, on
yuubin	mail
zutsuu	headache

Verbs

akemasu	to open
hairimasu	to enter
iimasu	to say
karimasu	to borrow
norimasu	to ride
ryoogae shimasu	to exchange currency
shomei shimasu, sain shimasu	to sign
watashimasu	to hand over, to turn in

Adjectives

itai	ache

Adverbs

sorekara	and then

Others

kedo, keredomo	but, although
kono hen	this vicinity
soshite	and

12.4 EXPLANATION

12.4.1 $\boxed{\text{V -te, ...}}$ (Sequence)

Kagi o watashite, onamae o itte kudasai.
Please turn in the key, and state your name.

When the subjects of the nonfinal clause and that of the final clause are identical, actions are sequential, meaning, *One does one thing, then does something else.*

Example:
Waikiki e itte, shokuji o shimashita.　　I went to Waikiki and had a meal there.

12.4.2 $\boxed{\text{V -te kara,}}$ (After doing V, or since V happened)

Kore o *yon'de kara,* sain shite kudasai.　　*After reading* this, please sign in.

Examples:

Uchi e kaette kara, repooto o kakimasu.
I'll write a report after I go home.

Tookyoo ni tsuite kara, tegami o kakimashita.
After arriving at Tokyo, I wrote a letter.

Compare this pattern with V-ta kara.

Omiyage o katte kara, hoteru e kaerimashita.
After buying the gift, I went back to the hotel.

Omiyage o katta kara, hoteru e kaerimashita.
Because I bought the gift, I went back to the hotel.

12.4.3 | V -te (mo) ii desu ka? | (Permission)

Kan'ji de kaite mo ii desu ka?   May I write it with kan'ji? *or*
                                  Will it be all right to write it with
                                     kan'ji?

In this pattern the particle mo means *even*, but it is optional.

The permission pattern is formulated as follows:

1. Verbal

| V -te mo ii desu ka? |

   Tabete mo ii desu ka?   Is it OK to eat?

2. Adjective: The te form of the adjective is formed by changing the final A -i
   to A -kute.

| A -kute mo ii desu ka? |

   Atsukute mo ii desu ka?   Is it OK if it's hot?

3. Adjective Noun or Noun: The te form of copula desu is de.

| AN }
| N } de mo ii desu? |

   Heta de mo ii desu ka?   Is it OK to be unskillful?
   Kore de mo ii desu ka?   Is it OK with this?

203

Kamaimasen ka? *don't you mind?* is also used.
Study the following.

Kite mite (mo) { ii desu ka? / kamaimasen ka?	Is it all right to try it on?
Hai, doozo.	Yes, please.
Hai, ii desu yo.	Yes, it's all right.
Hai, kamaimasen yo.	Yes, I don't mind.
Chiisakute (mo) ii desu ka?	Is it OK even if it's small?
Ee, chiisakute mo ii desu.	Yes, it's OK even if it's small.
Kono eiga wa kodomo de mo ii desu.	This movie is all right for children.
Ben'kyoo shinakute (mo) ii desu.	It is all right even if you don't study.

12.4.4 | V -naide kudasai | (Please do not do such and such)

Nakusanaide kudasai means *please do not lose it.* The polite negative request (imperative) *please do not do such and such* is formed as follows:

V pre-nai form + naide kudasai.

Ikanaide kudasai.	Please do not go.
Koko ni hairanaide kudasai.	Please do not enter here.
Mado o akenaide kudasai.	Please do not open the window.

This pattern is also used in the reply to a question asking permission:

Issho ni tomatte mo { ii desu ka? / kamaimasen ka?	Is it all right if I stay over with you?
Iie, tomaranaide kudasai.	No, please do not stay over.
To o akete mo ii desu ka?	May I open the door?
Samui kara, akenaide kudasai.	Please don't open it, because it's cold.

12.4.5 | . . . . . . ni norimasu | (To ride in / on)

The verb norimasu is used with the particle ni as in takushii ni norimasu.

Thus:

Basu ni norimasu.	I ride on the bus.
Hikooki ni norimasu.	I ride on the plane.
Fune ni norimasu.	I ride on the boat.

204

12.5 DRILLS

12.5.1 Substitution Drill

Example: Ryoogae o shimashita. Kaerimashita.
         Ryoogae o shite, kaerimashita.

1. Terebi o mimashita.
   Terebi o mite, kaerimashita.
2. Ban'gohan o tabemashita.
   Ban'gohan o tabete, kaerimashita.
3. Kagi o watashimashita.
   Kagi o watashite, kaerimashita.
4. Ippaku shimashita.
   Ippaku shite, kaerimashita.
5. Omiyage o kaimashita.
   Omiyage o katte, kaerimashita.

12.5.2 Substitution Drill

Example: Repooto o yomimashita. Kono zasshi o yomimashita.
         Repooto o yon'de kara, kono zasshi o yomimashita.

1. Ben'kyoo shimashita.
   Ben'kyoo shite kara, kono zasshi o yomimashita.
2. Den'wa shimashita.
   Den'wa shite kara, kono zasshi o yomimashita.
3. Tegami o kakimashita.
   Tegami o kaite kara, kono zasshi o yomimashita.
4. Uchi e kaerimashita.
   Uchi e kaette kara, kono zasshi o yomimashita.
5. Hirugohan o tsukurimashita.
   Hirugohan o tsukutte kara, kono zasshi o yomimashita.

12.5.3 Substitution Drill

Example: Ima hanashimasu. Ii desu ka?
         Ima hanashite mo, ii desu ka?

1. Ashita yomimasu.
   Ashita yon'de mo, ii desu ka?
2. Kyoo nomimasu.
   Kyoo non'de mo, ii desu ka?

3. Ima den'wa shimasu.
   Ima den'wa shite mo, ii desu ka?

4. Den'wa shimasen.
   Den'wa shinakute mo, ii desu ka?

5. Ookii desu.
   Ookikute mo, ii desu ka?

6. Tsumaranai desu.
   Tsumaranakute mo, ii desu ka?

7. Furui desu.
   Furukute mo, ii desu ka?

8. Basu desu.
   Basu de mo, ii desu ka?

9. Koohii desu.
   Koohii de mo, ii desu ka?

10. Gakusei desu.
    Gakusei de mo, ii desu ka?

12.5.4 Transformation Drill

Transform the following sentences into requests.

1. Mado o akemasen.	Mado o akenaide kudasai.
2. Eigo o tsukaimasen.	Eigo o tsukawanaide kudasai.
3. Namae o kakimasen.	Namae o kakanaide kudasai.
4. Shomei shimasen.	Shomei shinaide kudasai.
5. Purezen'to o tsutsumimasen.	Purezen'to o tsutsumanaide kudasai.
6. Heya ni hairimasen.	Heya ni hairanaide kudasai.
7. Sake o nomimasen.	Sake o nomanaide kudasai.
8. Terebi o mimasen.	Terebi o minaide kudasai.
9. Ashita kimasen.	Ashita konaide kudasai.

12.5.5 Question–Answer Drill

1. Kono juusu o non'de mo ii desu ka?
   Hai, non'de mo ii desu.
   Iie, nomanaide kudasai.

2. Ima chuumon shite mo ii desu ka?
   Hai, chuumon shite mo ii desu.
   Iie, chuumon shinaide kudasai.

3. Heya ni haitte mo ii desu ka?
   Hai, haitte mo ii desu.
   Iie, hairanaide kudasai.

4. Kagi o watashite mo ii desu ka?
   Hai, watashite mo ii desu.
   Iie, watasanaide kudasai.

5. Yamada-san o paatii ni yon'de mo ii desu ka?
   Hai, yon'de mo ii desu.
   Iie, yobanaide kudasai.

6. Seetaa wa ookikute no ii desu ka?
   Hai, ookikute mo ii desu.
   Iie, dame desu.

7. Omiyage wa chokoreeto demo ii desu ka?
   Hai, chokoreeto demo ii desu.
   Iie, dame desu.

8. Suteeki wa katakute mo ii desu ka?
   Hai, katakute mo ii desu.
   Iie, dame desu.

12.6 EXERCISES

12.6.1 Sentence Combining

Combine the following pairs of sentences to produce expressions meaning *after V-ing* as in the example.

Example: Gohan o tabemashita. Gohan o tabete kara, biichi e ikimashita.
          Biichi e ikimashita. After eating, I went to the beach.

1. Kaimono shimashita.
   Uchi e kaerimashita.

2. Mado o akemasu.
   Hon o yon'de kudasai.

3. Kusuri o nomimashita.
   Nemashita.

4. Nihon'go de iimasu.
   Eigo de itte kudasai.

5. Okinawa e ikimashita.
   Taiwan e ikimashita.

6. Tenisu o shimashita.
   Gorufu o shimashita.

7. Muumuu o kaimashita.
   Baggu o kaimashita.

12.6.2 Translation

Translate the following into Japanese.

1. I'll take you to the room after you check in.
2. After exchanging currency, I went shopping.
3. What do you do after reading the newspaper?
4. Will this one do?
5. Please don't go by boat.
6. Is it OK even if I call Mr. Tanaka to the party?
7. I returned to the hotel, listened to the radio, and went to bed.
8. After watching TV, I wrote a letter and went to a friend's house.

12.6.3 Questions and Answers

Pair up with a classmate and take turns asking each other for permission to do "such and such" and responding as in the examples given below.

Examples:

1. Verb
   Q: Ima koko de oyoide mo ii desu ka?
   A: Hai, oyoide mo ii desu.
   A: Iie, oyoganaide kudasai.

2. Adjective
   Q: Ocha wa tsumetakute mo ii desu ka?
   A: Hai, tsumetakute mo ii desu.
   A: Iie, dame desu.

3. Noun and Adjective Noun
   Q: Shomei wa nihon'go de mo ii desu ka?
   A: Hai, nihon'go de mo ii desu.
   A: Iie, dame desu.

   Q: Eigo wa heta de mo ii desu ka?
   A: Hai, heta de mo ii desu.
   A: Iie, dame desu.

12.7 SIMULATION AND SKITS

1. A hotel guest goes to the front desk to ask for a taxi to pick him up and take him to the Polynesian Cultural Center. The front desk employee arranges for the taxi to pick him up and tells him to wait for the taxi in front of the hotel.

2. A hotel guest has a stomachache so he goes to the front desk to ask where he can get some medicine. As the front desk employee, lead him to the hotel drug store.

208

3. A hotel guest from Japan wants to exchange 20,000 yen for American dollars. Explain to him what the current exchange rate is and how much he will receive.

4. As a front desk employee, help a hotel guest who wants to place some valuables in the hotel's safety deposit box. Ask him to fill out and sign the necessary papers.

5. A friend of one of the hotel guests comes to see her friend. She goes to the front desk and asks for her friend's room number. The front desk clerk instructs her to use the in-house phone. They then meet in the hotel lobby.

6. A hotel guest goes to the front desk and asks if he has any mail. As a front desk employee, you check to see if he has any mail. You tell him that he doesn't have any mail, but he does have a few phone messages.

7. A hotel guest asks the front desk employee to arrange a wake-up call for him at 6:30 in the morning. At 6:30 in the morning he gets a wake-up call from the hotel operator.

12.8   CULTURE ORIENTATION

12.8.1   A Day at a Japanese Inn

Since World War II, Westernization has affected various aspects of the daily lives of the Japanese people, including Japanese houses. The houses being built now are a combination of Japanese and Western styles, and a pure Japanese-style house is rarely found. However, the ryokan is one of the very few existing forms of the traditional Japanese home. In this lesson the Japanese ryokan will be viewed as encompassing a microcosm of the Japanese culture and way of thinking.

The word ryokan is made up of the words for *travel* and *mansion*. The ryokan is like a Western hotel where travelers can stay. In Japan, both Western hotels and Japanese ryokan are available to travelers. However, there is a definite distinction between the two. The ryokan allows the traveler to experience the atmosphere of the traditional Japanese lifestyle, whereas the hotel allows one to experience a Western lifestyle. The Japanese traveler chooses between the two according to his preference and needs. Since the Japanese lifestyle is such a mixture of Japanese and Western ways, the transition from staying at a traditional Japanese ryokan to a Western hotel can be made very easily for the Japanese person.

The ryokan is usually a two-story or three-story wooden building. The garden is typically Japanese with its carefully placed rocks, pond, pine trees, bamboo, and stone lantern. The ryokan is furnished in traditional Japanese style with straw tatami mats on the floor and sliding doors made of wooden frames and paper surfaces called shooji *(thin, translucent paper)* and fusuma *(thicker paper)*. The standard tatami is three feet by six feet. Tatami mats are placed side by side to cover the entire floor. In the center of the room a gleaming, polished, low table is kept with two zabuton *cushions* placed at its sides. Depending upon the ryokan, there may also be two Western-style chairs, with a small table placed between them on the indoor balcony overlooking the garden. Every room has a tokonoma, *an alcove* containing a hanging scroll painting and a flower arrangement. The tokonoma is considered the most important part of the room, and important guests are seated with their backs to the tokonoma. The fusuma usually has a painting of a scenic view of nature, and the guest is made to feel like an integral part of the setting when he sits down on the tatami. When the shooji is opened, the beautiful garden outside is revealed, and the guest is once again placed in nature. When one lies down on the tatami, he faces the ceiling made of wood revealing the beautiful patterns of its grain.

The tatami has a special strawlike smell of its own. When the tatami is newly changed, the fresh scent of straw in the whole room gives one a refreshing feeling. A ryokan located at a hot springs resort often has streams running close by; guests can hear the sound of the stream from their rooms. Sometimes one can even hear the carp splashing in the pond. Nature can be observed in the food served in the zashiki (tatami room). In these ways, the ryokan allows one to experience traditional Japanese life and immerse oneself in the beauty of nature through all the five senses of sight, smell, touch, taste, and sound. The ryokan illustrates how the Japanese people attempted to become one with nature even in their homes.

Arriving at a ryokan. As discussed in Lesson 1, Japan is a culture of form where the beginning and the end of a process must be properly carried out. At a ryokan, the way guests are greeted as they enter is an important detail to be considered. Usually the maids at the ryokan, dressed in their kimonos, greet the customers with smiles and repeated bowing. The customers are greeted at the gen'kan *foyer* where they take off their shoes and slip on some indoor slippers.

The gen'kan occupies a space not quite inside or outside of a house. It can be looked upon as an area where one gets prepared to enter the house from the outside. First one's shoes, which were directly in contact with the outside, are removed. Next, indoor slippers are put on, and then the guest enters the home. The gen'kan functions in a manner similar to the Buddhist concept of kekkai, which connects one world with another. Also represented by the gen'kan is the concept of kejime, which demarcates the physical and the mental worlds.

The maid brings in tea as soon as one is brought to one's room. Every guest is provided with a yukata, *a summer kimono for daily use.* Most people put on their yukata and go for a hot ofuro *bath* and relax afterwards. The concept of entering the inside world from the outside world is symbolically represented by entering the ryokan through the gen'kan and by taking an ofuro which removes the sweat and dirt from the outside world before entering the inside world. Cleanliness, ritualized in the form of misogi *purification*, is one of the essential tenets of the Shinto religion. In Japanese, the ideas of beautiful and clean overlap in the word kirei, reflecting the interrelationship between the concepts of cleanliness and beauty. Thus, the ofuro, an area to cleanse oneself in order to enter the inner world, can be seen as another area where the concept of kekkai is reflected.

The ofuro, especially at hot spring resort areas, are open all day to the guests who may go as many times as they like. An ofuro is generally communal in style and differs fundamentally from Western-style baths. First of all, soap must not be used in the tub water, and washing must be done outside of the tub. After the body is washed and rinsed, one may enter the tub. According to Shinto belief, clean things and dirty things cannot be placed together. Because of this, the toilet, which symbolizes uncleanliness, and the ofuro, which symbolizes cleanliness, are traditionally placed apart from each other.

The ofuro is an important part of a Japanese house. It is not only a place to cleanse oneself but also a place to relax and enjoy the hot water. Children love to play in the water and people often take hour-long baths. At hot springs, people take baths several times a day, not to clean but to enjoy themselves. Although most baths are now made of ceramic tile, a traditional ofuro is made of hinoki *Japanese cypress*. At a high-class ryokan one can still experience this cypress ofuro, enjoying the aroma of the wood as one relaxes in the shoulder-deep hot water. The ofuro made of hinoki not only smells good but feels very smooth to the touch.

Because the Japanese wash their bodies before entering the tub, there have been cases of "flooding" at Western hotels where Japanese people stay. Not knowing that one is supposed to wash one's body in the tub in a Western-style bath, the Japanese wash their bodies outside of the tub, causing a miniature flood in the hotels! Another cause for flooding in Western-style hotels is that the Japanese tourist sometimes takes a shower with the shower curtain hung outside of the tub instead of inside. Taking showers in Japan is still not as common as taking ofuro.

After a relaxing ofuro, one puts on the yukata and goes for a stroll in the garden. Thoroughly refreshed after the hot ofuro, and sometimes even a steam bath or sauna, a kan'pai over a nice cold beer would be ideal if the meal has not yet arrived. Otsumami *snacks and appetizers* and various drinks are available in the small refrigerators provided in each room. The maids keep track of what has been consumed, or the guest can submit a list when he pays for the services as he leaves. At some hotels, the small refrigerators are computerized, and as soon as one takes any object out, it is automatically computed at the front desk. In most cases, services are readily available for the guests.

Meals. A ryokan usually provides breakfast and dinner, which are included in the bill. Most of the time, these meals are served in each room, but sometimes, one must go to a hall where the food is served.

The menu is usually left up to the ryokan where meals are prepared according to what is seasonally available and according to what is the specialty of that particular area. Guests can learn a lot about the area and the food from the maid as she serves the food. The meal usually tastes especially good after a refreshing ofuro!

The Japanese attempt to create a microcosmic world of nature in their own homes. As discussed earlier, union with nature is sought even in the consumption of food. This holistic and aesthetic experience allows one to temporarily return to the natural setting of which man is a part, and draw energy from it. To the Japanese people, the concept of relaxation is intimately connected to returning to the natural condition.

Kotatsu. Unlike Western hotels, a ryokan may not have central heating or air conditioning. However, there are two ways of staying warm during cold winters. One way is to take a long, hot bath which will keep the body warm for the next few hours. Another is to sit in a kotatsu which the ryokan provides. The traditional kotatsu is like sitting at a Western table and chair, except the chair is the tatami floor, and the table is a low wooden frame placed over a pit dug exactly the same size as the frame. Traditionally, a live charcoal fire is placed in the pit to keep the people's legs warm. It is relatively safe from fire hazards. A warm futon *thick quilt* covers the top of the frame extending far enough to cover the lower body of everybody sitting at the kotatsu (Japan 1973:37). An additional square table top is placed on the frame and futon to prevent the futon from sliding and to create a flat surface to use as a table. (Live charcoal is generally not used anymore. Electric kotatsu or small portable heaters are placed inside the pit. Recently, since most homes do not have pits dug out in the floors, the kotatsu is just a low table with the futon to cover one's folded legs.) The kotatsu is an ideal place at which to eat, study, read, talk, and even conduct business. Since the modern ryokan provides television sets, watching T.V. while sitting at a kotatsu is comfortable also. During the cold winters, the kotatsu becomes the center of all activity and it becomes difficult to leave it.

Toilets. Although flush toilets are not traditional in Japanese houses, a ryokan is likely to have them. However, there are two types of flush toilets, one is the Japanese squatting type and the other is the Western sitting type. Unless the ryokan receives many foreign visitors, it will probaby have the Japanese squat-ting-type flush toilets. Since the Japanese people are accustomed to getting up and down from the floor, the squatting position is very natural for them. West-ern sitting-style toilets were very unnatural for the Japanese at first. The Japa-nese people also do not hygienically appreciate the sitting-style toilets since

212

every user sits on the same seat. For these reasons, the Western-style toilets are often left unused in public places like train stations, even though they are provided. Most hotels, Western or Japanese, provide both styles of toilet.

Sleeping on the floor. Traditionally there were no beds in a Japanese house. Every day the **futon** would be folded and put up in a closet. At a **ryokan**, the maid comes in every evening to prepare the **futon** and every morning to put it up in the closet. In this way, the **tatami** room serves as living room, dining room, and bedroom. The Japanese people have developed a lifestyle that efficiently utilizes limited available space. This ability to efficiently use space is typical of an agrarian people who attempt to get the maximum yield from a limited area. This ability in the Japanese people, as stated earlier, can be observed in their **makunouchi ben'too**, as well as their ingenuity in creating compact and portable objects out of complex mechanisms.

Although Western beds are becoming increasingly common in Japanese homes, most people still prefer to sleep on a **futon**. Some people use the Western bed frame and put a **futon** on it. Even in a warm place like Hawaii, Japanese **futon** are imported because of the large Japanese and Japanese-American population.

At night, when everything is quiet in the **ryokan**, one can hear the stream outside. In autumn, the singing of insects can be heard outside. One may hear the rustling of leaves and the wind, if the **ryokan** is located in the mountains. All these sounds of nature lull the guests into a peaceful slumber.

In the morning, an **ohayoo gozaimasu** will be heard from beyond the **shooji**. And once the guest is awake, the maid will come in and put the **futon** in the closet and tidy up the room. While the guest washes up in the bathroom down the corridor, the table is set and the room is transformed once again into a dining room where breakfast is served. Breakfast usually consists of **gohan** *steamed rice,* **omisoshiru** *miso soup* with **toofu** *bean curd,* **nori** *dried seaweed,* **namatamago** *raw egg,* **yakizakana** *hot broiled fish,* **takuwan** *pickled radish,* **umeboshi** *pickled plum,* and **ocha** *green tea.* Since two square meals are included in a stay at a **ryokan**, the charges are often higher than at a Western hotel. Depending upon the **ryokan** and its location, the cost runs from around 10,000 yen on upwards (as of 1984). In addition, a 15 to 20 percent service charge is added to the cost. Although entirely optional, an **okokorozuke** (a type of tip) of about 5 percent is given to the maid that took special care. However, unlike a Western tip, the **okokorozuke** is given at the beginning of the guest's stay. It can be given in the form of a gift, rather than money. As mentioned earlier, this tipping system is different from the evaluative Western type; it serves to insure good service and a good human relationship.

Leaving the **ryokan.** How guests are treated upon departure is as important as greeting them at a **ryokan**. With the Japanese emphasis on proper beginnings and endings, the guests are ceremoniously sent off by the maids, the owner of the ryokan, and sometimes even by the elders of the owner's family! They all repeatedly bow and say arigatoo gozaimashita and sayoonara. The shoes the guests took off upon entering are laid out at the gen'kan, sometimes polished at that! A shoe horn is handed over to help the guest put his/her shoes on. Sometimes travel towels, folding fans, or block-printed cotton napkins that bear the insignia of the ryokan are given out as omiyage (Japan, 1973:41).

In this way, the stay at a ryokan ends. If one wants to experience traditional Japanese lifestyle, staying at a ryokan can give a good feeling of it. One can experience, not only traditional Japanese lifestyle but also modern hospitality. There is an old Japanese saying, which translates as *the hand that extends even to an itch* which expresses what service should be. Also, the Japanese people have always said, *guests are the gods,* and therefore they must be served well.

12.8.2　The Ryokan and the Hotel

The ryokan also has its weak points as compared to a Western hotel. One of its weaknesses is that not much privacy can be maintained. Voices from next door can be clearly heard through the fusuma and shooji. This is a major drawback for foreigners wanting to stay at a ryokan, since they highly value privacy. Nowadays, however, inns with individual, compartmentalized rooms and increased privacy have begun to be built.

Another weakness lies in the lack of variety in meals. Since the guest does not have much choice as to what he can eat, he may become bored with the food. Many foreigners find that their bodies cannot handle rice every day. Western hotels, on the other hand, provide visitors with a choice of food to eat. In this way, a traveler may find that he prefers the Western-style hotel where individuality is honored and respected, as opposed to a Japanese ryokan. In a hotel, if one does not wish to be disturbed one can just hang the *Do Not Disturb* sign on his door, and privacy can be maintained. Japanese people stay at either a ryokan or a hotel depending upon their needs and the occasion. The existence of both the ryokan and the hotel is important in Japan, where Eastern and Western customs, as well as traditional and modern customs, coexist.

12.8.3　Various Kinds of Hotels

In Japan there are various kinds of hotels. One is called the bijinesu hoteru *business hotel* where mostly businessmen stay during their business trips. Since most of the businessmen use these hotels mainly for sleeping, the rooms are small; each has a small toilet and bathtub adjoining it. However, the services available are just the same as all other hotels. Because of the small space and efficency involved, however, the cost is about half that of the ordinary hotel.

Another kind of hotel is called the rabu hoteru *love hotel* which is oriented toward sexual activities. One can stay at these hotels anywhere from one or two hours to several nights. Often these love hotels are luxuriously furnished. There have been love hotels famous for their revolving beds or gold bathtubs! Interestingly, some foreigners have mistaken these love hotels for massage parlors because the Japanese pronunciation of rabu hoteru sounds like *rub hotel!* Many people prefer not to be noticed entering these hotels. Often the hotels are inconspicuous looking, but one can also find gaudy love hotels, colored pink with glaring neon signs. Very often, the color pink symbolizes sex, and x-rated pornographic films are called pinku eiga. A pink building can immediately be identified as a love hotel. Since love hotels are not available in foreign countries, Japanese tourists often bring prostitutes up to their hotel rooms and problems of robbery occur as a result.

12.8.4 Min'shuku

The Japanese compound min'shuku is made up of the words min for *people* and shuku for *dwelling place*. In other words, the min'shuku is a dwelling for people. A min'shuku is an ordinary home rearranged so that travelers can stay overnight. Since it is relatively inexpensive, staying at a min'shuku is popular among students. People utilize them in summer when they go mountaineering and in winter when they go skiing. Staying at a min'shuku can give one a good idea of how Japanese people in the countryside live. Like the ryokan, a min'shuku also serves breakfast and dinner, usually the local specialties. If one stays at a min'shuku in a fishing village, one is bound to taste fresh fish. Sometimes the owner of the min'shuku will go fishing himself. Most of the time, the min'shuku is even more personalized than a ryokan.

12.8.5 Japanese Sense of Security

Being an island, Japan has always had a natural barrier enabling her to ward off outside enemies. Japan was never occupied by another nation until World War II. (As mentioned earlier, Japan was attacked twice by the Mongols, but both attempts ended in failure.) In some ways, the Japanese people have taken their security for granted. Because of this, and in spite of repeated American demands for Japan to change, its defense budget makes up a relatively small percentage of the overall G.N.P. The lack of concern about defense matters, on the part of the Japanese people, stems from their sense of security. They are often surprised to hear comments of amazement on how Tokyo is one of the safest large cities in the world; such issues hardly seem worthy of comment. Tokyo is said to have a low crime rate as compared to other major cities. Possible explanations for this phenomenon will be discussed in order to understand the behavior of the Japanese people.

Ruth Benedict, the late, well-known American anthropologist, once wrote that Japan was a "culture of shame." Children are brought up with their parents telling them not to do this or that for fear that people will laugh at them. Through such an upbringing, the Japanese people have learned to look at themselves through others' eyes. One's own actions not only affect oneself, but also one's family and immediate ingroup, incurring both shame and honor depending on the situation. The fear of suffering shame prevents many people from committing crimes. In addition to this, since mass communication is extensively developed in Japan, incidents are publicized immediately. In order to "save face," the individual will not commit a crime carelessly.

Unlike the contractual society of America, trust between people is extremely important in Japan. When this trust is violated by some irresponsible act, it is extremely difficult to reestablish any relationship of trust. Thus, mass media, as they are structured in Japan, might contribute to Japan's low crime rate. There is a tacit understanding that trust between people is the fundamental element in conducting business and other affairs. According to one statistic, most Japanese people consider themselves to be members of the middle class. Because of this, they feel that there are not too many poverty-stricken people, and that a normal standard of living can be maintained without taking drastic measures such as committing a crime.

Japan's strict arms control laws also contribute to its low crime rate, as does its unique police system. There are several **kooban** *small police stations* in a city, where criminal, as well as neighborhood, problems are dealt with and resolved. The policemen are often considered part of the community and their assistance is available at all times.

We have discussed various sources of the Japanese people's sense of security. Because they travel abroad with this sense of security, they often end up in terrible trouble. For example, they may go to the restroom after arriving at a hotel, and leave their baggage in the lobby, only to find it gone upon their return. Or they may visit their neighbor in the hotel, leaving their door unlocked for several minutes, only to find their valuables stolen during their absence. Because Japanese people carry cash, they are often easy targets for theft.

Japanese women are especially vulnerable to crimes such as rape because they are not accustomed to protecting themselves from dangers. Because of the strong concept of haji *shame,* many cases of rape go unreported. Conductors of Japanese tours have to warn and advise their travelers on aspects of safety and security.

If a crime occurs in a hotel, Japanese travelers expect some responsibility to be assumed by the hotel. This responsibility often takes the form of emotional support, in addition to monetary compensation. The value of emotional support depends on the amount of sincerity expressed by the responsible party. This sincerity takes the form of an apology. Even if the hotel is not responsible, it must begin by apologizing. Sincerity can be felt when a genuine apology is expressed. When the victim realizes the sincerity in the apology, he comes to accept the situation with some degree of satisfaction. In Japan, the act of apologizing creates an emotional tie between people. The resolution of conflict cannot begin without this emotional tie between the two parties. At times, a criminal will be forgiven and can die in peace if he admits his guilt. He will be remembered not simply as a criminal, but also as an essentially good person who, for some personal reason, committed a crime.

However, the Japanese interpretation of an apology does not necessarily transfer to other cultures. For example, in America the court interprets an apology to be an admission of guilt and the sentence is pronounced accordingly. A person who admits to being guilty will automatically be held responsible for any damages. Therefore, an apology is the last thing one should utter in one's own defense. In Japanese courts, an apology will often go a long way toward reducing the terms of a sentence. Even such a seemingly simple act as an apology is subject to vast differences in interpretation and consequence depending on the culture.

If there is a robbery at an American hotel, the manager might apologize by saying "Our hotel cannot assume responsibility for this unfortunate occurrence. Therefore, we are sorry that we cannot do anything about it." Japanese tourists would find such a response extremely cold and insensitive compared to the Japanese hotel's apology which might be "We are sorry that you have experienced such inconvenience at our hotel." There is a difference in emphasis between the two apologies. The American apology refers to the fact that the hotel cannot do anything about the matter. The problem lies in the guest's hands, and not in those of the hotel. The Japanese apology refers to the fact that the guest has been greatly inconvenienced and that the hotel is expressing its sympathy.

When one delves further into the problems of security, one begins to realize the underlying cultural values which affect such problems. In order to resolve cross-cultural problems, underlying cultural values must be understood.

12.9 JAPANESE MODE OF COMMUNICATION

"Skin to Skin" Communication

The ofuro *bath* is an indispensable part of Japanese life. As mentioned earlier, the ofuro serves the utilitarian purpose of keeping one clean as well as providing pure enjoyment. When people go to an on'sen *hot springs,* they take baths several times a day for enjoyment. Some people sing in the baths, while others socialize. The ofuro serves a communal function. Traditionally, the ofuro was a place at which the villagers of both sexes and all ages gathered together following a day of hard work to discuss the happenings of the day.

Communal bathing, mixing men and women, can rarely be found nowadays, however. Nevertheless, segregated communal baths are still quite common, although the numbers are decreasing as more people install baths in their private homes. Even in private homes, baths are often taken together by parents and children who wash each others' backs. In this way, a skin-to-skin contact is maintained which is called communication by "skinship." This word was coined in analogy to the English word *kinship* and incorporated into the Japanese vocabulary. Sometimes "skinship" may be misinterpreted to include sexual connotations, but this is not a true meaning of the word at all. This "skinship" mode of communication is used to describe a close mother-child relationship. It is generally believed that "skinship" is necessary especially for the healthy emotional growth of the child.

On'sen *hot springs* are often chosen for annual company recreation trips. The company employees stay at a large ryokan and enjoy en'kai. They participate in "nomination" *communication through drinking* and in furo communication while sitting naked in the hot springs. A junior employee takes this chance to wash the backs of his seniors in the company, thus establishing sukin'shippu communication. Employees may even experience the rare opportunity of enjoying close communication with the company president at such locations. A much closer relationship can be established between workers through such "skinship" communication.

12.10 LANGUAGE AND CULTURE

A. Hai, nan deshoo ka?

Japanese people often begin their comments by using the word, hai. This hai does not necessarily indicate an English *yes*. In some cases, hai provides a pause before the actual comment itself. This pause is called ma and is an important part of conversation with a Japanese person. The expression Nan deshoo ka? *(What can I help you with?)* without the hai can sound too harsh and direct. The pause created by the hai softens the entire expression. In situations where the motive of the second party is very clear, one can just say Hai. For example, if a guest comes to a hotel desk, the receptionist can just say hai, alone.

The Japanese people also often use hai, along with a nod, to indicate that they are listening to the conversation. Even when a Japanese person understands and speaks English quite well, he or she may nod his or her head indicating, Yes, yes. However, this is often interpreted to mean *Yes, I understand*.

B. desu ga . . .
. . . kedo . . .

Japanese utterances often end in a subordinate clause. When both speaker and listener understand each other, the full sentence does not need to be said.

There are occasions when the use of a compelte sentence not only may sound awkward but may also seem offensive to the listener. Thus at times, one must sense the speaker's hidden intention, just by hearing only the subordinate clause ending with . . . desu ga . . . and/or . . . kedo. . . . In these cases, one knows that the speaker's responses are most likely negative. One puts the speaker in an awkward position if one waits for him or her to complete the sentence on such occasions.

C. Kusuriya

Kusuriya refers to stores selling medicines exclusively. (Sometimes supermarkets carry some medicine in a corner.) Therefore, *drug store* doesn't mean the same thing in Japan as in America. All pharmaceutical items are called kusuri *medicine; drugs* (or doraggu, as they are sometimes referred to today) usually mean marijuana and other narcotics. It may clarify the situation to say that there is a drug store in a kusuriya.

D. Anoo

This expression is often used at the beginning of a sentence in order to get attention. Like the expression hai it creates a pause in order to soften a more direct statement. Sometimes this expression can be translated as *Excuse me* . . .

12.11   CULTURE QUESTIONS

1. In the Culture Orientation, the Japanese concept that *guests are gods* at a ryokan was discussed. What kinds of behavior can be expected from a Japanese tourist at a foreign hotel because he is accustomed to Japanese forms of personalized service? Discuss the possible behavior of Japanese tourists at the front desk and in other situations.

2. Japanese bath customs were briefly described in the culture orientation. Discuss how Japanese customs and the customs of your country differ and explore some of the possible problems which may occur at a hotel due to the difference. Discuss further how you can cope with these problems with cultural sensitivity.

3. Having read the discussion on the Japanese idea of security, discuss what your country's ideas are. How are those ideas and values reflected in places like hotels?

12.12 SUGGESTED RESOURCE MATERIALS

12.12.1 Books and Magazines

Japanese Inn, Oliver Statler (Honolulu: University of Hawaii Press, 1982).
"The Japanese Inn," Neill Peter, *Winds* 6, no. 10 (March, 1985): 40–43.
The Japanese and the Jews, Isaiah Ben-dasan (New York: Weatherhill), pp. 3–25.

12.12.2 Films (16 mm) and Video Cassettes (Beta / VHS)

"A Cultural Journey into Japan." 27 mins. Color. Japan National Tourist Organization, 1980.

12.13 REFERENCE

Japan. New York: A Sunset Travel Book, 1973.

LESSON 13

INTERACTING WITH TOURISTS

13.1   USEFUL EXPRESSIONS

Ii oten'ki desu nee.	It's nice weather, isn't it?
Dochira kara irasshaimashita ka?	Where are you from?
Okuni wa doko desu ka?	Where is your hometown?
Guruupu de irasshaimashita ka?	Did you come with a group?
Kojin ryokoo desu ka?	Are you traveling alone?
Shin'kon ryokoo desu ka?	(Is this your) honeymoon trip?
Kan'koo ryokoo desu.	It is a sightseeing trip.
Ashita no goyotei wa?	What is your schedule tomorrow?
Watakushi, shihainin no Uchida desu.	I am Mr. Uchida, the manager.
Shitsurei shimashita.	I'm sorry for my rudeness.
	Excuse me. (*after* you do something)
Shitsurei shimasu.	Excuse me. (*before* you do something)
Tanoshiku osugoshi kudasai.	Have a good time.
Mata ato de.	See you later.

13.2   CONVERSATION

13.2.1   In the Lobby

Situation: A hotel manager approaches a female hotel guest who is relaxing in the lobby.

Shihainin: Yoku irasshaimashita. Watakushi wa kono hoteru no shihainin no John Smith desu. Dochira kara irasshaimashita ka?

Kyaku: Yamaguchi-ken kara desu.

Shihainin: Soredewa, Hawai ni goshin'seki no kata ga irasshaimasu ka?

Kyaku: Ee, oba ga imashite, kinoo aimashita.

Shihainin: Soo desu ka? Sore wa yokatta desu nee. Hawai wa hajimete desu ka?

Kyaku: Ee, hajimete desu.
Shihainin: Hawai wa doo desu ka?
Kyaku: Sora mo umi mo kirei de, hon'too ni subarashii tokoro desu nee.
Shihainin: Ashita wa don'na goyotei desu ka?
Kyaku: Hanauma Bei e iku tsumori desu.
Shihainin: Doozo tanoshiku osugoshi kudasai. Shitsurei shimashita.
Kyaku: Doomo arigatoo.

Manager: Hello. My name is John Smith, and I am the manager of this hotel.
         Where are you from?
Guest: From Yamaguchi Province.
Manager: Ah, do you have any relatives here in Hawaii?
Guest: Yes, I have an aunt whom I met yesterday.
Manager: Is that right? How nice. Is this your first trip to Hawaii?
Guest: Yes, it's my first trip here.
Manager: How do you like it?
Guest: The sky and sea are beautiful. It is really a splendid place.
Manager: What do you plan to do tomorrow?
Guest: I think I'll go to Hanauma Bay.
Manager: Please have a good time. Excuse me.
Guest: Thank you.

13.2.2   In the Cocktail Lounge

Kyaku: Mai Tai o moo ippai kudasai.
Ueitoresu: Doozo. Okyaku-sama wa okuni wa dochira desu ka?
Kyaku: Kyooto desu. Kyooto e itta koto ga arimasu ka?
Ueitoresu: Hai. Kookoo no toki, tenisu no guruupu to ikimashita. Ii tokoro
           desu nee, Kyooto wa.
Kyaku: Hawai to Kyooto to dochira no hoo ga ii desu ka?
Ueitoresu: Kuraberu no wa muzukashii desu kedo, watakushi wa fuyu ni
           wa Hawai ga suki desu.
Kyaku: Kikoo ga ii desu kara nee, Hawai wa.
Ueitoresu: Soredewa goyukkuri.
Kyaku: Doomo. Mata ato de . . .

Guest: May I have another Mai Tai please.
Waitress: Here you are. What country are you from, sir?
Guest: I'm from Kyoto city. Have you been there?
Waitress: Yes. When I was in high school, our tennis group went there. It's
          really a nice place, isn't it, Kyoto?
Guest: Which do you prefer, Hawaii or Kyoto?
Waitress: It's hard to compare, but in the winter, I like Hawaii better.
Guest: The climate is nice here in Hawaii, isn't it?
Waitress: Enjoy yourself.
Guest: Thank you. See you again.

222

13.3 VOCABULARY

Nouns

aki	fall
fuyu	winter
haru	spring
hon'too	true, real
imooto	younger sister
itoko	cousin
kazoku	family
ken	prefecture
kikoo	climate
kootoogakkoo, kookoo	senior high school
kuni	country, hometown
mago	grandchild
mei	niece
musuko	son
musume	daughter
natsu	summer
neesan, ane	older sister
niisan, ani	older brother
obaasan, sobo	grandmother
obasan, oba	aunty
oi	nephew
ojisan, oji	uncle
okaasan, haha	mother
okusan, kanai	wife
on'gaku	music
otoosan, chichi	father
otooto	younger brother
shin'seki	relative
shujin	husband
shuu	state
sora	sky
supootsu	sports
ten'ki	weather
tsumori	intention, plan
yotei	schedule

Verbs

aimasu	to meet
kurabemasu	to compare
sumimasu	to live

Adjectives

hiroi	wide

13.4 EXPLANATION

13.4.1 Family Terms

	Exalting or Honorific	Humble	Terms of Address
	Used when referring to other's family	Used when speaking about one's own family	Used directly to addressee
family	gokazoku	kazoku	
grandfather	ojiisan	sofu	ojiisan
grandmother	obaasan	sobo	obaasan
father	otoosan	chichi	otoosan
mother	okaasan	haha	okaasan
husband	goshujin	shujin	*first name*, anata
wife	okusan	kanai	*first name*
older brother	oniisan	ani	(o)niisan
older sister	oneesan	ane	(o)neesan
younger brother	otootosan	otooto	*first name*
younger sister	imootosan	imooto	*first name*
son	musukosan	musuko	*first name*
daughter	musumesan, ojoosan	musume	*first name*
uncle	ojisan	oji	ojisan
aunt	obasan	oba	obasan
cousin	oitokosan	itoko	
nephew	oigosan	oi	
niece	meigosan	mei	
grandchild	omagosan	mago	*first name*

Examples:

Taeko: Odekake desu ka?
Ken: Ee, chotto ani no tokoro made . . .
Taeko: Ken-san no oniisan wa kono hen ni sun'de irasshaimasu no?
Ken: Ee. Sobo to issho ni sun'de imasu.
Taeko: Soo desu ka?

Taeko: Are you going out?
Ken: Yes, just over to my older brother's place.
Taeko: Does your older brother live around here?
Ken: Yes. He lives with my grandmother.
Taeko: Is that right?

13.4.2 V (plain form) + { no / koto } (Verb nominalization)

Kuraberu no wa muzukashii desu.   It is difficult to compare.

The no after the plain form of a verb is a nominalizer meaning *act*. No is always preceded by a noun modifier, and **kuraberu no** is a nominative equivalent to *to compare, comparison,* or *comparing*.

Examples:

Biichi de oyogu no ga suki desu.   I like swimming at the beach.
Tomodachi to issho ni ryokoo   Traveling with a friend is enjoyable.
    suru no wa tanoshii desu ne.

Nominalization of a verb is also formed by using **koto** after the plain form of a verb.

Examples:

Kuraberu koto wa muzukashii desu.   It is difficult to compare.
Iu koto wa yasashii desu.   It is easy to say.

The nominalizers no and koto are similar in function and meaning, and they are sometimes interchangeable. However, koto cannot be replaced by no in the potential pattern of . . . koto ga dekimasu (see 9.4.4).

13.4.3 N1 to N2 to (de) / (dewa) { dochira (no hoo) / dotchi (no hoo) } ga { A desu ka? / AN desu ka? } (Comparison)

Which is more, N1 or N2?

Examples:

Hawai to Kyooto to dochira no hoo   Which is better, Hawaii or Kyoto?
    ga ii desu ka?
Ten'pura to sashimi to dotchi ga suki   Which do you like better, tempura or
    desu ka?   sashimi?
Tookyoo to Kyooto to dochira ga ii   Which is better, Tokyo or Kyoto?
    desu ka?

The word dotchi is an informal alternative of dochira meaning *which one of the two.*

A reply to the above question is usually made in one of the following ways:

. . . ga . . . desu.
. . . no hoo ga . . . desu.

Oahu shima to Hawai shima to dochira (no hoo) ga ookii desu ka?	Which is bigger, the island of Oahu or Hawaii?
Hawai shima ga ookii desu. (or Hawai shima no hoo ga ookii) desu.)	The island of Hawaii is bigger.

13.4.4 Other Comparison Patterns

1. | N1 wa N2 yori { adjective / adjective noun } desu. | (N1 is more . . . than N2)

Yori is a particle meaning *(more) than*.

Nihon no kuni wa Kariforunia shuu yori chiisai desu.
Japan is smaller than California.

Hawai wa hoka no shuu yori atatakai desu.
Hawaii is warmer than other states.

2. | N1 wa N2 hodo negative predicate | (N1 is not as . . . as N2)

Nihon wa Kariforunia hodo hiroku arimasen.
Japan is not as large as California.

Kono hoteru wa ano hoteru hodo kirei ja arimasen.
This hotel is not as pretty as that hotel.

13.4.5 | V (dictionary form) / V (plain negative form) } + tsumori { desu. / deshita. }

(One intends to do such and such)

Hanauma Bei e iku tsumori desu means *I intend to go to Hanauma Bay*. The tsumori is a dependent nominative meaning *intention* or *plan*. It is always preceded by a noun modifier (usually the dictionary form or the plain negative form of a verb).

When deshita is used after tsumori, the implication usually is that a person had the intention of doing such and such in the past but failed to do it.

226

Examples:

Ashita wa tomodachi ni au tsumori desu.	I plan to meet my friend tomorrow.
Yamada-san ni wa awanai tsumori desu.	I will not meet Mr. Yamada.
Kawanai tsumori deshita ga yasukatta kara kaimashita.	Although I did not plan to buy it, I bought it because it was cheap.

13.4.6 | **N1 to N2 o kurabemasu.**
N1 to N2 to kurabemasu. | **(Comparing N1 with N2)**

Kurabemasu is a transitive verb, which may take an object, meaning *to compare.* Some predicates that relate to two or more items or persons are used as follows:

N1 to N2 wa $\begin{cases} \text{onaji desu.} \\ \text{chigaimasu.} \end{cases}$ N1 and N2 are $\begin{cases} \text{the same.} \\ \text{different.} \end{cases}$

N1 to N2 to $\begin{cases} \text{onaji desu.} \\ \text{chigaimasu.} \end{cases}$ N1 is $\begin{cases} \text{the same as} \\ \text{different from} \end{cases}$ N2.

N1 to N2 $\begin{cases} \text{ga} \\ \text{wa} \end{cases}$ kekkon shimasu.   N1 and N2 will get married.

N1 to N2   to   kekkon shimasu.   N1 will marry N2.

13.5   DRILLS

13.5.1   Transformation Drill

Transform each of the following sentences into nominalized verbs and substitute them in the pattern sentence.

Tookyoo ni sumu no wa suki ja arimasen.

1. Nyuu Yooku ni sumimasu.
   Nyuu Yooku ni sumu no wa suki ja arimasen.

2. Shigoto o shimasu.
   Shigoto o suru no wa suki ja arimasen.

3. Nihon'go de hanashimasu.
   Nihon'go de hanasu no wa suki ja arimasen.

4. Fune ni norimasu.
   Fune ni noru no wa suki ja arimasen.

5. Omiyage-ten de hatarakimasu.
   Omiyage-ten de hataraku no wa suki ja arimasen.

6. Arubaito o shimasu.
   Arubaito o suru no wa suki ja arimasen.

7. Osake o nomimasu.
   Osake o nomu no wa suki ja arimasen.

8. Gakkoo o yasumimasu.
   Gakkoo o yasumu no wa suki ja arimasen.

9. Shachoo ni aimasu.
   Shachoo ni au no wa suki ja arimasen.

13.5.2 Question–Answer Drill

Produce questions by comparing the following sets of items. Use the pattern: *Which is more . . . , A or B?* Then reply to each of the questions using the second item in each set.

Example: on'gaku   supootsu
         Q: On'gaku to supootsu to dotchi ga suki desu ka?
         A: Supootsu ga suki desu.

1. jazu   kurashikku
   Q: Jazu to kurashikku to dotchi ga suki desu ka?
   A: Kurashikku ga suki desu.

2. rajio   terebi
   Q: Rajio to terebi to dotchi ga suki desu ka?
   A: Terebi ga suki desu.

3. Tookyoo   Kyooto
   Q: Tookyoo to Kyooto to dotchi ga suki desu ka?
   A: Kyooto ga suki desu.

4. haru   aki
   Q: Haru to aki to dotchi ga suki desu ka?
   A: Aki ga suki desu.

5. fuyu   natsu
   Q: Fuyu to natsu to dotchi ga suki desu ka?
   A: Natsu ga suki desu.

6. hikooki   fune
   Q: Hikooki to fune to dotchi ga suki desu ka?
   A: Fune ga suki desu.

7. San Furan'shisuko   Nyuu Yooku
   Q: San Furan'shisuko to Nyuu Yooku to dotchi ga suki desu ka?
   A: Nyuu Yooku ga suki desu.

13.5.3 Question–Answer Drill

Each student asks his/her partner what he or she is going to do today, and the partner replies.

Example:
Q: Kyoo nani o suru tsumori desu ka?
A: Hon o yomu tsumori desu.

13.6 EXERCISES

13.6.1 Translation

Express the following ideas in Japanese.

1. How many people are there in your family?
2. My mother and I are planning to take a trip.
3. Is your older brother living with you?
4. Which is harder, Japanese or French?
5. I like a hotel more than a Japanese inn.
6. I am not as good as Mr. Smith in speaking Japanese.
7. It is not easy to sing with karaoke.
8. Surfing is more interesting than swimming.
9. Will you attend tonight's party?
10. Which is more quiet, that hotel or this hotel?

13.6.2 Questions and Answers

Compare two items in the classroom. Prepare questions and answers regarding the items.

Example:
Q: Watakushi no hon to Yamada-san no hon to, dotchi no hoo ga atarashii desu ka?
A: Yamada-san no hon (no hoo) ga atarashii desu.

13.6.3 Situational Practice

Make comparisons concerning Japanese inns and Western hotels.

Examples:
1. Hoteru wa ryokan yori ookii desu.
2. Hoteru no furo wa ryokan no furo hodo ookiku arimasen.

13.7 SIMULATION AND SKITS

1. Two friends who have traveled to different countries are comparing the places they have traveled to.

2. You have just met a friend whom you haven't seen in a long time. Ask about each other's family using the appropriate family terms.

3. Two friends are discussing their plans for the summer vacation. They intend to do such things as work part-time or full-time, and go to summer school.

4. A hotel manager approaches a hotel guest in the lobby and carries on a "small talk" conversation with her.

5. As a hotel guard, interact with a guest standing near you, telling him what kinds of things are fun to do in Hawaii. Use the verb nominalizers **no** and **koto** in your conversation.

13.8 CULTURE ORIENTATION

13.8.1 Changing Trends in Japanese Overseas Travel

Over the past two decades, Japan's rapid economic growth has stimulated changes in lifestyles and consumer preferences. These changes have brought about changes in the Japanese international travel industry as well.

"The Emergence of New Japanese Travelers" is a film produced by Shozo Noda of Jetour, Inc. (presented at the Fifth Annual Conference on Japan-Hawaii Travel, Honolulu, February, 1984). It presents an analogy which categorizes Japanese overseas travel into four different stages: (1) 1964–1967—the birth, (2) 1968–1971—infancy, (3) 1972–1979—growth, (4) 1980–present—adolescence.

During the period of birth, from 1964 to 1967, only the rich could afford to travel abroad.

From 1968 to 1971, during its infancy, overseas travel was popularized by the introduction of the jumbo jet. However, to travel abroad was still considered a status symbol.

During the period of growth, from 1972 to 1979, the number of overseas travelers tripled, primarily due to a sharp decrease in airfares and an increase in disposable income. Another factor was the lifting of foreign currency restrictions.

The adolescent stage, 1980–present, has experienced continued growth in overseas travel, brought about by the growing diversity of consumer tastes and changes in the structure of the overseas travel market.

The following tables of figures give a good indication of the trends in Japanese overseas travel.

Japanese Visitors to Hawaii
From 1979 to 1984

	1979	1980	1981	1982	1983	1984
Japanese	653,600	658,100	690,400	715,000	729,000	816,000
Total Visitors	3,960,000	3,935,000	3,935,000	4,243,000	4,368,105	4,855,580
Japanese Percentage of Total	16.5	16.7	17.5	16.9	16.7	16.8

Source: State of Hawaii, Dept. of Planning and Economic Development, *State of Hawaii, Data Book, 1985*

Ten Selected Countries
Most Visited By Japanese
1982

Destination	Number Visiting
United States (including Hawaii and Guam)	1,220,000
(Hawaii)	(718,000)
Taiwan	575,686
Korea	518,013
Hong Kong	515,697
Singapore	378,501
(Guam)	(264,440)
Switzerland	244,449
Thailand	225,557
Macau	168,955
Philippines	159,918
Canada	139,447

Source: World Tourism Organization, Pacific Area Travel Association, Organization for Economic Cooperation and Development, and national tourist offices in Tokyo.

In 1982, the total number of Japanese overseas travelers was 4,086,138, a 14.8 percent increase from 1978. There has been a marked growth in overseas travel among women in their twenties and people in their fifties and sixties.

There was a 52.8 percent increase in women in their twenties traveling abroad. These women are generally unmarried office workers who live with their parents; therefore, their disposable income for leisure activities is large. They are called **dokushin kizoku** *privileged singles* or literally *single noble class.*

There was a 46.7 percent increase in women in their fifties and sixties and a 21 percent increase in men in their fifties and sixties traveling abroad. These people tend to be relatively secure financially, having attained their career goals. And they generally prefer to spend their retirement years enjoying various leisure-time activities. This age group is identified by the term shirubaa maaketto *silver market.*

On the other hand, overseas travel by men in their thirties and forties has leveled off and is beginning to decline. Thus, in the coming years, women in their twenties (dokushin kizoku), and people in their fifties and sixties (shirubaa maaketto), will be increasingly important target groups for the travel industry.

In the past, Japanese society has been termed as taishuu shakai, which simply means *mass society.* Recently, a new word has been coined to describe the changing nature of Japanese society. This new word is bun'shuu shakai *(society of divided masses).* It purports to mean that Japanese society is no longer made up of a generalized mass but of a multitude of people with different faces and needs. This expression bun'shuu, being used in the business world, implies that the recognition of individual differences in needs and taste is essential for business success. The travel industry is no exception. For example, until now, people traveling abroad had little to do with arranging and planning their trips. Today, overseas travelers are more closely involved with every stage of the planning. They are tailoring their trips to suit their lifestyles. Curiosity about life in other countries has contributed to their desire to travel abroad. They are interested in meeting people in other countries and doing more than just seeing the tourist sights. Examples of the variety of overseas travel enjoyed today include trips designed to watch and participate in sports activities, or to sample local culture and enjoy different food. These overseas trips satisfy the tastes and desires of the individual traveler.

Today, the concern of Japanese people is focused less on material gratification and more on emotional fulfillment. Thus, their interest in intangible forms of gratification, such as travel, has grown. And with a recovery of personal consumption projected in the near future, and an increase in leisure hours, further growth of overseas travel by the Japanese is also anticipated.

13.8.2 The Japanese and Group Travel

Recall an earlier discussion of travel in Lesson 11. Since childhood, Japanese people are required to travel; children are required to travel at least once a year during school from the first grade to the last year of senior high school. Younger children take one-day excursions called en'soku. But from junior high onwards, overnight trips of several days (sometimes as long as 10 days), called shuugaku ryokoo, are taken. Nowadays there are schools that even take their students abroad for these shuugaku ryokoo.

Most of these en'soku or shuugaku ryokoo are in the fall or spring when the climate is suitable for traveling. During these seasons, one cannot get away from hoards of students everywhere in Japan. Crowds of them can be found at tourist attractions and train and bus stations. Under these circumstances, individual movement is difficult as the students always travel in large groups. A bus guide, carrying a flag with the school name on it, leads a group of students. To some foreigners, they may look like a small unit of soldiers marching in uniform.

Such excursions do not end for most people, even after high school. Once a person joins a company, annual recreational trips are taken, with expenses covered by the company. These trips, called ian'ryokoo, are for recreation as well as to solidify group spirit among the employees, as was discussed earlier. Thus, Japanese are accustomed to traveling in large groups, as is easily observed in the case of Japanese tourists traveling abroad.

A trip teaches many things to the traveling student. One by-product of traveling in a large group is the sense of mutual accomplishment and the group spirit that naturally grows out of the experience. Actually trips taken by company employees are recreational only in theory; the real purpose lies in the creation of solidarity. With such a purpose in mind, the value of the excursion lies, not in where the trip was made, but simply in the experience of traveling together. For most people, the enjoyment comes from the latter, not the former. This can immediately be understood if one joins a bus chartered by such a group. The travelers enjoy drinking sake and singing together using the microphone and **karaoke** system installed in the bus. (**Karaoke** is a stereo system that produces the melody of songs to assist the singer.) Once they arrive at the **ryokan**, they begin their **en'kai**, enjoying themselves by drinking, eating, and singing together. It is important for Japanese people to share experiences by doing something together. Because of this, individual travel or family excursions are not as popular as group travel. This contrasts with the American and European independent traveling nature (Kato 1971:147–149).

13.8.3   Rituals of Adulthood and Japanese Overseas Travel

In the villages of Japan, the traditional ritual marking attainment of adulthood for boys consisted of completing a difficult climb atop a mountain such as Fuji or Ontake. This ritual complemented the Shinto worship of sacred mountains. A boy was considered a man if he could complete this difficult climb. During the middle of the Edo period, this was changed slightly so that the boys were expected to visit the sacred Ise Shrine. This custom was continued until the Second World War when elementary school children were taken to the Ise Shrine for their **shuugaku ryokoo**.

Although it appears the Japanese people have lost this "sacred" place in recent years, one can say that every interest group has their own "sacred" place or is in the process of establishing one. For example, the city of Kyoto holds a high ranking among Japanese tourists. For overseas tourists, Paris, New York, and even Hawaii seem to be sacred places. For that matter, there is a sense of novelty and "sacredness" in the mere concept of *overseas*. Just as failure to visit Ise Shrine brought shame at one time, not going abroad at least once in one's lifetime is a failure to participate in an important ritual in the life of a modern youth today. However, the difference between going to Ise Shrine as a pilgrimage in order to become an adult and going overseas as part of fulfilling one of life's goals is that the latter has become more the business of women than of men. Many single women work for about two or three years and then go abroad, using part of their pre-marriage savings to finance the trip. An increasing number of women feel that the opportunity for overseas travel becomes very limited after marriage. If traveling abroad is taken as a secularized form of the rite of passage for young people, the opportunity to attain adulthood would seem to be more open today to women than to men. But the honeymoon abroad in some sense offers both husband and wife an equal opportunity to make the pilgrimage and to undergo the rite of passage (Kato 1982:22–26).

13.8.4   The Philosophy of Pilgrimage and the Japanese Group Tour

The concept of the sightseeing tour is only about 150 or 160 years old, originating in England in the 1800s and in France during the 1840s. It is said that Thomas Cook, in the 19th century, established a sightseeing tour that was not religious in nature. Until then, all tours had been religious in nature.

It is also said that Alcoholics Anonymous established group tours for its members at this time. They reasoned that visiting beautiful areas and historic sites would compensate for giving up the habit of drinking alcohol (Tada 1981:121–122).

In Japan, too, travel was once mostly for religious purposes. Visiting places such as Koyasan and Ise Shrine was for the purpose of making a pilgrimage. However, these pilgrimages were slowly secularized. The idea of visiting various places along the way developed from the belief that more merits could be achieved if one visited and prayed at various shrines and temples. Even now, there are famous courses taken by group tours or individual travelers that stop at various shrines and temples. Many of these pilgrimage routes are now the courses taken by group tours. Many people are satisfied and feel a sense of security by traveling along these standardized routes. This tendency is not limited to domestic travel but also extends to travel abroad. Many of the tours abroad for Japanese tourists are highly organized, standard tours, reminding one of an assembly line. It is possible that Japanese people experience increased satisfaction whenever an additional site is added to their tour schedules, believing that each additional place increases the merits due them. For those that are traveling, the significance lies more in the act of visiting the various places rather than in seeing each place thoroughly. One can almost say that the modern group tours are a contemporary version of the traditional pilgrimage.

Earlier, in Lesson 9, the Japanese knack for assimilating all kinds of cultural and technological knowledge into their own culture, was discussed. The Japanese people also have an uncanny ability to rearrange these foreign elements to accommodate their own needs, in both social and cultural contexts. They are able to simplify and miniaturize when necessary. These special abilities that the Japanese possess were discussed by using the example of the makunouchi ben'too. It can be said that the Japanese group tours also illustrate how these special abilities function. These tours are able to incorporate numerous sites and elements into a compact and efficient course. Today's group tours can be seen as a sort of teishoku dinner, if not a makunouchi ben'too!

Taking another perspective on the Japanese group tours, one can observe that the industrious working schedules of the Japanese people don't allow any more than a few days off for travel. The Japanese are so industrious that they are sometimes seen as workaholics. It is almost a cardinal sin for an employee to take weeks off for vacation while others work. It is no wonder that the Japanese people take short compact group tours. The group tour reflects the lifestyle and the thinking process of the Japanese people.

13.8.5 The Japanese and Foreign Languages

One weak point of the Japanese is learning foreign languages. The various reasons behind this will be discussed with a focus on what form communication with the Japanese people can take.

The Japanese people launched the wakon-yoosai *Japanese spirit/Western knowledge* and technology modernization model right after the Second World War, as discussed earlier. As this process took place, Western knowledge was translated into Japanese with interpretations and nuances to suit Japanese taste. In this way, all sorts of knowledge from around the world was made available in Japanese, translated by those who felt that it was important. In some ways, Japan can be referred to as a "culture of translations." There is a pressing need to learn other languages in order to read and translate foreign texts.

Although Japanese students are required to study English from an early age, it is required largely to support this culture of translation and mainly stresses reading and writing. English is not really taught as a medium of communication. Since Japanese students are required to study English for their entrance examinations, many of them know grammatical rules better than native speakers. However, no matter how well-versed students may be in English grammar, their conversational ability lags far behind. Even those students who study conversational English are said to be rather slow in making progress. One of the reasons is that Japanese do not like to make mistakes which are embarrassing and may cause others to laugh at them. Most shy away from using English until they have considerable fluency. However, few achieve this fluency, and among those who have achieved it, many hesitate to use it for fear of appearing ostentatious and prefer to assume a silent humility instead. The "hammering of nails that protrude" is still very much at work in Japanese society. However, it cannot be denied that an increasing number of young people want to communicate with foreigners despite their errors in English. Some travelers even include this item as one of their travel objectives.

Sometimes these motivated students of English are disappointed when they are answered in Japanese, in response to questions asked in English. It would be considerate on the part of native English speakers to reply in English. If you spot such a motivated Japanese, why not let him/her practice English with you? Displaying such consideration to foreigners trying to learn English is an important aspect in furthering communication.

13.9 JAPANESE MODE OF COMMUNICATION

Japanese Nonverbal Communication

If the Italian people represent one pole in the degree of expressiveness in language, the Japanese people represent the other. Italians are known to be very expressive with their emotions and feelings, using words and facial and physical expressions. Japanese are quite the opposite of Italians. The Japanese language itself lacks adjectives which express many emotions. It is known to be as passive as a noh mask. Hand and body movements are not so heavily used while conversing. However, this does not indicate that the Japanese people are not emotional. On the contrary, Japanese culture heavily emphasizes emotions. But how these emotions are expressed differs greatly from other people, such as Italians. One of the virtues of the samurai class was to avoid outward display of emotions such as happiness, frustration, sorrow, or anger. As children, they were taught to restrain such emotional display.

The Japanese language does not have elaborate means of expressing love. Love is generally not conveyed through verbal expressions, but is something more to be felt. It would seem to be quite a task to be able to express and understand love without verbal or physical expressions. No wonder the Japanese are sometimes referred to by foreigners as the *inscrutable Japanese.*

An old Japanese saying, *Eyes say as much as the mouth,* explains how the Japanese express emotions such as happiness, sorrow, and anger. It is said that peasants used to watch the samurai's eyes when he talked because the emotions and feelings of the samurai could be captured through his eyes.

However, long eye-contact could not be maintained without being disrespectful. Only quick and short glances could be made. Even now, long eye-contact is not common since it makes both parties feel uncomfortable. A person should not maintain long eye-contact with a person senior to him since it is considered disrespectful. Women generally do not maintain long eye-contact with men since they would be perceived as having ulterior motives. As explained previously, elevator and escalator girls are trained to avoid eye-contact with customers. No wonder many foreigners find the Japanese people inscrutable when emotions are expressed through eyes but eye contact is discouraged.

Speaking of inscrutable, there is nothing more mysterious than Japanese laughter. As most people do, the Japanese laugh when they are pleased or when something is funny. Often, however, they also laugh when they are embarrassed or ashamed. If someone falls down while walking and there are others around him, he may laugh while getting up. Most people laugh when they experience failure or make mistakes, instead of expressing anger. This may be understandable to most people. What many people fail to understand is the laughter with which a Japanese person may convey his/her own unhappiness to others.

For example, one may convey the death of their loved one by saying, "Sorry I couldn't make the meeting yesterday. My father suddenly died last night . . . " followed by a slight smile. One way to perceive this would be that it is a cold and unfeeling response, but when one delves further into its meaning, one realizes that it is a way of sparing others from experiencing the same sorrow. It can then be understood to be far from cruel but rather considerate to the other party.

There are certain gestures used besides those made with the eyes. Although many similar gestures are used in different cultures, the meanings are often very different. For example, the gesture for *good-bye* used in America is used to indicate *come here* in Japanese. The American gesture of waving the index finger with the palm of the hand facing upward is insulting if used in Japan, because it is used to call a dog or a cat. In America, when someone points to himself, he may put his hand to his chest. However, in Japan, a person points his finger to his nose when he points to himself. The Japanese people use a fanning motion with the right hand in front of their faces if they don't understand something or are refusing something. This motion may mean that something smells bad in America! When Japanese men are embarrassed or troubled they may scratch the back of their ears. Women often cover their mouths with their hands or tilt their heads to the side. The American *OK* sign indicates money in Japan. The use of similar gestures can cause problems if one does not realize what each one means in a given cultural context. Understanding facial and physical expressions are important in conducting successful communication.

13.10 LANGUAGE AND CULTURE

A. Okuni wa doko desu ka?

When the word okuni is used inside Japan, it indicates hometown rather than country. But when used abroad, it means country, which would mean Japan. Asking an American, "Where is your hometown?" might not seem important or meaningful, since Americans lead such a mobile lifestyle. But in a traditionally agrarian society such as Japan, where mobility was limited and it was characteristic for people to remain in one area throughout their lives, most everybody has a hometown. However, with the development of industry and large cities, many people leave the agricultural areas. Although they leave, they always have a home to return to. It is known in Japan that those who don't have hometowns are people from Tokyo.

When a Japanese asks okuni wa doko desu ka? a consciousness of belonging is expressed. If both the parties' okuni are Hiroshima, an immediate sense of belonging is established. A kind of ingroup is developed where a common factor of okuni is emphasized. This concept of belonging is maintained even if one goes abroad. For example, there are organizations and meetings where people of Japanese ancestry who share a common okuni gather together to reaffirm their sense of belongingness.

B. Shitsurei shimashita

Shitsurei is written in kan'ji to mean *lose one's manners*. Shimashita is the past tense form of shimasu, which means *to do* or *commit*. Therefore, shitsurei shimashita means *I'm sorry for what I did*. If one wants to forewarn someone of rudeness or inconvenience, one says, Shitsurei shimasu. This expression is used when one passes in front of somebody, leaves a party or goes home early, takes someone's time, bumps into sombody, makes a mistake, or inconveniences someone.

Sumimasen, covered earlier, is also an expression of apology. Gomen nasai *Forgive me* is another commonly used expression of apology. Since there are so many expressions of apology, the Japanese people are sometimes thought to be apologetic by nature. However, one must be careful to distinguish between the use of sumimasen as a mere apology and as an appreciative expression meaning *Thank you for your trouble*.

13.11 CULTURE QUESTIONS

1. Many years ago, the State of Hawaii established a slogan, "Open yourself and your home to Japanese visitors," in order to encourage a more personalized atmosphere for Japanese tourists. There was quite a positive reaction within Hawaii, and many people volunteered their hospitality. All the necessary arrangements were made and they waited for Japanese tourists to apply for these services. But, to the disappointment of Hawaii's residents, there were only a handful of Japanese applicants, and the program fizzled out. Having read about the behavioral patterns of the Japanese and their thoughts from various perspectives, discuss what might have been some of the causes of this failure. Why didn't the Japanese tourists enthusiastically sign up for such a program? What kinds of considerations must be made in order to interact with Japanese tourists?

2. The video "The Emergence of New Japanese Travelers," discussed in the Culture Orientation, describes the changing trends in Japanese overseas travel patterns, namely from a group-oriented tour to an individualized tour. In other words, Japanese needs for traveling have been diversified. Identify what diversified needs are emerging, and discuss what sorts of conditions should be made to meet these needs.

3. Japanese people can be characterized as people who gather where there are people and don't go out of their way to visit areas where there aren't many others. With this in mind, what are some points to be considered in order to attract Japanese customers. Think and discuss.

4. Observe the nonverbal communication behavior of the Japanese people. Discuss what gestures you observe. Compare Japanese gestures and facial expressions with those of your own country.

5. There are many rules that go along with the use of gestures. For example, some gestures are used only by men. Discuss whether gestures in your country are influenced by factors such as age, sex, degree of acquaintance, education, time and place, social status, or rank.

13.12 SUGGESTED RESOURCE MATERIALS

13.12.1 Books and Magazines

From Bonsai to Levis, George Fields (New York: Macmillan Co., 1983), pp. 132–149.

Japanese: The Spoken Language in Japanese Life, Osamu Mizutani, trans. by Janet Ashby (Tokyo: The Japan Times, 1981), pp. 38–43.

Japanese Tourists Abroad, Kazuo Nishiyama (Honolulu: International Management Consultant, 1973), pp. 2–17.

Kodansha Encyclopedia of Japan, vol. 6 (Tokyo: Kodansha, 1983), p. 188.

Kodansha Encyclopedia of Japan, vol. 8 (Tokyo: Kodansha, 1983), p. 104.

Mock Joya's Things Japanese, Mock Joya (Tokyo: Tokyo News Service, 1968), pp. 663–664.

13.12.2 Films (16 mm) and Video Cassettes (Beta/VHS)

"The Emergence of New Japanese Travelers." Video. 60 mins. Color. Jetour, Inc., 1984.

"Pilgrimage to the Eighty-eight Sacred Places." Video. 30 mins. Color. Oliver Statler, 1980.

13.13 REFERENCES

Kato, Hidetoshi. *Toshi to Goraku.* Tokyo: Kajima Shuppan Kai, 1971.
———. *Shin Ryokō Yōjinshū.* Tokyo: Chuko Shinsho, 1982.
Tada, Michitaro. *Shinpen no Nihon Bunka.* Tokyo: Kodansha, 1981.

LESSON 14

CHECKING OUT OF THE HOTEL

14.1 USEFUL EXPRESSIONS

Onimotsu o omochi shimashoo.	I will carry your baggage.
Kaikei kaun'taa de oshiharai kudasai.	Please pay it at the cashier's counter.
Kore wa shinai den'wa-ryoo de gozaimasu.	This is the charge for the local calls.
Kore wa kokusai den'wa-ryoo de gozaimasu.	This is the charge for the international calls.
Owasure mono wa gozaimasen ka?	Did you forget anything?
Oki o tsukete, okaeri kudasai.	Please be careful as you return home.
Iroiro osewa ni narimashita.	Thank you for everything.
Mata doozo okoshi kudasaimase.	Please come again.
Omachi shite orimasu.	I will be waiting for you.

14.2 CONVERSATION

Checking Out of the Hotel

Kyaku: Moshi moshi. Kochira 531-goo shitsu no Satoo desu. Chekku auto shitai n'desu ga . . .

Furon'to: Hai. Furon'to ni irasshatte kudasai. Nimotsu o tori ni mairi-mashoo ka?

Kyaku: Hai, onegai shimasu.

. . . . . .

Beruman: Beruman desu. Onimotsu o omochi shimashoo.

Kyaku: Hai. Kono ni-ko onegai shimasu.

Beruman: Owasure mono wa gozaimasen ka?

Kyaku: Hai, nai to omoimasu.

. . . . . .

Kyaku: Chekku auto onegai shimasu. Kore ga heya no kagi desu.

240

Kaikei:	Okan'joo wa zen'bu de 253-doru ni narimasu. Gen'kin desu ka? Kurejitto desu ka?
Kyaku:	Kono ryokoo kogitte de onegai shimasu.
Kaikei:	Doomo arigatoo gozaimasu. 47-doru no otsuri desu. Mata doozo okoshi kudasaimase.
Kyaku:	Kuukoo e wa takushii ga ii desu ka?
Kaikei:	Rimujin ga ichiban ii to omoimasu. Juu ichi-ji han ni hoteru no mae de omachi kudasai.
Kyaku:	Iroiro osewa ni narimashita.
Kaikei:	Dewa, oki o tsukete okaeri kudasai.

Guest: Hello. This is Sato in room 531. I would like to check out.
Front Desk
Clerk: OK. Please come down to the front desk. Shall I have someone come to pick up your luggage?
Guest: Yes, please.

. . . . . .

Bellman: I'm the bellman. Can I take your luggage for you?
Guest: Yes, please. I have these two pieces.
Bellman: Are you sure that you haven't forgotten anything?
Guest: Yes, I don't think I have.

. . . . . .

Guest: I'd like to check out. Here is my room key.
Cashier: The total will be 253 dollars. Will you pay in cash or by credit card?
Guest: I'll be paying by traveler's check.
Cashier: That's fine. Here's 47 dollars change. Please come again.
Guest: Should I take a taxi to the airport?
Cashier: It's best to go by limousine. Please wait in front of the hotel at 11:30.
Guest: Thank you for all your kindness.
Cashier: Please have a safe trip home.

14.3 VOCABULARY

Nouns

byooki	illness
chekku auto	checking out
doobutsuen	zoo
gooruden uiiku	Golden Week
hisho	secretary
isha	doctor
kaikei	account
kan'joo	account, bill
kibun	feeling

kokusai den'wa ryoo	international telephone fee
kon'shuu	this week
naka	inside
raishuu	next week
sekai	world
sen'shuu	last week
shinai	within the city
shinai den'wa ryoo	local telephone fee
shoorai	future
Suisu	Switzerland
wasuremono	things left behind (things forgotten)
zen'bu	all, whole

Verbs

machimasu	to wait
mochimasu	to carry, to have
narimasu	to become
omoimasu	to think
san'po shimasu	to take a walk
shiharaimasu	to pay
torimasu	to take
torikeshimasu	to cancel
wasuremasu	to forget

14.4 EXPLANATION

14.4.1
V stem + ni + V	ikimasu	
	kimasu	
	kimasu	
	kaerimasu	(Purpose)
	dekakemasu	

Examples:

Nimotsu o tori ni mairimashoo ka?	Shall I come to pick up your baggage?
Nimotsu o tori ni kimashita.	He came for the luggage.
Eiga o mi ni ikimashoo.	Let's go see a movie.
Biichi e san'po shi ni ikimasen ka? *Biichi e san'po ni ikimasen ka?	Won't you go take a walk on the beach?

242

Ara Moana e kaimono shi ni
ikimasu.

I'm going to Ala Moana to shop.

*Ara Moana e kaimono ni
ikimasu.

*A nominative may replace the stem form of a verb if that nominative is part of compound action verb, such as san'po suru, ryokoo suru, ben'kyoo suru, kaimono suru.

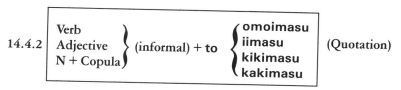

To is used to quote or report what one says, thinks, hears, writes, and so forth. It follows a direct or indirect quotation, which may be a word, phrase, or a sentence. When a quotation takes the form of a sentence, to is preceded by informal forms of the predicate. The tense of the quoted sentence is not affected by that of the sentence. Instead, it is determined by the tense of the final predicate.

Examples:

Hoteru ni tomaru to omoimasu.
I think he'll stay at a hotel.

Yamada-san wa hoteru ni tomaranai to omoimasu.
I don't think Mr. Yamada will stay at a hotel.

Ano kata wa Suzuki-san datta to omoimasu.
I think that person was Mr. Suzuki.

When the quoted phrase is rather long, the following formula is common and avoids ambiguity.

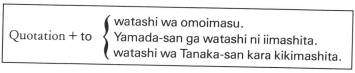

Examples:

Ano yoyaku wa moo torikeshita to watakushi wa shihainin kara kikimashita.
I heard from the manager that the reservation had been cancelled.

Sono resutoran no sushi wa totemo oishikatta to Yamada-san ga iimashita.
Mr. Yamada said that the sushi of that restaurant was very delicious.

14.4.3

| N1 {wa / ga} | N2 ni narimasu. |

. . . becomes such and such
. . . will be such and such

Example:
Zen'bu de 253-doru ni *narimasu* means *It will be 253 dollars altogether.*

Narimasu is intransitive and will not take an object. It means *become, get to be, come to be,* and so forth. In a sentence with structure *N1 becomes N2,* N2 is followed by the goal particle ni. This also applies to adjective nouns.

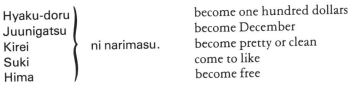

Hyaku-doru ⎫
Juunigatsu ⎪
Kirei   ⎬ ni narimasu.
Suki   ⎪
Hima   ⎭

become one hundred dollars
become December
become pretty or clean
come to like
become free

N {wa / ga} A -ku narimasu.

When an adjective precedes narimasu, the adjective is always in ku form.

Heya ga atsuku narimasu.
Ten'ki ga yoku narimashita.
Koohii ga tsumetaku narimashita
   nee.
Ocha o atsuku shimashoo.
Ryokoo ga omoshiroku narimashita.

The room gets hot.
The weather became nice.
The coffee has become cold, hasn't it?

Let me make the tea hot.
The trip became interesting.

14.4.4

| N {wa / ga} | . . . no naka / sono naka / an area | de ichiban | {A / AN} desu. | (Superlative) |

Example:
Rimujin ga ichiban ii to omoimasu.   I think that the limousine is the best.

In Japanese, adjectives do not have special superlative and comparative forms such as English *best, better,* and so forth. Instead, the superlative degree is indicated by using the noun ichiban meaning *number one.* The phrase . . . no naka de, *within a scope,* is used to indicate the scope or area to which the superlative description is applied.

244

Examples:

Guaba wa nomimono no naka de ichiban oishii to omoimasu.
Within the scope of drinks, I think guava is the most delicious.

Sono naka de dare ga ichiban (se ga) takai desu ka?
Within that group, who is the tallest?

Sekai de ichiban hito ga ooi kuni wa doko desu ka?
Which is the most populated country in the world?

Ichiban itte mitai kuni wa Suisu desu.
The country I want to visit most is Switzerland.

When several items are given for choice, a question is formulated as follows:

```
N1 to N2 to . . . N (to) de (wa),
  dore ga ichiban    ⎰A  ⎱
 ⎛dare ⎞             ⎱AN⎰ desu ka?
 ⎝doko⎠
```

The answer to the above question is as follows:

```
N ga ichiban  ⎰A  ⎱ desu.
              ⎱AN⎰
```

Ten'pura to sushi to sashimi to de wa dore ga ichiban suki desu ka?
Which do you like best: tempura, sushi, or sashimi?

Ten'pura ga ichiban suki desu.
I like tempura best.

14.5 DRILLS

14.5.1 Sentence Combining

Combine each pair of sentences into a single sentence.

1. Biichi e ikimashoo.
   Oyogi ni ikimashoo.

   Biichi e oyogi ni ikimashoo.
   Let's go to the beach and swim.

2. Raishuu Hawai e ikimasu.
   Ryokoo ni ikimasu.

   Raishuu Hawai e ryokoo ni ikimasu.
   Next week I will go on a trip to Hawaii.

3. Hoteru e kaeritai n'desu.
   Omiyage o tori ni kaeritai n'desu.

   Hoteru e omiyage o tori ni kaeritai n'desu.
   I want to return to the hotel to get souvenirs.

4. Ara Moana Sen'taa e ikimashita.
   Kaimono (shi) ni ikimashita.

   Ara Moana Sen'taa e kaimono (shi) ni ikimashita.
   I went shopping at Ala Moana Center.

5. Kapiorani kooen e ikimashita ka?
   Fura dan'su o mi ni ikimashita ka?

   Kapiorani kooen e fura dan'su o mi ni ikimashita ka?
   Did you go to Kapiolani Park to see the hula?

14.5.2 English–Japanese Response Drill

Use the English cues to formulate a response to each question below.

1. Karakaua Doori e ikimashita ka?   Cue: Yes, to see a parade.
   Hai, pareedo o mi ni ikimashita.

2. Honoruru doobutsuen e   Cue: Yes, to see a lion.
     ikimashita ka?
   Hai, raion o mi ni ikimashita.

3. Waikiki Sheru e ikimashita ka?   Cue: Yes, to listen to the concert.
   Hai, kon'saato o kiki ni
     ikimashita.

4. Disuko e ikimashita ka?   Cue: Yes, to dance.
   Hai, dan'su shi ni ikimashita.

14.5.3 Transformation Drill

1. Totemo gen'ki desu.   Totemo gen'ki ni narimashita.
2. Yamada-san wa isha desu.   Yamada-san wa isha ni narimashita.
3. Musume-san wa kirei desu.   Musume-san wa kirei ni
                                        narimashita.
4. Musuko-san wa han'samu desu.   Musuko-san wa han'samu ni
                                        narimashita.

5. Haha wa byooki desu.	Haha wa byooki ni narimashita.
6. Tomodachi wa shachoo desu.	Tomodachi wa shachoo ni narimashita.
7. Hoteru wa shizuka desu.	Hoteru wa shizuka ni narimashita.
8. Mise wa hima desu.	Mise wa hima ni narimashita.
9. Tanaka-san wa hisho desu.	Tanaka-san wa hisho ni narimashita.

14.5.4   Transformation Drill

1. Kyoo wa ten'ki ga warui desu.	Kyoo wa ten'ki ga waruku narimashita.
2. Kibun ga ii desu.	Kibun ga yoku narimashita.
3. Nihon'go no ben'kyoo ga omoshiroi desu.	Nihon'go no ben'kyoo ga omoshiroku narimashita.
4. Okyaku-san ga sukunai desu.	Okyaku-san ga sukunaku narimashita.
5. Okane ga nai desu.	Okane ga naku narimashita.
6. Kon'shuu wa isogashii desu.	Kon'shuu wa isogashiku narimashita.
7. Wasuremono ga ooi desu.	Wasuremono ga ooku narimashita.

14.5.5   Transformation Drill

1. Sono ueitoresu wa nihon'go ga wakarimasu.
   Omoimasu.

   Sono ueitoresu wa nihon'go ga wakaru to omoimasu.
   I think that the waitress understands Japanese.

2. Waikiki ni raamen'ya ga arimasu.
   Kikimashita.

   Waikiki ni raamen'ya ga aru to kikimashita.
   I heard that there is a Chinese-style noodle store in Waikiki.

3. Sono kata wa gin'koo ni tsutomete imashita.
   Iimashita.

   Sono kata wa gin'koo ni tsutomete ita to iimashita.
   That person said he used to work at the bank.

4. Hawai shima e ikitai desu.
   Kakimashita.

   Hawai shima e ikitai to kakimashita.
   I wrote that I wanted to go to the island of Hawaii.

14.5.6 Transformation Drill

1. Ashita wa ten'ki ga warui desu.
   Rajio de iimashita.

   Ashita wa ten'ki ga warui to rajio de iimashita.
   The radio announced that the weather tomorrow will be bad.

2. In'taanashonaru maaketto pureesu wa koko kara tooku arimasen.
   Omoimasu.

   In'taanashonaru maaketto pureesu wa koko kara tooku nai to omoimasu.
   I think that the International Market Place is far from here.

3. Sen'shuu wa amari isogashiku arimasen deshita.
   Omoimasu.

   Sen'shuu wa amari isogashiku nakatta to omoimasu.
   I think that we were not so busy last week.

4. Koko no sushi wa oishikatta desu.
   Keiko-san ga itte imashita.

   Koko no sushi wa oishikatta to Keiko-san ga itte imashita.
   Keiko said that the sushi here was delicious.

14.5.7 Transformation Drill

1. Sore wa hon'too desu.
   Omoimasu.

   Sore wa hon'too da to omoimasu.
   I think that that is true.

2. Yamada-san ga yomitakatta hon wa kore deshita.
   Omoimasu.

   Yamada-san ga yomitakatta hon wa kore datta to omoimasu.
   I think the book Mr. Yamada wanted to read was this.

3. Chekku auto no jikan wa ku-ji ja arimasen.
   Omoimasu.

   Chekku auto no jikan wa ku-ji ja nai to omoimasu.
   I think the check-out time is not 9 o'clock.

4. Mai Tai wa Hawai no nomimono desu.
   Kikimashita.

   Mai Tai wa Hawai no nomimono da to kikimashita.
   I heard that Mai Tai is a drink of Hawaii.

5. Yamada-san wa fura dan'su ga joozu desu.
   Kikimashita.

   Yamada-san wa fura dan'su ga joozu da to kikimashita.
   I heard that Ms. Yamada is a good hula dancer.

248

14.5.8 English–Japanese Response Drill

1. Tabemono no naka de nani ga ichiban suki
   desu ka?   Cue: steak
   Suteeki ga ichiban suki desu.

2. Ben'kyoo shita gaikokugo no naka de   Cue: French
   dore ga ichiban yasashikatta desu ka?
   Furan'sugo ga ichiban yasashikatta desu.

3. Suisu to Nihon to Oosutoraria to de wa   Cue: Australia
   doko e ichiban itte mitai desu ka?
   Oosutoraria e ichiban itte mitai desu.

4. Kono hon no naka de dore ga ichiban   Cue: this one
   omoshirokatta desu ka?
   Kore ga ichiban omoshirokatta desu.

5. Kaisha de ichiban isogashii kata wa dare   Cue: Keiko
   desu ka?
   Keiko-san desu.

14.5.9 Question–Answer Drill

Produce questions by comparing the following sets of items. Use the pattern:
Which one is most . . . , among A, B, and C? Then respond to each of the
questions.

Example: suiei, tenisu, gorufu
      Q: Suiei to tenisu to gorufu de wa, dore ga ichiban suki
         desu ka?
        Cue: gorufu
      A: Gorufu ga ichiban suki desu.

1. Tookyoo, Nyuu Yooku, Pari
   Q: Tookyoo to Nyuu Yooku to Pari de wa, doko ga ichiban suki desu ka?
   Pari
   A: Pari ga ichiban suki desu.

2. haru, natsu, aki
   Q: Haru to natsu to aki de wa, dore ga ichiban suki desu ka?
   haru
   A: Haru ga ichiban suki desu.

3. sushi, ten'pura, sukiyaki
   Q: Sushi to ten'pura to sukiyaki de wa, dore ga ichiban suki desu ka?
   sukiyaki
   A: Sukiyaki ga ichiban suki desu.

4. Kyooto, Oosaka, Tookyoo
  Q: Kyooto to Oosaka to Tookyoo de wa, doko ga ichiban suki desu ka?
    Tookyoo
  A: Tookyoo ga ichiban suki desu.

5. nihon'go, supein'go, chuugokugo
  Q: Nihon'go to supein'go to chuugokugo de wa, dore ga ichiban suki
    desu ka?
    nihon'go
  A: Nihon'go ga ichiban suki desu.

14.6 EXERCISES

14.6.1 Questions and Answers

Answer the following in Japanese.

1. Anata wa nan ni naritai desu ka?
2. Takushii to rimujin to basu de wa dore ga ichiban hayai desu ka?
3. Nihon'go wa muzukashiku narimashita ka?
4. Anata wa ryokoo suru no ga suki ni narimashita ka?
5. Anata wa hisho ni naru tsumori desu ka?
6. Toshokan e nani o shi ni ikimashita ka?
7. Doko e kaimono ni irasshaimasu ka?
8. Nihon wa don'na kuni da to omoimasu ka?
9. Yamada-san wa itsu ryokoo shitai to iimashita ka?
10. Anata ga ryokoo shite mitai kuni wa doko desu ka?

14.6.2 Translation

Express the following ideas in Japanese.

1. I want to become a front desk manager of a big hotel.
2. I wanted to become a medical doctor, but I could not (become one).
3. The Japanese tourist said that she likes guava juice best.
4. Which is the most expensive car in the USA?
5. Which is the most expensive hotel, the Kahala Hilton, the Waikiki
    Sheraton, or the Hyatt Regency?
6. The secretary will be very busy next week.
7. Mr. Brown went to the relative's house to borrow money.
8. I returned home to get things I forgot.

250

14.7 SIMULATION AND SKITS

1. Mr. and Mrs. Yamada, two hotel guests, are ready to check out of the hotel. As a front desk employee, help them with the check-out procedure.

2. As a front desk employee, you are helping Mr. Tanaka to check out of the hotel. He has made a local call, as well as an international call to Japan, so you must also explain his telephone charges to him.

3. John was not present when the tour guide told his group the plans for tomorrow, so Susan told John what the tour guide said. Speak as though you were Susan, for example:
   a. "Breakfast will be at 7:30."
   b. "Tomorrow at 9:00 we are going to Hanauma Bay."
   c. "Hanauma Bay is the nicest beach in Hawaii."
   d. "The Hawaiian show tomorrow will be fun."
   e. "It will be late when the show finishes, so please be careful as you come back."

4. Two friends meet while walking down the street, and they each ask where the other is going. Use ni to denote the purpose in your conversation.

5. Create a situation in which two friends are comparing three items and are asking each other which is the best or preferred item of the three.

6. Two Travel Industry Management majors ask each other about their career plans for the future.

14.8 CULTURE ORIENTATION

14.8.1 Holidays

National holidays, annual events, and festivals provide an opportune time for the Japanese people to engage in such leisure activities as traveling. It is during these festive periods that there is the greatest concentration of Japanese tourists at the more popular vacation destinations.

However, for students of various educational levels in Japan, school vacations determine the time available for traveling with family or friends. The school year in Japan starts in the Spring which is the opposite of the school year in America. From elementary to high school, the school year begins in April and ends the following March. The two months of summer vacation begin around mid-July. At the college level, vacations are between semesters. College students have a two-month break in July and August and a one-month break in March. During these school vacations there are many student travelers.

It may be interesting to know more about the holidays, annual events, and festivals which have influenced the travel patterns of the Japanese. These festivals, holidays, and other ceremonial occasions fall into two main categories—matsuri *festivals* and nen'chuu gyooji *annual events.*

Nen'chuu gyooji used to refer to the imperial court calendar, a schedule of recurring annual activities influenced by Chinese court schedules and astrology. However, over the centuries nen'chuu gyooji have undergone considerable change as many old practices have been eliminated and new ones have been added, influenced by politics, religion, agriculture, and commerce. For example, a fairly recent commercial nen'chuu gyooji is the hari kuyoo or *Needle Memorial Service,* an annual observance in which seamstresses collect their old sewing needles and take them to their local shrines to stick them into a cake of toofu and pray for improved sewing skill and safety from pricked fingers. Today, nen'chuu gyooji refers to both the ancient schedule of events as a historical phenomenon and to the annual events, including national and international holidays, that are observed by the Japanese today.

Japanese matsuri are chiefly of sacred origin related originally to the cultivation of rice and the spiritual well-being of local communities. The matsuri has two major aspects. The first is communion between the gods and people. The second aspect of matsuri is communion among people. Many Japanese festivals feature a parade of mikoshi *portable shrines* and contests or games that give community members opportunities to play together and match skills.

Among annual rites, spring and autumn matsuri are the most important. The spring festivals celebrate an anticipated good harvest; the autumn festivals are held in thanksgiving for a plentiful harvest. Besides spring and autumn festivals, there are summer festivals natsu matsuri and winter festivals fuyu matsuri as well.

In farming areas, summer matsuri have the role of driving away natural disasters that might threaten the crops, while in the cities, the role of such festivals has been to ward off plague and pestilence. In recent years matsuri in summer have gained remarkable popularity and have become the most colorful and lively of the year's festivities. The parades of brightly decorated floats attract thousands of spectators and visitors. One of the popular natsu matsuri is Kyoto's daimon'ji okuribi *Daimonji Bonfire.* This festival marks the close of the Bon Festival and bids farewell to the souls of ancestors. An enormous bonfire is laid out in the shape of the kan'ji dai *(great)* which is lit on the slopes of Nyogatake mountain (Daimonjiyama).

Winter matsuri, held between harvest and spring seeding, have elements of both autumn and spring matsuri. One of the more recent fuyu matsuri is Sapporo's yuki matsuri, which is a nonreligious contest of large snow and ice sculptures held in Sapporo's Odori Park. The different matsuri celebrate different themes, resulting in a variety of types of festivals in Japan.

The Japanese have a concept of two dimensions of life—hare and ke, as explained in Lesson 9. Hare correlates with the out-of-the-ordinary, and ke with the routine or everyday. Such occasions as New Year's Day, Bon Festival, birthdays, and weddings are termed hare. A symbol of hare is mochi. In pre-modern Japan, the precious rice was reserved for special occasions. Today almost all Japanese have preserved the custom of eating mochi rice during the New Year's holidays, although it is sold throughout the year everywhere in Japan. In recent years, festive hare occasions have spread over a wider spectrum of society. There are instances of hare on a national level, such as on Children's Day, Coming-of-Age Day, and Respect-for-the-Aged Day, which are national holidays.

In addition to such general observances as New Year's Day and the Bon Festival, numerous regional festivals of shrines and temples and agricultural rituals are still celebrated today. A few traditional events have even become national holidays, such as the celebration of the equinoxes and Children's Day. Labor Thanksgiving Day is celebrated on November 23. Certain Western or international events are now also celebrated in Japan, for example, May Day, when labor groups celebrate, and Christmas, which has become a round of parties termed boonen'kai *forget-the-year parties.* Listed below are some of the major national holidays observed in Japan.

NATIONAL HOLIDAYS

January	1	Oshoogatsu (New Year's Day)
	15	Seijin no Hi (Adults' Day or Coming-of-Age day)
February	11	Ken'koku Kinen no Hi (National Foundation Day)
March	21 or 22	Shun'bun no Hi (Vernal Equinox Day)
April	29	Ten'noo Tan'joobi (Emperor's Birthday)
May	3	Ken'poo Kinen'bi (Constitution Memorial Day)
	5	Kodomo no Hi (Children's Day)
September	15	Keiroo no Hi (Respect-for-the-Aged Day)
	23 or 24	Shuubun no Hi (Autumnal Equinox Day)
October	10	Taiiku no Hi (Sports Day)
November	3	Bun'ka no Hi (Culture Day)
	23	Kin'ro Kan'sha no Hi (Labor Thanksgiving Day)

The above is a list of the major national holidays of Japan. If all the different regional festivals and functions were listed, the entire calendar would be filled. The Japanese people must really enjoy festivals and special occasions since they even observe foreign holidays such as Christmas, Bastille Day, Valentine's Day, Mother's Day, and Father's Day. However, the way they observe some of these foreign holidays is somewhat unique. For example, in Japan it is customary for girls to give chocolates to boys they admire on Valentine's Day.

14.8.2   Holidays and the Japanese Mass Exodus

Tokyo is said to have two mass exoduses every year. The first takes place at the end of April and the beginning of May. This is Golden Week and begins with the Emperor's birthday on April 29th, which is a national holiday. This four-day or five-day vacation is a "golden opportunity" for people to visit their hometowns or to travel elsewhere. A large portion of the population in Tokyo leaves, and the city is left quite empty. This is often called the mass exodus. It is even said that during this time the usually smog-laden skies of the city clear because of the fewer number of cars. Traveling outside of Tokyo during this time, therefore, is not recommended. During Golden Week a large number of Japanese also travel abroad, and places such as Hawaii are, consequently, crowded with Japanese tourists.

The other mass exodus takes place from the end of December to the first week of January. This is another period during which employees are able to take a few days off in order to celebrate the New Year in their hometowns. Many people travel to warmer places such as Hawaii in order to escape the cold winter in Japan. Also, these people travel abroad in order to escape the crowds of guests that visit their homes for the first visit of the New Year. Some people feel that their vacations are spoiled if they spend most of their time entertaining guests.

There is also a collective feeling among people of being compelled to travel during this time, just because everybody else is. For such reasons, Tokyo becomes empty again. Japanese tourists rush to areas such as Hawaii, Guam, and Hong Kong. It would be a good idea to welcome Japanese tourists during these seasons with the understanding of the reasons compelling them to travel.

14.8.3   The Japanese and Festivals

According to the *Kojiki,* the gods formed the islands of Japan in the order of Awaji, Shikoku, Kyushu, and Honshu by traveling this route. The eight million gods travel anywhere when there is an order to do so from Izumo Shrine, the key Shinto Shrine. The gods move from the paddies to the mountains when they are called on by the people. These trips, taken by the gods, are called **otabi** (honorific expression for *trip*). These **otabi** can be said to be the prototypes of Japanese festivals (Tada 1981:125).

Omikoshi *portable shrines* are carried from one place to another during these festivals, finally returning to the beginning point. One can say that those who carry these **omikoshi** are not necessarily devout religious believers. Some of them don't even know which god is enshrined in the **omikoshi** they carry. It probably doesn't make much difference since the **omikoshi** serves as a symbol of collective action and cooperation among the people. What matters is the unison of effort as they carry the heavy **omikoshi** saying **wasshoi, wasshoi!** The **omikoshi** cannot be moved by one's individual will, and the joint effort

254

puts everybody in a trancelike state of mind. The Japanese people obtain a sense of freedom and satisfaction by immersing themselves in this collective action. The omikoshi itself moves back and forth, as though in a drunken stupor, but it somehow reaches its final destination and returns to its original position.

Through participation in this event, the individuals involved gain a sense of freedom (Tada 1981:140). This may seem like a slavish mentality within certain social contexts, but it presents a picture of freedom in the Japanese social context. This mentality, reflected in the omikoshi, may have been present in the minds of the Japanese during the Second World War. Furthermore, it may be present today in the minds and attitudes of company employees. In other words, there is a sense of belonging developed through entrusting and committing oneself to a mutual goal. A tremendous amount of energy and power develops as everyone gets together and says wasshoi! Although there may not be a clear-cut direction in the beginning, it may develop out of the energy created. The individual can attain a certain type of freedom through this collective action.

14.8.4 The Japanese and the Four Seasons

There are four distinct seasons in Japan. When the plum blossoms bloom, everyone knows spring has arrived and the cherry blossoms, the national flower, will bloom shortly thereafter.

The cherry blossom "front" begins slowly, advancing from the South—from Okinawa, to Kyushu, to Kansai, to Tokyo, to Tohoku, and finally to Hokkaido. At the beginning of the sakura season, TV stations regularly report on the varying degrees the sakura buds in different parts of Japan have bloomed.

The Japanese eagerly await the season of cherry blossoms. Why is it that they are so attracted by them? It isn't merely because they are so beautiful or bloom in abundance, but also because cherry blossoms are short-lived and fragile. They bloom one second and are gone the next. They don't wither away but are blown away by even the slightest breeze. The Japanese people say that the cherry blossoms do not want to lose their beauty, and so, while they are still fresh, they fly away.

There is some Zen influence in this thought, and even the samurai learned from it. It was thought that the life of a samurai was like the cherry blossoms. It may be peaceful at one moment but there may be warfare the next, and the samurai may lose his life. The kamikaze pilots were a modern version of these samurai. (The kamikaze pilots were symbolized as cherry blossoms in songs that were sung during the Second World War.) The Japanese perceive fallen flowers, or even fallen human life at an early but full age, to be aesthetically beautiful. It is understandable that Japanese has many different words referring to how things fall.

The Japanese enjoy hanami *flower viewing,* eating and drinking good food underneath the cherry blossom trees with their family and friends. After the cherry blossom season, the fresh green leaves come out almost at once. This season is called the season of shin'ryoku *fresh green.* This is followed by the rainy season, then the hot summer. At the end of summer, the typhoons begin, followed by autumn.

In autumn the leaves turn red, and the flower of this season, the chrysanthemum, reaches full bloom. Chrysanthemum shows are held all over the country, and crowds of people gather to see them. The chrysanthemum is the symbol of the Imperial family and is often mistaken for the national flower of Japan. Autumn is also known for its beautiful moons, and the Japanese enjoy moon viewing. Gradually, the crimson-colored leaves fall and winter begins. Mount Fuji begins to be cloaked in white, and the cold winds of winter commence. Gradually, winter passes and spring begins again.

The four seasons progress in a cyclical pattern. Often the seasons are likened to the life of man: spring as the beginning of life, summer as the dynamism of youth, autumn as old age, and winter as death. At this point, the cycle of life ends. But with the addition of religious philosophy, the winter of death brings forth the spring of a new life after death. The life of man repeats itself again and again as the four seasons repeat, and it may be said that the concept of reincarnation came from such ideas. These ideas also influenced the circling-around-the-point mode of communication which was mentioned earlier.

14.9 JAPANESE MODE OF COMMUNICATION

Adjusting Mode of Communication

Nature was always a friendly entity rather than an enemy to the Japanese people. Although Hokkaido, in the northern part of Japan, experiences severe winters, the climate of Japan is generally moderate. Nature is generally neither hostile nor harsh, though typhoons, earthquakes, and other natural disasters do occur. Life becomes easier if people cooperate with nature, which offers its abundance of water and fertile land. Fighting it would only prove to be an inconvenience. With favorable geographic conditions, the Japanese people developed a mode of solving problems that adjusted itself to its environment. The Japanese people developed a skill to adjust to situations.

In spring, people eat foods available during the season and wear clothes that are appropriate to the weather. In summer, people adjust to the heat, feeding and clothing themselves appropriately. In similar ways, the Japanese people adjust to the other party while communicating. Perhaps this is the reason why some foreigners feel that the Japanese are too agreeable. They try to avoid confrontation, which could occur if one continually presses one's own views. Problem solving, for example, between an employer and union, means adjusting to each other's situation and needs. American people also try to adjust. However, the adjustment is usually not made by the individual himself, as in Japan, but by trying to make others adjust to him. This aspect of the American character is well reflected in their problem-solving approach, that is, to solve problems by manipulating, controlling, and changing their environment rather than changing themselves first. For Americans, problems and conflicts are, first of all, isolated and identified as clearly as possible. Once they are clearly defined, they are directly confronted, for Americans generally believe that greater benefit is derived from confronting rather than avoiding or defusing conflict. As reflected in this type of problem solving, it can be said that the American mode of communication is basically confrontive and outer directed, while that of the Japanese is basically adjusting and inner directed.

14.10 LANGUAGE AND CULTURE

Owasure mono wa gozaimasen ka? and Oki o tsukete okaeri kudasai

The Japanese are known to be very helpful to others. This is apparent when one travels on a bus or a train. Warnings for safety and words of consideration never end: "Please be careful as you get on. The next stop is so-and-so." "In case of emergency, please hold the handles or the rails." These are repeated over and over. In addition, they warn passengers to be careful when boarding, and not to forget anything when leaving. There are signs all over train stations warning people to be careful while running or while the doors are closing, so that they do not jam their fingers.

Such warnings and reminders seem to be taken for granted in a nation where customers are considered gods. But to foreigners who are able to understand Japanese, this almost childish treatment may seem offensive. Such phrases of warning and reminders are used for store customers and hotel guests also, appearing frequently in the daily use of the Japanese language. The Japanese try to thoroughly serve their guests. Such services are not confined to guests only, but extend to the general public as well.

Mass communication is also greatly advanced where problems are presented, discussed, and solved for the people. In one respect, Japan is a nation where the thinking doesn't have to be done by the public, but is done for them by specialists. This may seem helpful at first; however, one is forced to question whether this may really be helpful to the people.

14.11 CULTURE QUESTIONS

1. May Day has become almost an international holiday. Japan also celebrates May Day, but there is a political image in the minds of the people, that they should march with placards and microphones. In Hawaii, May Day is called Lei Day and has a completely different connotation developed to suit

Hawaii. However, the Japanese people do not really know much about Lei Day, other than that it is a day of parades and lei exhibits. How would a program to teach lei making, including actual practice in making leis, be accepted by Japanese tourists? Discuss the pros and cons of this idea.

2. The Japanese people appreciate a proper beginning and ending to an event. So much emphasis is placed on this that many events are ritualized. From this standpoint, checking out of a hotel would be an important occasion for Japanese people. Discuss what considerations can be made by hotel employees in charge of checking out Japanese tourists.

3. Discuss what kinds of things should be considered in dealing with the adjustment-seeking Japanese. How is conflict resolution dealt with in Japan?

14.12   SUGGESTED RESOURCE MATERIALS

14.12.1   Books and Magazines

Kodansha Encyclopedia of Japan, vol. 2 (Tokyo: Kodansha, 1983), pp. 252–262.

Mock Joya's Things Japanese, Mock Joya (Tokyo: Tokyo News Service, 1968), pp. 99–125.

Things Japanese in Hawaii, John DeFrancis (Honolulu: The University Press of Hawaii, 1973), pp. 17–62.

We Japanese (Fujiya Hotel, 1949), pp. 52–54.

14.12.2   Films (16 mm) and Video Cassettes (Beta/VHS)

"Festival Japan." 20 mins. Color. Japan National Tourist Organization, 1968.

"The Four Seasons in Japan." 28 mins. Color. Japan National Tourist Organization, 1974.

"Nature's Patterns." 21 mins. Color. Japan National Tourist Organization, 1969.

14.13   REFERENCES

Tada, Michitaro. *Shinpen no Nihon Bunka.* Tokyo: Kodansha, 1981.

258

LESSON 15

REVIEW

15.1	Person **wa** + Predicate modifier + V-**ta koto** $\begin{Bmatrix} \text{ga} \\ \text{wa} \end{Bmatrix}$			arimasu/ arimasen.

maneejaa		biiru o non'da			
okyaku-san		kan'ji de sain shita			
Kinoshita-san		kokusai den'wa shita			
gaido		nihon'go de kaita		ga	arimasu.
haha	wa	oyoida	koto		
chichi		tomatta		wa	arimasen.
sen'sei		wasureta			
otooto		non'da			
ane		Amerika ni sun'da			
imooto		karita			
hisho					

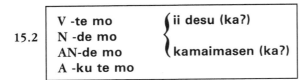

15.2	V -te mo N -de mo AN-de mo A -ku te mo	{	ii desu (ka?) kamaimasen (ka?)

tabete tomatte kaite watashite notte torikeshite non'de oyoide			
- - - - - - - - - - - - - - -			
pen de toraberaa chekku de tsuin de suteeki	mo		ii desu ka? kamaimasen ka?
- - - - - - - - - - - - - - -			
heta de joozu de			
- - - - - - - - - - - - - - -			
chikaku te tooku te			

15.3	**V-nai de kudasai.**

tabenai minai hairanai noranai oyoganai san'po shinai toranai torikesanai wasurenai shomei shinai	de kudasai.

260

15.4 | N1 **wa** N2 yori $\left\{\begin{array}{c}\text{A}\\\text{AN}\end{array}\right\}$ **desu.**

	wa		yori		desu.
Yamate-gawa no heya		umite-gawa			
ane		imooto			
doru		en		chiisai	
furon'to		robii			
ryokan		hoteru			
uisukii	wa	Buruu Hawai	yori		desu.
byuffe		teishoku		takai	
hoteru		ryokan			
Aroha Hoteru		Sheraton			
robii		furon'to			
doobutsuen		kooen			
tsuin		shin'guru		hiroi	
tonari		koko			

15.5 | V $\left\{\begin{array}{l}\text{dictionary}\\\text{plain negative}\end{array}\right\}$ + **tsumori** $\left\{\begin{array}{l}\textbf{desu.}\\\textbf{deshita.}\end{array}\right\}$

hairu		
hairanai		
nomu		
nomanai		
tomaru		
tomaranai		
san'po suru	tsumori	desu.
san'po shinai		deshita.
taberu		
tabenai		
kaku		
kakanai		
matsu		
matanai		
torikesu		
torikesanai		

15.6

$$N \begin{Bmatrix} wa \\ ga \end{Bmatrix} \text{A-ku narimasu.}$$

heya wa atsuku
kan'joo wa takaku
heya wa hiroku
umi wa tooku   narimasu.
Ara Moana Sen'taa wa chikaku
chuushoku wa osoku
atama ga itaku
kao (face) ga akaku

15.7

$$N \text{ wa} \begin{Bmatrix} AN \\ N \end{Bmatrix} \text{ni narimasu.}$$

kirei
shin'setsu
joozu
- - - - - - - - - - - - - - - - - -   ni narimashita.
shachoo
shihainin
hisho

LESSON 16

ON THE TELEPHONE

16.1   USEFUL EXPRESSIONS

Den'wa ban'goo wa 455-8730 (yon goo goo no, hachi nana san zero) desu.	The telephone number is 455-8730.
Moshi moshi . . .	Hello.
Tanaka-san no otaku desu ka?	Is this Mr. Tanaka's residence?
Iie, chigaimasu.	No, it isn't. (Wrong number.)
Yamada-san (o) onegai shimasu.	May I speak to Mr. Yamada.
	Mr. Yamada please.
Dochirasama desu ka?	Who's calling please?
Suzuki-san ni kawarimasu.	I'll give (the phone) to Mr. Suzuki.
Kyuu-ban o omawashi kudasai.	Please dial 9.
Den'wa ga tooi desu.	I can't hear you.
Den'wa de shitsurei shimasu.	Please excuse me for calling.
Den'wa o kirimasu.	I'll hang up the phone.
Ohanashichuu desu.	The line is busy.
Den'wa ni dete kudasai.	Please answer the phone.
Den'wa o totte kudasai.	
Okawari gozaimasen ka?	How have you been?
Seki o hazushite imasu.	He's not at his desk now.
Ima rusu desu ga . . .	He's out now, but . . .
Okotozuke ⎫	
Den'gon ⎬ o onegai shimasu.	Please take the message.
Messeeji ⎭	
Mata ato de.	(See you) later.
Gomen kudasai.	Well then, excuse me.
Shitsurei shimasu.	(Expression used before hanging up.)

263

16.2 CONVERSATION

16.2.1 Making an Outside Call

Kyaku: Moshi moshi, hoteru no soto e den'wa shitai n'desu ga . . .
Kookan'shu: Shinai desu ka?
Kyaku: Hai, soo desu.
Kookan'shu: Kyuu-ban o mawashite kara, den'wa ban'goo o omawashi
    kudasai.
Kyaku: Doomo arigatoo.

    . . . . . .

Araki: Moshi moshi. Yokoda-san no otaku desu ka?
Yokoda: Hai, soo desu ga . . .
Araki: Watakushi Araki Kazuko to iu mono desu ga, George-san iras-
    shaimasu ka?
Yokoda: Hai. Chotto omachi kudasai. Kawarimasu kara.

    . . . . . .

George: Boku, George desu ga . . .
Araki: A, George-san. Kinoo Hawai ni tsukimashita. Otegami o arigatoo
    gozaimashita.
George: Iie, doo itashimashite. Ima dochira kara?
Araki: Kahala Hilton ni imasu. Hoteru no hoo ni irasshaimasen ka? Iroiro
    ohanashi shitai koto mo arimasu kara.
George: Hai. Ukagaimasu. Kazuko-san wa biichi de oyogu no to san'po
    suru no to dochira no hoo ga ii desu ka?
Araki: Kyoo wa san'po ni shimashoo ka?
George: Soo desu ne. Dewa nan-ji ni oai shimashoo ka?
Araki: San-ji goro ni shimashoo ka? Robii de matte imasu ne.
George: Hai. Dewa, mata ato de. Sayoonara.
Araki: Sayoonara.

Guest: Hello. I would like to make an outside call.
Operator: Within the city?
Guest: Yes.
Operator: Dial nine, and then your number.
Guest: Thank you.

             . . . . . .

Miss Araki: Hello. Is this the Yokoda residence?
Mr. Yokoda: Yes, it is.
Miss Araki: My name is Kazuko Araki. Is George there?
Mr. Yokoda: Yes, just a moment please. I'll put him on.

             . . . . . .

264

George: This is George.
Miss Araki: Oh, George. I arrived in Hawaii yesterday. Thank you for your
             letter.
George: You're welcome. Where are you now?
Miss Araki: I'm at the Kahala Hilton now. Can you come to the hotel? I have
             so many things to talk to you about.
George: Yes, that will be fine. Which do you prefer, Kazuko, swimming at
             the beach or going for a walk?
Miss Araki: Shall we go for a walk today?
George: Sure. What time would you like to meet?
Miss Araki: About three? I'll wait for you in the lobby.
George: All right. I'll see you then. Good-bye.
Miss Araki: Good-bye.

16.2.2 Making a Hotel Reservation

Kyaku: Moshi moshi, Makaha Resort Hotel desu ka?
Furon'to: Hai, soo desu.
Kyaku: Heya no yoyaku o onegai shimasu.
Furon'to: Doozo. Itsu kara itsu made desu ka?
Kyaku: Kyoo kara asatte made, ni-haku mikka desu.
Furon'to: Wakarimashita. Onamae o doozo.
Kyaku: Shiraki Kazuo desu.
Furon'to: Nan-nin sama desu ka?
Kyaku: Futari desu.
Furon'to: Daburu to tsuin de wa, dochira no hoo ga yoroshii desu ka?
Kyaku: Tsuin no hoo ga ii desu.
Furon'to: Arigatoo gozaimashita. Chekku-in wa ichi-ji desu. Omachi shite
           orimasu.

Guest: Hello. Is this Makaha Resort Hotel?
Front Desk
Clerk: Yes, it is.
Guest: I would like to make a room reservation.
Clerk: Please go ahead. From when to when?
Guest: From today until day after tomorrow, two nights and three days.
Clerk: All right. Your name please.
Guest: Kazuo Shiraki.
Clerk: For how many?
Guest: Two.
Clerk: Do you prefer double or twin accommodations?
Guest: Twin please.
Clerk: Thank you. Check in time is one p.m. We will be waiting for you.

16.2.3 Making an Appointment

Situation: Mr. Akita, a front desk clerk, wants to make an appointment to see the manager of the section.

Akita: Moshi moshi, furon'to no Akita desu ga . . .
Hisho: Hai, shihainin shitsu de gozaimasu.
Akita: Shihainin ni oai shitai n'desu ga, nan-ji goro ga ii desu ka?
Hisho: Shihainin wa kaigi ni dete imasu ga, kyoo wa osoku naru soo desu. Ashita no asa de mo yoroshii desu ka?
Akita: Ee, kekkoo desu.
Hisho: Ku-ji han ni doozo.
Akita: Doomo. Dewa, ashita ku-ji han ni ukagaimasu. Gomen kudasai.

Mr. Akita: Hello. This is Akita from the front desk.
Secretary: Hello. This is the manager's office.
Mr. Akita: I would like to meet with the manager. What time would be good?
Secretary: The manager is out at a meeting just now and probably won't be back until late. Would tomorrow morning suit you?
Mr. Akita: Yes, that will be fine.
Secretary: Please come at 9:30.
Mr. Akita: Thank you. I'll see you at 9:30 tomorrow morning. Good-bye.

16.2.4 Wake Up Call

Satoo: Moshi moshi, moonin'gu kooru o onegai shimasu.
Kookan'shu: Nan-ji ni okoshimashoo ka?
Satoo: Shichi-ji han ni okoshite kudasai.
Kookan'shu: Hai wakarimashita. Onamae to oheya no ban'goo o doozo.
Satoo: 235-goo shitsu no Satoo desu.
. . . . . .
Kookan'shu: Ohayoo gozaimasu. Shichi-ji han desu. Okiru jikan desu yo.
Satoo: Hai, hai. Doomo arigatoo.

Sato: Hello. I would like to request a morning call please.
Operator: What time would you like to get up?
Sato: 7:30 please.
Operator: I see. Your name and room number please.
Sato: Room 235, Sato.
. . . . . .
Operator: Good morning. It is 7:30. Time to get up.
Sato: Yes. Yes. Thank you.

266

16.2.5 Telephone Conversations

1. A: Moshi moshi, Tanaka-san no otaku desu ka?
   B: Hai, soo desu ga . . .
   A: Anoo . . . Taroo-san irasshaimasu ka?
   B: Hai, shooshoo omachi kudasai.

2. A: Moshi moshi, Tanaka-san no otaku desu ka?
   B: Hai, soo desu.
   A: Teruya desu ga, Taroo-kun imasu ka?
   B: Hai, chotto matte kudasai.

3. A: Moshi moshi, Tanaka-san no otaku desu ka?
   B: Hai, soo desu ga . . .
   A: Anoo . . . Taroo-san irasshaimasu ka?
   B: Hai, orimasu. Dochira-sama de irasshaimasu ka?
   A: Sugimoto to mooshimasu.
   B: Shooshoo omachi kudasai.

4. A: Moshi moshi, Tanaka-san no otaku desu ka?
   B: Hai, soo desu.
   A: Taroo-san onegai shimasu.
   B: Boku desu ga . . .
   A: A, boku Sumisu desu.

5. A: Moshi moshi.
   B: Moshi moshi.
   A: Tanaka-san no otaku desu ka?
   B: Hai, soo desu.
   A: Taroo-san irasshaimasu ka?
   B: Ima chotto rusu desu ga . . .
   A: Nan-ji goro kaerimasu ka?
   B: San-ji goro kaerimasu ga . . .
   A: Ja mata ato de oden'wa shimasu. Sayoonara.

1. A: Hello. Is this the Tanaka residence?
   B: Yes, it is.
   A: Is Taro there?
   B: Yes, just a minute please.

2. A: Hello. Is this the Tanaka residence?
   B: Yes, it is.
   A: This is Teruya. Is Taro there?
   B: Yes, hang on a minute please.

3. A: Hello. Is this the Tanaka residence?
   B: Yes, it is.
   A: Well, is Taro there?
   B: Yes he is. Who is calling please?
   A: My name is Sugimoto.
   B: Please hold the line for a minute.

4. A: Hello. Is this the Tanaka residence?
   B: Yes, it is.
   A: Can I talk to Taro, please?
   B: This is Taro.
   A: Oh, this is Smith.

5. A: Hello.
   B: Hello.
   A: Is this the Tanaka residence?
   B: Yes, it is.
   A: May I speak to Taro please?
   B: He's gone out at the moment.
   A: When do you expect him back?
   B: I think around three o'clock.
   A: All right. I'll telephone again later. Good-bye.

16.3   VOCABULARY

Nouns

apoin'tomen'to	appointment
chookyori den'wa	long distance call
den'gon, messeeji, kotozuke	message
den'wa ban'goo	telephone number
den'wa choo	telephone directory
futsuu tsuuwa	station-to-station
kaigi	conference
kaigichuu	in a meeting
kokusai den'wa	international call
kookan'shu	operator
koshoo	out of order
mono	person
moonin'gu kooru	morning call, wake up call
naisen	extension
otaku	residence
seki	seat
shimei tsuuwa	person-to-person
shinai den'wa	local call

268

soto	outside
yakusoku	promise, appointment
yoyaku	reservation

Verbs

den'wa (o) shimasu (kakemasu)	to make a telephone call
kawarimasu	to change
okoshimasu	to wake (someone) up
mawashimasu	to dial, to turn around
tsutaemasu	to convey
ukagaimasu	to visit

Adverbs

ato de	later
zutto	by far, much (more)

Others

. . . kara . . . made	from . . . to . . .

16.4 EXPLANATION

16.4.1

V dict. 1 (no) yori	V dict. 2 **hoo ga**	$\left\{\begin{array}{l} \text{A} \\ \text{AN} \end{array}\right\}$	**desu.**
V dict. 2 **no wa**	V dict. 1 **(no) yori**		

(Comparison of actions)

Biichi de oyogu no to san'po suru no to dochira no hoo ga ii desu ka?
Which do you like more, swimming at the beach or taking a walk?

When actions instead of items are to be compared, the dictionary or nominalized forms of verbs are used, depending on the dependent words following these verbs.

Examples:

Tenisu o suru $\left.\right\}$ yori $\left\{\begin{array}{l} \text{gorufu o suru} \\ \text{sakana o taberu} \end{array}\right\}$ hoo ga ii desu.
Niku o taberu

It is better to $\left\{\begin{array}{l} \text{play golf} \\ \text{eat fish} \end{array}\right\}$ than to $\left\{\begin{array}{l} \text{play tennis.} \\ \text{eat meat.} \end{array}\right.$

Gorufu o suru $\left.\right\}$ no wa $\left\{\begin{array}{l} \text{tenisu o suru} \\ \text{niku o taberu} \end{array}\right\}$ (no) yori ii desu.
Sakana o taberu

Playing golf $\left.\right\}$ is better than $\left\{\begin{array}{l} \text{playing tennis.} \\ \text{eating meat.} \end{array}\right.$
Eating fish

269

A comparative question is formulated as follows:

```
V dict. 1 no to V dict. 2 no to  {(de),
                                  {(dewa),
dochira (no hoo)}      {A  }                    (Comparative question)
                 } ga  {   } desu ka?
dotchi (no hoo)  }     {AN }
```

A reply to the above question is formed in one of the following ways:

```
V dict. 1 hoo ga . . . desu.
V dict. 1 hoo ga V dict. 2 yori . . . desu.
V dict. 2 yori V dict. 1 hoo ga . . . desu.
V dict. 1 no ga . . . desu.
```

Examples:
Messeeji o onegai suru no to ato de moo ichido kakeru no to dochira no hoo
    ga ii desu ka?
Which would you prefer, to have (someone) take the message or to call back
    again later?
Ato de moo ichido kakeru hoo ga ii desu.
To call back again later would be better.
Den'wa suru no to tegami o kaku no to dotchi ga ii desu ka?
Which is better, to make a telephone call or to write a letter?
Den'wa suru hoo ga tegami o kaku yori ii desu.
To make a telephone call is better than to write a letter.

Superlative Expression

On'gaku o kiku no to un'doo o suru no to hon o yomu no (to) de wa,
    on'gaku o kiku no ga ichiban ii desu.
Among listening to music, exercising, and reading a book, listening to music is
    the best.
Hoteru ni iru no to, eiga o mi ni iku no to, san'po ni deru no (to) de wa dore
    ga ichiban ii desu ka?
Which is the best, staying in the hotel, going to see a movie, or going out for a
    walk?
San'po ni deru no ga ichiban ii desu.
Going out for a walk is the best.

Negative Comparison

Yomu no wa kaku hodo muzukashiku arimasen.
Reading is not as difficult as writing.

270

Shin'bun o yomu no wa anata ga omou hodo muzukashiku arimasen.
Reading a newspaper is not as difficult as you think.

The dictionary form of a verb before hoo ga (ii desu) can be replaced with the ta form of the verb. This is used for advice or suggestion to the hearer and is equivalent to *You had better do such and such.* The ta form makes the sentence more realistic or more emphatic.

Study the following:

Sugu uchi e kaetta hoo ga ii desu yo.
You'd better go home right away.

Sugu uchi e den'wa shita hoo ga ii desu yo.
You'd better call home right away.

Ima kusuri o non'da hoo ga ii desu.
You'd better take the medicine now.

Atama ga totemo itai toki ni wa kusuri o nomu hoo ga ii desu.
It's good to take medicine when you have a severe headache.

16.4.2	V Adj. (plain form) + **soo desu.** N Na	(Hearsay)

Kyoo wa osoku naru soo desu means *I understand that he will be late today.* The soo is the dependent nominative and conveys the meaning of *hearsay* when it is attached to the end of a plain form of a verb, an adjective, or a nominative. Soo is followed by the copula desu or da.

Examples:

Hoteru ni tomaru
          tomaranai
          tomatta
          tomaranakatta

Omoshiroi
Omoshiroku nai
Omoshirokatta   soo desu.
Omoshiroku nakatta

Kirei da
Kirei ja nai (*or* dewa nai)
Kirei datta
Kirei ja nakatta (*or* dewa nakatta)

271

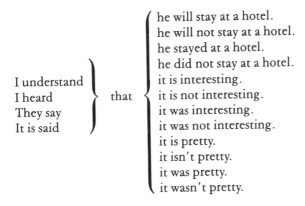

I understand I heard They say It is said	that	he will stay at a hotel. he will not stay at a hotel. he stayed at a hotel. he did not stay at a hotel. it is interesting. it is not interesting. it was interesting. it was not interesting. it is pretty. it isn't pretty. it was pretty. it wasn't pretty.

Basu wa san-ji ni tsuku soo desu.
I understand that the bus will come at 3 o'clock.

Ashita Yamada-san ga den'wa suru soo desu.
I heard that Mr. Yamada will call tomorrow.

Aoki-san wa Tanaka-san ni den'wa shinakatta soo desu.
They say that Mr. Aoki did not call Mr. Tanaka.

Sono resutoran no sushi wa oishii soo desu.
It is said that that restaurant's sushi is delicious.

Rusuchuu ni den'wa ga atta soo desu.
They said that there was a phone call during my absence.

16.4.3 **o- / go-** V stem **shimasu. / itashimasu.** (Humble style)

Nan-ji ni oai shimashoo ka? means *What time shall I meet you?* The polite prefix o or go, plus the stem form of a verb, plus shimasu is a humble sentence structure, and conveys the meaning, *The speaker or his ingroup member will do such and such.*

Examples:

Watakushi ga omochi shimasu.	I will carry it.
Imooto ga goan'nai shimasu.	My younger sister will guide you.
Sugu menyuu o omochi shimasu.	I'll bring a menu right away.
Yamada-san ni oden'wa itashimashoo ka?	Shall I call Mr. Yamada?

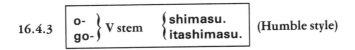

16.4.4 Mono (a person)

Araki Kazuko to iu mono desu means *I am a person called Kazuko Araki.*
Mono here means *a person*, not *a thing.*

Mono is also used to replace an individual's name when he/she feels it is not necessary to state his/her name, such as:

Watakushi wa Tookyoo Gin'koo no mono desu.	I am an employee of the Bank of Tokyo.

16.5 DRILLS

16.5.1 Number Drill

Read the following telephone numbers.

Example: 948-6851	Kyuu yon hachi no, roku hachi goo ichi
1. 973-6904	Kyuu nana san no, roku kyuu zero (or rei) yon
2. 546-7341	Goo yon roku no, nana san yon ichi
3. 395-0619	San kyuu goo no, zero roku ichi kyuu
4. 253-4904	Ni goo san no, yon kyuu zero yon

16.5.2 Substitution Drill

Use the English cues to guide your substitutions:

1. Please call Mr. Akita because he has a phone call.
   Akita-san o yon'de kudasai. Den'wa desu kara.

2. Please call Mr. Akita because he has an international call.
   Akita-san o yon'de kudasai. Kokusai den'wa desu kara.

3. Please call Mr. Akita because he has an appointment.
   Akita-san o yon'de kudasai. Apoin'tomen'to ga arimasu kara.

4. Please call Mr. Akita because he has a long distance call.
   Akita-san o yon'de kudasai. Chookyori den'wa desu kara.

5. Please call Mr. Akita because he has a meeting.
   Akita-san o yon'de kudasai. Kaigi desu kara.

6. Please call Mr. Akita because he has a message.
   Akita-san o yon'de kudasai. Den'gon ga arimasu kara.

7. Please call Mr. Akita because I want to see him.
   Akita-san o yon'de kudasai. Aitai desu kara.

16.5.3 Transformation Drill

Example: Nihon ryoori o tabemasu; Chuugoku ryoori o tabemasu.
Nihon ryoori o taberu yori Chuugoku ryoori o taberu hoo
ga suki desu.

1. Itaria ryoori o tabemasu; Amerika ryoori o tabemasu.
Itaria ryoori o taberu yori Amerika ryoori o taberu hoo ga suki
desu.
2. Eigo de hanashimasu; nihon'go de hanashimasu.
Eigo de hanasu yori nihon'go de hanasu hoo ga suki desu.
3. Fune ni norimasu; hikooki ni norimasu.
Fune ni noru yori hikooki ni noru hoo ga suki desu.
4. Furan'su ni sumimasu; Suisu ni sumimasu.
Furan'su ni sumu yori Suisu ni sumu hoo ga suki desu.
5. Hoteru ni tomarimasu; ryokan ni tomarimasu.
Hoteru ni tomaru yori ryokan ni tomaru hoo ga suki desu.
6. Tegami o kakimasu; den'wa o shimasu.
Tegami o kaku yori den'wa o suru hoo ga suki desu.

16.5.4 Response Drill

Example:
On'gaku o kiku no to hon o yomu no to, dotchi ga suki desu ka?
On'gaku o kiku . . . On'gaku o kiku hoo ga suki desu.

1. Eigo de hanasu no to, nihon'go de hanasu no to, furan'sugo de hanasu
no to de wa, dore ga ichiban muzukashii desu ka?
Nihon'go de hanasu . . . Nihon'go de hanasu no ga ichiban muzukashii
desu.
2. Yooroppa e iku no to, Amerika e iku no to, dotchi ga yasui desu ka?
Amerika e iku . . . Amerika e iku hoo ga yasui desu.
3. Shimei tsuuwa to futsuu tsuuwa to dotchi no hoo ga takai desu ka?
Shimei tsuuwa . . . Shimei tsuuwa no hoo ga (zutto) takai desu.
4. Biiru to wain to sake to uisukii de wa, dore ga ichiban suki desu ka?
Biiru . . . Biiru ga ichiban suki desu.

16.5.5 Transformation Drill

Example:
Tegami o kakimasu.
Den'wa o kakemasu.

Tegami o kaku no wa den'wa o
kakeru hodo yasashiku arimasen.

1. Asa otooto o okoshimasu.
Imooto o okoshimasu.

Asa otooto o okosu no wa imooto o
okosu hodo yasashiku arimasen.

274

2. Kan'ji de kakimasu.
   Hiragana de kakimasu.

   Kan'ji de kaku no wa hiragana de
   kaku hodo yasashiku arimasen.

3. Nihon'go de hanashimasu.
   Furan'sugo de hanashimasu.

   Nihon'go de hanasu no wa
   furan'sugo de hanasu hodo
   yasashiku arimasen.

4. Tenisu o shimasu.
   Gorufu o shimasu.

   Tenisu o suru no wa gorufu o suru
   hodo yasashiku arimasen.

16.5.6 Substitution Drill

Example:
You'd better *take the medicine now.*
Ima kusuri o non'da hoo ga ii desu yo.

1. Cue: call now
   Ima den'wa shita hoo ga ii desu yo.

2. Cue: leave a message now
   Ima den'gon o onegai shita hoo ga ii desu yo.

3. Cue: call person-to-person now
   Ima shimei tsuuwa shita hoo ga ii desu yo.

4. Cue: make a reservation now
   Ima yoyaku shita hoo ga ii desu yo.

16.5.7 Transformation Drill

Example:
Tashiro-san wa raigetsu kekkon shimasu.
    Tashiro-san wa raigetsu kekkon suru soo desu.

1. Asatte furan'su-jin ga dinaa shoo *(dinner show)* o mi ni kimasu.
   Asatte furan'su-jin ga dinaa shoo o mi ni kuru soo desu.

2. Kazuko-san wa eigo o hanasu koto ga dekimasu.
   Kazuko-san wa eigo o hanasu koto ga dekiru soo desu.

3. Tomodachi wa kon'ban Hawai ni wa tsukimasen.
   Tomodachi wa kon'ban Hawai ni wa tsukanai soo desu.

4. George-san wa Nihon bun'ka o ben'kyoo shimasen deshita.
   George-san wa Nihon bun'ka o ben'kyoo shinakatta soo desu.

5. Ima Yamaguchi-san wa seki o hazushite imasu.
   Ima Yamaguchi-san wa seki o hazushite iru soo desu.

275

16.5.8   Transformation Drill

Example:

Takaki-san wa kibun ga warui desu.

    Takaki-san wa kibun ga warui soo desu.

1. Ano shoo wa totemo omoshirokatta desu.
       Ano shoo wa totemo omoshirokatta soo desu.

2. Kore no hoo ga zutto yasukatta desu.
       Kore no hoo ga zutto yasukatta soo desu.

3. Ishii-san ga mita eiga wa amari omoshiroku arimasen deshita.
       Ishii-san ga mita eiga wa amari omoshiroku nakatta soo desu.

4. Smith-san wa kaban ga hoshii desu.
       Smith-san wa kaban ga hoshii soo desu.

5. Mise wa isogashiku arimasen.
       Mise wa isogashiku nai soo desu.

16.5.9   Transformation Drill

Example:

Yamamoto-san wa ima kaigichuu desu.

    Yamamoto-san wa ima kaigichuu da soo desu.

1. Hanashichuu desu.
       Hanashichuu da soo desu.

2. Kaigi wa mikka kara muika made deshita.
       Kaigi wa mikka kara muika made datta soo desu.

3. Yamada-san, chookyori den'wa desu yo.
       Yamada-san, chookyori den'wa da soo desu yo.

4. Ashita wa yasumi ja arimasen.
       Ashita wa yasumi ja nai soo desu.

5. Mise wa hima dewa arimasen deshita.
       Mise wa hima dewa nakatta soo desu.

16.5.10   Transformation Drill

Example:

Watakushi ga haraimasu.	Watakushi ga	{ oharai shimasu. { oharai itashimasu.
1. Watakushi ga yomimasu.	Watakushi ga	{ oyomi shimasu. { oyomi itashimasu.

276

2. Watakushi ga mochimasu.	Watakushi ga	⎰omochi shimasu. ⎱omochi itashimasu.
3. Watakushi ga den'wa o kakemasu.	Watakushi ga den'wa o	⎰okake shimasu. ⎱okake itashimasu.
4. Watakushi ga an'nai shimasu.	Watakushi ga	⎰goan'nai shimasu. ⎱goan'nai itashimasu.
5. Watakushi ga chuumon shimasu.	Watakushi ga	⎰gochuumon shimasu. ⎱gochuumon itashi-masu.
6. Watakushi ga hanashimasu.	Watakushi ga	⎰ohanashi shimasu. ⎱ohanashi itashimasu.

16.6 EXERCISES

16.6.1 Numbers

Read the following telephone numbers in Japanese.

1. 324-5910
2. 047-6858
3. 989-0047 extension 207
4. 831-6573 extension 959
5. 373-6024 extension 119

16.6.2 Situational Practice

You and Mr. Tanaka's secretary are on the telephone. Carry on the following telephone conversation in Japanese.

You say:

1. Hello, is this President Tanaka's office?
2. May I speak to Mr. Tanaka?
3. This is John Smith of the Waikiki Sheraton in Hawaii.
4. May I leave a message?
5. I'll arrive in Tokyo the day after tomorrow. I'll call him after arriving in Tokyo.

Secretary responds:

1. Yes, this is President Tanaka's office.
2. Who's calling please?
3. I'm sorry, but President Tanaka is in a conference right now.
4. Yes, please do.
5. Thank you very much. I will convey the message to him.

16.6.3 Translation

Translate the following into Japanese.

1. I think you'd better call Mr. Yamada tonight.
2. After arriving in Tokyo, I made reservations for a room at the Keio Plaza.
3. It is cheaper to buy it at that store than to buy it at this store.
4. Singing with **karaoke** was not as easy as I thought.
5. I think that it is more interesting to stay at a Japanese inn than to stay at a (Western) hotel.
6. They say that New York is not as lively as Tokyo.
7. Which do you like better, taking a walk or swimming in the hotel pool?
8. Mr. Yamada, there is a person-to-person international call for you.
9. Mr. Tsunoda, this is Mr. Tanaka of Fuji Travel Company. I'm sorry for calling, but I want to consult with you. Do you have time now?

16.7 SIMULATION AND SKITS

1. A Japanese tourist is visiting his aunt at her home. His aunt wants to know his hotel's telephone number so she can call him tomorrow for lunch. He looks up the hotel's number in the phone book for her and tells her the number.

2. A hotel guest calls the hotel operator and asks her to give him a wake-up call tomorrow morning at 7:00. At 7:00 the next morning, he receives the wake-up call.

3. A tour company manager wants to make a business appointment with the manager of a hotel. He calls the hotel manager's office, and the secretary sets up an appointment.

4. A Japanese tourist calls his Hawaiian friend as soon as he arrives in Hawaii. The two friends talk and make plans to meet.

5. John calls his friend's house, but he gets the wrong number. He tries again, but he's told that his friend is not home, so he leaves a message instead.

6. You try to call your section manager to let him know you're sick and won't be coming to work. However, you're told that he isn't at his desk at the moment. So you ask your colleague to take the message for you.

7. A hotel guest and a hotel employee are in the lobby discussing various activities that tourists would be interested in.

8. You and your friend are telling each other about the news you've just heard on the radio or read in the newspaper.

9. You want to make a dinner reservation at a restaurant for 7:00 tonight. Call the restaurant and make the arrangements with the hostess.

10. Upon arriving in Hawaii, a tourist calls a hotel in Waikiki to reserve a room. As the hotel's front desk employee, make a reservation for him.

16.8 CULTURE ORIENTATION

16.8.1 Telephone and Appointment

A Japanese person who is engaged in a conversation checks the expression and eyes of the other speaker while communicating. In order to adjust to the speaker, one must be very skillful at assessing their expressions with quick glances. In a culture where feelings are felt and understood, rather than verbally communicated, the observance of facial expressions becomes very important. For this reason, communication over the phone did not spread rapidly in Japan until recent years. It was a frightening idea for the Japanese people to have to communicate with someone without being able to see his face. However, radio and television use spread very rapidly. For some time there was a cultural bias against communicating over the phone, for it seemed somewhat rude. Even now, there is a tendency to consider it proper to talk in person if the matter at hand is very important. This is especially true if one is dealing with an older person. When a favor is being asked or something important is being conveyed, one begins a telephone conversation by saying, "Sorry for this rudeness over the phone (instead of visiting you)." Despite some avoidance of the telephone, increased usage is inevitable with the growth of the information society.

In the past decade or so, Japan finally reached the lower ranks of the advanced nations of the world in the propagation of telephone usage. If one family has five members, there is an average of one phone, or more, per family (Umesao et al. 1974:217–218).

The Japanese have overcome their phone phobias and have actually grown to like it. The most popular radio programs are programs that use telephones for people to call in and request songs. These cater mostly to younger people. Strangers talk to each other quite casually over the phone on these radio programs. Listeners tune in and some participate by calling. The speaker-vs.-many-listener system of radio programs is different from the typical communication between two people for which the telephone is normally used (Umesao et al. 1974:217).

We will discuss some of the reasons why the Japanese people now use the phone so extensively. One reason may be the immediate communication which the telephone provides. In this age of speed, the ability to communicate with people when one wishes is an attraction. Also, the Japanese have become reluctant writers of their own language. An increasing number of people are poor writers. Poor handwriting is considered an embarrassment, and much time is consumed in writing a letter in acceptable handwriting. The telephone avoids this problem. As urbanization spreads, the number of people who desire one-to-one communication increases. The number of lonely people increases, also. In typical radio and television programs, the speaker addresses a large, unknown audience. This is a relatively one-sided communication. But with telephones, the audience can also participate, making the shows more of a two-way communication. In some ways, the telephone bridges the space between sender and receiver, in addition to conveying information.

However, with the high rate of telephone usage, some social problems have arisen. It is said that telephones have contributed to a lack of maturity in young men and women. Children used to mature when they were separated from their parents. But with the availability of telephones, even students who leave home to go to college can remain closely tied to their parents. In spite of the distance, students can still turn to their parents for advice; they remain half adult and half child. It is said that immature young people are growing in numbers in Japan. In the case of women, even after marriage, their ties to their mothers remain very strong because of telephones. This can cause problems between partners; sometimes the woman is slow to learn household duties since her mother can advise her any time over the phone (Umesao et al. 1974:220–221). The propagation of telephones has made life easier in many ways, but it has been accompanied by problems as well.

16.8.2 Business Telephones

As in Western countries, telephones are available at offices, hotels, and even at ryokan. Interaction with customers is increasingly made over the phone. Because of this, a great deal of importance is attached to telephone manners which will give a favorable impression to customers. How one speaks, their tone of voice, and even accents become criteria for judgment. Because of this, telephone training programs are offered to secretaries, as well as to telephone operators. Such training is included in a company's in-service training for new employees.

16.8.3 Appointment

The word appointment is a difficult one to translate into Japanese. If made between friends or businessmen, the word **yakusoku** *promise* can be used. However, it is difficult to find an expression which conveys the meaning of the word in, for example, *a doctor's appointment*. Many simply use the English word for it. It is often abbreviated as **appoin'to**.

In Japan, there are occasions at which friends will drop in without calling first. *I was in the area, so I thought I'd drop in,* he might say. Visiting without warning may be considered rude in some Western countries, but in Japan it is quite acceptable. Since warning the other party of one's arrival would compel the other to tidy up the house and have something ready to serve, it would cause, rather than prevent, trouble. On the other hand, if one arrived without warning, no such expectation could be held, and it would save the other person a lot of unnecessary trouble. A well-prepared visitor will probably bring a small gift of cakes or sweets which can be eaten together.

Even among businessmen, if there is no urgent or specific matter to be dealt with, visiting without prior appointment is still a rather common practice. If the person is not there, it is simply accepted by the visitor. One takes the risk of wasting time in order not to waste the other's time making preparations for a guest. This type of behavior is a form of consideration for the other party, which allows him the freedom to carry on with his own plans.

In American universities, some professors notice that Japanese students often drop into their offices without making prior appointments. However, at times, they also make appointments for matters that could have been taken care of over the phone. This may happen because the student feels that he is burdening the professor by making an appointment ahead of time or that some matters are rude if treated by telephone. Regardless of how trivial the matter may have been, a student may prefer to meet the professor in person rather than use the phone. For students to drop in at the professor's office may actually take more time than if an appointment had been made, but Japanese students often do not interpret their own actions in this way. Differences in value systems of the people involved can complicate situations.

While appointments between people are still not common in Japan, restaurants, hotels, and ryokan do take reservations, and are doing so more and more frequently.

16.9 JAPANESE MODE OF COMMUNICATION

Aizuchi

The characters for the word aizuchi depict two people hammering steel to make a sword or pounding mochi *rice cake* for New Year's Day. In either case, this word indicates the timing with which two people hammer to create something. From this meaning, it came to signify the nodding movements of two individuals as they conversed. Earlier, it was mentioned that the Japanese basic rhythm was a synchronizing rhythm. The Japanese use this rhythm while they converse too. This rhythm is created through the aizuchi. When one speaks to a Japanese person there's always a hai, ee, hoo, a soo desu ka, or naruhodo *I see*, in response, or, if not these kinds of words, then a nodding of heads. There is a pattern between the speakers resembling waves that come and go. In order to maintain this synchronizing rhythm, it becomes necessary to adjust and more or less agree with the speaker, as was mentioned in the previous lesson. If one disagress, vague expressions are used, such as soo desu ka nee *I wonder,* instead of jeopardizing the rhythm by saying No or I *disagree*. This synchronizing rhythm is also used in a telephone conversation. Since the mere nodding of one's head cannot be observed over the telephone, expressions as hai, or ee become absolutely necessary. If one observes a Japanese speaker on the phone, one will notice that he is intermittently and continuously saying ee or hai or haa. These expressions allow the speaker to continue his conversation. If there is silence on the other end, the speaker checks for the other's presence by saying moshi moshi, moshi moshi. Although the Japanese appreciate silence as being meaningful most of the time, they find it unbearable over the phone.

Unlike the English *Yes, I understand you,* hai on the phone indicates, *I am with you,* or *Yes, go on; I'm listening.* Therefore, if there is silence on the other end, it is interepreted as an absence of the listener. The speaker will check by saying moshi moshi, to confirm that the listener is still present.

16.10 LANGUAGE AND CULTURE

A. **Moshi moshi**

This expression is used to begin a conversation over the telephone. Sometimes it is used in ordinary conversation to get somebody's attention (Mizutani 1981:102). It can also be used during a telephone conversation in order to get the other speaker's attention or to check that they are still there. It is also used if one cannot hear the other party very well.

Moshi moshi is also used when one asks for directions. One may get somebody's attention by saying Moshi moshi, shitsurei desu ga . . . In some ways it resembles the expression anoo, covered earlier. Moshi moshi gives a prior warning to the listener by subtly getting their attention. Once this is done, one can say what is substantial.

B. **Den'wa ga tooi desu.**
Den'wa o kitte kudasai.
Ohanashichuu desu.

The first expression literally means *the phone is far.* This is an idiomatic expression since the exact meaning cannot be understood from its literal translation. It simply means *I can't year you.* The second expression is also an idiomatic expression with a literal meaning of *Please cut off the phone.* It means *Please hang up.* The third expression literally translated means *(The person) is in the midst of conversing* and is used when English speakers would say *The line is busy.* This should also be learned as an idiomatic expression.

C. **Gomen kudasai**

This expression is used at the door of somebody's home and is equivalent to the English *Knock, knock* or *Hello, is anybody home?* However, it is also used at times at the end of telephone conversations following dewa *Well, then* or jaa. Instead of this expression, shitsurei shimasu, or shitsurei shimashita can also be used.

16.11   CULTURE QUESTIONS

1. It is often said that people or companies are judged by the tone of voice, manner of speech, or accent of the speaker on the phone. Is this true in your country? Are telephone operators or receptionists given special training on making a good impression? Discuss what manners of speech give favorable impressions to people over the phone.

2. On many occasions, Japanese behavior is based upon the criterion of how not to burden the other person. Furthermore, more importance is placed upon taking into consideration the needs and values of the other person. This takes precedence over saving time and efficiency in one's own schedule. An example of this kind of behavior can be seen in the discussion of making appointments. Are there similar tendencies in your country? Discuss and give examples.

3. Below is a telephone conversation between an American and a Japanese.

> Japanese: Hello, may I talk to Mr. Johnson?
> American: I'm sorry, he has just stepped out. Would you like to leave a message, or would you like to leave your number so that he can call you back when he returns?
> Japanese: That's OK. I'll call him again later.

Discuss some of the possible reasons why the Japanese did not leave his number.

4. There are certain kinds of aizuchi in English too. Discuss what kinds of expressions function as aizuchi and indicate their meanings. Discuss how they are used and whether they are similar to the Japanese expressions.

16.12   SUGGESTED RESOURCE MATERIALS

Books and Magazines

Japanese: The Spoken Language in Japanese Life. Osamu Mizutani, trans. by Janet Ashby (Tokyo: The Japan Times, 1981), pp. 81–86.
Nihongo Notes 1: Speaking and Living in Japan, Osamu Mizutani and Nobuko Mizutani (Tokyo: The Japan Times, 1977) pp. 14–15, 112–113.

16.13   REFERENCES

Mizutani, Osamu. *Japanese: The Spoken Language in Japanese Life,* trans. by Janet Ashby. Tokyo: The Japan Times, 1981.
Umesao, Tadao, et al. *Nihonjin no Seikatsu Kuukan.* Tokyo: Asahi Shinbun Sha, 1974.

LESSON 17

ASKING AND GIVING DIRECTIONS

17.1   USEFUL EXPRESSIONS

Chotto sumimasen . . .
Sumimasen ga . . .   } Excuse me, but . . .
Chotto ukagaimasu ga . . .

Ano kado o migi e magatte kudasai.   Please turn to the right at that corner.
Kono michi o massugu itte kudasai.   Please go straight ahead on this road.
Aruite go-fun gurai no tokoro desu.   It's about a five minutes walk from
                                       here.

Sugu wakarimasu yo.   You can't miss it. You'll find it easily.
Koko desu.   Here you are.

17.2   CONVERSATION

17.2.1   Asking about a Bus Stop

Kan'kookyaku: Sumimasen ga, kono hen ni basu no teiryuujo ga
               arimasu ka?
Gaado: Kono michi o massugu itte, ichiban'me no kado o migi e magatte
        kudasai. Basu sutoppu no sain ga miemasu.
Kan'kookyaku: Tooi desu ka?
Gaado: Iie, ni–san-pun no tokoro desu. Doko e irasshaimasu ka?
Kan'kookyaku: Ara Moana Sen'taa e ikimasu.
Gaado: Dewa, 8-ban no basu ni notte kudasai.
Kan'kookyaku: Doomo arigatoo.

Tourist: Excuse me. Is there a bus stop in this area?
Guard: Go straight along this road and turn right at the first corner. You will
        see a bus stop sign.
Tourist: Is it far?
Guard: No, it's just two or three minutes from here. Where are you going?
Tourist: To Ala Moana Center.
Guard: Then you should board bus #8.
Tourist: Thank you.

284

17.2.2 Asking about the Zoo

Kyaku: Sumimasen ga, doobutsuen e iku michi o oshiete kudasai.
Furon'to: Doobutsuen desu ka? Basu de ikimasu ka, aruite ikimasu ka?
Kyaku: Aruite ikitai desu ga, tooi desu ka?
Furon'to: Aruite 20-pun gurai no tokoro desu.
Kyaku: 20-pun kakarimasu ka?
Furon'to: Sono gurai kakaru deshoo. Chizu o kaite agemashoo. Kono michi
no niban'me no yotsukado o hidari e magatte kara, massugu itte
kudasai. Migi no hoo ni kooen ga miemasu. Doobutsuen no iri-
guchi wa sono kooen no mukai desu.
Kyaku: Doomo arigatoo gozaimashita. Kono chizu o itadakimasu ne.
Furon'to: Doozo.

Guest: Excuse me. Can you tell me which street to take to reach the zoo?
Front Desk
Clerk: The zoo? Do you want to go by bus or on foot?
Guest: I'd like to walk. Is it far?
Clerk: It takes about 20 minutes to walk.
Guest: It'll take 20 minutes?
Clerk: It takes about that long, I think. Let me draw you a map. Follow this
street to the second intersection, turn left and continue straight.
You'll see a park on your right. The entrance to the zoo is just oppo-
site the park.
Guest: Thank you so much. May I take this map?
Clerk: Sure.

17.2.3 Inquiries in the Street

1. A: Sumimasen ga . . . Kono hen ni den'wa ga arimasu ka?
   B: Den'wa desu ka? Ano eigakan no soba ni arimasu yo.
   A: Doomo arigatoo.

2. A: Anoo, chotto ukagaimasu ga, doobutsuen e wa doo ikimasu ka?
   B: Doobutsuen desu ka? Kono michi o massugu itte, niban'me no
   michi o hidari ni magatte kudasai. Doobutsuen wa migi no hoo ni
   arimasu.
   A: Doomo arigatoo gozaimashita.

3. A: Chotto sumimasen. Ara Moana e ikitai n'desu ga, basu no teiryuujo
   wa doko desu ka?
   B: Kono michi o massugu itte kudasai. Migi no hoo ni gin'koo ga
   arimasu. Sono mukai ni teiryuujo ga arimasu.
   A: Gin'koo no mukai desu ne. Doomo arigatoo.

4. A: Erebeetaa wa doko deshoo ka?
   B: Ano kaidan no ushiro no hoo desu.
   A: Doomo.

5. A: Hon'ya wa doko desu ka?
   B: Ano shiroi tatemono no naka ni arimasu yo.
   A: Aa, soo desu ka? Doomo.

1. A: Excuse me . . . Is there a telephone in this area?
   B: A telephone? Yes, there's one beside that theater.
   A: Thank you.

2. A: Excuse me, what's the best way to go to the zoo?
   B: The zoo? Follow this street and turn left at the second street. The zoo will be on your right.
   A: Thank you.

3. A: Excuse me. I would like to go to Ala Moana. Where is the bus stop?
   B: Go straight. On your right you will see a bank. Opposite the bank you will find the bus stop.
   A: Opposite the bank. Thanks.

4. A: Where is the elevator?
   B: Behind the stairway.
   A: Thank you.

5. A: Where is a bookstore?
   B: In that white building.
   A: Oh, thanks.

17.3 VOCABULARY

Nouns

bijutsukan	art gallery
byooin	hospital
chikamichi	short cut
chikatetsu	subway
chizu	map
eigakan	movie theater
eki	train station
erebeetaa	elevator
esukareetaa	escalator
gekijoo	theater
gakkoo	school
hakubutsukan	museum
hanaya	flower shop
hon'ya	bookstore
kado	corner
kaidan	steps, stairs
keikan, jun'sa	policeman
keisatsu	police station

286

kooban	police box
kooen	park
kyookai	church
kuukoo	airport
michi	way, street
otearai	restroom, bathroom
ryoojikan	consulate
shashin	picture, photo
soba	beside
taishikan	embassy
tatemono	building
teiryuujo	bus stop
tonari	next door (neighbor), adjoining
tsukiatari	dead end
ushiro	behind, back
yotsukado	intersection
yuubin'kyoku	post office

Verbs

agemasu	to give
itadakimasu, moraimasu	to receive
kakarimasu	to take (as in measuring time)
kudasaimasu, kuremasu	to give (to ingroup)
magarimasu	to turn
sashiagemasu	to give (to outgroup)
yarimasu	to give (to inferior)

Adverbs

massugu	straight

Others

dake	only
mukai	facing
mukoo	beyond

17.4 EXPLANATION

17.4.1 Verbs of Giving and Receiving

Always conscious of social hierarchy, Japanese are sensitive in the use of words expressing giving and receiving. Different words are used depending upon who is giving or receiving something from whom. These differences depend on social status, age, ingroup and outgroup relation, communicative distance, and so forth. Thus, for example, the English verb *to give* translates into different Japanese verbs as illustrated in the following:

1. Watakushi wa Yamada-san ni chizu o agemashita.
   I gave Mr. Yamada a map.

2. Yamada-san wa watakushi ni chizu o kuremashita.
   Mr. Yamada gave me a map.

Furthermore, the above sentence can be converted into:

3. Watakushi wa Yamada-san ni(kara) chizu o moraimashita.
   I received a map from Mr. Yamada.

The factors which determine the choice of these words, ageru, kureru, morau, are the grammatical *persons* (first, second, or third person) of the giver and the recipient. The verb ageru is used when I/we give something to you/him/her; you give to him/her; or he/she gives to him/her. The verb kureru is used when you/he/she give to me/us; or he/she gives to you. (In this, I identify you as my ingroup.) The verb morau is used when I/we receive from you/him; you receive from him/her; or he/she receives from him/her.

These three verbs also have their honorific counterparts which are used to express respect for the person(s) involved. Sashiageru, instead of ageru, is chosen when the recipient is older or superior to the giver in status; kudasaru, instead of kureru, when the giver is superior to the recipient; and itadaku, instead of morau, when the giver is superior to the recipient.

Study the following:

1.
$$\text{S} \left\{ \begin{array}{c} \text{wa} \\ \text{ga} \end{array} \right\} \text{P} \quad \text{ni} \quad \text{N o} \left\{ \begin{array}{l} \text{sashiagemasu.} \\ \text{agemasu.} \\ \text{yarimasu.} \end{array} \right.$$

S gives N to P. (S is the subject, N is the object, P is the person.) Yarimasu is used when the speaker or someone of the ingroup gives to an ingroup inferior such as the speaker's own children or a youngster. It is often used for inanimate objects, for example, *I gave water to the plant*.

Examples:
Watakushi wa okyaku-san ni kore o sashiagemasu.
I give this to the customers.

Watakushi wa tomodachi ni kore o agemasu.
I give this to my friends.

Watakushi wa otooto ni kore o yarimasu.
I give this to my younger brother.

Nani o sashiagemashoo ka?
What can I give you (help you with).

288

2.

$$S \begin{Bmatrix} wa \\ ga \end{Bmatrix} P \text{ ni } N \text{ o } V \begin{Bmatrix} \text{kudasaimasu.} \\ \text{kuremasu.} \end{Bmatrix}$$

S gives N to P. (P is the speaker.)

Examples:

Sen'sei ga watakushi ni kore o kudasaimashita.
My teacher gave me this.

Tomodachi ga watakushi ni kore o kuremashita.
My friends gave me this.

3.

$$S \begin{Bmatrix} wa \\ ga \end{Bmatrix} P \begin{Bmatrix} ni \\ kara \end{Bmatrix} N \text{ o } V \begin{Bmatrix} \text{itadakimasu.} \\ \text{moraimasu.} \end{Bmatrix}$$

$$S \begin{Bmatrix} \text{is given} \\ \text{receives} \end{Bmatrix} N \begin{Bmatrix} \text{by} \\ \text{from} \end{Bmatrix} P.$$

Examples:

Watakushi wa sen'sei ni (kara) kore o itadakimashita.
I received this from my teacher.

Watakushi wa tomodachi ni (kara) kore o moraimashita.
I received this from my friends.

17.4.2	(S wa *Person* ni) (N o) V -te +	sashiagemasu. agemasu. yarimasu. kudasaimasu. kuremasu. itadakimasu. moraimasu.

(Giving and Receiving Acts)

Chizu o kaite agemashoo means *I will draw a map for you.* Doing something for the benefit of someone else is treated as essentially the same as giving a thing to someone. A sentence indicating that someone does something as a favor has the te form of a verb plus one of the extenders ageru, kureru, morau, and so forth. The extenders retain their function of specifying direction of action: who does something and for whom it is done. The use of the compound verbs follow the same rules as in 17.4.1

Examples:

Tomodachi ni eigo o oshiete agemashita.	I taught English to my friend.
Tookyoo Eki e iku michi o oshiete kudasai.	Please teach me the way to Tokyo Station.
Hisho ga an'nai shite kuremashita.	The secretary guided me.
Sen'sei ga nihon'go o oshiete kudasaimashita.	The teacher taught me Japanese.
Michi o oshiete kudasaimasen ka?	Won't you please teach me the way?

The particle kara that occurs before morau in the pattern of *(a person)* kara *(a thing)* o morau is not used. Only ni is used, as in:

Watakushi wa tomodachi ni tegami o kaite moraimashita.
I asked my friend to write my letter.

Tomodachi ga tegami o kaite kuremashita.
My friend wrote a letter for me.

Kan'kookyaku wa michi o iku hito ni shashin o totte moraimashita.
The tourists had the passerby take their pictures.

17.4.3	Place N o	**arukimasu.**
		ikimasu.
		kimasu.
		magarimasu.
		etc.

Kono michi o massugu itte kudasai means *Please go straight along this street.* Place Noun + o followed by a motion verb (not a transitive verb) such as aruki-masu, ikimasu, kimasu, magarimasu, indicates the place through which the motion takes place. It is often translated as *through (the place)*, *along (the street)*, *at (the corner)*, and so forth.

Examples:

Waikiki o san'po shimashita.	I took a walk through Waikiki.
Kono michi o ikimashoo.	Let's go along this street.
Ano kado o migi e magatte kudasai.	Please turn right at that corner.

17.4.4	V (**te** form) +	**iku**
		kuru
		kaeru
	(How one goes, comes, returns)	

Aruite ikimasu means *I will walk.* The te form of verbs such as arukimasu and norimasu may be followed by the extender ikimasu, kimasu, or kaerimasu; the compound verbs indicate how one goes, comes, or returns, and so forth.

290

Examples:

Kuruma ni notte ikimasu ka? (Kuruma de ikimasu ka?)

Do you go by car?

Hakubutsukan kara aruite kaerimashita.

I walked home from the museum.

Shachoo wa basu ni notte irasshaimashita. (Shachoo wa basu de irasshaimashita.)

The company president came by bus.

17.5 DRILLS

17.5.1 English–Japanese Substitution Drill

Kyookai wa gakkoo no *soba* desu.

Example: next door   *tonari*
          Kyookai wa gakkoo no *tonari* desu.

1. front
   Kyookai wa gakkoo no *mae* desu.

2. left side
   Kyookai wa gakkoo no *hidari-gawa* desu.

3. right side
   Kyookai wa gakkoo no *migi-gawa* desu.

4. behind
   Kyookai wa gakkoo no *ushiro* desu.

5. beyond
   Kyookai wa gakkoo no *mukoo* desu.

6. facing
   Kyookai wa gakkoo no *mukai* desu.

7. side
   Kyookai wa gakkoo no *yoko* desu.

8. beside
   Kyookai wa gakkoo no *soba* desu.

17.5.2 Question–Answer Drill

Student A asks the following questions, and student B gives the answers based on Figure 1. Student A must locate the places based on B's responses, and fill in the answers on the blank Figure 2. (Student A must not look at Figure 1.) There are various answers for each question.

Figure 1

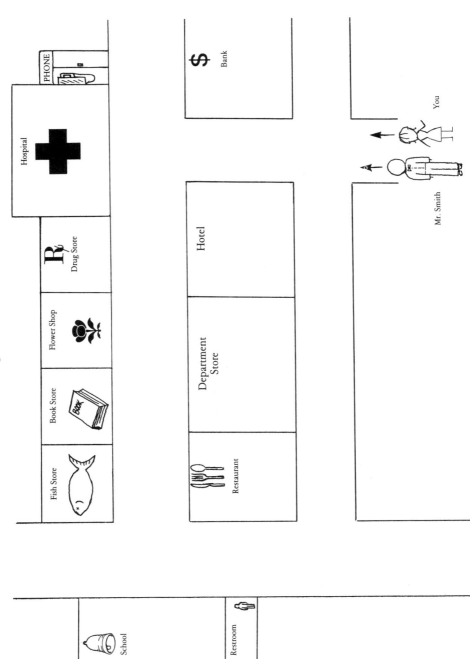

Figure 2

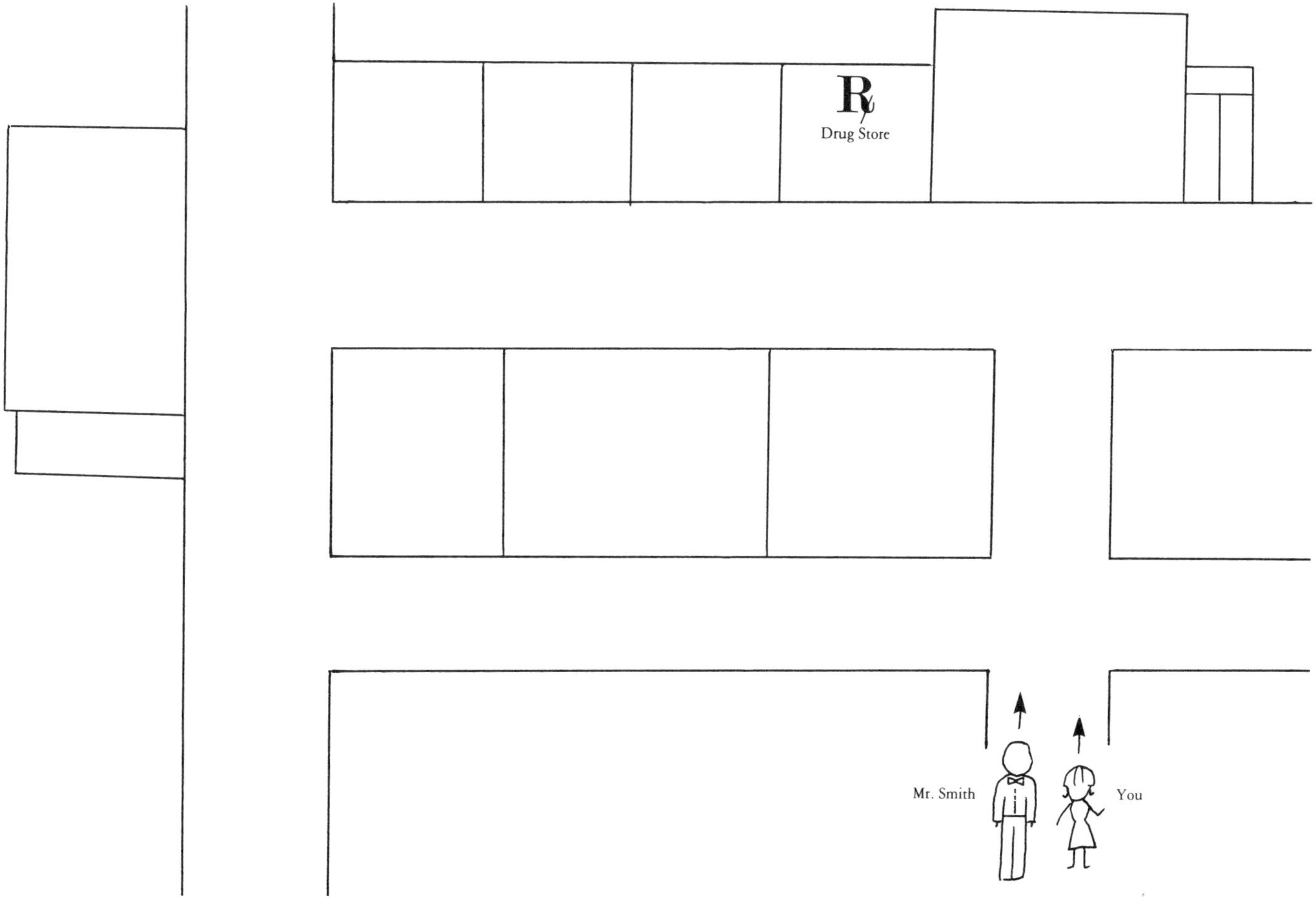

Examples: A: Hanaya wa doku desu ka?
            B: Hanaya desu ka? Kusuriya no tonari desu.

            A: Hon'ya wa doko ni arimasu ka?
            B: Hon'ya wa hanaya no hidari-gawa ni arimasu.

1. Hoteru wa doko desu ka?
2. Byooin wa doko desu ka?
3. Depaato wa doko ni arimasu ka?
4. Gin'koo wa doko ni arimasu ka?
5. Sakanaya wa doko desu ka?
6. Resutoran wa doko desu ka?
7. Gakkoo wa doko ni arimasu ka?
8. Otearai wa doko ni arimasu ka?

17.5.3   Situational Practice

Describe where you are by using the words in 17.5.1.

17.5.4   English–Japanese Substitution Drill

Eigakan e iku michi o oshiete kudasai.

Example: bank
        Gin'koo e iku michi o oshiete kudasai.

1. park
   Kooen e iku michi o oshiete kudasai.

2. museum
   Hakubutsukan e iku michi o oshiete kudasai.

3. zoo
   Doobutsuen e iku michi o oshiete kudasai.

4. train
   Eki e iku michi o oshiete kudasai.

5. embassy
   Taishikan e iku michi o oshiete kudasai.

6. consulate
   Ryoojikan e iku michi o oshiete kudasai.

7. airport
   Kuukoo e iku michi o oshiete kudasai.

8. police station
   Keisatsu e iku michi o oshiete kudasai.

9. police box
   Kooban e iku michi o oshiete kudasai.

10. hospital
   Byooin e iku michi o oshiete kudasai.

11. post office
   Yuubin'kyoku e iku michi o oshiete kudasai.

12. subway

Chikatetsu e iku michi o oshiete kudasai.

13. bus stop

Teiryuujo e iku michi o oshiete kudasai.

17.5.5 Mixed Drill

Watakushi wa tomodachi ni hana o agemashita.

1. Watakushi wa Yamamoto-san ni
   Watakushi wa Yamamoto-san ni hana o agemashita.
2. Yamamoto-san ga watakushi ni
   Yamamoto-san ga watakushi ni hana o kuremashita.
3. Watakushi wa ane ni
   Watakushi wa ane ni hana o agemashita.
4. Watakushi wa imooto ni
   Watakushi wa imooto ni hana o yarimashita.
5. Yamamoto-san wa Segawa-san ni
   Yamamoto-san wa Segawa-san ni hana o agemashita.
6. Segawa-san ga chichi ni
   Segawa-san ga chichi ni hana o kuremashita.
7. Watakushi wa Tanaka-san kara
   Watakushi wa Tanaka-san kara hana o moraimashita.
8. Imooto wa haha kara
   Imooto wa haha kara hana o moraimashita.
9. Tomodachi ga imooto ni
   Tomodachi ga imooto ni hana o kuremashita.
10. Dare ga anata ni
    Dare ga anata ni hana o kuremashita ka?

17.5.6 Mixed Drill

Watakushi wa John-san ni chizu o kaite agemashita.

1. Yamada-san wa Tanaka-san ni
   Yamada-san wa Tanaka-san ni chizu o kaite
   agemashita.
2. John-san ga watakushi ni
   John-san ga watakushi ni chizu o kaite kuremashita.
3. Watakushi wa imooto ni
   Watakushi wa imooto ni chizu o kaite yarimashita.

4. Tanaka-san ga otooto ni
    Tanaka-san ga otooto ni chizu o kaite kuremashita.

5. Watakushi wa tomodachi no otooto-san ni
    Watakushi wa tomodachi no otooto-san ni chizu o kaite
    agemashita.

17.5.7 Transformation Drill

1. Tomodachi ga kazoku no shashin o totte kuremashita.
    Tomodachi ni kazoku no shashin o totte moraimashita.

2. Jun'sa ga bijutsukan e iku michi o oshiete kuremashita.
    Jun'sa ni bijutsukan e iku michi o oshiete moraimashita.

3. Hisho ga den'wa shite kuremashita.
    Hisho ni den'wa shite moraimashita.

4. Sen'pai ga ogotte kuremashita.
    Sen'pai ni ogotte moraimashita.

5. Buchoo ga okane o haratte kudasaimashita.
    Buchoo ni okane o haratte itadakimashita.

17.5.8 Situational Practice

1. Okyaku-san ga omiyage o kudasaimashita.
    Okyaku-san ni omiyage o itadakimashita.

2. Sen'sei ga nihon'go o oshiete kudasaimashita.
    Sen'sei ni nihon'go o oshiete itadakimashita.

3. Musume ga tegami o kuremashita.
    Musume ni tegami o moraimashita.

4. Kachoo ga kore o kudasaimashita.
    Kachoo ni kore o itadakimashita.

5. Tomodachi ga shashin o totte kuremashita.
    Tomodachi ni shashin o totte moraimashita.

17.6 EXERCISES

17.6.1 Completion

Fill in the blanks in accordance with the English translation.

1. Tomodachi ga shashin o   My friend gave a picture to me.
   _____.

2. Koohii o ippai _____.   Please give me a cup of coffee.

296

3. Kan'kookyaku ni hana o
   _____.

I gave some flowers to the tourists.

4. Nani o _____ ka?

What shall I give you?

5. Ano ten'in ni go-doru
   _____.

I got $5.00 from the salesclerk.

6. Shachoo ni kono omiyage o
   _____.

I got this souvenir from the company
   president.

17.6.2 Translation

Translate the following into Japanese.

1. Shall I write this in Japanese for you?
2. I brought these souvenirs for my colleagues.
3. Please show (teach) me the way.
4. We gave the children delicious drinks.
5. Nancy ordered a meal for Mr. Yamada.
6. We had the secretary introduce the man from Japan to us.
7. Shall I take the picture for you?

17.6.3 Completion

Complete each sentence, inserting into each blank one of the following words:
teiryuujo, massugu, o, ni, de, e, kakarimasu, sugu, no, kuru, itte, aruite,
notte.

1. A: Basu no _____ wa doko deshoo ka?
   B: Kono michi _____ tsukiatari _____ migi _____ magatte, _____ itte
      kudasai. Aruite go-fun gurai _____. _____ wakarimasu yo.

2. A: Yamada-san wa kon'ban _____ deshoo ka?
   B: Ee, irassharu to omoimasu yo.

3. A: Koko kara bijutsukan made _____ ikemasu ka?
   B: Soo desu nee, chotto tooi desu yo. Kuruma _____ itta hoo ga ii
      deshoo.

17.7 SIMULATION AND SKITS

1. As you are walking near the East-West Center, a tourist stops you and asks
   you where the UH Bookstore is located. Give him the directions to the bookstore.

2. You are in front of the Waikiki Mitsukoshi building and a tourist asks you for
   directions to the Royal Hawaiian Hotel.

3. Some guests in the hotel where you work want to know where several famous places in Hawaii are located, such as the Honolulu Academy of Arts, the Honolulu Zoo, the University of Hawaii, etc. Describe the location of these places to them.

4. A visitor from Japan explains to you how the Japanese celebrate special days such as Children's Day. She wants to know what you do on special days such as, Mother's Day, Father's Day, and so forth. Explain to her what most people do to celebrate these special days.

5. At Ala Moana Center a tourist stops to ask you how to get back to Waikiki by bus. Give him directions to the bus stop.

6. You and your friend are going to a picnic in Laie. The picnic starts at 10:00, so you are discussing the time it will take to go from Honolulu to Laie by either bus or car.

7. For your birthday you received a nice shirt from your older sister. When you wear the shirt to school, your friends want to know who gave you such a nice shirt.

17.8 CULTURE ORIENTATION

17.8.1 Geography

Japan consists of four major islands: Honshu, Hokkaido, Kyushu, and Shikoku. If these four islands were put together, the size of Japan would be roughly equivalent to the size of California. That is to say that Japan is approximately one-thirtieth the size of the U.S.A. In terms of its general location and climate, Japan spans the same latitudes and has the same general range of climatic variation as the east coast of the U.S. For example, the northern island of Hokkaido corresponds to New England; the middle section of the country from Tokyo west to the Inland Sea corresponds to North Carolina; and the southernmost island of Kyushu resembles Georgia (Reischauer 1962:3).

The climate of Japan is a complicated mixture of continental and oceanographic elements. For example, winters are affected by the cold Siberian winds from the Asian continent. Although Hokkaido, in the north, remains extremely cold in winter, the island of Kyushu, in the south, remains relatively warm. In summer trade winds carrying moisture blow in from the Pacific Ocean. Okinawa, which is located on the same latitude as Florida, remains warm most of the year. Since Japan lies in the monsoon belt, it experiences a rainy season and typhoon season every year. With frequent encounters between warm currents from the Pacific and cold currents of the north, there is a constant change of climate with both low and high air pressure systems. Many different types of winds and rainfalls have names in Japanese.

298

As was mentioned in the previous chapter, Japan has four distinct seasons in the course of a year. However, the transition from one season to another is very subtle, and these transitions deeply influence Japanese lifestyle. Perhaps the Japanese became sensitive to the slow transformation of nature through their experience with the four seasons. The Japanese people adjust their taste for food and clothing according to each season. It can be said that these changing seasons heavily influenced the thoughts, philosophy, and aesthetic sense of the Japanese.

Japan, lying off the eastern side of the Asian continent, always led a relatively isolated existence from the rest of Asia. Even within the country, ocean channels (separating the various islands), mountains, and rivers isolated people, and pockets of closed societies developed (Komatsu 1980:15–26). Edwin O. Reischauer has commented, in *The Japanese,* on how this external, as well as internal, isolation affected the Japanese people:

> Isolation has made of the Japanese a highly self-conscious people, unaccustomed to dealing with foreigners individually or as a nation. The Japanese are always strongly conscious that they are Japanese and that all other peoples are foreigners. Isolation has made them painfully aware of their difference from other peoples and has filled them with an entirely irrational sense of superiority. Isolation has made it difficult for them to understand the attitudes and actions of other peoples. In short, the factors of geographic isolation during the past two thousand years helps explain the national traits which led Japan to political isolation and to the crushing defeat in the Second World War.

What had to be accomplished in divided Japan was to establish some sort of organization. The Japanese gan'bari spirit and ability to organize was dealt with in earlier lessons. Because of the small size of isolated villages, there was no pressing need for the establishment of large-scale irrigation and water-storage systems. Water sources could be adequately shared, and strict social rules were developed in order for people to live together in harmony. From such social organization, an inevitable closeness developed among fellow villagers, along with an ambivalence toward any outsiders. This fostered the uchi and soto consciousness of the Japanese people (Komatsu 1980:25–31).

These isolated societies were very small in scale and are referred to as hakoniwa *small box garden.* In recent years, many of these hakoniwa societies have become tourist attractions.

17.8.2   Volcanoes and the Japanese Personality

Japan is known for its numerous earthquakes. There are also quite a few active volcanoes. These volcanoes do not erupt very often, but once they do erupt, the results are violent. Some people have compared the characteristics of the Japanese personality to volcanoes. They say that the Japanese have a tendency to internalize emotions such as anger. They are able to bear long periods of stressful isolation and can maintain their cool and also remain cool on the outside. However, they may be boiling inside. Once these emotions explode, the result is often violent and uncontrollable. The comparison is not valid for all Japanese, however. Unlike the majority, the edokko (a person whose family has lived in Tokyo for at least three generations), is said to have a shorter temper. His emotions are not so repressed or internalized. Although the edokko doesn't fit the pattern, it is insightful to compare the Japanese personality to the volcano.

There are usually hot springs where there are volcanoes. Where there are hot springs, there are places where people can rest and relax. Japan has numerous such places in the countryside. These are usually tourist attractions.

Japan is also blessed with abundant water. Japan receives about 1700 millimeters of rainfall a year. This is about three times more than Europe (with 500 millimeters a year) or the U.S. (with 640) (Komatsu 1980:18).

There are many water-related phrases in Japan. For example, mizukusai *(watery = too formal, lacking in intimacy)* and mizu-irazu no naka *(relation without any water coming in between = intimate relation between/among ourselves without any outsiders)*. When problems cannot be solved, one is advised to mizu ni nagasu, or *to drain the problem into water and let it flow away.* Using water as the ultimate cure for all problems may have led the Japanese to pollute the oceans as well.

Air and land transportation systems are highly developed in Japan. Bullet trains travel from Kyushu all over Honshu. Soon they will be developed in Hokkaido and Shikoku as well. Recently, a bullet train system was developed to connect omote Nihon *front side of Japan* and ura Nihon *back side of Japan.* Because of this, one can get from omote Nihon to ura Nihon in a couple of hours. As transportation develops even more, tourism will also increase. Tourist attractions can be found in all parts of the country. Although one can go sightseeing all year around in Japan, spring and autumn are the most popular seasons. The weather is ideal at these times, and the views of cherry blossoms and autumn foliage are popular, particularly with foreign travelers.

17.8.3 Sightseeing Areas and Amusement Facilities

One of the characteristics of sightseeing areas in Japan is the amusement facilities that are also provided. These include pinball parlors, video game parlors, bowling alleys, omiyage shops, theaters, and various kinds of restaurants. There are many sex-oriented entertainment centers also. The reason why there are so many amusement facilities is probably related to the concept of shojin otoshi *(termination of days of abstinence),* which is documented from ancient times. After people traveled to Ise Shrine on a pilgrimage, it was customary for travelers to visit the red-light districts, called kan'raku gai. There was an understanding that on these trips there would be absolute freedom in order to relax.

300

Such amusement centers are important in Japanese culture probably because the Japanese lifestyle is necessarily puritanical, and there are no outlets for people's natural impulses and desires. Amusement and entertainment facilities popped up at sightseeing places where people could release their pent-up emotions. At these facilities, people become much more relaxed and are able to shed the seriousness of daily life. People's behavior here is very different from their daily behavior and almost exhibits a schizophrenic element in their personalities. The everyday sense of etiquette and common sense seem out of place at these locations (Kato 1970:150–151). There is no need to worry about meeting people one knows and one begins not to care about abiding by the daily rules of etiquette and manners. It is understood, even to an ordinarily well-mannered person, that actions of shame and rudeness are permissible while one travels. Such behavior is excusable while there are no acquaintances to witness them. However, there are those people who feel it is their duty to represent the Japanese people at these tourist locations by behaving courteously.

One can begin to understand why Japanese tourists prefer to band together in a lively area such as Waikiki rather than going to a peaceful beach resort while vacationing in Hawaii. Many Japanese band together at amusement centers in their own country. It is no wonder that one spots so many Japanese tourists congregating in Waikiki. One can, almost ironically, say that Japanese tourists do not feel they have come abroad if they do not see other Japanese tourists around them!

17.8.4 Asking and Giving Directions in Japan

Many tourists to Japan come back and speak of the very helpful and friendly Japanese people. For example, they explain that when asking for directions to some place, the Japanese would actually take them to that location. Does this sort of treatment really come from helpfulness and friendliness?

One can begin by saying that the Japanese people generally do not know enough English to give directions. Some may be able to say *Come with me.* In addition, Japanese may feel that giving directions, in general, is a difficult task, not only to foreigners, but even among themselves. This is because cities or towns were not built by a central and orderly plan, but were randomly built over the years. Giving directions in a randomly built city becomes a difficult task. Unlike American cities, the streets are not arranged in an orderly way.

The Japanese do not appreciate straight lines as being aesthetically beautiful. Straight lines were considered to be unnatural. As a result, asymmetric and winding roads were developed in cities and towns over the years. Perhaps it would be taking it too far to attribute winding roads in Japan to Japanese aesthetic concepts. However, straight streets and well-organized road systems are hard to find. The city of Kyoto is an exception to this general rule because it was modeled after the carefully planned capital of the T'ang Dynasty in China.

In recent years, with American influence on city planning, Hokkaido is the frontier of modern city planning in Japan. As a result, roads are broader and laid out in a more orderly manner in Sapporo. Except for a few cities like Sapporo and Kyoto, Japanese cities developed over centuries and, as a result, the city layouts are uneven and often disorderly. Street numbers are often given at random, and one wonders how letters are delivered in Japan! It is said that mailmen must learn the individual houses by heart.

For such reasons, giving directions can be a difficult task in Japan, especially in a city like Tokyo, where many people actually come from outside the city and are not able to give proper directions. If a foreigner asks for directions, the easiest thing to do is to take him directly to the place rather than trying to explain it verbally—in English at that! It is important to realize these difficulties and how they contribute to the perception of the Japanese people as helpful and friendly.

Foreigners are also surprised to find police boxes everywhere in Japanese cities. They are impressed by the Japanese high sense of security. The presence of police boxes in many areas undoubtedly gives the Japanese a sense of security, and the policemen are generally known to the Japanese as kind **omawari-san** who give directions and assistance to those who are lost.

17.9 JAPANESE MODE OF COMMUNICATION

The Ephemeral Mode of Communication

The Japanese people believe that everything is in the flow of constant change. Like the four seasons, man's life also passes and no moment will ever return to be the same. From this, a positive ideal of cherishing each of these changing and passing moments evolved. Since the lifetime of cherry blossoms is short, to capture and enjoy its momentary beauty become valuable experiences. The Japanese perceive human life to be "sad and beautiful" like the cherry blossoms.

This idea of everything in a flow of constant change is reflected in the concept of love as well. Love also has its changing seasons. There is spring, burning summer, the autumn of temporary beauty, and finally the winter where it all disappears. Love is both beautiful and sad. The concept of beauty reflected here is referred to as **mono no aware** and remains a very important aesthetic experience for the Japanese people.

To cherish each moment and to live every moment to the fullest extent is best understood by the well-loved expression of **ichigo ichie**. This expression was derived from the Buddhist teaching *one lifetime (in) one meeting*. It can often be seen written in beautiful calligraphy at the **tokonoma** of tea houses. This expression was often used in the fifteenth and sixteenth centuries during the Warring States period. Samurai lives were limited and they never really knew if they would die today or tomorrow. Therefore, the expression **ichigo ichie** was fitting for them, helping them to cherish and appreciate the moments that were available to them. They would often come to tea houses in order to seek spiritual comfort and calmness.

In order to enter a tea house, one had to stoop down and squeeze through a small door; this symbolized the entry into another world. The bowing of one's head showed humility. Once in the tearoom, everyone was equal, and that moment would never return. The tea master prepared the tea seriously and as best he could for the guest he may never see again. The guest also drank the tea seriously, appreciating every bit of it because it could be his last moment of peace. This spirit of ichigo ichie is being revived with the revival of tea ceremony in present-day Japan.

It would be difficult to live each day with such intensity. But it can be satisfying to experience the spirit of ichigo ichie for one moment every day through encounters with people or with nature. To be able to open up one's heart, for even a moment, to a small encounter, is expressed in the spirit of mono no aware. In English, aware has been translated as *being aware*. It has also been translated as "ahness"—the spirit of being able to open one's heart by saying "Ah!" This "ahness" captures the Japanese philosophy toward human encounters.

The Japanese people have a tendency to be overly concerned with the present moment. Some are attracted to this somewhat nihilistic lifestyle. There are many who feel that life is meant to be enjoyed and one only has one life. At the same time, the Japanese people feel that long-term commitments are very important. For example, most people like to establish long-term friendships and business partnerships. It often leads to misunderstandings if both the short-term and long-term desires of the Japanese are not kept in mind.

17.10 LANGUAGE AND CULTURE

A. Chotto sumimasen

This expression is used when one wants to get the attention of another person, for example, to get the attention of a store attendant, a waitress at a restaurant, or a stranger on the street.

B. Chotto ukagaimasu ga

This expression is used almost exclusively for asking directions. Chotto, used in both expressions above, has a softening effect. Literally, it means *a little bit,* but when placed before another phrase, it is used to soften the effect of the phrase itself.

C. Goan'nai shimasu. Issho ni kite kudasai.

This expression can be used if one doesn't want to verbally explain how to get to a certain location. As was explained in the Culture Orientation, it is often faster to show the way oneself rather than to explain verbally. The use of this expression will be enough to direct the other party.

17.11   CULTURE QUESTIONS

1. It is often said that geographic features of a nation affect the national character. How is this reflected in your own country?

2. Compare the tour habits of the Japanese with those of people from other countries, and discuss whether there are any differences.

3. Often a Japanese person changes his personality when he drinks alcohol at an en'kai. Also, he behaves differently when he is traveling than in everyday life. Many people have commented on the *split personality* of the Japanese. What is your opinion?

4. Explore further this dual aspect of Japanese behavior in terms of Japanese culture categorized as a "shame culture," to use anthropologist Ruth Benedict's term. Discuss how this view differs from "sin culture" as American culture is known.

17.12   SUGGESTED RESOURCES MATERIALS

17.12.1   Books and Magazines

Japan: Past and Present, Edwin O. Reischauer (New York: Alfred A. Knopf, 1962), pp. 3–8.

The United States and Japan, Edwin O. Reischauer (New York: The Viking Press, 1957), pp. 53–68, 99–108.

17.12.2   Films (16 mm) and Video Cassettes (Beta/VHS)

"Japan—Personality and Culture." 29 mins. B/w. University of Michigan, 1961.

17.13.   REFERENCES

Kato, Hidetoshi. *Toshi to Goraku*. Tokyo: Kajima Shuppan Kai, 1970.
Komatsu, Sakyo, "Nihonjin no Ningen Kankei." In *Nihonjin no Ningen Kankei Jiten*, ed. by Hiroshi Minami. Tokyo: Kodansha, 1980.
———. "Nihonjin no Seikatsu Kankaku." In *Nihonjin no Ningen Kankei Jiten*, ed. by Hiroshi Minami. Tokyo: Kodansha, 1980.
———. "Nihon no Shizen." In *Nihonjin no Ningen Kankei Jiten*, ed. Hiroshi Minami. Tokyo: Kodansha, 1980.
Reischauer, Edwin O. *Japan: Past and Present*. New York: Alfred A. Knopf, 1962.
———. *The Japanese*. Cambridge, Mass.: Harvard University Press, Belknap Press, 1977.

LESSON 18

HOTEL OPERATION

18.1 USEFUL EXPRESSIONS

Raishuu wa yakin desu.	I work the night shift next week.
Shachoo, oyobi desu ka?	Are you calling me, Mr. President?
Watakushi ga omochi itashimasu.	I'll carry it.
Itsu okaeri ni narimasu ka?	When are you coming back?
Kore o goran ni natte kudasai.	Please look at this.
Ashita no goyotei wa nan deshoo ka?	What's your schedule tomorrow?
Gokuroosama deshita.	Thank you (for your service).
Kaigi ga arimasu.	I have a meeting.
Kaigi ni demasu.	I will attend the meeting.
Kekka wa ato de oshirase shimasu.	I will notify you of the results later.

18.2 CONVERSATIONS

18.2.1 Job Interview

Maneejaa: Tsugi no kata, doozo.

Oobosha: Hajimemashite, Kon'doo Yaeko desu. Yoroshiku onegai itashimasu.

Maneejaa: Furon'to no shigoto wa yakin mo ooi n'desu ga, yoru hataraku koto ga dekimasu ka?

Oobosha: Ee, mon'dai wa gozaimasen.

Maneejaa: Soo desu ka? Soredewa, gojibun no seikaku ya shumi ni tsuite hanashite kudasai.

Oobosha: Seikaku desu ka? Majime de, akarui hoo da to omoimasu. Shumi wa tenisu desu.

Maneejaa: Dooshite kono shigoto ni oobo shimashita ka?

Oobosha: Sen'koo wa kan'koogyoo keiei desu. Desukara, furon'to no keiken kara hajimetai to omoimashita.

Maneejaa: Soo desu ka? Doomo gokuroo sama deshita. Kekka wa raishuu no mokuyoobi made ni oshirase shimasu.

Oobosha: Doomo arigatoo gozaimashita.

Manager: Next, please.

Interviewee: Hello. My name is Yaeko Kondo. I'm pleased to meet you.

Manager: There's a lot of night duty involved in front desk work. Can you work at night?

Interviewee: Yes, that's no problem.

Manager: All right. Please tell me something about yourself and your hobbies.

Interviewee: Myself? I think I'm serious and cheerful. My hobby is tennis.

Manager: Why do you want to do this sort of work?

Interviewee: My major is travel industry management. So I would like to start with experience at the front desk.

Manager: I see. Thank you for your time. We will make our decision by next Thursday and inform you.

Interviewee: Thank you very much.

18.2.2 To the Banquet Manager

The following is a short memo from the Dining Room Manager to the Banquet Manager.

Ban'ketto Maneejaa
Moriyama Hajime Sama

Yamaguchi Depaato no en'kai yoyaku ni tsuite oshirase shimasu.

Rokugatsu mikka suiyoobi gogo roku-ji kara juu-ji made, hachijuu hachi-nin no yotei desu.

Menyuu wa *"A-plan"* de, heya wa Aroha Hooru desu node, yoroshiku onegai shimasu.

1985-nen gogatsu hatsuka

Dainin'gu Ruumu Maneejaa
John Smith

306

May 20, 1985

Mr. Hajime Moriyama
Banquet Manager

I would like to inform you about the banquet for the Yamaguchi Department Store.

It will be held on Wednesday, June 3, from 6:00 to 10:00 P.M., with eighty-eight people expected.

Regarding the menu, it will be Plan A, and the room will be the Aloha Hall.

John Smith
Dining Room Manager

18.2.3 To the Dining Room Manager

Dainin'gu Ruumu Maneejaa
John Smith Sama

Yamaguchi Depaato no en'kai no ken, yoku wakarimashita. Aroha Hooru o yoyaku shite okimasu. Hyaku-doru no hoshookin o yoroshiku onegai shi-masu.

1985-nen gogatsu nijuugo-nichi

Ban'ketto Maneejaa
Moriyama Hajime

May 25, 1985

Mr. John Smith
Dining Room Manager

I received your memo regarding the banquet for the Yamaguchi Department Store. We will reserve the Aloha Hall. A $100 deposit will be appreciated.

Hajime Moriyama
Banquet Manager

Figures 3 and 4 give examples of organizational structures of American and Japanese hotels. Using the vocabulary provided in Figure 4, practice writing short memos between the various departments.

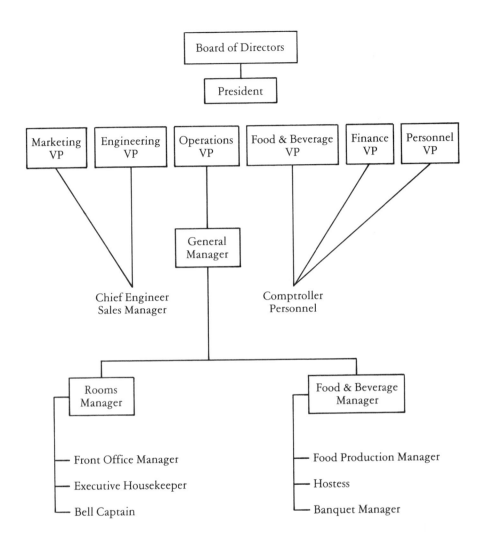

Line Management—Authority passed from top to bottom

Fig. 3. An example of the organizational structure of an American hotel

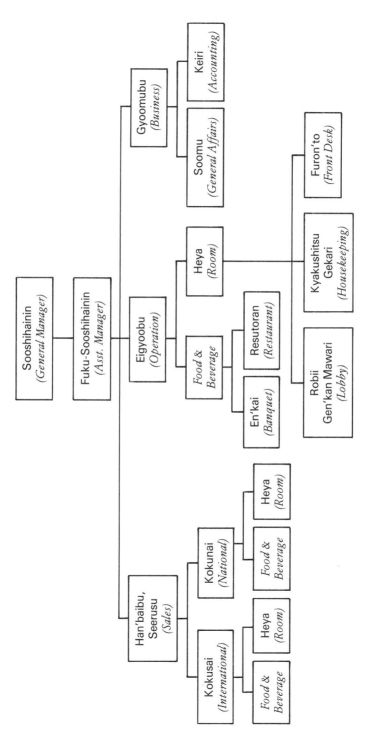

Fig. 4. An example of the organizational structure of a Japanese hotel

Nouns

ban'san'kai	dinner meeting
donata	who, polite form of dare
in'tai	retirement
kan'koogyoo	travel industry
keiei	management, operation
keigo	honorific expression
keiken	experience
kekka	result
kotobazukai	use of words
kyoochoosei	cooperative
men'setsu, in'tabyuu	interview
mon'dai	problem
nen'koo joretsu	seniority-based order
rirekisho	resumé
seido	system
seikaku	character
shumi	hobby
shuushin koyoo	lifetime employment
taishoku	quitting a job
teinen	retirement age
yakin	night shift

Verbs

hanashiaimasu	to discuss, talk over
oobo shimasu	to apply
shutchoo shimasu	to take an official trip, a business trip
shukkin shimasu	to report to work

Adjectives

akarui	cheerful, lighted

Adjective Nouns

majime	sincerity

Adverbs

moo	already, by now
mada	still, not yet

Other

. . . ni tsuite	about, concerning . . .
. . . made ni	by (a certain time)

310

18.4 EXPLANATION

18.4.1 Honorific Expressions

A speech level is determined by the speaker's evaluation of the social status and communicative distances of the people with whom he is talking. In this lesson, general formulations of honorific forms—promotion (exalted) and demotion (humble)—will be described. Promotion or demotion levels are ordinarily formulated in the following ways:

I. Nouns and adjective nouns are made into honorific forms by affixing o or go.

Examples:

otegami   ogen'ki   onamae   oshigoto   osuki   okaimono   ojoozu
gobyooki   gokekkon   goryokoo   goyotei   gotaizai   gokazoku

Sashimi wa osuki desu ka?   Do you like sashimi?

II. Verbs

1. | o + V stem desu. | (Promotion Form)

Shachoo ga oyobi desu.   The (Company) President is calling you.

Shachoo wa ima shin'bun o   The (Company) President is reading
  oyomi desu.   the newspaper now.
Odekake desu ka?   Are you going out?
Kachoo wa goshutchoo desu ka?   Is your section chief on an official trip?

2. | o + V stem + ni narimasu. | (Promotion Form)

Yamada-san ga okaki ni narimasu.   Mr. Yamada will write.
Suzuki-san wa oyomi ni   Mr. Suzuki will read.
  narimasu.

3. | o / go + V stem + { shimasu / itashimasu } | (Humble Form)

Watakushi ga goan'nai shimasu.   I will guide you.
Watakushi ga omochi shimasu.   I'll carry it.

III. Adjectives

Adjectives are usually made into promotion form by attaching the prefix o.

Ashita wa oisogashii deshoo ka?	Will you be busy tomorrow?
Okusama wa totemo outsukushii kata desu.	The wife is a very beautiful person.

Note: o is not added if the adjective begins with o, such as omoshiroi.

Some adjectives are made into formal polite form by adding gozaimasu. In this case, adjectives have the following inflection.

change final $\begin{Bmatrix} \text{-ai} \\ \text{-oi} \\ \text{-ui} \\ \text{-ii} \end{Bmatrix}$ of the informal to $\begin{Bmatrix} \text{-oo} \\ \text{-oo} \\ \text{-uu} \\ \text{-yuu} \end{Bmatrix}$

Examples:

chikai/chikoo gozaimasu.	It's near.
arigatai/arigatoo gozaimasu.	I'm grateful.
yasui/yasuu gozaimashita.	It was inexpensive.
yoroshii/yoroshuu gozaimasu ka?	Is it all right?

IV. Noun + Copula

The honorific forms of N + copula, N desu are de gozaimasu and de irasshaimasu. The form N de irasshaimasu is used only for exalting a human subject (N). N de gozaimasu is used for both human and nonhuman referents. When de gozaimasu is used for the speaker or his/her ingroup, it is regarded as a humble form. Otherwise, it is regarded as a neutral polite form which does not involve the ingroup versus outgroup dichotomy.

Study the following:

Tanaka-san de irasshaimasu ka? (exalting form)
Are you Mr. Tanaka?

Watakushi wa Aroha Hoteru no Sumisu de gozaimasu. (humble form)
I am Mr. Smith of Aloha Hotel.

Are wa Yamada sen'sei no heya de gozaimasu. (polite form)
That over there is Professor Yamada's room.

Ano kata wa Uchida-san de gozaimasu. (polite form)
That person is Mr. Uchida.

312

V. Special Lexical Item

There are special lexical items whose promotion and demotion forms must be memorized. Study the items in the following list:

(humble) *Demotion form*	*Neutral form*	(exalting) *Promotion form*	
oru	iru	irassharu	be, stay
mairu/ukagau	iku	irassharu	go
mairu/ukagau	kuru	irassharu	come
itasu	suru	nasaru	do
haiken suru	miru	goran ni naru	look
itadaku	taberu	meshiagaru	eat
moosu	iu	ossharu	say
ukagau	kiku	okiki ni naru	listen

18.4.2 The Forms moo *still* and mada *already*

The adverbs moo and mada have different meanings depending on their combinations.

moo	+	affirmative	=	already
moo	+	negative	=	no longer
moo	+	quantifier	=	more
mada	+	negative	=	not yet
mada	+	affirmative	=	still

Study the following examples:

Moo tabemashita.	I already ate.
Mada tabemasen.	I have not eaten yet.
Moo tabemasen.	I will not eat any more.
Mada tabete imasu.	I am still eating.
Moo hitotsu tabemashoo.	Let's eat one more.

18.4.3 The Forms made *until/as far as* versus made ni *by*

The particles made and made ni have quite different meanings.

Study the following:

San-ji made kaigi o shimasu.	I will hold a meeting until 3 o'clock.
San-ji made ni kaigi o shimasu.	I will hold a meeting by 3 o'clock.
Itsu made Hawai ni imasu ka?	Until when will you stay in Hawaii?
Ashita made ni repooto o kaite kudasai.	Please write the report by tomorrow.

18.5 DRILLS

18.5.1 Transformation Drill

Change each of the following into the humble form.

Example:

ikimasu	mairimasu
1. kimasu	mairimasu
2. imasu	orimasu
3. arimasu	gozaimasu
4. iimasu	mooshimasu
5. tabemasu	itadakimasu
6. omoimasu	zon'jimasu
7. shitte imasu	shitte orimasu
8. kikimasu	ukagaimasu
9. shimasu	itashimasu
10. ikimasu	mairimasu

18.5.2 Transformation Drill

Change each of the following into the exalted form.

Example:

ikimasu	irasshaimasu
1. kimasu	irasshaimasu
2. imasu	irasshaimasu
3. iimasu	osshaimasu
4. tabemasu	meshiagarimasu
5. shimasu	nasaimasu
6. shitte imasu	shitte irasshaimasu
7. ikimasu	irasshaimasu
8. shutchoo shimasu	shutchoo nasaimasu
9. in'tai shimasu	in'tai nasaimasu

18.5.3 Transformation Drill

Change each of the following into the humble form.

Example:

Watakushi ga kakimasu.   Watakushi ga okaki ⎰ shimasu.
                                              ⎱ itashimasu.

1. Ani ga haraimasu.   Ani ga oharai ⎰ shimasu.
                                           ⎱ itashimasu.

314

2. Hisho ga an'nai shimasu.	Hisho ga goan'nai	shimasu. itashimasu.
3. Haha ga hanashiaimashita.	Haha ga ohanashiai	shimashita. itashimashita.
4. Watakushi ga yomimashoo.	Watakushi ga oyomi	shimashoo. itashimashoo.
5. Imooto ga den'wa shimashita.	Imooto ga oden'wa	shimashita. itashimashita.
6. Sugu tsutaemasu.	Sugu otsutae	shimasu. itashimasu.

18.5.4 Transformation Drill

Change each of the following into the exalted form.

Example:

Buchoo ga kakimasu.	Buchoo ga okaki ni narimasu.
1. Tsugi wa Yamada-san ga hanashimasu.	Tsugi wa Yamada-san ga ohanashi ni narimasu.
2. Dare to hanashimasu ka?	Donata to ohanashi ni narimasu ka?
3. Kesa no shin'bun o yomimashita ka?	Kesa no shin'bun o oyomi ni narimashita ka?
4. Shachoo ga yon'de imasu yo.	Shachoo ga oyobi desu yo.
5. Tanaka-san ga matte imasu.	Tanaka-san ga omachi desu.

18.5.5 Question–Answer Drill

Answer each of the following in the negative; use mada.

Example:

Moo yomimashita ka?	Iie, mada yon'de imasen.
1. Moo hirugohan o tabemashita ka?	Iie, mada tabete imasen.
2. Moo in'tai shimashita ka?	Iie, mada in'tai shite imasen.
3. Moo taishoku shimashita ka?	Iie, mada taishoku shite imasen.
4. Moo oobo nasaimashita ka?	Iie, mada oobo shite imasen.
5. Moo ohanashi ni narimashita ka?	Iie, mada hanashite imasen.
6. Moo ryokoo shimashita ka?	Iie, mada ryokoo shite imasen.
7. Moo okai ni narimashita ka?	Iie, mada katte imasen.

315

18.5.6　Question–Answer Drill

Answer each of the following in the negative; use moo.

Example:

Mada ben'kyoo shite imasu ka?　　　Iie, moo ben'kyoo shite imasen.

1. Mada arubaito o shite imasu ka?　　Iie, moo arubaito o shite imasen.
2. Mada hataraite imasu ka?　　　　Iie, moo hataraite imasen.
3. Mada repooto o kaite imasu ka?　　Iie, moo kaite imasen.
4. Mada atama ga itai desu ka?　　　Iie, moo itaku arimasen.
5. Mada atsui desu ka?　　　　　　Iie, moo atsuku arimasen.

18.6　EXERCISES

18.6.1　Situational Practice

With a partner, conduct an interview with one of you as the interviewer and the other as a prospective front office employee. The interviewer wants the following information, and the prospective employee will answer his questions.

1. name
2. address
3. telephone number
4. marital status
5. information on family
6. personal charactger
7. availability for night shift
8. past job experiences

18.6.2　Situational Practice

Pair up with another student. One of you will play the role of a secretary receiving a telephone call from the other. Incorporate the following in your conversation. (Use polite forms.)

1. Who is calling?
2. Just a moment please.
3. Mr. Tanaka is in a meeting.
4. Would you like to leave a message?
5. I'll convey your message to Mr. Tanaka.

316

18.6.3 Sentence Building

Use each of the following in a sentence.

Example:
keiei   Kaisha no *keiei* wa yasashiku arimasen.

keiei	nen'koo joretsu
in'tai	seikaku
teinen	kyoochoosei
keiken	keigo
taishoku	kan'koogyoo

18.6.4 Multiple Choice

Choose moo, mada, made, or made ni, whichever is appropriate for the following blanks.

1. Hoteru wa _____ yoyaku shimashita ka?
   Did you already make reservations for the hotel?

   Iie, _____ shite imasen.
   No, not yet.

2. _____ nihon'go o ben'kyoo shite imasu ka?
   Are you still studying Japanese?

   Hai, _____ ben'kyoo shite imasu.
   Yes, I'm still studying.

3. Koohii o _____ ippai ikaga desu ka?
   How about another cup of coffee?

   Arigatoo gozaimasu. _____ takusan itadakimashita.
   No, thank you. I had enough already.

4. Tanaka-san wa _____ otaku ni irasshaimasu ka?
   Is Mr. Tanaka still at your home?

   Iie, _____ irasshaimasen.
   No, he is not any longer.

5. Raishuu _____ yakin desu ka?
   Are you still working the night shift next week?

6. Kon'shuu no doyoobi _____ oshirase shimasu.
   I will notify you by this Saturday.

18.7 SIMULATION AND SKITS

1. This interview requires four students. Students A and B are the prospective employers or interviewers, and Students C and D are the prospective

employees. Students A and B interview Student C. When C leaves the room, A and B discuss C's suitability for the job. The next prospective employee, Student D, is interviewed by A and B. When D leaves the room, A and B compare the suitability of C and D for the job.

2. The Food and Beverage Manager of a hotel calls the Banquet Manager and informs him of a banquet engagement. (Use the letter in 18.2.2 as a reference.)

3. A Japanese and an American hotel employee are discussing and comparing the differences in retirement and organizational policies between Japanese and American hotels, and the differences in personal plans between Japanese and American hotel employees.

4. As a student working part-time in the hotel industry, tell the class about your job experience.

5. Two hotel managers are discussing the kind of qualities they look for in prospective employees.

6. A Japanese and an American hotel employee are talking about the differences in management between Japanese and American hotels.

18.8   CULTURE ORIENTATION

18.8.1   Japanese Organization and Management

Japanese culture is holistic in nature. In terms of Gestalt Psychology, Japanese culture is more than the sum of its parts. The same can be said of Japanese companies. Rather than each employee being an isolated individual, the company treats individuals as part of the organizational body. The organization resembles a living body where none of the organs—the stomach, liver, or heart—can function by itself. Each organ can only function in relation to the other parts. The encouragement of mutual dependence is rooted in this holistic model of organization. With this holistic model, each individual who is a part of the whole, is an indispensable part.

On the other hand, America stresses a more mechanistic view of the world. For example, the human body can be treated as a machine, where parts are replaceable, and they can be treated individually. Similarly, individuals working in an organization can also be replaced if they are not functioning properly. The differences in organization are rooted in basic differences in world view (Yoshikawa 1982:5–11).

In Japan, the growth of the company is intimately related to the growth and profit of the individuals concerned. The company's prestige is the individual's prestige, and the company's profit is the individual's profit, which will be reflected in the size of his bonus paycheck. In such organizations, the longer one works, the better one becomes acquainted with the system. Lifetime

318

employment, under such circumstances, is encouraged. (Lifetime employment is characteristic of large corporations; the smaller companies often do not have lifetime employment available.) With lifetime employment, financial security is insured for the employee. The ability to support an average standard of living is guaranteed.

For the Japanese, however, the importance of psychological security surpasses that of financial security. One's emotional tie to a body larger than oneself creates a sense of security. There is a sense of belonging, like one experiences toward one's country. Before and during the Second World War, this sense of belonging was strongly felt toward the country as well as the Emperor who represented the country. However, since the war, the sense of unity and belonging to the country and the Emperor has greatly diminished.

The same emotional security is sought in companies and large organizations. The Japanese find such emotional ties to something to be necessary. By belonging to a larger body, there is a sense of security concerning even such things as one's marriage, the birth of one's child, and funeral arrangements after death. The company often functions as a Western church might, where ethics and morals are taught to individuals (Pascale and Athos 1981:86). In addition, it functions at times as an educational institution, teaching employees flower arrangement, tea ceremony, martial arts, and other hobbies. The company also provides broader education for individuals. Most large organizations require employees to go through shanai kyooiku which literally means *education in the company.* However, this does not mean only technical training, but also training for many aspects of life.

Lifetime employment not only implies commitment from the company, but from the individual, as well. The employee must commit his whole life to the company. As a result, loyalty is expected. In a system where one can change jobs for personal promotion and advancement, on the other hand, a company cannot expect a sense of loyalty from employees. In such cases, the company would not invest in its employees by offering programs such as shanai kyooiku.

In a company which works on a holistic system, personal traits valued in an employee are primarily harmony and cooperation. In other words, an ability to get along with others is often sought. American individualism would be discouraged. The desired skills are also not very specific. They usually seek people who have general skills and are able to learn quickly. This acquisition of general skills is facilitated by rotating a person's areas of specialty from time to time within the company. This method also enables workers to sample each other's work. Thus, company men are often lost when asked by foreigners, "What is your work?" because there is not one specialized job for which they are employed. Therefore, people often answer, "I am of X Company," merely relating himself to the company. Unlike America, where employees *participate* in their company, Japanese employees *belong* to their company.

Competition among coworkers in the same section or department is discouraged in companies where harmony and unity are important. As mentioned earlier *nails sticking out must be hammered down.* Promotions are given to all workers at the same time and are not based on individual ability or merit. Although promotions are given equally, individual ability and effort does affect, to a certain degree, how fast one can become a section chief. Characteristics sought in a section chief are personal ability, social ability, popularity, and respect among one's peers. It must be somebody who can create harmony rather than conflict in the section. What the company seeks most is leadership that can make the group a harmonious entity (Yoshikawa 1982:13–14).

Although Japanese companies work as holistic organizations, harmony and unity are not automatic. They are constantly being created through a conscious effort on the part of the company. Shanai kyooiku programs are conducted in order to create group spirit. In addition, there are annual entrance ceremonies for new company employees, annual company tours, and year-end parties. At the section level, there are the otsukiai where members are encouraged to create a sense of oneness. In day-to-day company life, the day begins with the ohayoo gozaimasu morning ritual. Unity is created through singing the company song, reciting the company pledge, or participating in the morning radio exercises. Harmony and unity are products of constant effort by the company itself.

18.8.2   The Japanese and Decision Making

Japanese companies employ a system called nemawashi while making decisions. The expression nemawashi had its origin in the method used to transplant a large tree. One or two years before a tree was to be transplanted, the smaller roots would be slowly dug out allowing only the main, large roots to remain intact. The smaller roots would be given time to grow onto the larger roots. This process made the transplant much easier (Yoshikawa 1982:48–49). Nemawashi was applied to the Japanese decision-making process in large companies. It described the prior adjustments that had to be made before major decisions could be made. Japanese decision making seeks a consensus. Therefore, major decisions are made only after a consensus has been reached. Much time and effort goes into creating consensus when there is a disagreement. The decision makers meet with the concerned individual or individuals, inside and also outside of the company, at coffee shops, restaurants, and bars. Often talks go smoothly when there is drinking and eating. Of course, such adjustment procedures can take place only after there is a foundation built ahead of time. There must be trust between coworkers. When the decision making involves sensitive, personal matters, nemawashi becomes very important. People working together cannot cause shame among each other. The more sensitive the problem at hand, the more time and energy must be spent on it. Many times, adjustments are made by going through individuals who are trusted by the person who disagrees with the group. Opinions and ideas are slowly changed and adjusted to fit the consensus.

320

This **nemawashi** approach is not typical only of the Japanese. It is often used in America also. However, there decision making requires a majority, and not a consensus. Thus, the process of adjustments is less time consuming. If value is placed on open discussion and open decisions, **nemawashi** remains a behind-closed-doors tactic, and thus could be viewed rather negatively. In Japan, **nemawashi** is publicly accepted and is generally not seen as anything negative.

There is another decision-making process called rin'gi. This process attempts to involve members in the decision by starting from the bottom (Ouchi 1981:42–45). It is a participatory exercise which fosters an egalitarian spirit, allowing its members to contribute opinions concerning the issue at hand. This approach encourages an atmosphere where both parties win the issue rather than allowing only one party to win while the other loses. If the final decision promotes positive results, the credit can be attributed to all who participated. And if the results are negative, everybody can take equal responsibility. This system also emphasizes the importance of unity and harmony in the group of decision makers. One disadvantage, however, is that it is extremely time consuming compared to the top-down decision-making process found in the U.S. However, once implemented, it can move rapidly.

The Japanese consider harmony, called **wa**, the most important thing, even while making decisions. If there are any negative feelings left between individuals when a problem is solved, it will only lead to further problems. For this reason, harmony between individuals becomes the most important issue while solving problems and making decisions.

18.8.3   Honorific System and the Japanese

It is often said that America has a horizontal society and Japan has a vertical society. This can be observed clearly if one studies their respective human relationships. For example, when an American addresses someone with *you*, there is no reference as to whether that person is superior, equal, or inferior. *You* could even refer to the President of the United States. However, in Japan, the choice of words changes depending on who the other party is. One must determine before speaking whether the party is superior to, equal to, or below oneself, and then use the appropriate vocabulary.

In Lesson 2, the three domains of ingroup, ritual, and stranger were discussed. While communicating within the ingroup, one does not have to worry too much about the honorific use of language. The plain form would suffice in such cases. In the ritual domain, however, one must be very careful of the usage of language, especially with those that are in a social status superior to one's own. (Social status is determined by age, education, sex, occupation, degree of familiarity, and family background.) For example, students would use the honorific language with their teachers. (The -masu and **desu** style is relatively safe to use—it is neither rude nor overly polite. It is appropriate to use among peers, other than in one's own family.)

There are two ways, within the honorific use of language, to speak with one's superior. One of them is to use the exalted form to speak of one's superior by essentially promoting him; this is called the promotion form. The other is to use the humble form while speaking of oneself; this is called the demotion form. By using either form, one's respect for the other's superiority can be expressed. Respect is shown, not by bringing one's level equal with the other, but by creating distance. The use of honorific language creates the social distance desired in order to show one's feeling of respect.

Using honorific language also allows one to keep distance from the other when desired. In this case, honorific speech functions, not to be polite, but to be cold. This type of honorific speech is often used when ingroup members are not on the best of terms. A certain degree of distance can be maintained. This may be somewhat equivalent to the situation when an American addresses a good friend *Mr.* rather than using his first name. The use of formal speech can put distance between two people.

Although Americans use formal speech to show respect, they prefer to overcome this level; a more informal, friendly situation is thought to be desirable. This can be seen as a cultural trait of Americans, who value friendliness and casualness. They often use first names at the start of a relationship to establish a friendly atmosphere. The Japanese, on the other hand, prefer to maintain distance between certain people. For example, it is natural for distance to be maintained between a student and a professor. No matter how friendly they may be with each other, a student would never call a professor by his first name. And in the office, subordinates would never call their superiors by their first names. The Japanese language itself does not accommodate this flexibility and it would sound very strange if used in this way.

As a general rule, honorific speech is used between elders and younger people, and always between customer and clerk. Use of honorific speech is extremely important in the business and service industry because the way employees behave determines the quality of that particular business or service. For this reason, training employees to use correct speech, even over the telephone, is extremely important.

18.9 THE JAPANESE MODE OF COMMUNICATION

The Holistic Mode of Communication

In a culture like Japan's where things are perceived holistically, even the human body is looked upon as a whole rather than as separate parts. All parts of the body are interrelated. Similarly, the Japanese people look upon their companies and organizations in a holistic manner. Americans, on the other hand, have a more mechanistic world view, where the whole is made up of distinctly separate parts. For example, the cognitive (thinking) domain of the brain is looked

322

upon as being separate from the affective (feeling) domain of the brain. How does the holistic world view and the mechanistic world view relate to respective modes of communication?

If one has a holistic world view, it is difficult to accept a person on the basis of liking his cognitive domain alone. He must be able to accept the entire person, rather than parts of him, since all parts are interconnected. Communication, for such a person, can become difficult at times, if he does not accept the other entirely. However, the person who carries a mechanistic world view can communicate well with many people because he is able to block out some parts of the other's personality as being separate from the rest. One can say that the person with the mechanistic view is more flexible in communication (Yoshikawa 1986:36–40).

In choosing business partners, the Japanese are very concerned about whether they can get along with each other as individuals, not only as profitable business partners. They have a difficult time separating the private person from the business person. Americans, on the other hand, can say without much difficulty, "I don't like him as a person, but I can work with him for the sake of mutual profit." They can separate business and private matters.

18.10 LANGUAGE AND CULTURE

A. Kaigi

As long as there are processes such as **nemawashi** and **rin'gi**, the Japanese interpretation of a **kaigi** will always remain different from what one would imagine of the English *meeting*. There are two types of **kaigi**: the **hon kaigi** and the **yobi kaigi**. The **hon kaigi** is a formal meeting where decisions have already been made ahead of time and members gather together to reconfirm their decision. At this meeting, there are no real discussions, and personal opinions on the issues are not dealt with. The **hon kaigi** offers no surprises, and members have an occasion to share their joint decisions at this time. The **yobi kaigi** is the preliminary meeting where real decisions are made and opposing opinions are adjusted. Here, there are open discussions as one would find in an American meeting.

B. Men'setsu

The **men'setsu** *interview* is an indispensible part of the hiring process in Japan. Literally, **men'setsu** means *face contact,* and this is the occasion at which an employer can directly see a prospective employee. The **men'setsu** allows the employer to see more than the personal resumé and entrance exam scores of the candidate. In Japan, much value is placed upon one's attitude. This can be observed by personal appearance and one's usage of language. The employer also asks questions such as what kind of hobbies one has and how long one has had them. If one has a blackbelt in judo and has practiced it for ten years, this may suggest the applicant is very disciplined. It may also indicate future loyalty of the applicant to the company. An attempt is made to look at the applicant as holistically as possible at these men'setsu.

The men'setsu is more or less like an interview held in Western countries. However, there may be certain differences in emphasis during these interviews. At the men'setsu, the chairman or president of the company usually participates. Because he does so, the responsibility of hiring a new employee can be shouldered by the company. If an employee turns out to be incompetent, fifty percent of the responsibility is taken by the company. For such reasons, the sha-nai kyooiku (in-service training and education) is important. The company is not merely a place for work, but also a place where personal growth can be developed.

C. Kyoochoosei

This term implies *the ability to get along with others* and is an indispensable quality in Japan where internal harmony is so highly valued. In addition to seeing that the prospective employee has the ability to be cooperative, the employer also looks for whether he is majime *serious and sincere*. They also look for akarusa *cheerfulness*. These are some of the characteristics looked for in prospective employees.

It must be noted here that while Japanese companies consider cooperativeness and the ability to get along with others indispensable qualities in their employees, they are also giving consideration to other attributes in recent years. According to the research report prepared by the Special Committee on Educational Problems Project chaired by Hideo Sugimura, adviser to Honda Giken Koogyoo, the kind of person highly sought by companies will be the one (1) who excels in the academic or cultural field or sports, (2) who has the ability not only to memorize facts but also to exercise sound judgment and make the appropriate application, (3) who knows how to observe social etiquette while being individualistic, (4) who is active rather than re-active, and (5) who is not a "workaholic" but one who balances work with recreational activities for personal enrichment. It is uncertain whether or not these criteria in personnel selection will be put into practice. What is certain is that change is taking place in Japanese society.

D. Taishoku

Large corporations in Japan have a mandatory retirement age of fifty-five. Although rather low in comparison to countries like the United States, in the past the retirement age reflected the average life expectancy in Japan. Until recently life expectancy was fifty years, so that working to fifty-five meant working longer than one's lifetime! However, with the average life expectancy having increased by more than twenty years, fifty-five becomes an age too early to retire. In spite of this, however, the retirement age has remained the same. Those people who wish to work after fifty-five must find employment elsewhere, unless they happen to be in administrative positions and their executive skills and experience are considered essential enough for them to be asked to continue on in their positions past the normal retirement age. Most often, however, retirees must resort to accepting salaries and positions lower than those they held before. This problem of forced early retirement has been rapidly growing in recent years.

18.11 CULTURE QUESTIONS

1. In recent years, American has begun to focus her attention on Japanese management practices. What are some of the things that can be learned from this system?

2. If your country were to adopt Japanese management practices, what would be some factors that would require close attention?

3. What are some areas that would require special attention if a foreign company were to open a joint venture with a Japanese company?

4. Many people have criticized Japanese kaigi as being shibai *fake or dramatic.* How do you feel about this?

5. In the Language and Culture section, desirable traits of a prospective employee were discussed. Discuss similarities and differences that can be found between Japan and your country when hiring a new employee. Which traits do you feel are desirable?

6. Now discuss how much weight is placed upon the job interview in Japan and in your country.

7. After reading and studying the Culture Orientation in this lesson, what type of shanai kyooiku would you design in your tourist-oriented company, if you were in charge of personnel training?

18.12 SUGGESTED RESOURCE MATERIALS

18.12.1 Books and Magazines

The Art of Japanese Management: Applications for American Executives, Richard Tanner Pascale and Anthony G. Athos (New York: Simon and Schuster, 1981).
From Bonsai to Levis, George Fields (New York: Macmillan, 1983).
A Book of Five Rings, Miyamoto Musashi, trans. by Victor Harris (New York: The Overlook Press, 1974).
Doing Business with the Japanese, Mitchell F. Deutsch (New York: New American Library, 1983).

Getting Your Yen's Worth: How to Negotiate with Japan, Inc., Robert T. Moran (Houston: Gulf Publishing Co., 1985).

Japan's Managerial System: Tradition and Innovation, M. Y. Yoshino (Cambridge, Mass.: The MIT Press, 1968).

The Japanese Way of Doing Business, Boye DeMento (Englewood-Cliffs, N.J.: Prentice-Hall, 1981).

Kodansha Encyclopedia of Japan, vol. 3 (Tokyo: Kodansha, 1983), pp. 224–226.

Managing Cultural Differences, Robert T. Moran and Philip R. Harris (Houston: Gulf Publishing Co., 1979).

Managing Cultural Synergy, Robert T. Moran and Philip R. Harris (Houston: Gulf Publishing Co., 1982).

"Melodrama in Japanese Negotiations," Robert March, *Winds* 3, no. 11 (April, 1982).

Theory Z: How American Business Can Meet the Japanese Challenge, William Ouchi (Reading, Mass.: Addison-Wesley Publishing Co., 1981).

Training for the Multicultural Manager, Pierre Casso (Washington, D.C.: The Society for Intercultural Education, Training and Research, 1982).

18.12.2   Films (16 mm) and Video Cassettes (Beta / VHS)

"The Colonel Comes to Japan." 28 mins. Color. WGBH, 1982.

"Doing Business in Japan: Negotiating a Contract." 30 mins. Color. Vision Associates Production.

"Kachōsan: The Section Chief and His Day." 30 mins. Color. Yomiuri Eigasha.

"The Kyocera Experiment." 30 mins. WGBH, 1982.

18.13   REFERENCES

Ouchi, William G. *Theory Z: How American Business Can Meet the Japanese Challenge*. Reading, Mass.: Addison-Wesley Publishing Co., 1981.

Pascale, Richard Tanner, and Anthony G. Athos. *The Art of Japanese Management: Applications for American Executives*. New York: Simon and Schuster, 1981.

Yoshikawa, Muneo Jay. "Japanese and American Modes of Communication and Implications for Managerial and Organizational Behavior." Paper presented at the Second International Conference on Communication through Eastern and Western Perspectives, July 20–30, 1982, held in Japan.

LESSON 19

REVIEW

19.1   Humble Form

beruman ga omochi maneejaa ga goan'nai haha ga omise hisho ga oshirase	shimasu.
- - - - - - - - - - - - - - - - -	
kachoo ni otsutae sen'sei ni owatashi okyaku-san ni oden'wa	itashimasu.

19.2 | V-te motion V-masu. |

basu takushii chikatetsu kuruma	ni notte	ikimasu. kimasu. kaerimasu.
- - - - - - - -	- - - - - - - -	
	aruite oyoide	

APPENDIXES

APPENDIX 1

EXPRESSIONS AND DIALOGUES—
KANA AND KAN'JI TRANSCRIPTIONS

LESSON 1

1.1 USEFUL EXPRESSIONS

おはようございます。

こんにちは。

こんばんは。

さようなら。

お休(やす)みなさい。

じゃあまた。

お元気(げんき)ですか。

いかがですか。

おかげさまで。

まあまあです。

おでかけですか。

ちょっと　そこまで。

しばらくですねえ。

1.2 会話

1.2.1

鈴木：こんにちは、 山田さん。
山田：ああ、 鈴木さん、 こんにちは。
鈴木：しばらくですねえ。 お元気ですか。
山田：ええ、 おかげさまで。 鈴木さんは？
鈴木：おかげさまで（元気です）。

1.2.2

内田：こんばんは、 課長。
課長：こんばんは、 内田君。
内田：おでかけですか。
課長：ええ、 ちょっと そこまで。

LESSON 2

2.1 USEFUL EXPRESSIONS

はじめまして。
どうぞ よろしく。
こちらこそ。
（ご）紹介します。
どうも。
ありがとう。
どうも ありがとう。
どうも ありがとうございます。
どういたしまして。
（ああ、） そうですか。
よろしく お願いします。

2.2 会話

渡 辺： こんにちは。

田 中： こんにちは。　先日は　どうも。

渡 辺： いいえ、　どういたしまして。　田中さん、　ご紹介します。
こちらは　木下さんです。　木下さんは　私の　日本の　と
もだちです。　こちらは　田中さんです。　田中さんは　ア
ロハ　ホテルの　マネージャーです。

田 中： アロハ　ホテルの　田中です。どうぞ　よろしく。

木 下： はじめまして。私は　東京ツアーの　ガイドです。
よろしく　お願いします。

田 中： ああ、　どうも。　こちらこそ。　よろしく　お願いします。

LESSON 3

3.1　USEFUL EXPRESSIONS

いらっしゃいませ。

どうぞ。

何を　さしあげましょうか。

いくらですか。

これは　いかがですか。

お願いします。

ほかに　なにか。

それだけです。

毎度　ありがとうございます。

3.2 会話

3.2.1

店員：いらっしゃいませ。
客　：その　チョコレートを　下さい。
店員：はい、　どうぞ。　おみやげですか。
客　：ええ、　そうです。
店員：ほかに　何か。
客　：それだけです。　いくらですか。
店員：6ドル　24セント　です。どうも　ありがとうございました。

3.2.2

ガイド：お帰りなさい。どこへ　行きましたか。
山田：おみやげてんへ　行きました。
ガイド：何を　買いましたか。
山田：チョコレートを　買いました。
ガイド：そうですか。　じゃ　また　あとで。

LESSON 4

4.1 USEFUL EXPRESSIONS

しょうしょう　お待ち下さい。
お待たせ　いたしました。
お待ちどうさまでした。
そうですねえ。
ちょっと　小さいです。
サイズは　ちょうど　いいです。
それを　見せて下さい。
4パーセントの　ぜいきんが　つきます。
かしこまりました。

4.2 会 話

4.2.1

店　員： いらっしゃいませ。

客　　： アロハ シャツを 見せて下さい。

店　員： どうぞ こちらへ。 サイズは 中ですか。

客　　： はい、 そうです。

店　員： これは いかがですか。

客　　： そうですねえ。 それは いくらですか。

店　員： 30ドルです。

客　　： じゃあ、 それを 1まい 下さい。

店　員： はい、 かしこまりました。

4.2.2

客　　： こうすいが ありますか。

店　員： はい、 あります。 こちらは フランスの こうすいです。
　　　　 そちらは ハワイの こうすいです。

客　　： この シャネル5は いくらですか。

店　員： 35ドルです。 それに 4パーセントの ぜいきんが つきま
　　　　 す。

客　　： それを 1個 ください。

店　員： 36ドル 20セントです。 つつみましょうか。

客　　： はい、 お願いします。

店　員： 3ドル 80セントの おつりです。 どうも ありがとう ご
　　　　 ざいました。

LESSON 5

5.1 USEFUL EXPRESSIONS

こちらは いま セール(バーゲン セール)です。

2割引で さしあげます。

どんな ものが よろしいでしょうか。

どんな　色が　よろしいでしょうか。

こんな　ものは　いかがでしょうか。

試着室(着付室)は　そちらです。

とても　おにあいですよ。

旅行小切手(トラベラー　チェック)で(も)　いいですか。

ええ、　けっこうです。

それは　いま　ございませんが…すみません。

ちょっと　すみません。

なにか　おみせしましょうか。

5.2　会話

店員：いらっしゃいませ。

客　：フェンディーの　ハンドバッグが　ほしいんですが…

店員：おきゃくさまの　ですね？

客　：ええ、　私の　です。　それを　みせて下さい。

店員：どうぞ。　こちらは　ぜんぶ　フェンディーです。　あちら
　　　は　ジバンシーと　クリスチャン　デオールです。

客　：きれいな　バッグですねえ。　この　バッグは　いくらです
　　　か。

店員：フェンディーですね。　160ドルで　ございますが、　1割引
　　　で　さしあげます。　ですから　144ドルです。

客　：タバコも　ありますか。

店員：はい、　ございます。　ダンヒルも　ラークも　ございます
　　　が…

客　：では　ダンヒルを　ください。　この　バッグも　いっしょ
　　　に　お願いします。

店員：どうも　ありがとうございます。　ダンヒルは　15ドルです。
　　　全部で　165ドル　36セントです。

客　：旅行小切手でも　いいですか。

店員：ええ、　けっこうですよ。　パスポートを　お願いします。

客　：どうぞ。

店員：どうも　ありがとうございました。

336

LESSON 7

7.1 USEFUL EXPRESSIONS

いただきます。

ごちそうさま(でした)。

予約 お願いします。

予約 なさいましたか。

何時に いらっしゃいますか。

何人様ですか。

お待ちしています。

何に なさいますか。

食券を お持ちですか。

ビュッフェ(バイキング)は セルフサービスです。

お勘定(チェック)は いっしょですか、 べつべつですか。

すぐ 持ってまいります。

もしもし ことぶきレストランですが・・・

ステーキの やきぐあいは?

7.2 会 話

7.2.1

ホステス	: いらっしゃいませ。 お2人様ですね。 どうぞ こちらへ。
森田さん	: どうも。
ホステス	: メニューを どうぞ。

· · · · · ·

ウエイトレス	: いらっしゃいませ。 食券を お持ちですか。
森田さん	: はい。
ウエイトレス	: では その 食券を 下さい。 昼食は ビュッフェです。 メニューからも 注文できます。

337

森田さん　　　：　私 は　ブッフェ。
内田さん　　　：　私 は　メニューから　注文します。
ウエイトレス：　何に　なさいますか。
内田さん　　　：　そうですねえ。　パパイヤが　好きですから、　パパ
　　　　　　　　　　イヤと　トーストと　コーヒーを　お願いします。
ウエイトレス：　はい、　すぐ持ってまいります。　ブッフェは　セ
　　　　　　　　　　ルフサービスですから、　どうぞ。
森田さん　　　：　はい、　どうも。

7.2.2

ホステス：　もしもし、　ことぶきレストランですが・・・
中田さん：　予約　お願いしたいんですが・・・
ホステス：　はい、　何時に　いらっしゃいますか。
中田さん：　6時半に　行きたいんです。
ホステス：　何人様　ですか。
中田さん：　3人です。
ホステス：　お名前を　お願いします。
中田さん：　中田春枝です。
ホステス：　ありがとうございます。　お待ちしています。

7.2.3

ホステス　　　　：　いらっしゃいませ。　予約なさいましたか。
中田さん　　　　：　はい、　中田です。
ホステス　　　　：　3人様　ですね。　こちらへ　どうぞ。

カクテル
ウエイトレス：　カクテルは　いかがですか。

中田さん　　　　：　ビール、　ミラーを　2本　下さい。

カクテル
ウエイトレス：　はい、　すぐ持ってまいります。

ウエイトレス：　お待たせしました。

338

中田さん　　　　：　この　サーロインステーキを　3人前　下さい。

ウエイトレス：　やきぐあいは？

中田さん　　　　：　ミディアムです。

ウエイトレス：　サラダの　ドレッシングは　何に　なさいますか。

中田さん　　　　：　フレンチです。

ウエイトレス：　ライスと　ポテト、　どちらに　なさいますか。

中田さん　　　　：　ライスを　おねがいします。

ウエイトレス：　はい、　わかりました。　しょうしょう　お待ち下さ
　　　　　　　　　　いね。

中田さん　　　　：　お勘定　お願いします。

ウエイトレス：　はい、　あちらの　レジで　お願いします。　ありが
　　　　　　　　　　とうございました。

LESSON 8

8.1　USEFUL EXPRESSIONS

ごはんが　食べたいなあ。

おなかが　すいています。

おなかが　いっぱいです。

のどが　かわいています。

お茶を　もう　いっぱい　いかがですか。

いいえ、　もう　けっこうです。

おすみですか。

かしこまりました。

私　が　おごります。

ごちそうに　なります。

8.2 会話

8.2.1

ウエイトレス ： いらっしゃいませ。

良夫 ： ああ、 ごはんが 食べたいなあ。

順子 ： あたしも。

ウエイトレス ： きょうは 観光でしたか。

順子 ： そうです。 ハナウマベイへ 行きました。 すみません、 おひやを 下さい。

ウエイトレス ： どうぞ。

・・・・・・

ウエイトレス ： 何に なさいますか。

良夫 ： 僕は 定食B。

順子 ： あたしは おすし、 にぎりの「竹」を お願いします。

ウエイトレス ： はい。 お飲み物は?

順子 ： きりん 一本と グアバ ジュースを いっぱい お願いします。

ウエイトレス ： はい、 かしこまりました。

―――――――＊―――――――

順子 ： ねえ、 チップは いくらぐらい おくの?

良夫 ： 10パーセントから 15パーセントぐらいだよ。

順子 ： では 行きましょう。 ごちそうさまでした。

ウエイトレス ： どうも ありがとうございました。

8.2.2

山田 ： せんぱい、 何を 食べていますか。

佐藤 ： てんどんだ。 僕が おごるよ、 山田君。 いっしょに どう?

山田 ： どうも ありがとうございます。 では せんぱい、 ごちそうに なります。

佐藤 ： ちょっと すみません。 てんどんを もう ひとつ 持ってきて下さい。

ウエイトレス ： かしこまりました。

LESSON 9

9.1 USEFUL EXPRESSIONS

ひさしぶりに　いっぱい　やりましょう。

おひやを　もう　いっぱい　いただけますか。

おさけに　つよいですねえ。

そうですか。

そうですねえ。

（これで）　よろしいですか。

いつも　おせわに　なっています。

これからも　どうぞ　よろしく　お願いします。

おたがいに　がんばりましょう。

これは　何で　できていますか。

カクテルは　すぐ　できます。

パンチは　フルーツ　ジュースで　できています。

しかたが　ありません。

かんぱい！

9.2 会話

9.2.1

ブラウン：　ああ、　小林さん、　しばらくでしたねえ。

小　林：　ああ、　ブラウンさん、　本当に　しばらくでした。　い
　　　　　つも　おせわに　なっています。　ブラウンさん、　こん
　　　　　ばんは　おひまですか。

ブラウン：　ええ。

小　林：　じゃあ、　こんばん　いっしょに　飲みませんか。　金曜
　　　　　日ですから…

ブラウン：　いいですねえ。　ひさしぶりに　いっぱい　やりましょう。

小　林：　いい　ところを　知っていますか。

ブラウン：そうですねえ。　ああ、「クラブ　サンシャイン」へ　行きましょう。　カラオケも　ありますよ。
小　林：そうですか。　じゃあ、　そこに　しましょう。

　　　　　　　　　　　・・・・・・

小　林：ブラウンさん、　何に　しますか。
ブラウン：そうですねえ、　私は　水わり。
小　林：じゃあ、　私も　水わり。
ブラウン：じゃあ、　水わりで　かんぱいしましょう。
小　林
ブラウン：かんぱい！

ブラウン：これからも　どうぞ　よろしくお願いします。
小　林：こちらこそ。
ブラウン：日本の　景気は　どうですか。
小　林：あまり　よくないですね。
ブラウン：そうですか。こちらも　きびしいですよ。
小　林：さあ、　どうぞ　どうぞ。
ブラウン：ああ、　どうも　どうも。
小　林：まあ、　おたがいに　がんばりましょう。
小　林
ブラウン：かんぱい！

9.2.2

客：マイタイは　何で　できていますか。
バーテンダー：マイタイですか。　ラム酒で　できています。　ハワイの　ゆうめいな　カクテルです。　少しつよいですよ。
客：チチは何で　つくりますか。
バーテンダー：ウォッカ、　ココナツ　シロップ、　フルーツ　ジュースなどで　つくります。　おいしいですよ。
客：マイタイを　いっぱい　飲んでみましょう。
バーテンダー：はい、　どうぞ。

LESSON 11

11.1 USEFUL EXPRESSIONS

予約が　ございますか。

はい、　予約してあります。

いつまで　ごたいざいですか。

海(手)側が　いいですか、　山(手)側が　いいですか。

ごあんないします。

ハワイは　はじめてですか。

海が　よく　見えます。

この　かぎを　どうぞ。

どうぞ　ごゆっくり。

お心づけを　どうも　ありがとう。

お休みなさい。

11.2 会話

11.2.1

フロント：　いらっしゃいませ。

客　　　：　へやを　お願いします。　佐藤春男です。予約してありま
　　　　　　す。

フロント：　しょうしょう　お待ち下さい。　佐藤春男さんですね。
　　　　　　いつまで　ごたいざいですか。

客　　　：　今日から　5月9日までです。

フロント：　3泊ですね。　おへやは　531号です。　5階の　海(手)側
　　　　　　です。　この　かぎを　どうぞ。　ベルマンが　ご案内し
　　　　　　ますから、　しょうしょう　お待ち下さい。

客　　　：　どうも。

11.2.2

ベルマン： この　お荷物　ですね。　どうぞ。　エレベーターは　右
　　　　　　の方です。

客　　　： 食堂は　何階に　ありますか。

ベルマン： 一階です。　よなかの　二時まで　あいています。

客　　　： プールは　どちらですか。

ベルマン： ホテルの　よこの方です。　ハワイは　はじめてですか。

客　　　： いいえ、　前に　一度　来たことがあります。

ベルマン： そうですか。　さあ、　こちらです。　エアコンのある
　　　　　　おへやですよ。　どうぞ　ごゆっくり。

客　　　： どうも　ありがとう。　これは　少しですが　どうぞ。

ベルマン： お心づけ　ありがとうございます。

LESSON 12

12.1　USEFUL EXPRESSIONS

はい、　何でしょうか。

何か　ごようですか。

きちょうひんを　あずけたいんですが・・・

私に　何か　伝言が　ありますか。

おへやの　番号は？

お急ぎですか。

かぎを　なくさないで下さい。

だめです。

12.2　会話

12.2.1

フロント： はい、　何でしょうか。

客　　　： 手紙が　きて　いますか。　342号室の　鈴木ですが・・・。

344

フロント： お手紙は　きていませんが、　伝言が　ございます。
客　　　： どうも。

12.2.2

客　　　： あたまが　いたいんですが、　このへんに　くすりやが
　　　　　　ありますか。
フロント： あのロビーの　入口の方に　ありますよ。
客　　　： どうも。

12.2.3

客　　　： 両替　できますか。
フロント： はい、　できますよ。
客　　　： レートは　いくらですか。
フロント： 1ドルは　160円です。
客　　　： 1万円　おねがいします。
フロント： はい。　62ドル　50セントです。　どうぞ。
客　　　： どうも。

12.2.4

客　　　： あのう、　アラモアナ　センターへ　行きたいんですが。
　　　　　　タクシーは　どこで　のりますか。
フロント： タクシーを　よびますから、ホテルの入口の前で　お待ち
　　　　　　下さい。
客　　　： どうも　ありがとう。

12.2.5

客　　　　： かしきんこを　借りたいんですが・・・。
フロント　： となりの　カウンターへ　どうぞ。
客　　　　： あ、　そうですか。

客　　　　　：あのう、　かしきんこを　借りたいんです　けど…

キャッシャー：はい。　これを読んでから、　下に　サインして下さい。

客　　　　　：漢字で　書いても　いいですか。

キャッシャー：いいえ、　ローマ字で　書いて下さい。　それから、　このかぎを　なくさないで下さい。　そして、　きんこを　あけたい時には、　かぎを　わたして、お名前を　言って下さいね。

客　　　　　：分かりました。　どうも　ありがとう。

LESSON 13

13.1 USEFUL EXPRESSIONS

いいお天気ですねえ。

どちらから　いらっしゃいましたか。

おくには　どこですか。

グループで　いらっしゃいましたか。

個人旅行ですか。

新婚旅行ですか。

観光旅行です。

あしたの　ご予定は？

私、　支配人の　内田です。

しつれいしました。

しつれいします。

楽しく　おすごし下さい。

また　あとで。

346

13.2 会話

13.2.1

支配人： よく いらっしゃいました。 私は この ホテルの
支配人の ジョン スミスです。 どちらから いらっしゃ
いましたか。

客 ： 山口県からです。

支配人： それでは、 ハワイに ごしんせきの 方が いらっしゃい
ますか。

客 ： ええ、 おばが いまして、 きのう 会いました。

支配人： そうですか。 それは よかったですねえ。 ハワイは は
じめてですか。

客 ： ええ、 はじめてです。

支配人： ハワイは どうですか。

客 ： 空も 海も きれいで、 ほんとうに すばらしい ところ
ですねえ。

支配人： あしたは どんな ご予定ですか。

客 ： ハナウマ・ベイへ 行くつもりです。

支配人： どうぞ 楽しく おすごし下さい。 しつれいしました。

客 ： どうも ありがとう。

13.2.2

客 ： マイタイを もう いっぱい下さい。

ウエイトレス： どうぞ。 お客様は おくには どちらですか。

客 ： 京都です。 京都へ 行った ことが ありますか。

ウエイトレス： はい。 高校の時、 テニスの グループと 行きま
した。 いい ところですねえ、 京都は。

客 ： ハワイと 京都と どちらの方が いいですか。

ウエイトレス： くらべるのは むずかしいですけど、 私は 冬には
ハワイが 好きです。

客 ： 気候が いいですからねえ、 ハワイは。

ウエイトレス： それでは ごゆっくり。

客 ： どうも。 また あとで・・・。

LESSON 14

14.1 USEFUL EXPRESSIONS

お荷物を　お持ちしましょう。

会計カウンターで　おしはらい下さい。

これは　市内電話料で　ございます。

これは　国際電話料で　ございます。

おわすれものは　ございませんか。

お気をつけて、　おかえり下さい。

いろいろ　おせわに　なりました。

また　どうぞ　おこし下さいませ。

お待ちしております。

14.2 会話

客　　　：もしもし、　こちら　531号室の　佐藤です。　チェック・
アウトしたいんですが・・・

フロント：はい。　フロントに　いらっしゃって下さい。　荷物を
取りに　まいりましょうか。

客　　　：はい、　お願いします。

　　　　　　　　・・・・・・

ベルマン：ベルマンです。　おにもつを　お持ちしましょう。

客　　　：はい。　この　2個　お願いします。

ベルマン：おわすれものは　ございませんか。

客　　　：はい、　ないと　思います。

　　　　　　　　・・・・・・

客　　　：チェック・アウト　お願いします。　これが　おへやの
かぎです。

会計　　：お勘定は　全部で　253ドルに　なります。　現金ですか、
クレジットですか。

客　　　：この　旅行小切手で　お願いします。

会　計　：どうも　ありがとうございます。　47ドルの　おつりです。
　　　　　　また　どうぞ　おこし下さいませ。

客　　　：空港へは　タクシーが　いいですか。

会　計　：リムジンが　一番　いいと　思います。　11時半に　ホテ
　　　　　　ルの前で　お待ち下さい。

客　　　：いろいろ　おせわに　なりました。

会　計　：では　お気を　つけて　おかえり下さい。

LESSON 16

16.1　USEFUL EXPRESSIONS

電話番号は　455-8730です。

もしもし…

田中さんの　おたくですか。

いいえ、　ちがいます。

山田さん（を）　お願いします。

どちらさまですか。

鈴木さんに　かわります。

九番を　おまわし下さい。

電話が　とおいです。

電話で　しつれいします。

電話を　きります。

お話し中です。

電話に　出て下さい。

電話を　取って下さい。

おかわりございませんか。

せきを　はずしています。

今　るすですが…

おことずけ⎫
伝言　　　⎬を　お願いします。
メッセージ⎭

また　あとで。
ごめん下さい。
しつれいします。

16.2 会話

16.2.1

客　　　：もしもし、　ホテルの　外へ　電話したいんですが・・・
交換手　：市内ですか。
客　　　：はい、　そうです。
交換手　：9番を　まわしてから、　電話番号を　おまわし下さい。
客　　　：どうも　ありがとう。

・・・・・・

荒木　：もしもし。　横田さんの　おたくですか。
横田　：はい、　そうですが・・・
荒木　：私　荒木和子と　いうものですが、　ジョージさん　いらっしゃいますか。
横田　：はい。　ちょっと　お待ち下さい。　かわりますから。

・・・・・・

ジョージ：ぼく、　ジョージですが・・・
荒木　：あ、　ジョージさん、　きのう　ハワイに　つきました。お手紙を　ありがとう　ございました。
ジョージ：いいえ、　どういたしまして。　今　どちらから？
荒木　：カハラ・ヒルトンに　います。　ホテルの　方に　いらっしゃいませんか。　いろいろ　お話ししたい　ことも　ありますから。
ジョージ：はい、　うかがいます。　和子さんは　ビーチで　泳ぐのと　さんぽするのと　どちらの　方が　いいですか。
荒木　：今日は　さんぽに　しましょうか。

350

ジョージ： そうですね。　では　何時に　お会い　しましょうか。

荒木　： 3時ごろに　しましょうか。　ロビーで　待っていますね。

ジョージ： はい。　では　また　あとで。　さようなら。

荒木　： さようなら。

16.2.2

客　　　： もしもし　マカハ・リゾート・ホテルですか。

フロント： はい、　そうです。

客　　　： へやの　予約を　お願いします。

フロント： どうぞ。　いつから　いつまでですか。

客　　　： 今日から　あさってまで。　二泊三日です。

フロント： わかりました。　お名前を　どうぞ。

客　　　： 白木和男です。

フロント： 何人様ですか。

客　　　： 二人です。

フロント： ダブルと　ツインでは　どちらの方が　よろしいですか。

客　　　： ツインの方が　いいです。

フロント： ありがとうございました。　チェック・インは　1時です。
　　　　　　お待ちして　おります。

16.2.3

秋田： もしもし、　フロントの　秋田ですが・・・

秘書： はい、　支配人室でございます。

秋田： 支配人に　お会いしたいんですが、　何時ごろが　いいですか。

秘書： 支配人は　会議に　出ていますが、　今日は　おそくなるそうです。　あしたの朝でも　よろしいですか。

秋田： ええ、　けっこうです。

秘書： 9時半に　どうぞ。

秋田： どうも。　では　あした　9時半に　うかがいます。　ごめん下さい。

16.2.4

佐　藤：もしもし、　モーニング・コールを　お願いします。

交換手：何時に　起こしましょうか。

佐　藤：7時半に　起こして下さい。

交換手：はい、　分かりました。　お名前と　おへやの　番号を　ど
　　　　うぞ。

佐　藤：235号室の　佐藤です。

・・・・・・

交換手：おはようございます。　7時半です。　起きる　時間ですよ。

佐　藤：はい、　はい。　どうも　ありがとう。

16.2.5

1. A：もしもし、　田中さんの　おたくですか。

　　B：はい、　そうですが・・・

　　A：あのう・・・　太郎さん　いらっしゃいますか。

　　B：はい、　しょうしょう　お待ち下さい。

2. A：もしもし、　田中さんの　おたくですか。

　　B：はい、　そうです。

　　A：照屋ですが、　太郎くん　いますか。

　　B：はい、　ちょっと　待って下さい。

3. A：もしもし、　田中さんの　おたくですか。

　　B：はい、　そうですが・・・

　　A：あのう・・・　太郎さん　いらっしゃいますか。

　　B：はい、　おります。　どちら様で　いらっしゃいますか。

　　A：杉本と　もうします。

　　B：しょうしょう　お待ち下さい。

4. A：もしもし、　田中さんの　おたくですか。

　　B：はい、　そうです。

　　A：太郎さん　お願いします。

　　B：ぼくですが・・・

　　A：あ、　ぼく　スミスです。

5. A：もしもし。

  B：もしもし。

  A：田中さんの　おたくですか。

  B：はい、　そうです。

  A：太郎さん　いらっしゃいますか。

  B：今　ちょっと　るすですが。

  A：何時ごろ　帰りますか。

  B：3時ごろ　帰りますが。

  A：じゃ　また　あとで　お電話します。

     さようなら。

LESSON 17

17.1　USEFUL EXPRESSIONS

ちょっと　すみません・・・

すみませんが・・・

ちょっと　うかがいますが・・・

あの　かどを　右へ　まがって下さい。

この　道を　まっすぐ　行って下さい。

歩いて　五分ぐらいの所です。

すぐ　分かりますよ。

ここです。

17.2　会話

17.2.1

観光客：すみませんが、　このへんに　バスの　停留所が　あります
　　　　か。

ガード：この道を　まっすぐ　行って、　一番目のかどを　右へ　ま
　　　　がって下さい。　バス・ストップの　サインが　見えます。

観光客 ： とおいですか。

ガード ： いいえ、 二、三分の所です。　どこへ　いらっしゃいます
か。

観光客 ： アラモアナ・センターへ　行きます。

ガード ： では　八番の　バスに　のって下さい。

観光客 ： どうも　ありがとう。

17.2.2

客　　 ： すみませんが、　動物園へ　行く道を　教えて下さい。

フロント： 動物園ですか。　バスで　行きますか、　歩いて　行きま
すか。

客　　 ： 歩いて　行きたいんですが、　とおいですか。

フロント： あるいて　二十分　ぐらいの　所です。

客　　 ： 二十分　かかりますか。

フロント： その　ぐらい　かかるでしょう。　地図を書いて　あげま
しょう。　この道の　二番目の　四つかどを　左へ　まが
ってから、　まっすぐ　行って下さい。　右の方に　公園
が見えます。動物園の　入口は　その公園の　むかいです。

客　　 ： どうも　ありがとうございました。　この地図を　いただ
きますね。

フロント： どうぞ。

17.2.3

1. A：すみませんが・・・このへんに　電話が　ありますか。
   B：電話ですか。　あの映画館の　そばに　ありますよ。
   A：どうも　ありがとう。
2. A：あのう、　ちょっと　うかがいますが、　動物園へは　どう行き
   ますか。
   B：動物園ですか。　この道を　まっすぐ　行って、　二番目の　道
   を　左に　まがって下さい。　動物園は　右の方に　あります。
   A：どうも　ありがとうございました。

354

3. A：ちょっと　すみません。　アラモアナへ　行きたいんですが、
　　　バスの　停留所は　どこですか。
　 B：この　道を　まっすぐ　行って下さい。　右の方に　銀行が　あ
　　　ります。　その　むかいに　停留所が　あります。
　 A：銀行の　むかいですね。　どうも　ありがとう。
4. A：エレベーターは　どこでしょうか。
　 B：あの　かいだんの　うしろの方です。
　 A：どうも。
5. A：本屋は　どこですか。
　 B：あの白い　たてものの　中に　ありますよ。
　 A：ああ　そうですか。　どうも。

LESSON 18

18.1　USEFUL EXPRESSIONS

来週は　夜勤です。
社長、　およびですか。
私が　お持ちいたします。
いつ　お帰りに　なりますか。
これを　ごらんに　なって下さい。
あしたのご予定は　何でしょうか。
ごくろうさまでした。
会議が　あります。
会議に　出ます。
結果は　あとで　お知らせします。

18.2.1

マネージャー：次の方、　どうぞ。

応募者　：はじめまして、　近藤八重子です。　よろしくお願い
　　　　　　いたします。

マネージャー：フロントの仕事は　夜勤も　多いんですが、　夜働く
　　　　　　ことができますか。

応募者　：ええ、　問題は　ございません。

マネージャー：そうですか。　それでは　ご自分の性格や　趣味につ
　　　　　　いて　話して下さい。

応募者　：性格ですか。　まじめで　明るい方だと　思います。
　　　　　　趣味は　テニスです。

マネージャー：どうして　この　仕事に　応募しましたか。

応募者　：専攻は　観光業経営です。　ですから、　フロントの
　　　　　　経験から　始めたいと　思いました。

マネージャー：そうですか。　どうも　ごくろうさまでした。　結果
　　　　　　は　来週の木曜日までに　お知らせします。

応募者　：どうも　ありがとうございました。

18.2.2

バンケット　マネージャー
森山一様

山口デパートの宴会予約について　お知らせします。
6月3日水曜日、午後6時から10時まで、88人の予定です。

メニューは「Aプラン」で、へやはアロハ　ホールですので、よろしく
お願いします。

　　　　　1985年5月20日

　　　　　　　　　　　　ダイニング　ルーム　マネージャー
　　　　　　　　　　　　ジョン　スミス

356

18.2.3

ダイニングルーム　マネージャー
ジョン　スミス　様

山口デパートの　宴会の件、よく分かりました。アロハ　ホールを　予約しておきます。100ドルの　保証金を　よろしく　お願いします。

1985年 5 月　25 日

バンケット　マネージャー
森　山　一

APPENDIX 2

KAN'JI SIGNS AND SYMBOLS

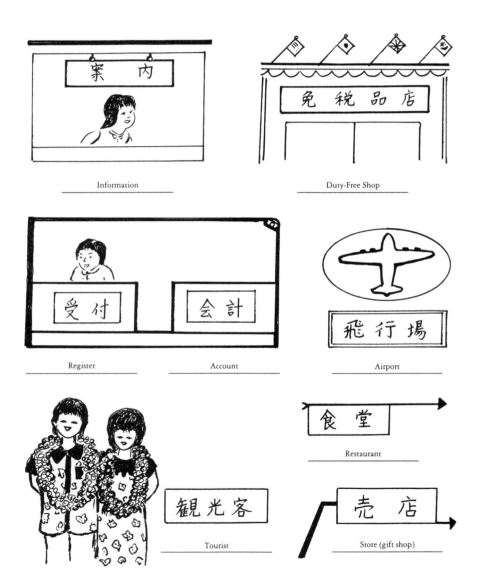

Information

Duty-Free Shop

Register

Account

Airport

Restaurant

Tourist

Store (gift shop)

Taxi

Waiting Room
push   pull

Bus Stop

Adult

Emergency Exit

Entrance

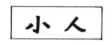

Child

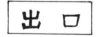

Exit

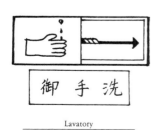

Lavatory

Women

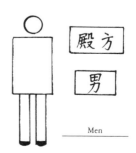

Men

359

Mail

Telephone

No Smoking

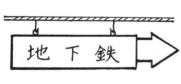

Subway

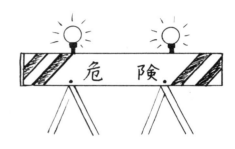

Danger

School

Temple

Shrine

Hot Spring

旅 館

Japanese Inn

Fire Extinguisher

APPENDIX 3

GLOSSARY

The glossary is a compilation of the vocabulary lists in this book. Numbers refer to lessons.

agemasu	8,17	to give
aimasu	13	to meet
akai	3	red
akarui	4	cheerful, lighted
akemasu	5	to open
aki	13	fall
akimasu	11	to open
amai	9	sweet, flat taste
amari-nai	9	not very
Amerika	4	America
anata	2	you
ane	13	older sister
ani	13	older brother
an'na	5	that kind of . . . over there
an'nai shimasu	11	to guide, to show the way
ano (+ noun)	3	that, those (distant)
apetaizaa	9	appetizer
apoin'tomen'to	16	appointment
are	2	that, those (distant)
arimasu	4	to exist (inanimate), to have
aroha shatsu	3	aloha shirt
arubaito	8	part-time job
arukoru	9	alcoholic beverages
asa	7	morning
asagohan	7	breakfast
asatte	12	day after tomorrow
ashita	4	tomorrow
atama	12	head
atarashii	5	new
ato de	16	later
atsui	9	hot (weather, heat)

baagen seeru	5	bargain sale
baggu	4	bag
baikin'gu	7	buffet
-ban	11	counter for night
ban'gohan	7	supper, dinner
ban'goo	11	number
ban'san'kai	18	dinner meeting
ben'kyoo shimasu	4	to study
betsubetsu ni	7	separately
bifuteki	7	beefsteak
biichi	2	beach
biiru	7	beer
bijutsukan	17	art gallery
buchoo	1	department chief
buran'do hin	5	brand made
buran'do seihin	5	brand-name products
byooin	17	hospital
byooki	14	illness
byuffe	7	buffet
chekku auto	14	checking out
chichi	13	father
chiisai	4	small
chikai	11	near
chikamichi	17	short cut
chikatetsu	17	subway
chippu	7, 11	tip
chittomo	9	(not) at all
chizu	17	map
chokoreeto	3	chocolates
choodo	11	just right, just about
chookyori den'wa	16	long distance call
chooshoku	7	breakfast
chotto	4	a little bit
chuu	4	medium
chuumon shimasu	7	to order
chuushoku	7	lunch
dai	4	large
daigaku	4	university
dake	17	only
deguchi	12	exit
dekakemasu	3	to go out
dekimasu	9	can do, possible

den'gon	12	message
den'poo	12	telegram
den'wa bango	16	telephone number
den'wa cho	16	telephone directory
den'wa (o) shimasu (kakemasu)	16	to make a telephone call
depaato	3	department store
dezaato	7	dessert
-do	11	counter for repititions (ichido = once)
dochira	7	which one, which side
doko	3	where
donata	18	who, polite form of dare
don'na	5	what kind of
dono (+ noun)	3	which
doobutsuen	14	zoo
dooryoo	9	collleagues
doresshin'gu	7	dressing
ea kon	11	air conditioner
eiga	11	movie
eigakan	17	movie theater
eigo	3	English language
eki	17	train station
en'kai	9	dinner party
erebeetaa	17	elevator
esukareetaa	17	escalator
fasshon	5	fashion
fuku-shihainin	1	assistant manager
-fun	7	counter for minutes
fune	9	boat, ship
Furan'su	4	France
furon'to	11	front desk
furui	5	old
futsuu tsuuwa	16	station-to-station
fuyu	13	winter
gaido	2	guide
gakkoo	17	school
gakusei	2	student
gekijoo	17	theater
gen'kin	5	cash
gochisoo	8	feast
gogo	7, 11	p.m., afternoon

-goo (shitsu)	11	room number
gooruden uiiku	14	Golden Week
goro	8	approximate (point of time)
gorufu	11	golf
gozen	7, 11	a.m., morning
gurai	8	approximate (amount, quantity)
hade	5	loud (color)
haha	13	mother
hai	1	yes (ee is less formal)
-hai	7	counter for glasses of drinks
hairimasu	12	to enter
-haku	11	counter for night's lodging
hakubutsukan	17	museum
hana	9	flower
hanashiaimasu	18	to discuss, talk over
hanashimasu	3	to speak
hanaya	17	flower shop
han'baagaa	7	hamburger
han'dobaggu	5	handbag
(han'do bakku)		
haru	13	spring
Hawai	4	Hawaii
hayai	11	early, fast
heya	11	room
hidari	11	left
hikooki	9	airplane
hima	7	free time
hiroi	13	wide
hiru	7	afternoon
hirugohan	7	lunch
hisho	14	secretary
hito	5	person
hon	2	book
-hon	7	counter for slender objects
hon'too	13	true, real
hon'ya	17	bookstore
hoo	11	side, direction
hoteru	2	hotel
ii (yoi)	4	good
iie	2	no
iimasu	12	to say
ikimasu	3	to go

ima	3, 7	now
imasu	4	to exist (animate)
imooto	13	younger sister
inarizushi	8	fried bean curd stuffed with sushi rice
in'tabyuu	18	interview
in'tai	18	retirement
ippin ryoori	8	ala carte
iriguchi	12	entrance
iro	5	color
iroiro	9	variety
isha	14	doctor
issho ni	5, 7	together
itadakimasu	17	to receive
itai	12	ache
Itarii	4	Italy
itoko	13	cousin
itsu	11	when
-ji	7	counter for time
-jikan	7	counter for hours
jimi	5	conservative (color)
jimusho	3	office
joobu	5	strong
jun'sa	17	policeman
juusu	7	juice
kachoo	1	section chief
kado	17	corner
kaerimasu	3	to return
kagi	11	key
-kai	11	counter for floors
kaidan	17	steps, stairs
kaigi	16	conference
kaigichuu	16	in a meeting
kaikei	14	account
kaimasu	3	to buy
kaimono	4	shopping
kaimono shimasu	4	to go shopping
kaisha	3	company
kakarimasu	17	to take (as in measuring time)
kakimasu	3	to write
kakuteru	7	cocktails
kanai	13	wife
kan'ji	12	Chinese character

kan'joo	7, 14	account, bill
kan'koo	8	tour
kan'koogyoo	18	travel industry
kan'pai	9	a toast
-kara	11	from
. . . kara . . . made	16	from . . . to . . .
karai	9	hot (taste)
karaoke	9	taped music for singing along
karimasu	12	to borrow
kashikin'ko	12	deposit box (for valuables)
katachi	5	shape
katai	9	hard
kawarimasu	16	to change
kazoku	13	family
kedo (keredomo)	12	but, although
keiei	18	management, operation
keigo	18	honorific expression
keikan	17	policeman
keiken	18	experience
keiki	9	business condition
keisatsu	17	police station
kekka	18	result
kekkon shimasu	8	to marry
ken	13	prefecture
kibishii	9	harsh, severe, strict
kibun	14	feeling
kichoohin	12	valuables
kikoo	13	climate
kimasu	3	to come
kinoo	4	yesterday
kissa-ten	9	coffee shop
-ko	4	counter used for number of pieces
kochira	2	this side (this person), this way, here
kokorozuke	11	tip
kokusai den'wa	16	international call
kokusai den'wa ryoo	14	international telephone fee
konna	5	this kind of
kono (+ noun)	3	this, these
kono hen	12	this vicinity
kon'shuu	14	this week
kooban	17	police box
koocha	7	black tea
kooen	17	park
koohi	7	coffee

kookan'shu	16	operator
kookoo	13	senior high school
koosui	4	perfume
kootoogakkoo	13	senior high school
kore	2	this, these
koshoo	16	out of order
kotobazukai	18	use of words
kotozuke	16	message
kudamono	7	fruit
kudasaimasu	17	to give (to ingroup)
-kun	1	informal suffix, a form of address used among men, equals, or towards those of lower status
kuni	13	country, hometown
kurabemasu	13	to compare
kuremasu	17	to give (to ingroup)
kuroi	5	black
kusuri	12	medicine
kusuriya	12	drug store
kuukoo	17	airport
kyaku	3	customer, guest
kyoo	4	today
kyoochoosei	18	cooperative
kyookai	17	church
machimasu	14	to wait
mada	18	still, not yet
made	11	until
. . . made ni	18	by (a certain time)
mado	12	window
mae	7, 11	front, before
magarimasu	17	to turn
mago	13	grandchild
-mai	4	counter used for flat pieces
majime	18	sincerity
makademia nattsu	3	macadamia nuts
makizushi	8	rolled sushi
makunouchi	9	makunouchi dish
maneejaa	1	manager
massugu	17	straight
mawashimasu	16	to dial, to turn around
mazui	7	not delicious
mei	13	niece
meishi	2	business card

men'setsu	18	interview
menyuu	7	menu
mezurashii	5	unusual
michi	17	way, street
miemasu	11	is visible, can see
migi	11	right
mise	3	store, shop
misoshiru	8	miso soup
mizuwari	9	whiskey and water
mochimasu	14	to carry, to have
mon'dai	18	problem
mono	16	person
moo	18	already, by now
moo hitotsu	8	one more
moonin'gu kooru	16	morning call, wake up call
moraimasu	17	to receive
mukai	17	facing
mukoo	17	beyond
musuko	13	son
musume	13	daughter
muumuu	3	muumuu
muzukashii	4	difficult
-nado	9	et cetera, and so forth
naisen	16	extension
naka	14	inside
nama biiru	9	draft beer
nani (nan)	2	what
narimasu	14	to become
natsu	13	summer
neesan	13	older sister
nen'koo joretsu	18	seniority-based order
. . . ni tsuite	18	about, concerning . . .
nigirizushi	8	hand-rolled sushi with raw fish
nigiyaka	5	lively
Nihon	2	Japan
nihon'go	2	Japanese language
niisan, ani	13	older brother
niku	9	meat
nimotsu	11	baggage
-nin	7	counter for people
nin'ki	9	popularity
-nin'mae	7	counter for portions of food
Nippon	2	Japan

nomimasu	7	to drink
nomimono	7	drinks
nomiya	9	drinking place
norimasu	12	to ride
oba	13	aunty
obaasan	13	grandmother
obasan	13	aunty
ocha	7	green tea
ogorimasu	8	to treat
(o)hashi	8	chopsticks
ohiya	8	cold water
oi	13	nephew
oishii	7	delicious, tasty
oji	13	uncle
ojisan	13	uncle
okaasan	13	mother
okimasu	8	to place
okoshimasu	16	to wake (someone) up
okusan	13	wife
okyakusan	3	customer, guest
omiotsuke	8	miso soup
omiyage	3	souvenir
omiyage-ten	3	gift shop
omoimasu	14	to think
omoshiroi	4	interesting
onaji	8	same
onaka	12	stomach
on'gaku	13	music
on'na mono	5	things for women
oobo shimasu	18	to apply
ookii	4	large, big
oouri dashi	5	big sale
osoi	11	late, slow
otaku	16	residence
otearai	17	restroom, bathroom
otoko mono	5	things for men
otoosan	13	father
otooto	13	younger brother
ototoi	12	day before yesterday
otsuri	4	change
oyogimasu	11	to swim
papaiya	7	papaya

raamen	8	Chinese-style noodles
raishuu	14	next week
reeto	12	rate
reji	7	register
restoran	7	restaurant
rirekisho	18	resumé
robii	12	lobby
roomaji	12	Roman letters (romanization)
ryokan	11	Japanese-style inn
ryokoo	11	trip
ryokoo kogitte	5	traveler's checks
ryokoo shimasu	11	to travel
ryoogae	12	currency exchange
ryoogae shimasu	12	to exchange currency
ryoojikan	17	consulate
ryootei	9	a Japanese teahouse (with **tatami** rooms)
ryuukoo	5	fashion
sain	12	signature
sain shimasu	12	to sign
saizu	4	size
sake	8	Japanese rice wine
-san	1	suffix attached to a person's name, similar to Mr., Miss, or Mrs.
san'go	4	coral
san'po shimasu	14	to take a walk
sarada	7	salad
sashiagemasu	17	to give (to outgroup)
sashimi	8	sliced raw fish
seeru	4	sale
seido	18	system
seikaku	18	character
sekai	14	world
seki	8, 16	seat
sen'jitsu	2	the previous day
sen'pai	8	senior person
sen'sei	1	teacher
sen'shuu	14	last week
serufu saabisu	7	self-service
setsumei	9	explanation
shachoo	1	company president
shashin	17	picture, photo
shigotoba	2	place of work
shihainin	1	manager

shiharaimasu	14	to pay
shimasu	2	to do
shimei tsuuwa	16	person-to-person
shinai	14	within the city
shinai den'wa	16	local call
shinai den'wa ryoo	14	local telephone fee
shin'bun	2	newspaper
shin'seki	13	relative
shin'setsu	5	kind, polite
shirimasu	8	to know
shiroi	5	white
shita	12	beneath, under
shizuka	5	quiet
shokudo	7	restaurant
shokuji	9	meal
shokuji shimasu	9	to dine
shomei	12	signature
shomei shimasu	12	to sign
shoo	4	small
shoorai	14	future
shujin	13	husband
shukkin shimasu	18	to report to work
shumi	18	hobby
shutchoo shimasu	18	to take an official trip, a business trip
shuu	13	state
shuushin koyoo	18	lifetime employment
soba	8	buckwheat flour noodles
soba	17	beside
sobo	13	grandmother
sochira	2	that side (that person), that way, there
son'na	5	that kind of
sono (+ noun)	3	that, those (nearby)
soo	2	so
sora	13	sky
sore	2	that, those (nearby)
sorekara	12	and then
soshite	12	and
soto	16	outside
sugi	7	past (in telling time)
sugu	7	right away
suiei	11	swimming
Suisu	14	Switzerland
suki	7	like
sukoshi	11	a little, a few

sumimasu	8	to finish
sumimasu	13	to live
sunakku	9	snack bar
supootsu	13	sports
sushi	8	rice with vinegar
sutairu	5	style
suteeki	7	beef steak
tabako	3, 5	cigarettes, tobacco
tabemasu	7	to eat
tabemono	8, 9	food
taishikan	17	embassy
taishoku	18	quitting a job
taizai shimasu	11	to stay over
takai	4	expensive, high
takusan	11	a lot, many, much
tan'joobi	9	birthday
tanoshii	9	joyous
tatemono	17	building
tegami	3	letter
teinen	18	retirement age
teiryuujo	17	bus stop
teishoku	8	a meal of set items
ten'don	8	a bowl of rice with fried shrimp or fish on top
ten'in	3	salesclerk
ten'ki	13	weather
ten'pura	8	tempura, deep fried Japanese foods
toki	12	time, when
tokoro	5	place
tomarimasu	11	to sleep over
tomodachi	2	friend
tonari	12, 17	next door (neighbor), adjoining
ton'katsu	8	pork cutlet
tooi	11	far
toraberaa chekku	5	traveler's checks
torikeshimasu	14	to cancel
torimasu	14	to take
toshokan	4	library
totemo	4	very, quite
tsuin	11	twin, double occupancy
tsukemono	8	pickled vegetables
tsukiai	9	association, company
tsukiataru	17	dead end

tsukimasu	8	to include, to attach
tsukurimasu	9	to make
tsumami	9	hors d'oeuvres
tsumaranai	4	uninteresting
tsumetai	9	cold
tsumori	13	intention, plan
tsutaemasu	16	to convey
tsutsumimasu	4	to wrap
tsuyoi	9	strong
uchi	3	house, home
udon	8	thick wheat flour noodles
ue	12	above, on
uisukii	4, 9	whiskey
ukagaimasu	16	to visit
uketsuke	11	receptionist
umi	11	ocean, sea
umi(te)gawa	11	ocean side (view)
ushiro	17	behind, back
uta	9	song
utaimasu	9	to sing
wain	9	wine
waribiki	5	discount
warui	4	bad
wasuremasu	14	to forget
wasuremono	14	things left behind (things forgotten)
watakushi	2	I
watashimasu	12	to hand over, to turn in
yakin	18	night shift
yakusoku	16	promise, appointment
Yamada-san	1	Mr. (Miss, Mrs., Ms.) Yamada
yama(te)gawa	11	mountain side (view)
yarimasu	17	go give (to inferior)
yasai	9	vegetables
yasashii	4, 5	easy, gentle, kind
yasui	4	inexpensive, cheap
yawarakai	9	soft, tender
yoi (ii)	4	good
yoko	11	side
yoku	11	well, frequently
yomimasu	4	to read
yonaka	11	midnight

yoru	11	night
yotei	13	schedule
yotsukado	17	intersection
yowai	9	weak, mild
yoyaku	16	reservation
yukkuri	11	slowly, leisurely
yuubin	12	mail
yuubin'kyoku	17	post office
yuumei	9	famous
yuushoku	7	supper, dinner
zasshi	2	magazine
zeikin	4	tax
zen'bu	5, 14	all
zen'sai	9	appetizer
zuibun	5	very, relatively
zutsuu	12	headache
zutto	16	by far, much (more)

ABOUT THE AUTHORS

Kyoko Hijirida holds a master's degree in teaching Japanese as a second language and a doctorate in education from the University of Hawaii. She has taught Japanese language for over twenty years and has done research on foreign language instruction for specialized use. She is the author of a number of articles on Japanese language teaching and was instrumental in developing the Japanese language and culture curriculum for the University of Hawaii's School of Travel Industry Management. She is presently an associate professor of Japanese language at the University of Hawaii.

Muneo Yoshikawa received an M.A. in teaching Japanese as a second language from the University of Hawaii. He received his Ph.D., also from the University of Hawaii, in American studies, specializing in comparative cultures and cross-cultural communication. He is currently an associate professor of Japanese at the University of Hawaii. Professor Yoshikawa also conducts seminars and training programs in international business communication for multinational company executives.

Production Notes

This book was designed by Roger Eggers.
Composition and paging were done on the
Quadex Composing System and typesetting
on the Compugraphic 8400 by the design
and production staff of University of Hawaii
Press.

The text typefaces are Garamond No. 49
and Univers, and the display typeface is
Garamond No. 49 bold.

Offset presswork and binding were done
by Malloy Lithographing, Inc. Text paper is
Glatfelter Offset Vellum, basis 50.

DATE DUE